D0392562

The Performance of Politics

The Performance

of

Politics

Obama's Victory and the Democratic
Struggle for Power

JEFFREY C. ALEXANDER

OXFORD
UNIVERSITY PRESS

2010

OXFORD
UNIVERSITY PRESS

Oxford University Press, Inc., publishes works that further
Oxford University's objective of excellence
in research, scholarship, and education.

Oxford   New York
Auckland   Cape Town   Dar es Salaam   Hong Kong   Karachi
Kuala Lumpur   Madrid   Melbourne   Mexico City   Nairobi
New Delhi   Shanghai   Taipei   Toronto

With offices in
Argentina   Austria   Brazil   Chile   Czech Republic   France   Greece
Guatemala   Hungary   Italy   Japan   Poland   Portugal   Singapore
South Korea   Switzerland   Thailand   Turkey   Ukraine   Vietnam

Copyright © 2010 by Oxford University Press, Inc.

Published by Oxford University Press, Inc.
198 Madison Avenue, New York, New York 10016

www.oup.com

Oxford is a registered trademark of Oxford University Press

All rights reserved. No part of this publication may be reproduced,
stored in a retrieval system, or transmitted, in any form or by any means,
electronic, mechanical, photocopying, recording, or otherwise,
without the prior permission of Oxford University Press.

Library of Congress Cataloging-in-Publication Data
Alexander, Jeffrey C., 1947
The performance of politics : Obama's victory
and the democratic struggle for power / Jeffrey C. Alexander.
p.   cm.
Includes bibliographical references and index.
ISBN 978-0-19-974446-6
1. Presidents—United States—Election—2008.   2. Obama, Barack.
3. Performance art—Political aspects—United States.
4. United States—Politics and government—2001–2009.
I. Title.
E906.A44 2010
324.973'0931—dc22   2010007928

1 3 5 7 9 8 6 4 2

Printed in the United States of America
on acid-free paper

For Morel, who shared it all

A Symbol...always partakes of the Reality which it renders
intelligible.

—Coleridge

Contents

Part III Victory and Defeat

Acknowledgments

F ROM JANUARY TO MAY 2009 I WAS A SENIOR FELLOW AT THE Kluge Center at the Library of Congress in Washington, D.C., and was supported also by a sabbatical leave from Yale University. The Kluge residency greatly facilitated the completion of this book, and I thank the Kluge staff and especially its director, Carolyn Brown, for their assistance; I also thank Yale for its continuing support. Andreas Hess and Isaac Reed were especially helpful readers of this manuscript. I benefited also from suggestions by Peter Beilharz, Werner Binder, Elizabeth Breese, Donald Green, Mark Haugaard, Ron Jacobs, Wade Kenney, Peter Kivisto, Richard McCoy, Giuseppe Sciortino, Steven Skowronek, Norma Thompson, Vered Vinitsky-Seroussi, and student fellows at the Yale Center for Cultural Sociology. Marshall Ganz made possible my connection with the Obama ground game in Denver, Colorado. I am grateful to four *New York Times* journalists who covered the 2008 presidential campaign—John M. Broder, Jodi Kantor, Michael Powell, and Janny Scott—for allowing me to interview them at length. Katherine Venegas, a Field Organizer for the Obama campaign in Colorado, extended me the same privilege, and included me in her Pueblo group at Camp Obama in Denver in September, 2008. Nadine Amalfi supplied much-appreciated administrative assistance. James Cook, my editor at Oxford University Press, offered helpful editorial suggestions. I owe a significant debt as well to my research assistant on this project, Nadya Jaworsky.

Preface

WHY ANOTHER BOOK ABOUT OBAMA AND MCCAIN WHEN THERE have been so many and after all this time? That was 2008, after all. It was only yesterday, but it often seems so long ago, almost ancient history.

The answer, I hope, is that this book is different from other "campaign books" in ways that are more likely to stand the test of time. *The Performance of Politics* is very much about that 2008 presidential campaign, but it is about a lot more as well. My ambition is to provide a new explanation of victory and defeat in 2008, but also a new way of looking at the democratic struggle for power in America and beyond.

Three types of books are written about presidential campaigns. One is by insiders, the people who organize and run them. Another is by journalists, the people who report on them as they unfold. The third is by academics, who make claims for greater objectivity because they have observed the campaign from the outside. The best of each genre has its virtues that make them essential reading for every student of political life, but in their more conventional forms they fall short. Books by insiders often become too personal, veering from game plans to bragging and score settling. Books by social scientists often become too objective, putting what are nuanced and uncertain events into neat and tidy conceptual boxes, passing off broad demographic correlations as causal explanations, and presenting outcomes as if they were determined in advance—by "society." Journalistic accounts too often focus on individuals and their biographies. They can veer from recounting to gossip, turning off-the-record interviews into juicy nuggets that make news for a day.

Insider accounts provide us with new backstage knowledge, but they are way too inside to give us perspective on the whys and whats of the campaign. Academic accounts provide all sorts of contextualizing knowledge, but they are far too outside to provide convincing explanations of victory and defeat at this time and in this place. Journalists are actually in a better position. Reporters create what the public sees, hears, and reads every day about the campaign, and sophisticated political journalists produce narrative streams of nuance and complexity. Neither an insider nor an academic has ever produced a great book about a political campaign. Political journalists have, though they have been few and far between. Theodore H. White's *The Making of the President 1960* was the best book written in the last century about an American political campaign.[1]

The Performance of Politics is between inside and outside. I look carefully at the strategies and statements of those who planned and directed the 2008 campaign, and I pay close attention to the broader contexts that defined its social backdrop. I also enmesh myself in the day-to-day reports of political media not only to glean detailed information but also to gain access to the symbolic flows that decide campaigns, the cultural frameworks that journalists not only referee but also help create.

In the pages that follow I investigate the back and forth between Barack Obama and John McCain from June to November of 2008. My focus is microscopic, but the big picture is never left entirely behind.

Chapter 1 is mainly about this big picture, and it's a bit abstract, a little academic. My argument is that the democratic struggle for power is not much determined by demography or even substantive issues and that it's not very rational, either. Political struggle is moral and emotional. It's about "meaning," about symbolically "constructing" candidates so they appear to be on the sunny rather than the shadowy side of the street. When they run for office, politicians are less public debaters, public servants, or policy wonks than they are performers. They and their production teams work on their image, and political struggle is about projecting these cultural constructs to voters. Political journalism mediates these projections of image in an extraordinarily powerful way.

My discussion of these broad issues is mercifully brief. Soon we enter into the concreteness of the 2008 presidential campaigns.

Part I describes how Obama and McCain tried to become symbols of American democracy, each in his own way. Obama often succeeded. People saw him as real and authentic, if sometimes too earnest. McCain couldn't seem to make his political performances fly. He was such a bad actor that voters often felt he seemed to be acting, following a script rather than being himself. But there was another reason for McCain's difficulty to symbolize effectively. In 2008, concerns about terrorism were fading. McCain could be narrated as a hero pretty easily in a time of military crisis but not so easily on the domestic scene. Obama was inexperienced in foreign affairs and had nothing to do with the military, but he could fill out the hero role in civil society, having formed his political identity and rhetoric in wake of the titanic black struggles for civil rights.

Political performances are not only carried in the airwaves by mass media but are also organized on the ground as volunteers go door to door and communicate terminal to terminal. But are the ground game and the war of the airwaves really so different? Organizing, too, depends on emotional energy and image projection. In an hour-by-hour ethnography of a training day for "Hispanics for Obama" in Denver, Colorado, I show that this day of organizing the organizers projected democratic symbols and organized emotional rituals around them. The result was an energy and solidarity that inspired volunteers to project political performances to their neighbors back home, with the hope of creating the same kind of fusion between them and the people in the street.

Part II is about binaries and boundaries. The moral and emotional framework that inspires American democracy has little room for ambiguity. For better and for worse, it is organized in simple, deeply believed dichotomies that evaluate actions and paint motives in starkly contrasting shades of black and white. When candidates symbolize, they struggle to align themselves with the sacred side of these binaries and their opponents with the profane. Even in a democratic public sphere—so often idealized as rational and respectful—politics is about "working the binaries." It is also about connecting these anchoring moral dichotomies to issues that are not really about governing at all, to gender and family values, to whether one is god fearing and faithful, and to whether one is of a respectable ethnicity and racial stripe. This is what I call "walking the boundaries." The 2008 campaign featured the first major nonwhite candidate, two female superstars, and rumors about Islamic affiliations, and it continually returned to concerns about virility and strength. Binaries were worked, and boundaries were walked in strenuous, disconcerting, and sometimes alarming ways.

The first two parts of *The Performance of Politics* are not organized chronologically. My discussions of performance, heroes, ground games, binaries, and boundaries are about particular campaign events and minicrises. Certainly, these are nested in the backward and forward flows of momentum in summer and fall of 2008. Only in part III, however, do I examine the actual horse race and identify the events that produced victory and defeat.

Using composite data reconstructed from the most representative political polls, I identify three critical periods of flux for Obama and opportunity for McCain. Obama's triumphal overseas trip in late July set off anxieties he was overreaching and arrogant. This opened the door for Republican image makers to sculpt him as a superficial, out-of-touch celebrity. This crisis of "celebrity metaphor" lasted five long weeks, during which Obama's fortunes fell and McCain's rose substantially. It subsided only with the ritual power of the Democratic convention in Denver, where Obama delivered a stem-winding, thoughtful, and hard-hitting speech to an enormous "all-American" crowd.

Yet it was immediately after Obama's revitalizing speech, at the end of August, that Sarah Palin exploded as a symbol on the political scene. The Alaskan governor presented herself not only as devoted mother but also as a feisty and scrappy political reformer, and to many she seemed genuine, a new American hero on the domestic scene. Within a week, the "Palin effect" allowed Republicans once again to take the lead. The Palin symbol deflated as quickly as it had inflated, however, as investigative journalists made discoveries that seemed to place her on the shadowy side of the street.

Just as Obama regained the lead in mid-September, the nation's financial institutions melted down. Analysts of the 2008 campaign typically describe the "financial crisis" as a kind of automatic game changer. Because Republicans presided over deregulation and the bubble economy, they reason, economic failure led voters to decide that they should not put a Republican back in the presidency. This reasoning is false. It assumes voters act in terms of rational interest and that image and symbolic performance are not central to campaigns. I demonstrate that there was actually a lot of wiggle room during the first two weeks of the financial crisis. McCain seemed awkward, impulsive, and bumbling; Obama presented himself as poised, calm, and rational. It was these sharply contrasting performances that sealed the campaign. Within two weeks, Obama gained a statistical advantage for the first time and never gave up his lead.

After explaining Obama's victory and McCain's defeat, I append an epilogue about postelection time. Once one is responsible for running the machinery of government, it is not easy to be a hero, despite the ruffles and flourishes of the presidency. But this book is not about today, when President Obama is governing; it is about yesterday, when he was winning the right to try. After the epilogue, readers who are academically interested will find a "Note on Concept and Method." I discuss here the intellectual choices that inform this book, the theories I am working with, my choices about "data," and my reasons for bringing theory and data together in particular ways.

Let's move on to politics and the 2008 campaign.

The Performance of Politics

Prologue

On the evening of Nov. 4, 2008, Barack Obama stepped onto the stage of a country maimed by war, cleaved by greed, riven by a collapsing economy, and I walked outside my new York apartment with my 5-year-old son in my arms [and] up and down the street, people shouted out the windows of their cars [and] strangers were hugging one another.... When 2008 is crushed and lying in the smithereens of memory, far from now, when it has taken on new shape, or when it has been undone by other years, when it has been dissected and torn, when it has been transformed into novels, shot through with language, reinventing the president, and indeed us, I will still return to that November evening, a moment that...was the marker of a beginning and an end.[1]

T HE OLD GREEKS DISTINGUISHED BETWEEN *KAIROS* AND *CHRONOS*. Chronos is calendar time, measured by the spoonful, orderly and linear. Kairos is the right time, the opportune moment, improvised for the occasion, "a point in time filled with significance, charged with a meaning derived from its relation to the end."[2] The election of Barack Obama in November 2008 was *kairos*, not *chronos*. It did not come by virtue of time's unfolding. It was an intervention that shifted the arc of history, and it depended on creativity, perseverance, and fortune—as this book explains.

Democratic politics swings like a pendulum from right to left and then back again.[3] However, the movements of a pendulum are determined by invariant laws of physics, each side symmetrical, its movement gradual and predictable. The pendulum of democratic politics is different. It swings back and forth from right to left and from left to right but without any necessary balance. The movement of politics can veer dangerously out of kilter. The swing can stay on the left for a long time and then suddenly and sharply move toward the right and seem stuck there. That's what happened to American politics from the late 1960s until 2008.

The ideals of liberty, equality, and community are buried in the heart and soul of American society, the sources of the promises it must keep. For centuries, group after oppressed and excluded group—classes, religions, ethnicities, races, genders, regions, and sexualities—have struggled to compel the nation to make good on these promises. Their efforts have created great lurches forward. They have stimulated progressive political movements, triggered liberal electoral victories, and created pioneering pieces of social legislation. But great leaps forward create backlash movements. Inevitably, conservative movements and rightward-leaning, reactive politics have pushed back and eventually displaced the political forces of the progressive side.

From the early 1930s, when Franklin Roosevelt created the New Deal during the Great Depression, to the mid-1960s, when Lyndon Johnson launched the Great Society during a much more affluent time, the pendulum of American politics swung magisterially and seemingly inexorably to the left side. In the four decades following, the same pendulum swung to the right. In 1964 Johnson won the presidency with the greatest landslide in U.S. electoral history, a 61.1 percent victory over Barry Goldwater, the immoderately conservative, out-of-step candidate of the Republican Right. Two years later Republicans gained control over half of the nation's state legislators, including seven of the ten most populous states.[4] When President Johnson signed the Civil Rights Act of 1964, one of the most radical pieces of legislation in U.S. history, he ruefully observed that its passage could transform the American South from Democrat to Republican and cost progressives national power for a generation. Johnson was right. Democrats lost seven of the next 10 presidential elections, only once winning more than half of their fellow citizens' votes—when Jimmy Carter, in the wake of Watergate, won 50.1 percent of the vote in 1976.

Richard Nixon pioneered the "Southern strategy" of reactive, backlash politics in his successful run for the presidency in 1968 and went on to crush the avowedly leftist candidacy of George McGovern in 1972. After the Watergate interregnum, the nation's political pendulum continued its rightward swing. Ronald Reagan's election in 1980 marked the demise of twentieth-century liberalism and the rise of neoconservative hegemony. Republicans were elected president for three consecutive terms. While Democrat Bill Clinton ruled formally between 1992 and 2000, he was often outfoxed and fenced in by conservatives. In 1994, the ever more rightward-leaning Republicans took control of both houses of Congress for the first time in 40 years. The Democratic president responded by virtually renouncing the liberal faith and proclaiming the era of big government over and done. Even so, Clinton was mortally wounded when House Republicans impeached him in 1998 and, while he escaped Senate indictment and eviction from office, the political pendulum continued its swing to the right. Republicans squeaked back into power in 2000, but they won a more decisive victory in 2004, with the fear of terrorism in full bloom and energetic political participation from the maturing religious Right. It looked like Republican rule was here to stay. The Democrats, in the words of one academic observer, were "a party largely devoid of power and subservient to the opposition for decades."[5]

The decades-long decline of liberal political fortune came in part because of social backlash. From the New Deal to the Great Society, there had just been too much equality, too much progressive social change, too much government, and too much disruption of settled manners, mores, and entrenched elites. There was bound to be growing resistance and the return to political power of the Republican side. Nonetheless, it would be a mistake to see the extent or the timing of this rightward swing as inevitable or determined. While political movements are deeply affected in part by social forces, their fate is decided to some extent by whether they provide these social forces with effective rhetoric and voice. If Bobby Kennedy had not been assassinated in 1968, Nixon would not have won his first election, and American politics would not have swung as rapidly and sharply to the right.[6] If Teddy Kennedy's car had not careened off the bridge that night at Chappaquiddick, he might well have run against Nixon in 1972 and defeated him, and the hapless Jimmy Carter would not later have gained political leadership.

Progressives remained exiled from national power for decades because they did not have a Moses to lead them out of the wilderness. Their presidential candidates were either worn out retreads like Hubert Humphrey and Walter Mondale or political rubes like Carter and Michael Dukakis. Bill Clinton was neither, but he suffered from being deeply implicated in the polarizing politics of the sixties, the period that gave the new conservative politics its vitality, its very reason for being. The Republicans did have effective leaders. Goldwater was a man of narrow conviction but political prescience and integrity, and his call for conservative renewal rang with enthusiasm and clarity. Nixon was a brilliant if unscrupulous street-fighting man, and Ronald Reagan an extraordinarily gifted politician. Without Reagan, there would have been a conservative renewal but no revolution. The Republicans also had fortune on their side. Their leaders were shot but did not die. Reagan survived his assassination attempt and became a hero. By a cruel irony, even mass murder seemed to help the Republican side. If terrorists had not destroyed the Twin Towers and killed thousands on September 11, 2001, George W. Bush would not have soared to unprecedented popularity in the years immediately after, nor would he have been able, only a decade after the Cold War, to so effectively employ conservative us-versus-them politics.

Yet a paradox haunted this long Republican rise. During the very same decades as its exile from the political center, social liberalism experienced an enormous efflorescence in the culture and society of the United States. In the worlds of law and collective feeling, a rights revolution gradually transformed every nook and cranny of the nation—women's and environmental movements emerged and presided, affirmative action became powerful and legitimate, multicultural ideas and practices flourished, and gays and lesbians came out of the closet.[7] A kind of double movement took place, a decidedly conservative triumph in national politics, a society that became emphatically more equal and more liberal underneath. But to the latter, the Democrats could not give voice. There was not a national leader who could symbolically refashion these new emancipations and speak about them in an American idiom that would make them seem not radical or deviant or marginal but down to earth, patriotic, center rather than left, and as American as apple pie.

It took a long time for such a voice to emerge—a generation, in fact—but it seemed forever to the progressive side. Barack Obama was the beneficiary of the 1960s' social legislation. His career outside and inside politics rode the waves of the new social movements following in the wake of that decade. However, Obama himself was not implicated by the politics of polarization. He was not a boomer and did not look back nostalgically but forward to a different kind of progressive time. The Democratic Party's candidates in 2000 and 2004, Al Gore and John Kerry, were each regarded, in different ways, as spokesmen for the sixties' generation. Barack Obama could break away. He could represent the idealistic promise of American society, but differently, in a less angry, more soothing and potentially unifying way. Obama spoke with the thrusting cadence of twentieth-century America's greatest political figure, African American Martin Luther King Jr., but his voice also resonated with the democratic eloquence of Abraham Lincoln, the white president who saved the nation in the nineteenth century.

Americans first heard Barack Obama's voice in 2004 at the Democratic convention, when he delivered his optimistic, often stirring keynote address. The presidential election that followed marked another discouraging Democratic defeat, but the Republicans' hold on national political power turned out to be much thinner than it seemed. Scandalous deceit at the highest levels of government about weapons of mass destruction, American humiliation in the Iraq War, corruption locally and in the national capital, soaring budget deficits and economic slowdown, conservative callousness and ineptitude in the face of Hurricane Katrina—by the beginning of the 2008 campaign, the poll ratings of President Bush had fallen 60 points—to the lowest level ever recorded since opinion surveys began during Franklin Roosevelt's reign.

It was time for the pendulum of American politics to swing to the left again. But the moment could be seized only if improvisation were clever and performance right. It was a matter of kairos, not chronos. The voice was ready. Would it be able to sing? What would the audience's response be?

PART I

Power, Performance, and Representation

CHAPTER ONE

Civil Sphere and Public Drama

THE STRUGGLE FOR POWER IS NOT INTERNALLY DEMOCRATIC. Political campaigns are centralized battles run by generals, organized by captains, energized by foot soldiers, and disciplined, if possible, in the extreme. What is democratic about this struggle for power is simply that it must take place.

In order to gain power in a democratic society, one must win the formal consent of one's fellow citizens. It is these members of the democratic public—what I call the "civil sphere"—who call the shots. They are putatively equal to and immensely more numerous than candidates for power, and it is their votes, every single one of them, that decide to whom power will go. Earlier, in simpler democratic societies, candidates for power appeared directly before the electors and asked for their support. As societies became larger, more complex, and more inclusive, this asking gradually took the form of an extended campaign. The struggle for power is democratic insofar as power becomes a privilege that must be campaigned for. One asks the members of the civil sphere to become their representative. Only if they agree can the reins of power be seized.[1]

In the course of political campaigns, those struggling for power are subject to a terrible scrutiny. This is critical because, once power is achieved, it gains significant independence from civil society. In the middle of the past century, America's finest political reporter, Theodore White, spoke of "the most awesome transfer of power in the world—the power to marshal and mobilize, the power to send men to kill or be killed, the power to tax and destroy, the power to create and the responsibility to do so, the power to guide and the responsibility to heal—all committed into the hands of one man."[2] In the first democracy, in ancient Greece, there were no political campaigns. Athenians chose their governors by lot in regular rotation. Because the duties of domestic government were light, the Greeks required neither state nor professional bureaucracy. Indeed, in their entire lifetimes, Athenians were allowed to serve as governors no more than three one-year terms. Without extensive government, there was no need for specialization.

Today's states are immense and intricate. The behavior of those who wield power inside this vast apparatus is subject to moral norms and to legal sanctions of office; reported upon by news media; and monitored by nongovernmental groups. While these indirect controls—along with institutional checks and balances—are critically significant hedges against unlimited state power, the machinery of governing is nonetheless, merely as a practical matter if not by purposeful design, largely hidden from view.[3] It is during the publicly visible campaign to take state power, as well as in the knowledge that, even if successful, the candidates and their parties will be subjected to the same scrutiny time and again, that the most critical exercise of civil control over state power actually lies.

Intellectual efforts to understand democratic struggles for power have muted the voice of civil society and its citizens—the hopeful discourses about courage and conviction, honesty and integrity—that subject candidates to moral scrutiny. Reducing democracy to demography, students of politics have focused upon interests, making broad correlations between political opinion and stratification position. Class, race, gender, religion, region, age, ethnicity—such prior commitments are said to determine the vote. In fact, however, interest determination, whether established by speculation or statistic, has never been the case. Demography is not destiny, at least not in a political campaign. In the first place, one's "objective" or "structural" position is always subject to subjective interpretation. What does it mean, in this time and this place, to be a working man, woman, black, Catholic, or Southerner? In the second place, parties and candidates struggling for power must present themselves not as slavishly serving a particular demographic but as speaking and acting on behalf of democratic ideals that go beyond circumscribed interests to embrace the aspirations of society. Even in the class-bound society of nineteenth-century Britain, one-third of manual workers voted regularly for the conservative side. Whether for reasons of religion, region, ethnicity, or reverence for monarchy and tradition, to vote in such a manner violated the material interests of working people narrowly conceived.[4]

If position in the social hierarchy actually determined party identification and vote, how could there ever be any alternation in the struggle for power? The same relatively fixed "interest" can express itself in widely and sometimes wildly different political forms and ideologies. While ideological commitments are fixed on the right and left sides of the spectrum, as one moves toward the center, political opinions about representation become fluid and subject to continuous slip and slide. In the contemporary United States, the looseness of fit between demography and democracy has frayed further still. In 1954, self-declared independents constituted 22 percent of the electorate; in 2004, that number had almost doubled in size.[5] During the decades he has been writing about politics for the *Washington Post*, David Broder has observed the same thing:

> The fastest-growing portion of the electorate consists of people who have no strong partisan allegiance. These political independents are now as numerous as self-identified Republicans and are closing the gap on the Democrats. Though badly underrepresented in Congress, where districting rules and campaign finance practices reinforce the two-party hegemony, the independent voters make up the swing vote in almost every contested election—including the presidential race.[6]

If candidates cannot reliably count on the objective interests of citizens or their official party affiliations to guarantee votes, they must struggle to gain them. Rather than direct interaction with the political candidates, the voters who referee the struggle for power have available only symbolic representations of candidates, which the mass media supply. Projected to citizens over vast space, these symbolic representations are interjected into the campaign by politicians, and they are pushed this way and that by journalists. Politicians are compelled to enmesh themselves in a devilishly complex and unpredictable process of symbolic representation, projecting images of themselves not only to voters who are close at hand but also, and primarily, to those who are far away.

For all of these reasons, the struggle for power becomes theatrical. Candidates work to present compelling performances of civil competence to citizen audiences at a remove not only geographically but also emotionally and morally. It is the success of these performances that determines how whites, blacks, Jews, Catholics, and women distribute their precious votes, and the opinions of these supposedly demographic groups shift significantly in response to coding, narrative, tone, metaphor, setting, and performance in the course of campaign time.[7] Cultural mattering is not a matter of Left versus Right—the Left's interest in class versus the Right's in tradition; nor is it a product of one particular historical moment—of loopy postsixties' culture wars versus pocketbook concerns brought on by the Great Recession.[8] Meaning matters all of the time. That demographic position and historical context are significant, there is no doubt. However, in a democratic society it is the attribution of meaningfulness that determines who will exercise power.

The public space of civil society provides an arena for the democratic struggle for power. Making democracy real depends on this public space having some autonomy from others. The civil sphere is more than legally guaranteed rights, private associations, and voluntary groups. It is also a structure of feeling. It is defined by the experience of solidarity, by a feeling of identity with, or at least empathy for, every other member of one's society. What makes solidarity democratic and civil rather than authoritarian and primordial is its breadth, on the one hand, and its autonomy, on the other. *Civil* solidarity is a big tent. It is universal rather than particular, not a community of love, friendship, or kinship but something more abstract and broad, a societal community that, in principle, goes beyond any particular religion, class, ethnicity, race, region, gender, and sexuality to embrace the ideal of humanity. Such a broad solidarity paradoxically rests upon the autonomy of its members and requires each person to realize the individuality of every other.

What makes this civil solidarity powerful and not merely a utopian ideal is its independence from other spheres. Though it depends on schools, families, religion, economy, and state, it is not the same as these spheres. It is different in that it is conceived as broader and more voluntary than any other. It is neither ruled by prescriptive or dogmatic beliefs nor directed by hierarchies and powers. It is empowered from the bottom up by individuals to whom are attributed self-control and rationality; openness, altruism, and generosity; honesty and independence; and the capacity to criticize without being aggressive. That democracies are really peopled by such ideally cooperative persons is inscribed deeply in the public opinion that circulates through the civil sphere like a gust of warm spring wind. This "discourse of liberty" constitutes the positive and hopeful side of the collective; it is taken-for-granted language to which every action inside civil societies must refer.

There is, however, another and more negative side to this collective language. There is a "discourse of repression" that defines antidemocratic qualities preventing persons from being allowed inside the civil sphere or at least from being fully so and certainly from being allowed the privilege of representing the civil sphere in the state. If people are viewed as out of control, impulsive, dependent and subservient, dishonest and secretive, and prone to conspiracy rather than open and as selfish rather than generous—then they do not deserve civil membership. Indeed, civil societies must defend themselves against such persons, for they would damage the capacity for thoughtful and mutual cooperation upon which the very possibility of dispensing with hierarchical power depends. Sometimes this repressive discourse is attributed to persons and forces that pose real dangers. Often, however, it is not. Projecting anticivil qualities upon others is like a chilly wind sweeping across the fields of political campaigns on a winter day.

The discourse of civil society is divided into either/or binaries. In real life, political actors are not *either* rational *or* impulsive, honest *or* deceitful but more than a little of each. Inside the moral rhetoric of democratic politics, however, this is exactly how they are symbolically constructed as being. The nuance and ambiguity of empirical actions does not often make an appearance in the public language of civil society. It seems, instead, that action must be clearly and cleanly categorized, put into boxes in neat and tidy, black-and-white ways. The bright side of this moral binary enjoins civility and tolerance, energizes liberation, sustains hope, inspires democratic rituals of purification, triggers progress, and allows injustice to be repaired. The dark side of the symbolic dichotomy justifies exclusion from civil society and sometimes repression inside it. It can make perfectly decent human beings seem dirty, dangerous, incompetent, incapable of exercising the franchise, and unworthy of ever holding public office. Sometimes, of course, such evaluations are accurate and fair. Corrupt power holders should be polluted, and impulsive and incompetent politicians condemned. Inspiring and rational men and women with justice in their hearts should be described in bright and positive ways. Often, however, the relationship between moral category and political action is arbitrary and fuzzy. The binary language of democratic communication is not an empirical description of real political action but a set of preexisting and prescriptive judgments.* It constitutes a symbolic reality that those who struggle for democratic power must align themselves with or go down trying.

The civil sphere is more than a symbolic discourse. It is sustained also by a web of powerful institutions. Some of these are communicative, such as mass media organizations, whose business it is to project evaluations and opinions in the form of factual and fictional reports, and public opinion polls, which regularly project evaluations via statistically generated samples of civil society. Other institutions are more regulative. While these also speak the language of civil society, they can enforce their black-and-white evaluations through sanction and coercion. Law is one of these regulative institutions; the electoral system another. Underpinned by the franchise, fueled by political parties, and brought to closure by voting, the electoral system selects representatives of the civil sphere for the most powerful positions of the state. It is with this regulative institution that the present work is concerned.

Political campaigns unfold inside the civil sphere. Success in a campaign depends on making the civil sphere's binary language walk and talk. Live human beings must seem to embody the hopeful discourse of liberty, all the while pushing the dark and brooding qualities that mark the discourse of repression to the other side. Political theory says that democratic actors are deliberative and that the force of better argument prevails—the argument that is fairer, more truthful, and more honest. Jürgen Habermas, the most influential contemporary philosopher of democracy, conceptualizes public conflict in just this way, as if it is about presenting truth claims and propounding rational justifications.[9] If this were only so, the

---

*For more about this collective language at the center of civil society, including a systematic model of the "good and bad" qualities that are applied to motives, relationships, and institutions, see "Note on Concept and Method."

world would be a much better place. It would also be a lot easier to understand. Truth, honesty, and fairness do matter, but it is less a matter of being those qualities than of seeming to be them, of embodying truth, narrating honesty, projecting fairness, and doing so in a persuasive way. Being truthful, honest, and fair are discursive *claims;* whether these claims take root is a matter of performative success. Throughout the 2008 presidential campaign, operatives and journalists alike spoke of "painting" the other side.[10] Painting is an aesthetic activity, not a cognitive or a moral one. It depends on stagecraft rather than ethical worthiness or empirical accuracy.

Meaning is relative, not objective. Good and bad are established by comparison and difference, not by pointing to the real actions of good or bad people or things. Political struggle achieves clarity and persuasive power by defining the difference between one's own side and the other's, connecting "us" to the sacred civil qualities that sustain liberty and linking "them" to the anticivil qualities that profane political life, undermine liberty, court repression, and open the door to corruption. "A man sees himself as a member of a group only in opposition to other groups," wrote the British anthropologist Evans-Pritchard it seventy years ago.[11] In the 2008 campaign, Barack Obama put it more colloquially: "I'm a big believer that if something's good, then there's a bad to it, and vice versa."[12] One's goal in the democratic struggle for power is to become a powerful representative of the sacred and to embody and project it in such a compelling manner that one seems a natural symbol of what it means to be right and good. If our opponents are successful, however, we will be constructed in precisely the opposite way; they will make us seem cunning and aggressive, dependent and deferential, not fit to rigorously represent the ideals of civil life.

At the end of July 2008, presidential candidate John McCain and his staff launched a powerful "celebrity" campaign against Barack Obama. Reporting on this new development, the *New York Times* implicitly references both the demand for meaning through difference and the challenge of performing to the citizen audience. Describing the celebrity campaign as "the most full-throated effort to *define* Mr. Obama," the nation's leading liberal paper explains that "by creating a narrative"—about the Democratic candidate as an arrogant celebrity—the Republican campaign hoped "to turn the public off to an opponent."[13] The analysis is accurate, but stating it so publicly presents a potential danger to the Republican side. Politics is signifying, but if it appears to *be* symbolic action, it is bound to fail. Because political performance succeeds only when it seems natural, it must not betray its own construction.[14] When Steven Schmidt, chief strategist of the McCain campaign, responds to reporters' inquiries about the success of the Republicans' new celebrity tactic; he carefully insists that it is not metaphor but empirical fact. It "speaks to a truth," he suggests, "that people get instantly."[15]

When candidates in the democratic struggle for power address citizen audiences, they make every effort to deploy the language of civil society, but they may not have success. In November 2008, on the day after the presidential vote, the *Wall Street Journal* looks back on the failure of the Republican campaign. According to the nation's leading conservative newspaper, the problem was that McCain "had struggled to find a message that would resonate."[16] To resonate is to find a pathway that leads from the words that come from the mouths of political performers and from the pictures drawn by their hands to the eyes and ears of the citizen audience and, via these receptors, into the center of their throbbing democratic hearts. To resonate is to fuse actor and audience. However, the more complex society becomes, the more difficult is this task. As the expanse of society grows, actor and audience become more separated physically. As society becomes more stratified, actor and audience become more separated by background and disposition. When Athenians spoke directly to their fellow citizens in the face-to-face intimacy of their ancient polis, they employed not only rational argumentation but also a rhetoric shaped by instruction and skill. How much more self-conscious artifice, organization, self-styling, and image control are required when those who struggle for power must convince audiences with whom they do not share a way of life, cannot see, and will never know?

More than half a century ago, when Theodore "Teddy" White began writing about presidential politics, he already recognized how the candidate "sits at the center of a web of affairs so complex as to be dehumanized," how "his ideas, his phrases, his finances, his schedules, are all prepared for him by others," how "wherever he pauses to consult with staff, he must already make the detached executive decision." Yet, White could still insist in those relatively early days of the performative struggle for power that "becoming President is an utterly personal business."[17] White traced this personal thread through each of the "two audiences to the ordeal of a man seeking the Presidency."[18] To reach the larger, national audience, the candidate addresses "the two score or more newsmen, broadcasters, analysts who doggedly trail in his wake," mediators who "feed the great opinion-making press and networks" by offering "their distillation of his speeches, film clips of his action, sound-snatches of his voice." Through this layered intermediary, the presidential "candidate reaches the national audience, the many millions who idly watch the evening television news or hastily scan the morning newspapers." Despite this easy connection, however, political effectiveness cannot be ensured. "Not for days or weeks," White acknowledges, "will the candidate know the effect of any speech or statement on the national mood or on the minority to which it is specifically addressed,"[19] "what posture or image he has established in the mood or emotions" of his listeners.[20]

The second audience for presidential aspirants is local, "so small in numbers as to be minuscule in scope." For such face-to-face campaigning, the impact of political performance is easier to judge because it presents itself directly, without mediation. This audience "gathers in the flesh, in shirt sleeves and house dresses, to listen to the candidate as he pauses in his travels." Whether there is fusion between candidate and audience in this intimate setting "is more important than [in] any other." It is also very easy to discern:

> The laughter of the personal audience, its scowl, its silence, its cheering are the only clues in the mystic communication between the leader and the led that tell, truly, whether he has reached those he seeks to lead.... The candidate must feel the best of the people he hopes to lead; their heart is his target; and by their immediate response, whether it be a thousand at a whistle stop or ten thousand in an auditorium, he knows whether he has ranged the target or failed.[21]

While White certainly did not ignore the uncertainty of political performance, he was relatively sanguine, not only about the primacy of face-to-face engagement and the possibility of connecting with audiences small and large but also about the transparency of political performance and whether the politicians struggling for power will know whether they have struck the citizen's heart.

It is different today. The personal audience has been relegated to the "retail politics" of Iowa and New Hampshire, the first two primary states, and, even there, the national audience is always the most significant surround. The dehumanized apparatus of the message giver, the political candidate, has expanded exponentially. The campaign has become a floating crap game of press secretaries, spinners, speechwriters, advance personnel, poll takers, focus groups, lighting and stage designers, personal assistants, and bodyguards. Arrayed against this effort is the opposing candidate, who sits at the center of an equally large and depersonalized political staff. Each side wishes to appear authentic and sincere, and in fact they may be. Inspired by democratic ideals, "we" present ourselves as embodying freedom and liberty. "They" seek to undermine the power of this performance by making it seem artificial, to denaturalize it by declaring it to be only a performance, and to make our sincere and very human candidate seem like an automaton reading a script from a machine:

> It was the bleary-eyed end of a 16-hour day, and the strategists in the Republican war room were about to call it quits. Then an image from the Democratic National Convention flashed across their banks of television sets. Sen. Barack Obama appeared on stage via video conference, greeting his wife from what he said was a living room in St. Louis. In fact, he was in Kansas City. Sen. Obama quickly corrected himself. But the Republican operatives who had been tasked with undercutting the

Democratic message here in Denver were electrified. "Woo-hoo!" one shouted, pumping his fist in the air. "Boo-yah!" another yelled. Within minutes, Alex Conant, communications director for the Republican National Committee, had blasted an email to more than 600 reporters nationwide and scores of GOP strategists. The subject line: "Obama Gaffe Machine Rolls into DNCC." This was exactly the type of moment Mr. Conant had been sent to Denver to seize. In an alleyway office a short drive from the downtown convention hall, two dozen staffers from the Republican National Committee and Sen. John McCain's presidential campaign are doing their best to disrupt Sen. Obama's big week.... The heart of the Republican counterattack is what they call the "war room," a small space lined with TVs and red, white, and blue posters that proclaim that Obama is "Not Ready" to lead. Here, hunched over laptops and cold coffee, bloggers, researchers, advisers and press secretaries dissect every minute of the Democratic festivities and fire off a steady stream of criticism. The goal is to shape reporters' coverage and throw the Democrats off stride. "We're jamming them a little," said Michael Goldfarb, deputy communications director for the McCain camp.[22]

The struggle for power is not dialogical, a political version of "American Idol," where two contestants vie for the judges' approval or the audience's vote. Between the two political sides sits a morass of mediating mass communication, one that dwarfs the posse of "two score and more" upon which White so portentously remarked in that earlier, much simpler political day. Reporters, editors, and other commentariat constitute a giant digital prism through which every candidate's performance must pass, distorting the light and displacing the verbal and visual images that pass in between. "For the broad public," Obama rues in *The Audacity of Hope,* "I am who the media say I am. I say what they say I say. I become who they say I've become."[23] Those who have this say—the journalists who create mass media content—are finely attuned to the performative dimension of politics. They know that the citizen audience is always on guard and believe that, if it is not, it certainly should be. In an interview after the election, this is what a senior *New York Times* reporter who had covered the 2008 campaign told me:

It's theatrical even when it's incredibly authentic.... There is a huge performative aspect.... People know that campaigns are designed down to the very last second. And I think the public is incredibly suspicious of what even seem like spontaneous moments. People know how it works.... Throughout the campaign, I found that the public was incredibly suspicious and skeptical on every level.... I don't think the public sees anything connected with presidential politics as pure.[24]

So those who mediate political events employ the same standards of performative effectiveness and civil discourse as those who create them. What's different—and this is critical—is that journalists do so in a less partisan, more professionally organized, and more consistent way.

In the concluding days of the Republicans' failed campaign, a member of the *Wall Street Journal*'s editorial board writes that he has discovered a "useful prism to view the current presidential race."[25] Describing the "Axelrod Method," the journalist reports that it had been "field tested" three years earlier in the campaign of Duval Patrick, who went on to become the first African American governor of Massachusetts. "The Patrick campaign," he suggests, "is the model for Barack Obama's effort, down to the messages of 'hope' and 'change' and the unofficial Patrick slogan of 'Yes, We Can!'" The implication for performativity seems unavoidable: Candidate Obama is merely a cipher, a talented actor reading from a script that had already been successfully previewed elsewhere, in an out-of-town run. According to the *Journal*'s report, it is Obama's chief strategist, the "image maker and political guru" David Axelrod, who has created the powerful representations of Barack Obama that have dominated the presidential campaign. Apparently, these representations have nothing to do with the candidate himself. The implications for civil discourse are clear, for if Obama is a fake, then he must also be a liar. Rhetorical construction and performative deconstruction go hand in hand. If candidates are not themselves but instead puppets whose strings are pulled behind the scenes, then they are not sincere and honest but anticivil in the extreme.

Because politics and reportage are each centrally concerned with performance and binary discourse, these realms, so different in many aspects of their culture and organization, are during political campaigns tightly intertwined. Two weeks after the *Journal*'s deconstruction of Obama, the Democratic candidate makes an extraordinary purchase of three, 30-minute segments of evening prime-time TV. He does so, according to his campaign, so that he can better project his message of hope and civil repair throughout the nation on election eve. On the morning before these broadcasts, John McCain warns Americans that "the sales job is always better than the product" and adds, "Buyer beware."[26] This caustic comment attributes to Obama artifice and manipulation. The Republican wants to transform Obama's pure and sacred image into something polluted and profane.

It is revealing how closely this effort by McCain echoes the *Journal*'s critical account two weeks earlier. In making and promoting judgments, politicians and the media employ the same overarching moral categories and think about failed and successful performance in the same way.

CHAPTER TWO

Becoming a Collective
Representation

I N MID-SEPTEMBER 2008, WITH THE TRIUMPH OF THE DEMOCRATIC
convention long past, the unnerving challenge of Sarah Palin well under way,
and the financial situation entering meltdown, Barack Obama's campaign
continues to generate anxieties bordering upon desperation among his supporters. Precisely at this moment the *Times* publishes an extraordinarily pessimistic
story about the opportunity in contemporary political life for performative success. Under the headline "Carefully Shaped Message Now a Campaign Relic," the
paper's chief White House correspondent and campaign reporter, Adam
Nagourney, describes "Mr. Obama's efforts to break through the day's crush of
blog postings, cable television headlines, television advertisements, speeches by
other candidates and surrogates, video press releases and countercharges—not to
mention the old-fashioned newspaper article or broadcast report on the evening
news."[1] In a speech at a Norfolk, Virginia, high school, the Democratic candidate
had "offered one of his most scathing attacks on his Republican opponent, Senator
John McCain, accusing him of 'lies and Swift boat politics' and denouncing his
campaign tactics as insulting to the American public."[2] Yet, Nagourney writes,
"Mr. Obama's attack barely broke through." The next morning "Mr. Obama tried
again, this time with the 6 A.M. release of two new attack advertisements, followed
by a memorandum from Mr. Obama's campaign manager...telling the world
exactly what Mr. Obama was doing and why attention must be paid." Once again,
the message did not break through; the audience was still not paying attention.
According to the *Times'* correspondent, this "episode reflects one of the most frus-
trating challenges the candidates face." Because there has been a "fracturing of
mass media," candidates must "stumble through what has become a daily campaign

fog." Even "senior campaign aides say they are no longer sure what works." For broader perspective, Nagourney turns to Matthew Dowd, chief strategist for President Bush's 2004 reelection campaign. "There is just so much stuff," Dowd observes ruefully, that "at this point, the ability to create and drive a message narrative is all but impossible."

The perceptions shared by journalist and consultant reveal the anxiety with which even the most seasoned political observers view the performative struggle between political actors and citizen audience in the course of political campaigns. If politicians' symbolic projections cannot enter into the heart of the citizen audience, the candidates will not be seen as embodying the discourse of civil society; as a result, they will not be selected by the members of the civil sphere to represent them in the state. If such connection has, indeed, become impossible, if new structural conditions prevent fusion, there would be a political crisis of massive proportion not just for this or that political campaign but also for democracy itself. Fortunately, even in contemporary, mass-mediated civil society, this is not the case. In fact, the searing criticisms that Democrats made against Republican Sarah Palin often did take hold. Moreover, almost immediately after the *Times* issued its dire warning about successful campaign messages becoming relics of the past, candidates Obama and McCain both captured rapt national attention with their dramatic showdown during the financial crisis. Despite the enormous increase in mass mediation and the uncertainty it exacerbates, those who struggle for democratic power frequently do establish powerful connections with citizen audiences.

Ritual and Representation: Political Success

To struggle for power in a democratic society one must become a collective representation—a symbolic vessel filled with what citizens hold most dear.[3] More than simply a smart, experienced, and competent politician, one needs to become a broad expression of the moods and meanings of the nation's democratic life. Moreover, for political performance to be successful, one must become a symbol not only of the civil sphere but also of some of the extracivil realms that form its boundaries, realms organized around issues such as gender, family, religion, class, ethnicity, and race. To become such a collective representation, one must achieve powerful symbolic status not only with one's immediate supporters but with other groups inside and outside civil society as well. Struggles for power project meanings and styles to citizen audiences both nearby and far away and who are fragmented in all the familiar demographic ways. Winning power depends on creating performances that successfully breach these supposedly great divides.

Created by active processes of symbolic communication, collective political representations become carriers of intense social energy, and they project this energy back to society in turn. A former comrade from Barack Obama's early Chicago days, interviewed by the *New York Times,* remembers the young community organizer as somebody who displayed a remarkable "*energizing capacity* to connect with the people in these neighborhoods."[4] Political life is a back-and-forth process of interaction and communication, one in which psychic energy flows between symbolic public texts and actual living and breathing persons. This explains why, even in the virtual age, politicians must mingle and be seen to do so with real voters, and why they shake so many real hands and speak not only digitally but also in all their throaty sweatiness to throbbing and heaving rallies in real time.

Candidates experience and channel the energy of human contact. These intense, face-to-face encounters look a lot like old-fashioned rituals.[5] The emotions they generate are connected to civil discourse, and culture and emotion are digitized and circulated. The sounds and images of audiences whistling and applauding and of beaming, back-slapping, and fist-pumping candidates reflect collective psychic energy to the candidate and upward, via communicative institutions, into the broader civil sphere. This circulating energy cannot be supplied simply from studio performance. While virtual, digitally created political performances are technically feasible, it would be considered immoral to employ them. They would not trigger the recursive processes of ritual and symbolic representation so critical to performative success. Barack Obama often feels compelled to counter criticisms that he is merely a performer separated from real human interaction:

> Fighting the perception that he is only a razzle-dazzle speechmaker who is aloof in small settings, Mr. Obama devoted most of his time on the campaign trail in the past week to intimate appearances, hosting round-table discussions with the public and touring a hospital in St. Louis, a retirement facility in Columbus, Ohio, and an all-girls charter school in Chicago.... Mr. Obama's chief strategist, David Axelrod, said large rallies in the primaries had energized the candidate and his supporters, but were also on some level "isolating" lectures rather than conversations. In the general election, Mr. Obama wanted to interact more intimately with voters.... A participant in a round-table discussion about credit in Chicago, Rosa Figueroa, who was driven into bankruptcy by credit card debt after her divorce, said in an interview afterward: "I think he understands the need for change. A lot of families are going through what I went through." Ms. Figueroa said [Mr. Obama] had quickly put her at ease when they met before the event. "I was not afraid of him," she said.... "He's just very warm and comforting, an average Joe."[6]

Political rallies aim at becoming rituals, fused performances in which charismatic leaders touch the voters' hands, the tremendous effervescence of the crowds flowing into the symbolic figure who is the collective political representation. In the presidential campaign season, the ritual process begins with small groups in living rooms in Iowa and New Hampshire. It segues into larger settings in later primary contests, morphs into advertisements that condense collective energy into texts and images on YouTube and television advertisements, and culminates in the carefully choreographed scenes of mass hysteria, laced with almost religious gravitas, that characterize party conventions. In the personal contact process, which defines the ground game of political campaigns, "advance staff" are crucial. They create the conditions for fused performances. Campaign image makers aim to extend this ritual experience, via the mass media, to larger audiences of voters. They organize the candidate's websites, write blogs, send reporters spinning messages throughout the 24-hour news cycle, and address millions of digital messages daily to contributors and fans, all the while arranging face-to-face meetings with journalists and interest group representatives in private and in public.

Reporting on Hillary Clinton's June 7, 2008, concession speech in the historic National Building Museum in Washington, D.C., CNN's Washington correspondent John King talks about "the drama building," about how "you hear the excitement building inside the hall." Identifying the object of this spiraling emotion, King reports that "the many thousands of people in here have been asking us, where is she? Is she here yet?"[7] Wolf Blitzer agrees, "we're listening to this crowd getting *excited*." remarking that the museum's immense interior space, with its vaulting modernist arches, provides a dramatic and imposing setting for the denouement of Senator Clinton's powerful and controversial campaign. As Senator Clinton arrives and addresses her cheering fans, Blitzer observes that she is elevated on a platform high above them. Another CNN correspondent suggests it is as if the politician were in a great church, offering a sermon to devoted worshippers. "Hillary"—the chants are ubiquitous—offers thanks to her staff and all the volunteer workers, the priests and the laity, respectively, of her political religion. We witness the production of myth, of fallen heroes and martyrs in the struggle for civil power. The next day, the *Times* describes the event in a manner that attested to its performative success. "A dramatic—and at times theatrical—end to a candidacy that transfixed the country," the newspaper calls it, reporting that "many of her supporters watched, some weeping, turning out to witness and appreciate the history of this latest turn in the Clintons' story."[8]

The ritual-like nature of such fused performances, the manner in which deeply affected, often breathless journalists break down the barrier between actor and audience, and the extraordinary collective energy and symbolic power produced—all these dimensions of the struggle for power are quintessentially on display much later that summer in Denver, Colorado, at the Democratic convention. During the roll-call vote on the evening of Wednesday, August 27, it is not only the actual casting of votes but also the emotional power of ritualized personal interaction that closes the intensive primary conflict between Obama and Clinton, replacing party schism with broadened solidarity:

> The unanimous vote made Mr. Obama the first African-American to become a major party nominee for president. It brought to an end an often-bitter two-year political struggle for the nomination with Senator Hillary Rodham Clinton of New York, who, standing on a packed convention floor electric with anticipation, moved to halt the roll call in progress so that the convention could nominate Mr. Obama by acclamation. That it did with a succession of loud roars, followed by a swirl of dancing, embracing, high-fiving and chats of "Yes, we can."[9]

The next day Barack Obama formally accepts his party's nomination in a speech delivered in a different and much larger setting, Mile High Stadium. What follows is a media ethnography of MSNBC's television coverage on the afternoon and evening of August 28. The cable channel's long afternoon run-up to its coverage of Obama's evening acceptance speech mixes political religion with entertainment. Through observations, interpretations, and interviews, the coverage displays—and at the same time helps to create—a sense of ritual occasion and performative power.[10]

Looking forward to the big moment, the Reverend Al Sharpton evaluates its potential significance—and simultaneously tries to ensure its performative success—by quoting from Martin Luther King's "I Have a Dream" speech, delivered forty-five years before on this very day to the March on Washington. Presenting that earlier, historic speech as an eerie adumbration of Obama's candidacy, Sharpton recalls how Reverend King had proclaimed his faith that "someday people will be judged not by the color of their skin but by the content of their character." Sharpton tells NBC correspondent David Gregory that Obama's victory in the primary is perfect proof that King's prophecy has come true.

Then, Congressman John Lewis is interviewed. The former civil rights activist had been a key organizer of the March on Washington in 1963, where King had delivered his famous speech. Lewis proclaims, "We are dedicated this evening to Reverend King and his Dream speech." There

(continued)

follows an evocative video about King and his tragic-heroic quest. We are presented with his iconic face and reminded that he believed in the glory of God and the egalitarian promises of the American civil sphere. Bernice King, daughter of Martin and the recently deceased Coretta Scott King, offers the benediction.

Afterward, Keith Olbermann, MSNBC coanchor, narrates a video about racial discrimination that focuses on the great Yankee baseball player Elston Howard. Chris Matthews, Olbermann's coanchor, frames the world-historical importance of what is to follow by declaring that the United States will become "the first western hemisphere country" to nominate a person of African origin for president. Olbermann equates the nomination with other "completely unforeseen" and dramatic historic events such as the fall of Germany's Berlin Wall and the end of South Africa's apartheid. The two anchors exchange remarks about historical significance. Matthews calls this "an amazingly democratic moment." The essence of democracy, he avers, is that everything is open. In the struggle for power, nobody knows what will happen in advance. "Elections matter," he observes. "If you sit at home" and do not participate, you are "an idiot in the Greek sense," somebody with no connection to the polity. Olbermann characterizes Obama's nomination as an undeniable demonstration of the possibility for "concrete change," something that is "real for many, many people." For David Gregory, it "represents the future, not the past"—it's "change, that's the key."

This inflationary framing is momentarily brought back to earth by NBC correspondent Andrea Mitchell, who reveals what she clearly believes to be the wires behind the evening's event. "The whole point of coming," Mitchell says, is "organizing," getting attendees to sign up to do grunt campaign work. The events at Mile High Stadium, in other words, amount to simply "a massive recruitment effort." You get a free ticket if you agree to do six hours of volunteering. This is good reporting in a professional, journalistic sense. Reducing the event from rhetoric and dreams to planning and base, it implies fakery, not idealism, and exchange, not altruism. In the present context of ritual fusion, however, Mitchell's observations appear discordant, symbolically out of place even if empirically true. Anchor Chris Matthews is affronted, warning, "Andrea, this seems to me immensely Machiavellian!"

What follows on screen is a performance by African American recording artists Will.i.am and John Legend performing Obama's campaign slogan, "Yes, we can." For the commentators and perhaps many white viewers, these back-to-back screen events are beginning to appear too black, enmeshing the Obama symbol in a minority, still partially stigmatized subculture. Such a segmented performance would prevent the wider connection with whites that political performances in the contemporary American civil sphere need to succeed. Obliquely addressing this performative anxiety, Olbermann observes, "That's one of the dangers here"—the "need to keep these people entertained for two hours" before the evening's main speakers arrive.

Then something rather surprising happens. The televising of Obama's acceptance speech is wrenched out of its black-versus-white frame, out of the world of entertainment, and pulled from the past and anniversary to the future and celebration. Joe Scarborough, a conservative ex-congressman who is now an influential MSNBC morning talk show host, proclaims, "I can't think of any event that approaches this. They are hitting a home run here, I'll tell you that. After this speech, none of us will have any questions at all about what 'change' means." This skeptical observer has judged the ongoing event at Mile High Stadium to be authentic, and he has declared admiration. Asked by Matthews about Senator McCain's sarcastic references to the link between large stadiums and arrogant celebrities, Scarborough reminds viewers that "JFK took over the L.A. coliseum" for his acceptance speech in 1960, repeating information published earlier that day in the *Times*. "I need to tell you again," Scarborough insists, "that this is the most extraordinary event I've ever seen. Watch for Colorado to swing Obama's way." This outspokenly conservative commentator has been engaged by the dramaturgy and meaning of the ritual process. His testimony suggests the performative power of the occasion and its capacity to create a cathartic moral experience after the up-and-down narrations of the convention's previous days.

The MSNBC coverage now turns to "youth reporter" Luke Russert, who is interviewing John Legend, the recording artist who wrote and performed "Yes, We Can." Legend is articulate and forceful. Asked about the celebrity attacks on Obama by McCain and others, he issues a warning to conservatives and predicts their performative failure: "Don't be jealous because you haven't aroused emotion." Russert describes Legend's song as a media sensation, with 15 million hits on YouTube alone. Russert paraphrases Legend's remarks in a generational way: "You [aging] boomers think seeing a woman or black in power is a big deal, but to us it isn't. For us, it's not 'cause we've grown up with this."

(*continued*)

Coverage moves to the stadium's stage, where Sheryl Crow is rocking out. After projecting this bite of popular culture, televised attention shifts to Olbermann interviewing Chicago mayor Richard Daley. "What a throwback to yesterday," the coanchor remarks, referring to the tumultuous 1968 Democratic convention in Chicago, over which Daley's father had presided, contrasting today's civil ceremony with the provocative displays of youth culture, violent political protest, and controversial police repression of that earlier time. On split-screen, the television displays Sheryl Crow in skintight white jeans and cowboy hat, still singing her heart out. Daley responds to Olbermann's remark by mentioning Michelle Obama's address earlier in the week. He asserts that, in her speech, "she connected." The Chicago mayor insists that today, just as 40 years ago, "it's the economy" that matters, thereby identifying Obama not with sixties' radicals but with the most popular liberal president of the twentieth century, Franklin Roosevelt. Matthews asks, "How did you in Illinois manage to elect two black Americans senators?" Daley continues to emphasize the contrast by answering that today, "We have an open society."

This insistence on the contemporary reality of civil solidarity is underscored as the camera shifts to Stevie Wonder singing about "the united people of these United States." He calls out, "Now everybody repeat after me: Barack Obama, yes, we can, yes, we can." Enthusiastically joining in, the crowd applauds loudly, offering shouts of "We love you, Stevie." The singer replies by underscoring this moment of civil fashion: "I gotta do this, I gotta do this, I gotta do this one: 'Signed, Sealed, Delivered (I'm Yours).'" Here, at the center of contemporary popular culture, African Americans are being fully incorporated, at least performatively. Stevie Wonder has been Barackobamized. As Wonder sings, the camera scans the booth to find Rachel Maddow, Maureen O'Connell, and Eugene Robinson—two white MSNBC correspondents and an African American reporter from the *Washington Post*—swinging and dancing to Wonder's "Signed, Sealed, Delivered."

The camera scans the mixed-race stadium audience, much of which is also standing and swaying back and forth to the music. Amid this aura of fusion, there is a complaint. The right-wing political commentator Pat Buchanan, sporting dark wraparound sunglasses that give him a rather sinister Darth Vader look, seems bemused. "God bless our country, the United States of America," he intones sarcastically. "Pat, don't you want to join the MSNBC dance back-up band?" Olbermann asks. Even if Buchanan refuses to dance, Olbermann quips, he has contributed to the scene by looking like one of the "Blues Brothers."

Connecting this ritual buildup more directly with the struggle for power, the attention shifts in the next scene to the speech by former vice president Al Gore, the hard-luck Democratic presidential candidate who lost the disputed vote to George W. Bush in 2000. Since that loss, Gore has become famous as an environmental campaigner, winning a Nobel Peace Prize and an Academy Award for his documentary about global warming.

Democracy gives us an opportunity to change, Gore exclaims. Elections do matter. Remember the 2000 election. Let's not allow that to happen again. This election matters so much. Throughout Gore's remarks—as it had with the remarks of those who had preceded him—the camera shifts revealingly back and forth between the speaker and individual faces in the audience. This shifting indicates whether speaker and audience are connecting, whether the performance is hitting home or not. As Gore speaks, we see the audience laughing and joking with each other, not particularly engaged. America cannot continue, Gore thunders, with an "indifference to facts," subordinating the general good to the benefit of the few. Global warming is a "planetary emergency." McCain has allowed his party to browbeat him into abandoning measures that could prevent an imminent environmental apocalypse. Gore attacks "the special interests who control" the Republican party "lock, stock, and barrel." He declares that we can restore solidarity and rationality at the same time: "You understand that this election marks a clean change from the politics of partisanship and division." Drawing a parallel between President Abraham Lincoln and Obama, Gore asserts that our present crisis is as great as the Civil War. Obama represents "the best of America." He "will restore E Pluribus Unum" and "allow us Americans to speak with moral authority to other nations."

The MSNBC commentators now discuss the content of Obama's upcoming speech, selections from which have just been supplied. Noting its confident, sometimes even aggressive, tone, Olbermann says this is "an alpha male moment," recalling Bill Clinton's acceptance speech in 1992, when he proclaimed that if "Bush doesn't want to use the powers of the presidency, I'll do it." Matthews proactively deepens the civil moment. "This is not something cute and personal," he instructs viewers, but "something serious and powerful." The speech shows, "Here is my order of battle, here's what I bring to the table." It "will be a dramatic and compelling

(continued)

speech by Barack Obama, by all accounts—at the top of the hour." Olbermann increases the anticipation: "You can't just read from this and get what it's going to be like. You need to think stylistically because of the optics." Buchanan himself concedes that "it may be the most decisive moment of the entire election, it's that important a speech." Allowing it a sacred place, Buchanan describes the upcoming speech as possessing "gravitas." Rachel Maddow immediately agrees, but she points to the performative challenge of the speech: "It is long! How will he be able to manage that?" Buchanan, a former speechwriter for Richard Nixon, explains that "you've got to 'talk through' the applause." Olbermann adds, "This is *his* voice." Buchanan responds, "This is written for the ear, not for the eye." It's not Al Gore. "It should be a tough man's speech," he says.

Once again, the camera scans the crowd. The sun has set, and the stadium is now filled to overflowing as for a popular festival or a sell-out football game. Thousands of tiny American flags are waving. Old folks with grandchildren, blond-haired all-American girls and Ivy-League-jacketed preppies, and men and women of every color and shape are cheering, while banners proclaiming "Latinos for Barack" are held high.

Illinois Senator Durbin steps to the podium and offers the formal introduction. He declares that there is a "hunger for more authenticity" and a need "to renew the faith of the American people in a leader." "Americans want to believe," Durbin explains, suggesting the reason Barack Obama has become a collective representation. "I've been close to Barack Obama for many years, but now, many Americans feel close to this man." Averring fusion, the senator prophesies that Obama embodies the sacred discourse of liberty in a transcendental way. Obama has "judgment" and "wisdom," and with him, "the future of our nation is in the hands of hard-working Americans, who want to believe that America's best days are still to come. Tonight, as the stadium's lights are going dark, we will come to the dawning of the new day!" If we accept his "message…that the greatness of America will return," we "can turn the page and welcome a new generation. Yes, America can; yes, we can." Barack Obama and Joe Biden "will lead us to a better place." Fused with them, "we will be by their side every step of the way." We are in the realm of the civil sacred, passing from the evil past and the mundane present into the idealized space of the future. Grasping the hands of caring and prophetic leaders, we can make the American dream of a perfect civil society come true.

Barack Obama has been well and truly introduced, his imminent speech lauded for its power and meaning, liminally set off from mundane reality, and his person adulated in a salvationary way. The flesh-and-blood nominee now emerges. His face set in serious demeanor, Barack Obama strides forcefully to the podium.

As the Democratic nominee delivers his speech, the camera pans the crowd to show whites, blacks, old folks, and youngsters nodding in affirmation. Obama directly challenges the recent withering criticism of his Republican opponent. "I don't know what kind of lives John McCain thinks celebrities lead, but this is mine." Offering ambitious proposals to repair the nation's torn social fabric, Obama's speech fluidly moves from the practical and mundane to the utopian premises of the civil sphere—"That's the idea of America, the promise that we rise and fall together, that I am my brother's keeper, my sister's keeper."

The commentarial responses are filled to overflowing with praise. When Andrea Mitchell likens Obama's words to those of President Andrew Shepherd in Aaron Sorkin's movie *The American President*—which morphed into the long-running, legendary television show *The West Wing*—the factual and the fictional media of communication meet halfway, merging poetry and prose.[11] Declaring, "the hell with my critics," Chris Matthews underscores the intensity of the personal-cum-civil connection Obama has achieved: "I think what he said was about us, and that's why we care. Our strength is not in our money or military but in the American promise." Adding, "let me tell you how" Obama did this, Matthews explains that Obama asked, "Was my upbringing a celebrity's upbringing? How dare you say this election is a test of [my] patriotism!" Obama was declaring "Enough!" He supplied not only his usual inspiration but also all the specifics that his critics said he had until now neglected in the campaign—"twenty-nine specific policy pledges and at least nineteen failures of the McCain campaign." He supplied "four direct punches to George Bush and four more to the Republican party. No shots were left unthrown. There has been an extraordinary laying down of the glove."

As if to prevent critics from intervening between Obama's speech and his audience, the MSNBC commentators provided responses before the potential critics of Obama's speech have a chance to reply. They attribute their positive reactions not to their interpretive powers but to the actual speech and its performative effect. Olbermann asks, "As political theater, where *doesn't* this rank in our recent history?" Brian Williams, anchor of

(*continued*)

NBC Nightly News, answers by drawing an analogy between Obama's rhetoric and the fictional prose of *West Wing* writer Aaron Sorkin. Chuck Todd, NBC pollster and political analyst, observes, "I was struck by the little nods here to political responsibility." Obama is "trying to appeal to Missourra [*sic*], not Missouri. He is saying I'm going to fight. The toughness of the speech is what's still going to stand out." McCain won't "know how to react to this speech. I'll tell you, I don't know how the Republican Party is going to be able to go against this show." Tom Brokaw, the iconic former NBC news anchor and best-selling popular historian, adds: "Barack felt a certain license to throw a punch back. There was something personal and combative here that I haven't got so far.... This guy is just a step above no matter what you think of him or his politics." After "three days of *mishigas*," Williams observes, "we can now look at this as a narrative, a four-day narrative." Matthews turns to his normally cool, rather politically conservative colleague Michelle Bernard. The African American commentator states that, immediately after the speech, she fled to a room backstage "so I could weep alone." Matthews asks, "Is this nomination of Obama a 'willingness of the heart'? Are we beyond an ethnic nation? There was a sea of black, white, and Asian faces. Is the era of ethnic politics over?" Iowa did it first, he recounts, on the day of Obama's early primary victory. Responding that "Iowa was the greatest day in our nation's history," Bernard affirms that, after today, "America will never be the same again." Mitchell recalls how, during Obama's speech, "people jumped to their feet and started shouting when he attacked McCain." She states, "I've never witnessed anything quite like this. The stagecraft was so phenomenal. I don't know how they could have made it any better." These commentarial remarks are repeated in the *New York Times* the next day.[12]

As postconvention media reporting confirms, the performative fusion that transpires inside the Mile High Stadium generates not only local ritual but amplifies widely outside, gaining the largest audience in the history of televised conventions, larger by one-third than the opening night of the Beijing Olympics. Evidently, the media commentators' aahing and oohing over that Thursday afternoon and evening scene appeared as felicitous to millions of Americans as to the journalists themselves.

This television ethnography provides a textbook illustration of how to become a collective representation. The audience is emotionally engaged for hours before the speech, and sound, images, and cultural texts circulate rapidly back and forth between them and the performers on stage. When Obama walks onto the stage, he absorbs the swelling energy of the crowd and sends it back encoded in democratic themes. This cresting fusion is recorded by the television and print media and projected to tens of millions in the citizen audience, who feel themselves inspired by the democratic themes.

Becoming a collective representation is much more than having performative success at this or that particular event, however. It is a matter of establishing broad and compelling connections between political actors and citizen audiences over the course of a long campaign. Barack Obama succeeded not only in the moment of the convention but also over the long haul. His principal opponents did not. Hillary Clinton, Sarah Palin, and John McCain each had dramatic moments, but they did not succeed in becoming collective representations over the long run. This performative failure explains their defeats.

Failed Representation: Weakness, Restriction, Artifice

If political success depends on becoming a collective representation, then political failure emerges from not being able to be one. Candidates become collective representations when their image and meanings are inflated with energy. If the energy is not there, the image deflates. Instead of a collective representation symbolizing civil society, the image seems to be only a hollowed-out shell. The hollowing-out process unfolds in different ways.

McCain: Thin Performance, Weak Audience

During the summer of the general election campaign, John McCain is finding it difficult to become a collective representation. His poll numbers are falling behind Obama's, and news stories report his appearances drawing sparce audiences. In early July, the *Wall Street Journal* is already worrying that McCain "remains over-shadowed by the *excitement* surrounding Sen. Obama's candidacy."[13] Later that month, the failure to become symbolic is more concretely observed. In a story headlined "Picturing Obama," the *Journal* reports that "collectors, investors, and fund-raisers—many of them looking to cash in on the [Democratic] candidate's popularity and place in history—are snapping up campaign posters and other works depicting the presumptive nominee."[14] This is in striking contrast to the Republican side, for "there appears to be little demand for art promoting Sen. John McCain." According to statistics from eBay, "only six McCain-related art items sold on the site in the past 60 days, with an average price of $57," which "compared with 889 Obama-related art items that have sold in the last 60 days, with an average selling price of $127." As summer turns into the fall campaign,

McCain's inability to draw large audiences becomes increasingly noted, and diverse explanations are offered for this failure. When McCain speaks spontaneously, he is frequently unfocused. When, in order to correct this performative problem, the Republican nominee delivers prepared comments from the teleprompter, he seems wooden and detached. There are more substantive concerns as well. The message that the Republicans image makers have crafted is not fitting with the country's mood in 2008.

We explore the reasons for McCain's political difficulties in great detail throughout this book. Our concern here is not why but what. Time after time, John McCain gives speeches at which only relatively few persons show up. One cannot become a collective representation without attracting others. Only by concentrating an audience's energy can a politician powerfully project it back not just to the immediate listeners but beyond as well. By the tense days of late October, reports in the *Wall Street Journal* are beginning with leads such as "John McCain proclaimed Sunday that his presidential campaign remained viable," its coverage vividly contrasting the weak resonance of the Republican's speeches with his Democratic opponent's performative effect:

> The candidates campaigned in similar parts of the same states over the weekend, but drew crowds of different sizes. In Albuquerque, N.M., on Saturday, Sen. McCain had roughly a thousand people at his morning rally. That evening in the same city, Sen. Obama drew an estimated 35,000, according to a University of New Mexico fire marshal. In Denver, Sen. McCain's rally attracted several thousand; Sen. Obama spoke before more than 100,000 there Sunday, according to the Denver Police Department.[15]

The veteran Republican candidate puts on a brave front, proclaiming long and loudly that ritual energy is there even if size is not. Enthusiasm at campaign events "is at a higher level than I've ever seen," McCain reassures a *Journal* reporter, reminding him that "I've been in a lot of presidential campaigns." Insisting that the energy circulating is more than enough, the Republican contends, "I see intensity out there, and I see passion." The skepticism in the conservative newspaper's coverage is palpable, nonetheless. Reporters know that, in becoming a collective representation, numbers do matter, for psychic energy must circulate and be spread around.

Palin: Strong Performance, Narrow Audience

It was to overcome this looming crisis of representation that John McCain picked Alaska governor Sarah Palin as the GOP's vice-presidential nominee. From the moment of her unveiling, Palin's iconic power is immediately evident. As the conservative *Washington Times* puts it, "Sarah Palin went from an unknown moose hunter to a mass phenomenon" in a "media instant."[16] The *New York Times* attests that Palin's nomination has created "a jolt of energy" that "energized" the Republican Party.[17] On the eve of Governor Palin's acceptance speech at the Republican convention, John McCain declares, "America's excited" and predicts that "they're going to be even more excited once they see her" tonight.[18] Indeed, 37 million Americans tune in for Palin's speech, an astonishing audience for such an address, and, in the weeks of campaigning that followed, the Republican candidate enters deeply and passionately into the hearts of increasingly large and enthusiastic crowds. "When she hits the stage, audiences erupt and they don't calm down," the conservative opinion journal *Weekly Standard* reports in late October, adding "they want to touch her." A Republican senator accompanying the vice-presidential campaign states, "I've never seen anything like it."[19]

The fact of the nominee's becoming a collective representation is not in dispute. "Mrs. Palin's crowds have been enormous and enthusiastic, shaking red-and-white pompons and filling minor league baseball stadiums, airplane hangars, and warehouses," the *New York Times* reports, adding "she whips crowds into a frenzy."[20] What is very much in dispute, however, is just how widely the intense energy attached to the Palin representation has spread. It is certainly true, as one *Times* headline proclaims, that "With Palin at His Side, McCain Finds Energized Crowds."[21] A senior McCain advisor later recollects how Palin's presence had created "large events that got us back to our energy and momentum."[22] Yet from the day this collective political representation first appeared, awed attestations about its symbolic power are carefully paired with anxious concerns about the narrowness of its audience reach. In its very first paragraph of reporting on the Palin nomination, the *Journal* suggests that, while her "solid conservative positions" have "thrilled the Republican base," the choice has "also thrilled some Democratic strategists."[23] The antiabortion group United for Life Action, while reporting itself "thrilled," also expresses the hope that the ritual chain reaction will extend farther, suggesting that Palin is "a brilliant pick" because "in one move she energizes pro-lifers *and* reaches out to Hillary supporters."[24] Three days later, when the *Journal* reports that $10 million had poured into party coffers after the Palin nomination, it warns at the same time that the "selection was not risk free."[25] The day after, McCain professes optimism not only about Palin's impact but also about the breadth of its reception, telling the conservative *New York Post*, "I'm very, very proud of the impression she's made on all of America."[26] That same day, an influential conservative journalist supports this prediction that the new icon possesses not just depth but breadth as well: "With Gov. Sarah Palin of Alaska as John McCain's running mate, the party now has a new national leader whose personal story resonates [with] Sam's Club Republicans."[27]

Within weeks, however, the ambiguous performative implications of the Palin representation are resolved and, for the Republican side, not in a happy way. Palin's audiences, while indeed extraordinarily energetic, have proven to be dangerously narrow. By late September, her approval rating has fallen 37 percent from its high of 54 percent, and she now has garnered significantly less support than her Democratic counterpart, Joe Biden.[28] Three weeks later, even as the *New York Times* affirms that Palin "has emerged as the most electrifying speechmaker among the four politicians on the major party ticket" and that she "generates enormous fervor at her events," polls reveal that the Republican nominee has slipped 10 more points. Less than one-third of the American public now give her favorable ratings.[29]

Clinton: Phony Performance, Deceived Audience

Nonetheless, even if the connection between candidate and audience is tight, the energy powerful, and the audience broad as well as deep, collective representation may still not be achieved. There is the matter of how this dialogical communication will be recorded by the third party, which stands with neither the performer nor the audience.

While contemporary journalists view politics as performative, this does not mean they evaluate any particular political performance as contrived. Journalists are as acutely aware as any other party to the electoral process that democratic politics demands from its citizens the same quality of indulgence as dramas of a more traditional kind. If "poetic faith" is to be established, Coleridge wrote, audiences must, "for the moment," engage in the "willing suspension of disbelief"—the willingness not to see the artificiality that they know is actually there.[30] Without such suspension, plays would not seem real; there could be no verisimilitude, narratives would be dismissed as fantasies, identification would fail, and there would be neither moral learning nor cathartic relief.

Nonetheless, political journalists often see the suspension of disbelief by citizen audiences as too willing. They respond by creating empirical accounts that destabilize political symbolization, sometimes in fateful ways—media representations that now vie with those projected by candidates. Caught inside the swirl of conflicting representation, citizen audiences find it difficult to achieve a sense of verisimilitude—truthfulness—and they are less able to evaluate authenticity. To resolve such dissonance, citizen audiences condemn sophistry either in the media or in the political candidates. If media reports are accepted as true, then a politician's performance seems phony, and becoming a collective representation becomes difficult.

In a front-page story on the day of the Democratic primaries in Indiana and North Carolina, a veteran *Times* political reporter, Jodi Kantor, looks back skeptically on the recent string of successes garnered by Hillary Clinton's campaign. The double primary is crucial for Clinton; commentators agree that without wins in both contests her candidacy is bound to fade. That such a double victory actually seems possible is due in no small part to Clinton's newfound ability to project herself as an earthy, rough-talking populist candidate. Kantor begins by describing the tight and intense connection between Clinton and the grass roots, explaining how broad swaths of the citizen audience profess to see in her some significant part of themselves:

> All over North Carolina and Indiana, crowds of teachers and truckers, salespeople and small business owners, have been hailing Hillary Rodham Clinton as one of their own. "She's a working mom," Tracy Zettel, who works for a health insurance company, said Saturday while waiting for Mrs. Clinton to appear in Cary, N.C., "that's what I am." "A good ol' girl," Clyde Swedenberg, owner of a small jewelry story, called her in Kalkeside Park, N.C. After listening to her speak in Fort Wayne, Ind., on Sunday, Joe Jakacky, a warehouse worker, remarked that Mrs. Clinton had started out just like he did, in a menial job.[31]

After this initial recounting of actor-audience connection, however, Kantor seems to take a step back, reflecting on campaign dynamics from a position that is decidedly outside. In the paragraph immediately following her description of the audience's enthusiasm, she suggests that the persona of candidate Clinton has undergone a radical shift:

> Whatever the results of the primaries on Tuesday in Indiana and North Carolina, Mrs. Clinton has accomplished the seemingly impossible. Somehow, a woman who has not regularly filled her own gasoline tank in well over a decade, who with her husband made $109 million in the last eight years and who vacations with Oscar de la Renta, has transformed herself into a working-class hero.

The candidate so energetically addressing folks in the Midwestern and Southern states, Kantor informs her readers, is not Clinton the actual person but Clinton the representation. On display in her recent campaign events is the "Story of Hillary Clinton," which has taken a "surprising turn." Contrasting representation and reality, Kantor suggests that the newly populist Clinton employs the true facts of her biography only "minimally." In her real autobiography, *Living History,* Clinton had "never mentioned earning money." In her recent speech at a community college in Greenville, N.C., however, she testifies that, during her college years, "if I wanted a book or a cup of coffee, I had to pay for it with money I made." In her new campaign role, Clinton "never mentions the name Wellesley," the elite women's college where she first made her name. Indeed, "Mrs. Clinton says very little about herself at all," and "she focuses instead on her audience's concerns":

> Exuding empathy, Mrs. Clinton bellows accusations at the villains of her speeches—oil companies, the Chinese government and George W. Bush—and returns to a plaintive voice to plead the case of hard-working Hoosiers or Tar Heels. She raises eyebrows and arms in exaggerated indignation...."I don't think folks in Washington listen enough," Mrs. Clinton said in Greenville, a catch developing in her voice. "Because if we listen we will hear this incredible cry: 'Please just pay attention to what's going on in our lives.'" Many voters at these events marvel at Mrs. Clinton's understanding....Like Oprah Winfrey interviewing a tearful guest...even as Mrs. Clinton shifts herself down market, she moves her audience up market, speaking in flatteringly aspirational language. Choosing a president is like choosing a builder for your dream house, she told an audience in North Carolina. She tells histories of wealthy people who struggle with, would you believe, the same problems as her audiences.

The clear implication is that, even if performatively successful, Hillary Clinton the collective representation is a histrionic fake. The headline for the *Times'* front-page story says it all: "With Right Props and Stops, Clinton Transforms into Working-class Hero."

In a later interview, Kantor disavows any deflationary ambition: "I hope the story did not communicate that 'this is all a sham' or 'this is totally fake.'"[32] Her goal has been simply to allow distant readers to imagine themselves as close up rather than far away: "The first thing I would do is make the reader feel like they were there." To bring the audience into the performance requires not literal description but interpretive accuracy. "Just taking a general snapshot," Kantor explains, "that's not that interesting. There's a real art to listening to...candidates' speeches, to really hear the incredible differences between them and to be able to sort those out for readers." Listening closely involves distinguishing the artificial, the merely performative, from the authentic, separating political representations from the real person underneath:

> The goal was to figure out what she was up to in terms of her salesmanship, and one of the really interesting things about following Hillary's campaign in particular is that her persona kept evolving over the course of the campaign, and we were watching that very closely....My goal in

writing that story was to really capture that moment and to capture what she was trying to do for readers—to really witness it....You can write a sort of literal, one-dimensional accounting of what she said or did that day. But my aim was to figure out how that fit into the greater story of Hillary as we know it. This is a woman that we've watched for 16 years now....Clinton sort of had to search for a new persona for herself....This was a really important chapter in explaining how Hillary had become the candidate of the working-class, Democratic voter. And the way that she connected with them was part of what I was trying to capture...the actual sort of amazing narrative of watching this woman work her way through politics and figure out what she wants to be at each turn of the game.

Another veteran *Times* reporter, John Broder, contributed to the working-class hero story, though he did not share the byline. Broder is more blunt:[33]

When you're on the campaign trail, we are all quite sensitive to those moments of artifice. Artificial moments in which your candidate is playing a role....Hillary is an interesting character because she's just so bad at it, frankly. It's transparent when she does that....Her father was an upper-class businessman. They were fairly prosperous, they lived in the suburbs. She went to Wellesley and Yale. She's hardly a woman of the soil. But when she...would get into certain parts of the country, she would go dropping her *g*'s [and talk about] "drinkin'" and "workin'" and "thinkin'" about "ya all the time." And it was so transparently phony that it was almost endearing....These are the things—the costumes that a candidate has to wear. And she's not really fooling anybody, but it does help to build a comfort level with her audience....It would be a little bit too clever to [cite] the willing suspension of disbelief, but I think that's what American voters do with their politicians....And I think it's easy to lapse into mockery or cynicism about it....I would like to think that story, and I contributed on the ground observation...describe[d] the process—the play—in a sympathetic way, in an explanatory way, as opposed to in a mocking way.

Clinton's do-or-die double primary effort does not come off. She wins in Indiana but loses in North Carolina. The result devastates her chances of securing the Democratic nomination, and commentators begin repeating the phrase "the numbers just aren't there." Clinton herself denies this is an objective reality. Vowing to continue her campaign, she competes in all the remaining primaries and battles for so-called super delegates all the way to the convention floor. In its news pages, the *Times* does not directly call Clinton's bluff, but its reporters continue, now even more critically, to deconstruct her political effort as performance. In contrast to its report on primary day, the newspaper's postprimary coverage suggests not only phony performance and deceived audience but also weak audience and thin performance. In his seemingly purely factual report on the launch of Clinton's West Virginia campaign, Broder's lead starkly separates person from political actor:

> Senator Hillary Rodham Clinton's greatest gift may be her ability to remain upright and smiling as chaos and chagrin surround her. On what was probably one of the toughest days of her campaign so far, with pundits and analysts of all stripes declaring her presidential candidacy finished, Mrs. Clinton put on her battle face Wednesday.... A smile was fixed on Mrs. Clinton's perfectly made-up face—not a hair was out of place.[34]

Broder reports Clinton reading from a weak, hastily written, and ineffective script:

> Her remarks on the steps of 19th-century McMurran Hall on the main street of town were an abridged cut-and-paste job of her standard stump speech. It was not her most fluid effort. While discussing incentives for education and public service, she took a sharp detour into trade policy and vowed to get tough with oil-producing nations before circling back to preschool programs.... She betrayed only an occasional glimmer...of the exceedingly narrow straits she must now navigate. At one point in her 19-minute remarks, Mrs. Clinton promised that the United States would have universal health care "if I'm president," a deviation from her customary "when I'm president" and [she] made no mention of her 14-point loss in North Carolina. Nor did she speak the name of her rival, Senator Barack Obama, or even refer to him as "my opponent."

The effect of this woefully inadequate performance is to sever any connection between audience, actor, and script. The moment is so fraught that it prompts Broder to recall the breakdown of civil solidarity in another, much earlier time, and other bloody battles that had been fought but lost:

> [Mrs. Clinton] confronted what was at times a hostile crowd at a hastily arranged speech here at Shepherd University. Shepherdstown, a quaint and hippieish town on the Potomac River in the Western Virginia Panhandle, is where Robert E. Lee led his Confederate Army in retreat after the battle of Antietam, the single bloodiest day of the Civil War. Mrs.

Clinton endured boos when she mentioned her proposal for a gasoline tax holiday, catcalls when she spoke of ending the Iraq war, and, most difficult of all, the heckling of her daughter, Chelsea, who introduced her. "End the dynasty!" a young man holding an Obama poster shouts when Chelsea Clinton stepped to the microphone.

If the *Times'* account of this event possessed verisimilitude, then Mrs. Clinton was living in a delusional, fictional world:

A pop psychologist might say that Mrs. Clinton was showing symptoms of denial or of being divorced from reality, but she has said for months that she will not quit....At a brief news conference after her remarks at the college, she said, "It's a new day, it's a new state, it's a new election," her upbeat tone never wavering.

Interviewed later about this postprimary story, Broder recalls that Clinton's long struggle for power had been at stake:[35]

It was West Virginia after North Carolina and Indiana, when everybody, [MSNBC political commentator] Chris Matthews and others, had written her off the night before....She was sailing into some very still winds of public opinion or at least media chatter that it was over for her.

Broder attributes the lack of audience resonance to sloppy prep work, a departure from the normally high production values maintained by the Clinton campaign:

Most of her crowds up until then had been more carefully screened. Her events had been noticed two to three days in advance. This one literally was put together on the spot, virtually in an hour or two. We were woken up in the middle of the night and told we would be traveling in the morning. This was in Washington. There was nothing on her schedule, and suddenly we were on buses into Shepherdstown.

Broder also vividly recalls that his factual description of the West Virginia event was immediately challenged by Clinton staff:

We had some heated discussion about this afterwards, Hillary's people and I. [They claimed] the crowd was not "hostile" as a group [but that] there were protestors and unfriendly voices *in* it....I commented on it because it was rare—because she seldom drew protestors in her crowds.

Such heated political confrontation with journalists does not frequently occur in political campaigns, but for Clinton the stakes were high. She was on the verge of losing her struggle for power. The last thing she needed was the nation's most powerful newspaper reporting her political performance as contrived.

Political success depends on becoming a collective representation. Effective performances so powerfully project energy and message that audiences fuse with political performers. Failed performance means that the distance between politicians and the breadth and depth of the citizen audiences remains great. Communication is spotty and mutual understanding weak. This means political defeat.

CHAPTER THREE

Spirit of the Ground Game

PROPOSING THAT THE DEMOCRATIC STRUGGLE FOR POWER IS about becoming a collective representation, we have examined successful and failed performances, as well as the mass media's commentaries upon them, in both primary and general election campaigns. In this chapter, we confront the conventional wisdom that money and organization really decide what happens in politics. We begin with media observations that collective sentiment is critical to both finances and the ground game. We follow with an ethnographic account of grassroots organizing by the Obama campaign.

Money and Organization

When political professionals, journalists, academic intellectuals, and everyday citizens think of themselves as realists, as being practical rather than idealists with their heads in the clouds, they are inclined to emphasize the absolute centrality of money and organization to political campaigns. There are the proverbs about money being the mother's milk of politics, about paying the piper and calling the tune, about the purse strings controlling the campaign. There is also the folk wisdom that winning depends on political organization. It is not a matter of symbolic representation but numbers and planning. Staffing and rational knowledge are alleged to be the keys to political success.

In late October 2008, the *Wall Street Journal* reports on the unprecedented fundraising of Obama's presidential campaign. Its premise is that financial resources translate directly into symbolic and organizational power:

Sen. Barack Obama set a new record for presidential fund raising in September, with more than $150 million in contributions, allowing him to swamp Republican rival Sen. John McCain in spending on advertising and organizing in the final days of the campaign. The Democratic candidate's one-month figure is nearly double what Sen. McCain received in public financing for the final two months of the campaign. Sen. Obama...enjoys the biggest money advantage over an opponent since Richard Nixon easily defeated George McGovern in 1972....The money advantage is clearly helping Sen. Obama get his message out. For the week ending Monday, Sen. Obama spent nearly $39 million on TV ads versus about $11.9 million for the McCain campaign.... "McCain is in a shouting match with a man with a megaphone," said Evan Tracey of TNS Media Intelligence/CMAG, who tracks ad spending.[1]

According to this syllogism, (a) monetary advantage confers (b) strategic communicative advantage, and (c) strategic communicative advantage confers political victory. But this logic is false. Even at this early point in our empirical discussion it has become apparent that possessing a megaphone hardly guarantees communicative success. Certainly, money is vital even if, in democratic societies, votes cannot be directly purchased. Money buys access to the creation of symbols and their distribution. It can purchase the skills of expert consultants who craft messages and scripts for political performance, and it can pay for the stagecraft that allows these messages to be presented in dramatic forms from video to television and radio ads. It can buy television and radio time, billboard space, print ads, and campaign literature.

However, if financial contributions are crucial, they are not determinative. One way of putting this is that controlling "the *means* of symbolic production" has little to do with whether the *ends,* the symbols themselves, are compelling. Controlling the symbolic means allows a campaign to buy access to symbolic production and distribution but cannot guarantee performative success. In the private sector, as both empirical studies and practical experience continually demonstrate, even the most expensive advertising campaigns largely fail.[2] When the scripted and crafted "commodities" are living and breathing human beings, and when messages are patterned by the codes and institutions of civil society and mediated by critical third parties of journalists, and when contexts are swiftly changing, chances for success fall farther still. As every practitioner of modern politics has learned the hard way, hitting the center of the citizen heart is a rare and difficult thing.

The chance that money actually constitutes the "base" for politics is further diminished when we consider that access to money is usually not a first- but a second-order cause. In democratic politics, access to financing over the long run depends on energy, on performative fusion, and on ritual. It is rarely generated simply by a tit for tat of material exchange. Symbolic power attracts money, which then facilitates the production of more symbolic force in turn. In June 2004, Barack Obama was an unknown state legislator from Illinois who struggled mightily to raise money for his first senatorial campaign. Only after performing his electrifying 17-minute keynote speech at the Democratic National Convention in Boston later that summer did the African American politician succeed in becoming a collective representation on the national stage. Only after Obama achieved such symbolic power could he begin to develop a strong financial base. Yet, when he formally launches this bid in February 2007, the war chest of his opponent, Hillary Clinton, seems so formidable that experts predicted failure for Obama's relatively underfinanced, mostly grassroots campaign. Only after candidate Obama begins generating the intense excitement and attachment that crystallize in his Iowa primary victory does his campaign begin amassing its extraordinary material base. In democratic politics, the distribution of money eventually becomes a function of the allocation of symbolic power and emotional energy.

Political effectiveness is also reduced to material base by emphasizing political organization. If voters are described as already committed either by preexisting habit or ideology, then political victory depends not on symbolic process but upon which side gets its voters out. Political candidates and professionals call this process of getting out the vote the "ground game," contrasting it with images circulating via mass media in the "air war." A campaign's ground game unfolds not all at once but over a significant period of time. It involves trained organizers meeting and speaking with citizen audiences in person, in their homes or in public places; sometimes registering them; keeping track of those who are on their side; staying in touch throughout the campaign; checking on Election Day to see whether they have voted and, if not, making sure they get to the polls before closing time. In academic literature and among political consultants and journalists as well, ground games are often likened to the top-down field operations of the military or to the well-oiled efficiencies of a bureaucratic or technological machine. Getting out the vote becomes a mechanical, quasi-mathematical process. It is size that matters, and it is financing that decides how many salaries can be paid. Staff members are soldiers for hire, mercenaries who do the banal, uninspired, and uninspiring dirty work of campaigns.

Noting two weeks before the vote that "the Obama campaign is spending money at a prodigious clip," the *Wall Street Journal* describes the organizing challenge facing the Republicans:

> Sen. Obama's field operations, which have become his campaign's trademark, are ... of a size unprecedented in presidential politics, stunning even

seasoned veterans such as New Mexico Gov. Bill Richardson. "Obama has 40 local offices in my state—40."…The McCain campaign said it has about "a dozen" in that state. The McCain campaign, working with his party's national committee, has scrambled to catch up in [the] newly competitive states of North Carolina and Indiana, but it has not come close to the Obama organization. In North Carolina, the Republicans opened about 10 offices in July and another 10 around Labor Day, according to a senior McCain campaign official. But that's less than half of Sen. Obama's 47 offices, according to his Web site. The Republicans recently opened a handful of offices in Indiana, nowhere near the 43 in place for Sen. Obama. In Ohio, Sen. McCain and the RNC have 45 offices; Sen. Obama has 76. The mismatch is even larger in Democratic-leaning Pennsylvania, where Sen. McCain has 30 offices compared with 83 for Sen. Obama.[3]

Later, on election eve, the *Journal* declares that, in 2008, "after years of ceding the advantage in ground-level organizing to the Republican voter-turnout machine, national and state Democratic parties are spending far more heavily than their Republican counterparts on field operations." The result is that "Democrats have set up 770 offices nationwide," whereas the Republicans only "have about 370 offices." Asserting that "the year's change is made possible by Democratic Sen. Barack Obama's historic fundraising," the *Journal* reports that "Democrats have increased their staff expenditures from $30 million to $56 million." They have "employed an estimated 4,500 workers making more than $1,500 a month as of mid-October," whereas "Sen. McCain and the Republicans had about 1,100 at that point."

Such reasoning is not partisan. The *New York Times* argues in a similar way. Citing "Mr. Obama's fund-raising advantage over Mr. McCain" and how it allowed "an unprecedented investment of money to push the get-out-the-vote effort to a new level," the *Times* explains the "organizing principles" of Obama's field offices in a quasi-scientific, technological, and machinelike way:

> Falls Church, Va.—Lukas McGowan was sitting in an old barber's chair, a cell phone pressed to his ear, as he contemplated a critical assignment for the closing chapter of the presidential campaign: the ground game. The most pressing matter inside this field office for Senator Barack Obama was not the next debate or the latest scorching exchange with Senator John McCain, but getting every possible voter to the polls. As Mr. McGowan surveyed an assembly line of activity, a more immediate question popped into his mind. Have all the spots been filled in the 6 to 8 P.M. shift for walking neighborhood precincts? "When we identify sporadic voters, we want to go back to their house until they can't stand

us anymore," said Mr. McGowan, 23, who oversees the Obama operation in Fairfax County, which is Virginia's largest.... If the primary race was an experiment in building the capacity of the Obama organization, the general election will show whether [Obama's] army of employees and volunteers [can] shift the electoral map.... Mr. Obama, whose career in public service began in community organizing in Chicago, dropped by a training session on Friday evening in Ohio. And even through his encouraging words, he sounded a note of wonder about whether the system will work. "We've been designing, we've been engineering and we've been at the drawing board and we've been tinkering," Mr. Obama said. "Now, it's time to just take it for a drive. Let's see how this baby runs."... These satellite offices, a campaign trademark that contributed to Mr. Obama's first victory in Iowa, have been set up with the swiftness of a Starbucks franchise. While local buy-in is encouraged at the more than 700 field offices across the country, the uniformity is remarkable, down to the cardboard cutout of Mr. Obama near the front door in many locations.... The Obama campaign has broken the country into a collection of battleground states, which are dissected into precincts that are parceled one more time into neighborhood teams. (Ohio, for example, is divided into 1,231 neighborhoods.)... A sophisticated battery of databases has been tapped to find voters [who are] culled from a variety of sources, including magazine subscriptions, the types of cars people drive, where voters shop and how much they earn. Commuting patterns are analyzed. Voting history in local races is factored in. The data, after it is studied and sorted at campaign headquarters in Chicago, is sent to every battle ground state. The names are bar-coded and ultimately show up on the lists given to volunteers.[4]

Yet political organizing actually does not proceed in quite this way. It is hardly so efficient and rational as a well-oiled military field operation or even a bureaucratic organization. If campaign financing swells and narrows according to circulating political energy, even more so do organization and ground game. Party membership and registration are deeply affected by the great waves of political sentiment that begin blowing through the civil sphere long before the down-and-dirty, face-to-face organizing of the actual political campaign. Organizing efforts for the 2008 presidential campaign, for example, unfolded in the context of President Bush's drastic slide in popularity, intensified by the Democratic victory in the midterm elections of 2006:

In Pennsylvania, the number of registered Democrats has grown by 350,000 since 2004, while the number of registered Republicans fell by

285,000. In Florida Democrats have added 130,000 new voters, while Republicans have remained even. Democrats are particularly hopeful about trends in a trio of Western states that voted Republican in 2004: New Mexico, Colorado and Nevada. In Nevada, Democrats have added 80,000 more voters than Republicans in a state that Mr. Bush won by 20,000 votes. In New Mexico, Democrats have gained a net 7,000 voters since 2004, more than the president's 6,000-vote margin of victory.[5]

The effectiveness of field organization cannot be attributed to financing or to any other mechanical kind of thing. Face-to-face organizing requires not only intensive but also extensive moral commitment and emotional energy.[6] It takes not only perspiration but also inspiration to build, maintain, and participate in the ad hoc organization of political campaigns, which may last for months and sometimes even years. In the early months of its general election effort, Democrats recruited thousands of "Obama Fellows" as organizers, and, as the *Wall Street Journal* attested, most of them are unpaid:

Nationally, the Obama campaign is training 3,000 volunteers to conduct voter-registration drives as part of its "Obama Fellows" program. These volunteers pledged to work 30 hours a week for six weeks this summer, focusing on blacks, Latinos and young voters in select states. Among those states is Florida, which President Bush won by 380,000 votes four years ago and 537 votes in 2000. Four hundred Obama Fellows are targeting an estimated 500,000 qualified African-Americans who sat out the 2004 election.... In North Carolina, the Obama campaign has nine paid staff and about 150 near-full-time volunteers registering new voters—an unusually large force for this period of the election cycle. An estimated 343,000 black citizens there were eligible to vote in 2004 but didn't; President Bush won the state by 400,000.[7]

Organizational power depends on feelings of connection. As the *Journal* explains, "Deondra Ramsey, a 24-year-old Raleigh native and political science student, began pulling full-time volunteer shifts as an Obama Fellow even before the program officially started. 'I need to get my foot in the door—I want to be part of this.'"[8]

By contrast, Republican "party strategists said elections were...won by...a committed core of voters who cast ballots like clockwork every four years," according to the *Times*. The GOP is confident that "robo-calls" will be enough to get this committed core out to vote.[9] The Obama campaign knows better. Grass roots must be fused with collective representation. There must be person-to-person contact—the ground game—for organization to be motivated and sustained.

Energy and Fusion at Camp Obama

"We tend to think of organizing as a mechanical, instrumental thing," Barack Obama observed in 1988, reflecting on his years of organizing in Chicago's underprivileged racial communities. But what organizing is really about, he insists, is "building a culture," which means "building up stories and getting people to reflect on what their lives mean and how people in the neighborhood can be heroes, and how they are part of a larger force."[10] Twenty years later, when he struggles for national power, Obama puts this cultural approach to organization into effect.

It's early Saturday morning at Su Teatro, which is located in a well-kept, working-class Hispanic neighborhood of Denver.[11] Formerly an elementary school, now a flamboyantly decorated community arts center, the setting has been transformed into "Camp Obama," an oft-repeated but under-the-radar training exercise that today is aimed at massively enlarging the vote of the state's Latino population. Standing in line for coffee, fruit, tortillas, and *huevos mexicanos,* between 150 and 200 first-, second-, and third-generation Americans of Hispanic origin gather in the school's elegant indoor amphitheater, the seats sloping dramatically downward to the spotlit stage.

These volunteers arrived in vans and buses the evening before, traveling from towns such as Greely and Pueblo and Boulder, coming in from all over the state. They are accompanied by their local organizer-recruiter, some 20, mostly youthful "FOs," field organizers hired to work full time for the national campaign and paid a minimal salary. Recently recruited by the national staff and often identified by other recently hired FOs, they have taken leave from graduate school, business or professional careers, and often from partners and spouses to live with local families and organize neighborhood teams throughout this key western state. Choosing to put their normal lives on hold, they entered into a liminal, morally elevated, and energized space of Obama representation and campaign. An FO who organized the Pueblo group explains her gradual immersion into the full-time campaign.

In the spring of 2007, I helped coordinate a visit by Barack Obama to Boston University, and that was sort of my first motivation for being part of the campaign, because his speech was really fantastic and we had a really wonderful turnout for it…He was gaining a lot of momentum nationally—and I had read his book *Dreams from My Father,* and I loved it and I just felt somehow really touched by his candidacy. He seemed like an honest person, very genuine…I got to meet him at the event—it was lovely…Then the following fall, I canvassed in New Hampshire, just one day, in Derry in the rain with a friend of mine. And I made phone calls for the Massachusetts primary…And then, after graduation, I literally just drove my stuff up to Chicago, dropped everything in my room, got on a plane, flew to San Juan and stayed with a friend of mine who is a volunteer coordinator for the Puerto Rico primary. And I was there for about three weeks, as a full-time volunteer, so on my own dime, and from that experience I was hired to go to Colorado.[12]

As the newest recruits to the campaign sit clustered around their FOs in the theater seats, they are presented with a carefully planned and tightly sequenced performance from a team of "NOs," the national organizers, who take turns occupying center stage. These are the dozen or more persons who have traveled to Denver from Obama campaign headquarters in Chicago, among them three senior staff officials in charge of national "Latinos for Obama," and an equal number of state organizers in Colorado. Explaining to me why she had taken leave from her position as chief of staff for a U.S. senator to join the campaign in Chicago and from her new husband as well, one of the national Latina organizers relates that "there was just something about Obama; he reached inside of me."

For the group of thirty staff organizers in attendance—the NOs and FOs employed by the Democratic campaign—the rationale, if not the motivation, for staging this Denver Camp Obama is absolutely practical. A former community organizer himself, Obama believes that ground games make a difference, and his campaign strongly reflects this conviction. Because of Latino underrepresentation in key states that had gone to Bush in 2004, the national campaign's senior Latino staffer explains to me that "the ground game is worth 2 percent on voting day—all over, in Nevada, New Mexico, Colorado, and Florida." Yet the challenge of building an effective ground game in these states is daunting. "Thirty-six thousand new voters have been registered in Colorado in the last three months," the campaign's state director tells me, "but only 5,000 [of these] are from Latinos. To win in November, we'll need 20,000 new Hispanic registrations in the next 26 days." On October 1 the window for new registration will close.

In the days following this Denver Camp Obama, the 20 volunteer groups are to return home and organize 300 neighborhood teams of five to ten persons each. The team members will make phone calls, knock on doors, fill out registration forms, and make sure the newly registered will eventually vote. The national staff has explained detailed goals beforehand. Presented in tabular form, they distribute these one-page handouts to the FOs in an organizers' meeting convened prior to the day's main event (figure 3.1).

This handout explains the campaign's organizing strategy in a neat, efficient, cut-and-dried way. Winning seems a matter of numbers and probabilities, of multiplying contacts, attempts, and shifts so that the necessary 20,000 extra registrations can be made. In fact, these objective achievements depend on securing and

Neighborhood Team Goals for | East Eagle Team 1A01 | Sept 8th–14th

Goals Key

| What is a Contact? |
| A Contact is a person that you actually speak to. You will be finding out who they support for President, as well as answers to other questions. |

Team Goals for Sept 8th–Sept 14th	Daily Goals	How Many Attempts?	How Many Shifts?	Goals for the Next 10 Days	How Many Attempts?	How Many Shifts?
Phone Calls	66 Contacts	329 Calls	5	660 Contacts	3290 Calls	50
Door Knocks	45 contacts	180 Knocks	4	450 Contacts	1800 Knocks	40
New Voter Registration Forms	6 New Voters	36 Forms	3	60 New Voters	360 forms	30

| What is an Attempt? |
| Attempts show how many calls, knocks or registration forms you need to complete to reach the contact goals. It takes 70 calls to make 14 contacts and 50 knocks to make 13 contacts. |

Your Individual Goals in a Team of Five Vols	Daily Goals	Daily Attempts	Daily Shifts	Goals for the Next 10 Days	Attempts for the Next 10 Days	Shifts for the Next 10 Days
Phone Calls	14 Contacts	70 Calls	1.00	132 Contacts	658 Calls	10.0
Door Knocks	12 Contacts	40 Knocks	0.72	90 contacts	360 Knocks	8.0
New Voter Registration Forms	1 New Voters	6 Forms	0.6	12 New Voters	72 Forms	6.0

| What is a Shift? |
| Shifts are blocks of 3 volunteer hours. There should be 70 calls made in one shift. Similarly, there are 50 knocks or approx. 2.2 new voter registration forms collected in one shift. |

Your Individual Goals for a Team of Ten Vols	Daily Goals	How Many Attempts?	How Many Shifts?	Goals for the Next 10 Days	How Many Attempts?	How Many Shifts?
Phone Calls	7 contacts	37 Calls	0.50	90 Contacts	329 Calls	5.0
Door Knocks	6 contacts	26 Knocks	0.40	45 Contacts	180 Knocks	4
New Voter Registration Forms	.5 New Voters	2 Forms	0.3	6 New Voters	36 Forms	3

FIGURE 3.1.

intensifying symbolic connection, building energy, creating emotional identification, and extending moral commitment. Going from 20 FOs and their small band of followers to 300 neighborhood teams means that—on average—15 new and closely knit teams will have to be created and nurtured in every organizing region of the state. And each of these neighborhood teams will have to register 60 to 70 new Latino voters before October 1.

Camp Obama aims to create motivational power so that these objectives can be achieved. It is no doubt exactly because the FOs are so attuned to motivation that, as soon as they are handed the one-page worksheet, they launch a fierce and totally unexpected resistance. They are worried that, written down in black and white, the goals will seem like demands coming to their neighborhood teams from the outside. If this were the case, it would undermine the motivational purpose of the day, which is to create energy and to build emerging relationships that will allow intensive organization and goal achievement to seem like natural extensions of solidarity.

Faced with this resistance, Obama's national staff quickly concede. The goal sheet will not be distributed to the assembled volunteers. The only tactical goals that the FOs will give to their neighborhood teams will concern the next week.

The daylong volunteer training that follows has been carefully choreographed by a revered veteran of decades of movement organizing. Now an academic expert who serves as a trusted consultant to national staffers, Manny has researched and written extensively about narratives and emotion in organization. As he directs the day's festivities, they alternate between active, tightly choreographed assemblies of the entire group—assemblies that featured directed participation and call-and-response sessions—and breakout sessions of goal setting and team building. During the breakout sessions, the 20 regional groups disperse from the general assembly to meet in more intimate settings by themselves—in empty classrooms or outside on the school grounds.

The morning session begins rather awkwardly. As master of ceremonies, Manny faces the seated volunteers and declares, "Last night our goal was telling our story." Things begin to warm up when he asks, "What was good about last night?" He is addressing anything but a passive audience. They are not simply listeners but activists, potential leaders. They are here to become organizers. After a brief hesitation, hands shoot up, bodies stand up, voices are raised:

> "It made me feel wanted."
> "It made me understand why I'm here."
> "I realized I'm not alone."
> "What I learned is that the reasons I'm here are not only rational. It's related to who I am."

"Then what are we here for?" Manny demands, in a passionate, rousing, almost shouting voice. A response emerges from somewhere in the dimness of the upper reaches of the theater. It is highly rhetorical, as the drama of the occasion seems to demand: "We're here to bring the children out of the shadows of illegality, to pride and their rights, to citizenship."

Today, Manny explains, "We will learn what is organizing." Organizing is not, he tells the assembly, about interests and resources, at least not at first. It's about "sharing your *story*" and "working together for the common good." Don't "*lecture* the people you're trying to organize," he cautions. You need to "*allow them* to change," and you do this by relating their story to yours and through yours to the campaign's. Organizing is about building a relationship. Manny addresses a critical question to the audience: "What makes a relationship?" And he answers it himself: It's "trust, respect, interaction, commonality, getting to know each other—openness." Relationships start with an exchange, with a conversation that is an exploration. "But then you need commitment. That's the bottom line." Manny turns and writes quickly in large letters on the big green chalkboard behind him, below a giant red and green "Latinos for Obama" banner strung across the top of the room. What he sketches is a contrast between different conceptions of an organizing relationship, one civil and reciprocal, the other mechanical and manipulative. This is what Manny actually writes on the chalkboard:

IS	: IS NOT
Story	: Task
Mutual	: Interview
Conversation	: Prying
Curiosity	: Fact
Why, How	: What
Specific	: Abstract

Turning back to the assembly, Manny launches into the summation of his case. He is inspiring and moralistic but also deeply practical:

> Our resources are our idealism. It is our sense of social justice! Barack Obama wants us all to be Americans, to be there for our country! Barack Obama believes that a motivated base is something he has that the others didn't. That's how we won the primaries. Motives come first, energy and meaning, and only then strategy. Strategy begins with imagination. Motivation—that's the story of this campaign! None of this strategy means anything unless we change the world. Which is what power is all about. You're offering somebody a gift, the opportunity to change the world, to experience what you're experiencing. You're helping them to break the belief barrier.

After this speech, Manny turns back to the chalkboard and scrawls out another set of contrasts. When people are organized, they move from the left to the right side. This is what Manny writes:

BREAKING THE BELIEF BARRIER

Fear	→	Hope
Apathy	→	Anger
Inertia	→	Urgency
Isolation	→	Solidarity

The first breakout session is announced, the audience whistling and clapping as they get up to leave. The FO leading my group is a recent graduate of Boston University. Half-Hispanic, half-Irish, part of an old New Mexican family, Katie dislikes identity politics and majored in international relations. After arriving six weeks ago in Pueblo, her Colorado target city, she networked among churches, schools, trade unions, and local party activists; organized two community forums; and ended up with "this amazing group of eight," the core group of volunteers who are sitting around her now. She invites a round of introductions, asking her proté-gés to reprise the stories that brought them there, and starting with her own.

> I did my best not to let my nerves show, but I was very nervous. I had probably practiced my story 30–40 times before that, on a one on one basis, and in small group meetings. But it's a hard thing to ask someone to speak really honestly about themselves—so that's why I went first, and I thought that really helped. I think everything I asked everyone to do I modeled for them first, and that helped them be comfortable with one another too. Because—everyone that came up—each and every one of them had a relationship with me when they got there.[13]

After Katie speaks about her reasons for being here, a 17-year-old boy offers his own: "It's our country." His 14-year-old companion, a precocious ninth-grader who is the youngest volunteer attending this Camp Obama, proudly confides that, after 19 years in the United States, his immigrant parents will be taking their citizenship oath that very evening in a town on the other side of the state. Warm congratulations are offered around the circle. A nurse speaks quietly about the urgent need for more health care, which she observes firsthand every day. A librarian describes budget cuts for books, school supplies, and services. Nods and more verbal affirmations circulate again. A shy high school honor student reveals that she wants to one day become a librarian herself but tells us there is no way she can afford college after graduation. Heads are shaken, sympathetic smiles offered, and the two middle-aged women offer verbal support. "Don't give up hope," the nurse says; "I know you'll make a great librarian someday," the librarian offers. Two army veterans, now government office workers, speak bitterly and fatalistically about the human detritus of the Iraq War. "It's as bad as Nam. Nobody knows shit about why we're there; we gotta get out—and soon." A worn-out-looking former union organizer, now local politician, tells us that he has come here so that these two young boys and others like them will be able to experience the thrill of patriotism and hope he had felt when he was their age. After these shared confidences, Katie switches on a VCR, which is plugged into an outdoor socket by a long cord. The group becomes intensely absorbed in a video that strings together stirring passages from recent Obama speeches about hope and justice.

When the volunteers and FOs return for the second assembly, Manny begins by highlighting themes from the campaign video they have just heard. Then he tells the audience that he is going to ask them a crucial question. "Why did you come here?" he asks and then warns them to think carefully before they answer. The responses come flying in:

"To get more effective."
"To get more confidence."
"To get honor."
"To make it constructive."
"I want to meet other people in my community."
"We want to feel the movement from ground up."
"We want to multiply."
"Building our community gives us a sense of belonging."

Throughout these animated audience responses, the national campaign's senior Latino organizer has been writing in thick blue letters on a very large white pad attached to poster board and mounted on a tripod on the stage. It is as if he is translating this call and response into a recipe for organizing civil repair and democratic social change. Here is what he writes:

DISORGANIZATION	→	LEADERSHIP	→	ORGANIZATION
Divided	→	Building Relationships	→	Community
Confusion	→	Interpretation	→	Understanding
Passive	→	Motivate	→	Participate
Reaction	→	Strategize	→	Initiate
Inactive	→	Mobilize	→	Action
Drift	→	Accept Responsibility	→	Purpose

When he finishes writing, the national staff director turns around and passionately exclaims: "This is what organizers do! This is what we do! And this is what you will do, too!" He grabs a pointer and speaks directly to each of the sequences he's written on the white pad. Afterward, Manny takes the stage and announces lunch and the second breakout session: "Come back with some solid plans for organizing your communities."

After picking up food, our team heads to what is now our special outdoor place. Katie decides to lay it all out to us—the organizing goals for the coming weeks. We need to knock on 100 new doors each day, she tells us, which means about 2,000 new doors before the end of the month. We will have to make 500 new calls a day, she warns, which will add up to the extraordinary figure of 20,000 calls before the month is over. Our campaign office back in Pueblo has a phone bank of eight separate lines, she explains, so lots of calls can be made at the same time. We need to schedule canvassing teams, with shifts changing every three hours, from 9 A.M. to 9 P.M., seven days each week. We'll need data inputters. The results from canvassing and calling must be entered into the office computer, separating the "maybe" Obama voters from the definite "nos" and "yeses"—so that the maybes can be revisited and all registered voters who are potential Obama supporters can be tracked to make sure they get to the polls. To get all of this done, we will have to multiply ourselves to generate a bunch of new neighborhood teams.

Katie's information is a blast that for a moment seems to take everybody's breath away. Can our small group of volunteers really handle such a large and imposing task? Katie expresses total confidence in our abilities. She says we know without knowing that we know—how to make sure that this stuff gets done. She asks the group for concrete ideas.

> "Well, we gotta use food and music. That'll get more folks to come."
> "There's my church. Can we get out there Sunday when people are coming out of services?"
> "The American Legion hall is where Latinos hang out. There's always a lot of guys there."
> "There's people around the library, especially late afternoons and Saturdays."
> "Don't forget the chili festival in two weeks. Don't you think that's going to be a terrific place to organize? There's going to be hundreds of our people there."
> "In three weeks, there's the state fair."
> "Do any of you know about the Latino film festival? That'd be great organizing territory, I think."

Nodding and smiling, Katie says, "We'll need a couple of people at all these places with clipboards. Take everybody's name who wants to help out. Make sure you have registration forms and know how to use them, too." Then she asks us to sign up for shifts. Nobody complains and every person offers at least 20 hours a week, some a lot more. The volunteers sort through their schedules verbally—school, work, days off, spouses' needs and work, their lunch hours, church times, club times. Soon Katie has the entire week mapped out: who will be at the office greeting drop-ins and when will they be there, who will be doing phone bank, and who will be canvassing and inputting. The librarian asks whether the door knocking will be singly or in pairs. "I felt so isolated going door to door during the Kerry campaign," she apologizes, "I was all by myself." Katie reassures her that "the Obama campaign is investing in communities" and promises she'll have a partner if she wants.

The last item of business is finding a time for us to meet face to face once each week. "Is it really necessary for us all to get together in person?" one of the vets asks. "It's going to be really hard to find a common time." Katie responds that a weekly meeting for this core group is not negotiable. Even as they themselves are organizing new neighborhood teams, the leaders must touch base in person. After much back and forth, Fridays from 7 to 8 P.M. is chosen as the weekly meeting time. Katie warns that everybody must "be on time" and promises that we will move quickly through an agenda she will distribute in advance. "Don't come late," she exhorts us, "Don't ever be late!" She reminds us, "Barack says taking time seriously is a way of taking power." "What will happen if we do come late?" the younger boy asks.

"You'll have to make 25 cold calls after the meeting ends!" the nurse jokes.

"You'll have to bring popcorn to the next meeting," the older boy warns.

"You'll have to spell 'Obama' with your butt!" exclaims the high school senior. This irreverent remark brings down the house. Our group returns in good spirits to the assembly back in the theater inside.

"We're going to talk now about how to do a one-on-one," Manny announces to the mass of seated volunteers. Exchanging stories is the first step, he reminds us. "Remember, the purpose here is not to extract resources but to build a relationship. You need to find out what's moving the other person, for his children, his spouse, himself. These are the things that interest is built on." As Manny speaks, another national organizer draws two stick figures on the chalkboard, the organizer on the left and the "neighbor" on the right. Between those two figures she lists the qualities upon which building their relationship depends (figure 3.2).

Once the national organizer finishes writing she takes the microphone: "One-on-one is not just a conversation. It is rooted in a story; it's not just a task. Make yourself a little vulnerable. Let yourself be driven by curiosity. Don't ask 'what' questions but get into motivation. Doing a good one-on-one is an art." Manny chimes in: "Don't think about extracting resources from people—money, time, whatever. Think about them as another human being." There will now be role

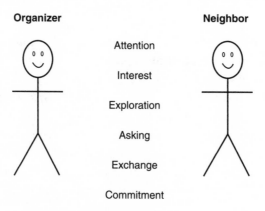

FIGURE 3.2. Relationship Building

playing, he announces. Two other persons from Obama's national organizing staff come onto the stage.

> ORGANIZER: Hi, my name's John. I live around the corner from you, and I'm from the Obama campaign. I was in law school, but I've taken a leave. I wanted to be part of this thing. This just is what feels right.
>
> NEIGHBOR: Well, I heard his speech the other night, and I liked it.
>
> ORGANIZER: He made a lot of good points, didn't he?

Manny explodes: "No, no, no!!! What should the organizer have asked at this point? He should have said, 'Why did you like it?' Instead of focusing on facts and information, he needed to think about motivation." The role playing continues.

> ORGANIZER: Why did you like it?
>
> NEIGHBOR: I liked when he said we have to get beyond race. For me, to be an American is what I always wanted to be, and here I saw a guy running for president saying the same thing.
>
> ORGANIZER: We're all Americans!
>
> NEIGHBOR: I never felt truly accepted. There's all these barriers that keep you out. I see the future being much brighter with Obama if he's president.
>
> ORGANIZER: That's the American dream. You know, first one group fights for their rights, then another. It's our turn now with Obama.
>
> NEIGHBOR: Actually, a bunch of guys and me had the idea of putting a storefront office up for Obama on the main street to hand out bumper stickers and stuff, but we found out it costs $2,000 a month. So we just started using my garage. The problem is this is not a good side of town.
>
> ORGANIZER: I think I can help you find a better place. I know some business people who might like to help!

When the skit ends, the assembly laughs, cheers, and applauds at the excellent outcome. Manny speaks over the applause. "What did they do well?" he asks. "They were open. It's important for an organizer to reveal who she is! You know, to go deeper than 'we both like Obama.' You need to say…what in your background it is that makes you like him, and then you direct it back to them, asking questions that probe into their motivations. Once you get this out, then you have their real interests on the table, and they'll offer you some kind of resources. This will lead to action, to storefront offices, to house meetings, to commitments to do something." Another national organizer adds, "It'll kind of merge into a collaboration."

The volunteers are excited and relaxed as Manny announces another break-out. "Go out there and get names for your group," he tells them. "And think of a song, a poem, or a skit that tells us about you, who you are, what you want, where you live. When you come back, we're going to call you up here on stage."

Our group returns to our outdoor place. The idea that we are to decide on a group name and compose a dramatic presentation seems, to me, awkward and artificial. It seems highly appealing, however, to the other members of our group. They trust Katie implicitly, and they buckle down to the task. They create a totemic name, a plant virtually unknown outside their own section of the state. Then, led by the two high school boys, they proceed to write a song. What emerges is a rap poem laced with saucy Spanish argot, about gringos, Obama, Latinos, getting to be citizens, and the wish to be free. They will sing the chorus together, and the boys will step out for solo parts.

"So what do you have?" Manny asks the volunteers as we reassemble in the amphitheater. "What's your name?" he demands of each group, writing them down on the big green board as he calls each one up to the stage. The volunteers run, straggle, and sometimes need to be urged up by name. Awkward, grinning, serious, abashed, poised, enthusiastic, amateurish, and skillful, each group per-forms its story, then returns to become audience again. The responses begin with appreciative applause, but soon the hall is rocking with catcalls, whistles, and orga-nized waves of syncopated clapping between each act. The lines between audience and actors, organizers and organized, paid staff and volunteers—all these have broken down. The Obama campaign's script of civil repair has been made to walk and talk. An extraordinary performative fusion has unfolded at Su Teatro in the late afternoon of Camp Obama that day.

It would seem to be a fitting time to bring the curtain down, but other acts remain. Trying to bring the high-flying volunteers back to earth, Manny gives notice about a major new task. In the next breakout, he announces, the volunteers will set up as many house parties as possible for next week. House parties, Manny explains, are "the key to political organizing":

> You sit around and tell stories. They're like Tupperware parties. That's how we won Nancy Pelosi's first congressional campaign back in the 1980s. We had 90 house parties, and Nancy came to 89 of them, and we won. Now, each of you is going to think of 50—yes, 50!—names in your closest network. You're going to—right now—call as many of them as possible. When? Right now! Keep track of the calls, the contacts, the com-mitments, and, once somebody says they'll do it, be specific about the time and place of the party. You're going to have an hour and 20 minutes to get this list together and make these calls, and then you'll come back

here and report to the big group. I know, I know—nobody likes to make calls! It's awful, but you have to do it.

"How many of you have cell phones?" Manny asks. Hundreds of hands shoot up. "Well, get out there and use them!" he exclaims.

This new demand to organize these house parties sets off an intense and worrisome moment in our breakout meeting. As we sit in a circle around Katie, the tone borders on panic. The resistance is almost palpable.

> "We're never going to find that many people!"
> "My husband and I live mostly alone. We just don't have that many people we
>   know!"
> "My mother wouldn't let me do this. No way."
> "Can I do it at your house?"
> "I work at odd times. I'm way too shy, anyway. Could I substitute phone
>   banking for being at these parties?"

The same feelings of inadequacy circulate through the other groups, whose meetings spot the grass in the late afternoon sun. Nonetheless, Katie expresses her usual serene confidence, the anxiety abates, the group relaxes and begins to get into it. As Katie goes around the circle, the volunteers start making associations, pulling faces and names out of their memories, constructing their personal network. "Give 'em a call," Katie encourages:

> Just tell them straight what you want them to do. You want them to come
> to a party. In fact, you want them to host one! If they don't answer, leave
> a message that explains what you want. Keep track of these calls and then
> the actual contacts you make and also the commitments you get. You
> really only need to be five people for a party, but try for more. The first
> thing we'll do at each house party is play the Obama video. Then we'll
> have a conversation and engage. Then, at the end, we'll sign people up.

New energy pulses through our group. It must be surging through the other groups, too. Soon the grassy front and back playgrounds of the former elementary school, its hallways, and its classrooms are filled with people making calls on their cell phones. Snatches of conversation ricochet around Su Teatro about food, places, and times. Coiled by the dramatic fusion of this day, the ritual energy now begins spreading outward. The next stage of organizing has begun.

The breakout over, we return to the assembly. Manny and the Colorado state director stand aside the long green chalkboard. On the left side they have made a vertical list of the 20 group names. Now, in a call-and-response, they make horizontal entries to the right of each name, recording the number of calls each group made during the preceding breakout, the number of contacts that were logged, the commitments garnered, and finally the number of actual house parties arranged. It is a volunteer, not the FO, who stands and shouts out these results in response to the call from the stage. After each number is reported, there are cheers or cries of sympathy. If reassurances are needed after a group's report is complete, the assembled audience has them in ready supply.

Group ideals and solidarity are now crystallized into lists of concrete tasks. After the last group makes its report, applause ripples through the amphitheater, and Manny steps forward with a broad smile and congratulations:

> See, what do we learn? That making the calls *does* work—that people *will* be responsive. You've generated about twice as many high payoffs as I would have predicted. That's because you dug deep and approached people you really know, and you spoke to them from your heart. Asking people for something big, for a sacrifice—you know that can have a surprising effect.

Glancing at his watch, Manny announces, "Hey, it's dinner time. Go get some of that great food, get back with your teams, go over what your next week is like. And tell one another how much you like each other and what you've meant to one another today."

We do this, and what unfolds is truly touching. Strangers have become comrades and friends, a fused group, telling one another what has never been confided to such short-lived company. The volunteers reach out to one another and exude mutual appreciation. There's a sense now of being a prepared team and of confident anticipation about the weeks ahead. "How enthusiastic you've been, how eager to join in, how willing to step up!" Katie exclaims. She addresses each person in turn. She tells the older, former union organizer, "You've given us your wisdom, your experience as a political man"; to the two vets, she says, "You brought your experience and your age"; she thanks the nurse for bringing "your skills and real experience"; she lauds the boys for their "extraordinary youth, sincerity, and bravery—you are our future"; she thanks the librarian for "your gentleness." Our group warmly returns Katie's compliments. "Katie, you're really the greatest," one vet acclaims, and the sentiments are repeated from girl to woman, from man to boy. "We love you," the librarian says, and they do. "The point of the program," Katie later confides to me, "was for them to have relationships with one another so that their accountability was greater and their drive was greater as they moved forward. I was nervous that they wouldn't take to some of the team building strategies. But they did—beautifully, and I felt like my confidence was reflected back to me in them."[14] The relationship between the organizer and her group has become fused; they can hardly wait for the next nine weeks of furious organizing to begin.

We return to the amphitheater as darkness descends, preparing our good-byes. But there are still more acts to come. First comes a surprise speaker, Federico Peña, one of the best-known Hispanic political figures in the United States and still Colorado's leading Latino politician. A two-time cabinet member of the Clinton administration, Peña strides to the stage, and the audience comes to its feet. Wearing a starched and brocaded white shirt, blue jeans, and cowboy boots, Peña speaks of being the first Latino elected mayor of Denver and of how nobody had thought it could be done. He had won by a margin of only 6,000 votes, this number matching the new registrations his campaign workers had amassed in the open registration period's final three days. His campaign volunteers, Peña emphasizes, had gone everywhere to find these potential Hispanic voters. "I love going door to door, talking to the people about anything, no matter what their politics—about abortion, about health care, about taxes, you name it." Finally, he urges, "Don't be afraid to speak to people about your love for Obama," and leaves the stage to a standing, thunderous, whistling, foot-stamping ovation.

The floor is taken by the national campaign's senior Latino organizer, who, intense and unsmiling, bounds onto the stage. "You have energized me," he declares loudly and triumphantly. "This is what refills my batteries." He continues in a less rhetorical, more confiding way:

> We are in the fight of our life, of our times. We are going to change the world. Here is the importance of Latino states. It is critical. We are going to have a major meeting in D.C. this week, with Hispanic immigrant rights groups, Hispanic radio DJs, churches, and labor unions. Barack is going to come, and he's going to tell them we must all get together, and he'll ask them what they can do to help. He will promise them that this new spirit that is beginning here will last, that it must last long after the election. It is essential to the Obama presidency.

Next the state director climbs up onto the stage. Holding in his hands a three-foot-long computer printout, he looks over it and announces: "We have the most recent numbers, and here's bad news: We need 20,000 new registered voters." Bedlam breaks out. The volunteers are going nuts not because they are shocked but because they are so happy. They're cheering. Cries of "Yes, we can" and "We can do it" ricochet around the theater. Rock-and-roll music starts blaring from the loudspeakers, along with traditional Hispanic songs.

There is a graduation ceremony. Every member of every group matriculates from Camp Obama. Diplomas, T-shirts, hugs, tearful thank yous, and goodbyes. The NOs and FOs retire for a debriefing session. Manny recounts how, earlier that day, an organizer had described the assembled volunteers as mere "*hypothetical groups.*" He asks them how they feel now.

"How much I admire these people."

"I feel not only do I have their back, but they have mine."

"Today brought home to me why I do this."

"Sometimes I feel it's hopeless, but it's not."

"I cold-called a Republican today, and he said he'd organize a house party."

Manny reminds them about the upcoming two-day staff retreat.

When Colorado went into the Democratic column on Election Day two months later, many analysts were surprised. It would not have surprised anybody in attendance at Su Teatro that day.

The Digital Ground Game

Political performances attempt to fuse candidate and audience "in the air" via the mass media. As this chapter suggests, these efforts at fusion are complemented by organization "on the ground." It is not only door-to-door engagement that connects citizen and candidate, however, but terminal-to-terminal engagement as well. The Obama campaign is the first national struggle for power to bring the Internet age to the ground game in a massive and organic way.

The circulating energy that fuses symbol to audience in the face-to-face rituals unfolding at Camp Obama extends outward in the civil community via door-to-door campaigning. Energetic, symbol-projecting volunteers encounter less committed but potentially sympathetic members of the citizen audience, hoping the meetings will become fused and intimate. Energized symbols are also projected digitally to members of the citizen audience who sit in front of computers at home or office or when they are on the go and working mobile messaging machines. These are virtual, not face-to-face encounters, but the possibility for intimacy and symbolic fusion remains. The Obama campaign's official social networking site, "My BO," operates under the ethos "Keep it real and keep it local," according to Chris Hughes, the cofounder of Facebook, who joins the campaign in early 2007 as director of online organizing.[15] This networked community organizes more than 200,000 offline, local events in real, face-to-face time. In September 2008, it also launches an online phone-banking tool called Neighbor to Neighbor (N2N), under the aegis of an exhortation from Obama himself, posted on the Barack Obama HQ blog: "The single most important thing you can do is talk to voters. There's nothing more powerful than everyday people reaching out to their neighbors."

In addition to providing a virtual venue for person-to-person fusion, the net campaign creates symbolic connections by projecting iconic representations of the candidate and his message via music and video. If these symbolic performances are compelling, they are picked up and circulated by public and private blogs. Of

the more than 1,800 videos the campaign creates and posts on its YouTube channel, BarackObamadotcom, well over 100 received at least a quarter-million views,
with the top 20 getting more than one million views each.[16] Will.i.am's "Yes We
Can" music video is posted on YouTube on February 28, 2008.[17] The campaign's
most popular online presentation, it receives nearly 20 million views since going
viral.[18] At McCain's official YouTube channel, by contrast, only three videos ever
hit the one-million mark, dropping below 350,000 at the 20th most viewed.[19]

From the outside, meeting, registering, and even motivating voters can seem
merely technical, an organizational chart of calls and contacts, lists of "maybes" and "yeses," store-front offices, and tracking "not yet" voters at polling
stations on Election Day. From the inside, however, organizing—whether it is
face to face or virtual—is about connection, engagement, emotion, morality,
and identification. The organizer aims the collective political representation at
the citizen's heart. It seems as if such a short shot would be easy, but it is not.
If the organizers can pierce this citizen heart, then the struggle for power can
succeed. For only then will the civil sphere allow the candidate to represent it
inside the state.

PART II

Heroes, Binaries, and Boundaries

CHAPTER FOUR

Imagining Heroes

C AMPAIGNS ARE ALWAYS 'WHAT'S THE NARRATIVE OF THE RACE?'"
an Illinois political consultant remarks in September 2007.[1] He is
explaining to the *New York Times* why Barack Obama lost his first effort
to enter the national scene back in the fall of 2000, when he had opposed incumbent Bobby Rush in a Chicago congressional race. Candidates and their advisors
struggle to find their stories, and journalists spin their own narratives even as they
evaluate candidates' success at telling their own.

Predestination and Redemption

Political stories are all about heroes. It is because Obama could not be a hero in
south Chicago's black community that he lost that long-ago congressional race.
Bobby Rush had been an activist in the Student Nonviolent Coordinating Committee (SNCC) and a leader of the local Black Panther party. He had fought on
behalf of an oppressed and vulnerable people against the white power structure,
and he remains a hero to the African American community in Chicago's south
side. Narratives are elastic, however, and from the standpoint of the present,
Obama's defeat can be framed as a blessing in disguise. As time passes, new and
more encompassing narratives can emerge. If Obama had won in 2000, the Illinois
political consultant tells the *Times,* he would have remained a mundane everyday
figure, "an African-American congressman" instead of the "transcendent" political
figure he is becoming today. Only by losing could Barack Obama become a hero
on the larger historical stage.[2]

Heroes rise above ordinary political life, and the narratives we spin about them allow us to understand how they are able to do so. Stories about heroes create meaning by looking back to the past from the present and by projecting the plot's next act into the future, all at the same time. In their earlier lives, heroes were tested and suffered, usually on behalf of something greater than themselves. In the present, however, their suffering and their causes will be redeemed. Unlike an actual flesh-and-blood person, who is materially rooted in time and space, the narrative character of a hero is not moved by a cause immediately preceding it but by a goal that is to come. The actions of a hero are caused by a meaning that becomes clear only after the heroic journey is complete. There is a purpose to a hero's life. It is this goal that defines an arc stretching from the past to the future via the present, moving the heroes and the greater causes for which they fight from earlier despair to contemporary redemption and on to future glory. Persons who become heroes are predestined to traverse this rainbow arch. This is what the plot to their story is all about.[3]

In 2007, Bobby Rush is serving his eighth term as a congressman from south Chicago. He needs to make sense of—to be able to tell a meaningful story about—the fact that he had earlier opposed and defeated the very same man who today offers historical salvation not only for the African American people but beyond as well. Rush creates this coherence by weaving a new narrative about Obama as a predestined hero. Obama had to suffer and be defeated, or else he and America's black community and perhaps even America itself could not now be redeemed. In telling the story of Obama's 2000 campaign and the dilemma Bobby Rush faces, the *Times* recounts the trials, tribulations, and ultimate goal of a hero's journey.

THE DOWNFALL

In his book, *The Audacity of Hope,* Mr. Obama wrote: "Less than halfway into the campaign, I knew in my bones that I was going to lose. Each morning from that point forward I awoke with a vague sense of dread." [In that campaign] Mr. Obama's Ivy League education and his white liberal-establishment connections [had] become an issue. Mr. Rush told [the African American newspaper] *The Chicago Reader,* "He went to Harvard and became an educated fool. We're not impressed with these folks with these Eastern elite degrees." Mr. Rush and his supporters faulted him for having missed experiences that more directly defined the previous generation of black people. "Barack is a person who read about the civil-rights protests and thinks he knows all about it," Mr. Rush told *The Reader.* Mr. Obama was seen as an intellectual, "not from us, not from the 'hood,'" said Jerry Morrison, a consultant on the Rush campaign. [Obama mentor and former congressman Abner] Mikva said, "It indicated that he

[Obama] had not made his mark in the African-American community and didn't particularly have a style that resonated there."[4]

Because he could not be a hero for Chicago's African American community in 2000, candidate Obama's campaign for Congress failed to resonate. He was defeated and humiliated. But this downfall was followed by a rise. The *Times* continues its story this way:

THE CANDIDATE MATURES

Mr. Mikva recalls telling him [Obama] about advice once given to John F. Kennedy by Cardinal Richard Cushing: "The cardinal said to him, 'Jack, you have to learn to speak more Irish and less Harvard.' I think I recounted that anecdote to Barack. Clearly, he learned how to speak more Chicago and less Harvard in subsequent campaigning."…In March 2004, Mr. Obama won the Democratic primary for the United States Senate with nearly 53 per cent of the vote, racking up huge totals in wards he had lost to Mr. Rush in 2000. (Mr. Rush, still stung by Mr. Obama's challenge to him, endorsed a white candidate in the race…)….Today, Mr. Rush, a practicing Baptist minister in his eighth term in Congress who is backing Mr. Obama's presidential candidacy, still seems to be ruminating about the Obama phenomenon with grievance and wonder…."For what he is doing now, he didn't need to march against police brutality," Mr. Rush said [and] has an explanation for Mr. Obama's emergence after the dark days of 2000 as a political star four years later. [Obama] vanquished a field of multimillionaires, some more experienced and better known, and benefited from fortuitous domestic scandals that sidelined two opponents and left him facing a Republican widely seen as unable to win. "I would characterize the Senate race as being a race where Obama was, let's say, blessed and highly favored," Mr. Rush said…."That's not routine. There's something else going on." What was he suggesting? "I think that Obama, his election to the Senate, was divinely ordered," Mr. Rush said, all other explanations failing. "I'm a preacher and a pastor; I know that that was God's plan. Obama has certain qualities that—I think he is being used for some purpose. I really believe that."[5]

Crisis and Salvation

In early June 2008, *Times* reporter Michael Powell explains that Obama "has the gift of making people see themselves in him."[6] Such identification allows collective representation, the candidate's performance becoming so powerful that it creates fusion with an audience. To explain the source of identification, Powell evokes the miraculous, even eerie qualities of heroes and their relation to temporality. "Obama is a protean political figure," Powell suggests, "inspiring devotion in supporters who see him as a transformative leader." It is "as if there were a Barack-the-immaculate-pol quality to his rise." Employing allusive terms that evoke prophecy, Powell writes that Obama "has taken just 11 years to run the course from state senator to the first black presumptive nominee who holds thousands spellbound." The modern political journalist reaches for a narrative about supernatural qualities associated with premodern religious life. Hope for transcendence remains a vivid and powerful secular motif, and the idea of the hero is deeply imbedded in political campaigns.

In a *Times* report on the publication of comic books devoted to candidates Obama and McCain, the paper's tone is mildly ironic and "sophisticated." However, the prose style barely conceals the liberal newspaper's recognition that the stakes in the struggle for power are such as to suggest a parallel between the superheroes and contemporary presidential campaigns (figure 4.1).

FIGURE 4.1. From *The New York Times*, "The Candidates, Comically Drawn," George Gene Gustines, July 22, 2008. (Illustrations: J. Scott Campbell/IDW Publishing)

COMPANY FOR BATMAN AND ROBIN

Comic books are filled with stories about protagonists who overcome seemingly impossible odds as they fight for truth, justice and the American way.
Where better to chronicle the stories of Senators John McCain and Barack
Obama and their campaigns for the White House?...Each cover depicts its
presidential candidate looking skyward. They each have a trace of color out-
lining their bodies: naturally, red for Mr. McCain and blue for Mr. Obama.[7]

Characters become heroes by overcoming great odds and by resolving what
seem to be overwhelming challenges. Struggles for big-time political power are
narrated in terms of crisis and salvation. According to those who would be president, Americans face a unique moment in our history. There are unprecedented
dangers and opportunities; a world-historical crisis domestically and interna-
tionally threatens to derail the nation's triumphant, mythical history. America
has fallen on tough times. The dream lies in tatters. The nation has fallen off
the hill. With national collapse looming, the present moment is precarious and
burdened with terrible significance. Desecrated and polluted—not least by the
outgoing president and his administration—the nation must be purified. For this
we need a hero. Only one man can save the day. If he is defeated, there will be
apocalypse; if he wins, there will be salvation and transformation. Only by resolving the "crisis of our times" can heroes be made.[8] Not just survival but also transcendence and refounding are at stake. At the most critical early moment in his
campaign for the Democratic nomination, late in the evening of November 10,
2007, Barack Obama climbed onto the stage in Des Moines, Iowa, at the Jeffer-
son-Jackson Day dinner, two months before the Iowa caucus and just moments
after Hillary Clinton had finished a speech earnestly highlighting her experience.
Here is what Obama had to say.

> We are in a defining moment in our history...Our nation is at war. The
> planet is in peril. The dream that so many generations fought for feels as
> if it's slowly slipping away. We are working harder for less. We've never
> paid more for health care or college. It's harder to save and it's harder
> to retire. And most of all, we've lost faith that our leaders can or will do
> anything about it. And that is why the same old Washington textbook
> campaigns just won't do in this election.[9]

Barack Obama on the Hinge of History

To become a hero, one must establish great and urgent necessity. A hinge is created in history and the candidate inserted into that break. Heroes are constructed

by shoehorning a political actor into world-historical time. It's about narrating time, about building a new temporality that is radically discontinuous, and about weighting the imminent break with immense significance. The hero's opponent is so dangerous that electing that person will plunge the nation into apocalypse. Rather than transcending the troubled present, history will be set in reverse. If the antihero is elected, the progressive arc of our collectivity will be broken, and we will no longer be able to move into future time and change for the better. Facing the millennium during the 1996 Clinton-Gore reelection campaign, the Democratic Party promised voters "A Bridge to the 21st Century."

The past is anticivil and dark, but the future will be good and bright. Jack Kennedy memorably announced in his 1960 inaugural address that "a new day is dawning," recalling the prowess of Olympic heroes with his proclamation that "the torch has been passed to a new generation." Half a century later, Barack Obama draws the same kind of bright, redolent line between sullied past and golden future. He presents himself as a force that mediates between darkness and light. He will purify the American project, pulling it from the past to the future and into the bright sunshine of a new day. The present is a hinge. "This is our time, this is our moment," candidate Obama declares not only in his postprimary speech on June 4, 2008, but over and over again as well. One week later, in a major economic address, Obama insists that his opponent, John McCain, is only nominally in the present and that his real attachment is to the past. "Mr. Obama said again that a McCain presidency would be a continuation of President Bush," the *Times* reports.[10] "We've been there once," Obama declares, and he assures his audience that "we're not going back." According to the *Times*, "Mr. Obama posed the choice between him and Mr. McCain as a fundamental one between the future and the past," and it describes this framing as "the ground on which he hopes to fight his campaign." The present becomes critical because it sits between polluted past and transformed future. "This is the choice we face right now," Obama proclaims to his audience, "a choice between more of the same...or change." It is not a matter of issues or ideology but of temporality. Voters must choose the candidate who can connect the present to the future. Rather than "an argument between left or right," Obama contends, "it is time to try something new." As the Democratic candidate sees it, McCain believes the nation is somehow already in the future: "He says we've made great progress in our economy these past eight years." If McCain is right, then the contrast between the Republican and the Democratic candidates is lost. There is no hinge. The present looks exactly like the past. Difference disappears. Meaning cannot be made.

From the very first days of his appearance on the American political stage, Barack Obama has presented a character perched on the very hinge of history. If his candidacy is accepted, he promises his audiences, he will play a transformational role in turning the historical page. In a television ad that runs just two weeks before the election, Obama proclaims that we face a "defining moment in our history," invoking a great temporal urgency: "The question is not are you better off than you were four years ago—we all know the answer to that. The real question is will our country be better off four years from now?"[11] Obama's opponents—the critics of his political performances—have insisted on the deceptiveness of his character and the strategic nature of his plot. They are unable to deny, however, that for many Americans the Obama story does exert performative power and that the Obama character does display a hero's integrity.

In the July 21, 2008, *New Yorker* magazine, Ryan Lizza writes an exposé detailing what he depicts as the Machiavellian quality of Obama's Chicago years, the period stretching from Obama's 1991 post–law school arrival in the Windy City to his 2004 election to the U.S. Senate.[12] The article quickly becomes notorious, inspiring commentators to reach for Al Capone–style similes about "Chicago politics" and for metaphors about Obama as "fast Eddie." Lizza hopes his story will deflate Obama's hero narrative by pointing to "a realization among his supporters that superheroes don't become President; politicians do." Tellingly, these revelations about Obama playing Chicago-style politics emerge at the same time as the *Times'* reports on superhero "candidate comics." In fact, even as Lizza recounts Obama's climb upward through the nooks and crannies of Chicago politics, the *New Yorker* narrative suggests that the bedazzling story of a hero stuck to Obama like glue throughout this early phase of his political career. "Obama's rise has often appeared effortless," Lizza acknowledges, describing how his "breathtakingly rapid political ascent" and "lightning transition from Hyde Park to legislator to Presidential nominee" created a "zealous corps of campaign workers" who were "passionate" and "crazed."

The *New Yorker* narrates Obama's 1995 campaign for the Illinois state senate as the beginning of an arc stretching from darkness to light. Writing that Obama "was able to capture the imagination of some young African-Americans frustrated by their local leadership," Lizza quotes from a staffer recalling that first campaign:

> You have to understand, it's 1995. It's the year after the Republicans have taken over control of Congress, and in Illinois all three branches of government were also controlled by the Republicans. So it was a really dark point. I was looking to be engaged in something that would mean something.

It is in this context of decline and weakness, Lizza explains, that on September 19, 1995, at a lakefront Ramada Inn in Chicago, the thirty-four-year-old Barack Obama announced, "I want to inspire a renewal of morality in politics." A well-known politician introducing the neophyte spins a narrative connecting the emerging Obama candidacy to the Democratic Party's earlier heroic past and to the young candidate's glorious future. It was "in this room," she declares, that "Harold Washington announced for mayor." Washington had been Chicago's first African American mayor. Mourned and beloved, he had died shortly after his 1987 reelection to a second term. Connecting the young candidate with the discourse of civil society, the political veteran announces that "Barack Obama carries on the tradition of independence in this district," prophesying that "his candidacy is a passing of the torch."

Twelve years later, when Obama announces his campaign for a much larger office, the hinge of history is still in full swing. In the final weeks of the presidential campaign, the conservative *Weekly Standard* provides this retrospective account of Obama's announcement, constructing an interpretive grid to explain why Obama is now on the verge of winning that race:

> When Barack Obama announced his presidential candidacy in Springfield, Illinois, on February 10, 2007, he promised to change the practice of American politics. "This campaign must be the occasion, the vehicle, of your hopes, and your dreams. It will take your time, your energy, and your advice—to push us forward when we're doing right, and to let us know when we're not." Obama told the crowd on that chilly day that he was running "not just to hold an office, but to gather with you to transform a nation." He was particularly concerned with the way politicians run for office. He decried "the smallness of our politics" and "the chronic avoidance of tough decisions" and politicians who win by "scoring cheap political points." All of this, he said, had led voters to look away in "disillusionment and frustration." "The time for that politics is over," Obama said.[13]

Two months earlier in 2008, the liberal *New York Times* columnist Maureen Dowd observes candidate Obama's speech at the Victory Column in Berlin before a crowd of 200,000 people. Dowd reports that Berliners have christened Obama the "Redeemer" and "Savior" and how, according to the German press, French president Nicolas Sarkozy "was also Obamarized, as the Germans were calling the mesmerizing effect." She describes Obama's meeting the next day with Sarkozy "a moment of transcendent passion."[14]

One year before, in 2007, *Times* reporter Janny Scott interviews the campaign manager of Obama's losing 2000 congressional campaign. As I recounted earlier, he describes Obama's defeat to Scott as if it were a turning point in a pilgrim's progress. Because of Obama's shattering loss, the African American political aspirant had progressed from "thoughtful, earnest policy wonk/civil rights lawyer/constitutional law expert to Barack Obama the politician, the inspirer, the speaker."[15]

Another Obama friend and former state senator tells Scott that, because of that early loss, Obama had moved from an earthbound concentration on contemporary, concrete issues to the politics of transcendence, aspiration, utopia, and hope:

> He stumbled on the fact that instead of running on all the issues, quote unquote, that [*sic*] hope is the real key. Not only the black community but less privileged people are looking for that hope. You don't have to talk about health care, you have to talk about "the promise" of health care. Hope is a pretty inclusive word. I think he is very good at selling that.

All of these former comrades of Obama, as well as those reporting on their observations, understand that Obama is presenting himself as a hero who promises salvation. They are wrong, however, to describe this merely as "performance." The promise of salvation has been there from the beginning, as real for Obama and his citizen audiences as any fictional or spiritual truth can be. Obama character has always promised big things. It stands on the hinge of history, in "the fierce urgency of now." Obama character inspires audiences to believe that they and their nation can be resurrected, that the mundane can be transcended, that, as the Democrat so eloquently promised in his speeches, it "is time, America, time for us to believe again!" Whether this is seen as making meaning or selling it depends on whether the arrow from the hero's bow has firmly entered into the citizen heart.

The Immortal Body

To successfully become a hero is to enter into myth. It is to cease being merely a mortal man or woman and to develop a second, immortal body.[16] The second body is an iconic surface, and contact with it conveys a powerful feeling of connecting with the idealized nation that lies just underneath. Because the hero's iconic body is symbolic and immortal, it will not die. It can be remembered no matter what happens to the biological woman or man. Most political figures cannot grow such second skin. They are respected or well liked and maybe even deferred to, but their public body is weak and insubstantial. Because they do not have a second skin, they remain politicians rather than myth. They are overshadowed, sometimes even wimpified, by their opponents. Wounded in political battles, they reveal their mortal natures.

In 1960 Richard Nixon's five o'clock shadow, not properly covered by makeup, darkened and polluted the Republican candidate; this allowed Jack Kennedy to shine like a bright young god during the first nationally televised debate. In 1980 Jimmy Carter was damaged by Teddy Kennedy's late primary run and injured further by the prophetic "The Dream Will Never Die" speech Kennedy delivered to the Democratic convention on the eve of Carter's nomination. In that televised oration, widely circulated later via record and tape, Kennedy declared himself the once and future king. A mere administrator by contrast, Carter faltered in the subsequent general election campaign, watching helplessly as the once mundane, even comic figure of Ronald Reagan grew a sacred and mythical second body during the course of that campaign. The immortal, second body of American liberalism sequestered itself inside the Kennedy mystique for three decades until the "lion of the Senate" and his fairy-tale niece Caroline conferred the sacral blessing on Barack Obama himself.

The Suffering and Redemption of John McCain

For many years before he put himself forward as a candidate for president, McCain had embodied a story of sacrifice and redemption for the American people. In 1966 and 1967, as a U.S. Navy fighter pilot, he flew dangerous bombing missions over Hanoi, a city that was not merely the capital of North Vietnam but also, for many Americans, the heart of antidemocratic darkness. The cold war against communism was experienced by the vast majority of Americans as a hinge in history, a long twilight struggle that would decide the fate of all humankind. When John McCain was shot down over Hanoi in late 1967, it was not only his individual life but also this higher cause that was at stake.

By narrow circumstance, McCain did not die when his plane crashed into a Hanoi lake. He was, however, seriously injured and later brutally tortured and for five years submerged in a gulag of Vietnamese prisoner-of-war camps. During the early months of this imprisonment, McCain's suffering became widely known. As the son and grandson of navy admirals, his captivity presented a public relations bonanza for the Vietnamese, who interrogated him—in bandage and body cast—and distributed the film worldwide. As the brutal and tragic conflict in Vietnam wound down, the cause of the POWs, the American prisoners of war, heated up. They became a cause célèbre, idealized by many Americans as symbolic representations of the nation's anticommunist ideals and of the suffering that fighting for them entailed. When McCain was released along with the other POWs in 1973, his redemption transfixed the nation. "HANOI TO RELEASE ADMIRAL'S SON," proclaimed a huge banner headline in the *Los Angeles Times*.[17] Still hobbling on crutches and resplendent in his gleaming white naval uniform, McCain was lauded by President Nixon and a grateful if weary nation in a celebration at the White House.

Staying on in Washington, D.C., McCain learned politics from the inside as a naval liaison to Congress, moving to Arizona and eventual parlaying his national reputation as a war hero into a series of successful political campaigns. In 1999, as prelude to his first run for the Republican presidential nomination, McCain published an autobiography depicting his youth and early years of imprisonment. "Whenever I am introduced at an appearance, the speaker always refers to my war record first," McCain acknowledged. "My public profile is inextricably linked to my POW experiences," he continued, and "such recognition has benefited my political career."[18]

Faith of My Fathers, written in the first person but coauthored with McCain's close friend and political advisor Mark Salter, narrates the story of a young man who was destined at birth to become a hero. Born into a long line of military men, a "martial lineage" traced "through many generations of our family,"[19] McCain attended the U.S. Naval Academy as his father before him, yet finished near the bottom of his class and compiled a string of demerits for bad behavior. McCain recalls the "crude individualism" of his childhood and how he had been a "rowdy and impetuous young man."[20] Only in his thirties, after he had been shot down and come close to death, when he had suffered humiliation, powerlessness, and years of loneliness at the hands of his nation's enemies, did McCain discover the higher calling that would allow him to redeem himself and others in his postmilitary life:

> When you're alone with your thoughts for years, it's hard not to reflect on how better you could have spent your time as a free man....I regretted much of the foolishness that had characterized my youth [and that] I hadn't worked harder at the Academy....I gained the insight, common to many people in life-threatening circumstances, that the trivial pleasure of life and human vanity were transient and insignificant. And I resolved that when I regained my freedom, I would seize opportunities to spend what remained of my life in more important pursuits....I thought glory was the object of war, and all glory was self-glory. No more. For I have learned the truth: there are greater pursuits than self-seeking. Glory...is not a prize for being the most clever, the strongest, or the boldest. Glory belongs to the act of being constant to something greater than yourself, to a cause, to your principles, to the people on whom you rely, and who rely on you in return.[21]

This narrative of courage, sacrifice, suffering, and redemption had an extraordinary impact on citizen audiences, powerfully amplifying the performative effect of McCain's hero story from three decades before. Advance reviews prepared citizen audiences to read the book as a deeply affecting, archetypical narrative. *Kirkus* called it "impressive and inspiring, the story of a man touched and molded by fire who loved and served his country in a time of great trouble, suffering, and challenge." *Publishers Weekly* judged it "the most engrossing book to appear in a long time from a presidential candidate." After publication, the reviewers agreed. *Faith of My Fathers* became a *New York Times* bestseller, the newspaper's book reviewer suggesting that, even "if he never presents himself as a hero...it is impossible to read this book without realizing that a hero is what he is." According to *USA Today*, McCain's memoir was "hard to top and impossible to read without being moved," and the *Seattle Times* predicted that "by the end of this book you will undoubtedly like and admire John McCain."[22]

After McCain lost to George W. Bush in 2000, he and Salter authored a string of similar accounts. These kept the politician's hero character in the public eye, highlighting the redemptive arc that *Faith of My Fathers* first inscribed. With September 11, the invasion of Afghanistan, and the war in Iraq, the character of military hero became particularly powerful in the performances McCain projected to Republican audiences. It was in large part on the basis of this narrative promise that the senator launched his campaign for his party's nomination in 2008.

Achilles and Hector

In the presidential campaign, McCain played Achilles to Obama's Hector, even if the outcome of their epic confrontation inverted the tragic ending Homer earlier prescribed. The *Iliad* provides the mold for the Western hero story. Its major protagonist, the Greek warrior Achilles, was half god, half man. Achilles' antagonist, the Trojan Hector, was fully a human being, described by Homer as not simply a great warrior but also the champion of the civilization of Troy. The outcome of the Trojan War between Greece and Troy was decided by the battle between Achilles and Hector. As Achilles dragged Hector's body around the walls of Troy, Homer made it clear that might—not right—had won on the field that day. During the siege of Troy, Achilles had sulked in his tent because King Agamemnon had taken away his war prize, a woman named Briseis, and eventually joined the fight only out of the spirit of revenge for a fallen friend. Hector, though also a great fighter, was motivated much more by familial and ethical concerns. He worried about abandoning his wife and young children, and his decision finally to engage Achilles was made not because of blood lust but because of the desire to save his city:

> Achilles' greatness is a greatness of force and of negation. He is different from other men by his greater capacity to deny, to refuse, to kill, and to face death....Hector, by contrast, is a hero [who] affirms all that Achilles denies....Hector is a human creature, with wife and child, parents and brothers, friends and fellow citizens. Achilles' acts are always true to his

shifting visions of himself; Hector has placed his life at the service of others.[23]

Even as they struggle for civil power, political heroes can be more and less democratic, centering their representative narratives more inside or more outside the promises and institutions of civil society. Obama presents himself as a decidedly democratic hero. The crisis he constructs and promises to transform is most of all an internal, domestic one, sparked by what he decries as massive violations of civil ties, dangerous corruptions of office obligations, and the growing inequalities that threaten the broad solidarity upon which democracy is based. Obama promises to overcome not only divisions internal to American society—"we are not red states or blue states but the United States of America"—but external ones as well. Like Hector, he is reluctant to make war on his nation's enemies and worries about the costs to hearth and home. Preferring to negotiate, Obama would employ common sense and goodwill to reach over boundaries that rest upon suspicion and reflect merely physical divides. Like Hector, Obama's most fervent obligations are to families and fellow citizens, to the civil sphere of the United States. Obama's mythical body molts from the iconic forms of Lincoln, Franklin Roosevelt, and Martin Luther King Jr., American heroes who promised civil repair and possessed the practical, political skills to carry them out.

The Obama hero addresses internal boundaries and divisions and promises to transcend intra- and international tensions and to expand inclusive solidarity. For John McCain it is a different story. His hero concentrates on the nation's external boundary. The suffering and redemption of the McCain hero comes from engagement in war and violence, from victory in military confrontations, not from struggles for civil repair. For the Republican candidate, being an American means living within the legally defined territory of the nation-state. For the Democratic protagonist, Americanism is defined by the moral boundary of the civil sphere, by the creed of liberty and justice for all. Obama's heroic ethic centers squarely on the discourse of civil society, emphasizing the significance not only of honesty but also of criticism, not only of respect but also of transparency, and not only autonomy but also a rough equality of social conditions for every human being.

McCain's heroic ethic is of a different sort. As a warrior hero, he struggles to maintain separations between inside and outside, not to overcome them, and he succeeds not by offering moral recognition but by securing physical domination. When the Republican candidate clinches the votes for his party's nomination in March 2008, the *Wall Street Journal* records the scene of a hero triumphant, but in a military, not a civil way, providing an implicit contrast to the hero then emerging on the Democratic side:

In his victory speech Tuesday night, John McCain ticked off his muscu-
lar foreign-policy plans and then, with clenched jaw, urged the rowdy
crowd to "stand up and fight for America." The Republican presidential
nominee's resolve will now be tested on a national stage. His record in
Congress suggests that a McCain White House could assume a tougher
posture overseas than has the current administration, which has itself
been criticized as too bellicose. Sen. McCain has joked about bombing
Iran, ruled out talks with North Korea and, earlier this week, condemned
the new leader of Russia.... "He's more confrontational, he's more coercion, he's more sticks," said retired Air Force Maj. Gen Scott Gration, who
advises Sen. Obama on foreign policy and national security. "It's time
to go back and do carrots."...Sen. McCain has a long record of urging
the use of force from North Korea to Iran. In 1994, he accused President
Clinton of trying to appease North Korea over its nuclear program. "To
get a mule to move, you must show it the carrot and hit it with a stick at
the same time," he wrote in the *Los Angeles Times*. Five years later, when
the Clinton administration led a North Atlantic Treaty Organization
bombing campaign against then-Yugoslavia, Sen. McCain was one of
the loudest voices in the Senate urging the White House to prepare for a
potential ground invasion.... Sen. McCain wrote in *Foreign Affairs* magazine last fall that, when it comes to Iran, "military action, although not
the preferred option, must remain on the table."...Sen. McCain, whose
father, grandfather and sons served in the military, has also vowed to
increase the size of the armed forces.[24]

Warrior heroes do not suffer and conquer for themselves. They, too, act on
behalf of others. The McCain hero is selflessly committed to national solidarity.
Certainly, honesty and respect are intrinsic to the ethic of the military hero. However, as the *Wall Street Journal* editorializes about McCain in the closing days of
his campaign, "the former Navy pilot's politics" revolve around "core convictions"
of a distinctly noncivil kind.[25] The military virtues of "duty, honor and country"
are McCain's primary moral concerns. Courage plays the central role in his memoir, defined more in a physical than a moral sense. In *Profiles in Courage*, John
Kennedy had lauded the courage of nonconforming conscience, the strength to
go against one's fellow citizens for the sake of moral right. In *Faith of My Fathers*,
McCain admires the courage to stand with one's fellows, to withstand violent
blows for their sake. He writes that "the great test of character" is war and describes
courage as "finding the will to act despite the fear and chaos of battle."[26] Another
cardinal virtue is loyalty, whether manifest in soldierly absorption in a band of
brothers or in the deference and paternalism of which military hierarchies are

made. Portraying his father and grandfather as extraordinary warriors, McCain announces, on the very first page of his book, that "earning their respect has been the most lasting ambition of my life," and when he lays out "the terms of their approval" he avers that these forefathers "were honest, brave, and loyal all their lives." Duty and honor follow from courage and loyalty. Testifying to the virtue of a fellow prisoner who withstood the physical pain of torture and the moral temptation of appeasement, McCain writes that "no one I knew in prison, Army, Navy, Marine, or Air Force officer, had greater loyalty to his country or derived more courage from his sense of honor."[27] All of these virtues are rolled together into the ethic of faith, which means accepting earthly and divine authority without fear or doubt. "Faith in God, faith in country, and faith in your fellow prisoners," McCain avers, were "the three essential keys to resistance," which "our senior officers always stressed" and which "we were to keep uppermost in our mind…when we were isolated or otherwise deprived of their guidance."[28]

This is not to suggest that John McCain has problems with democracy. He presents himself as fighting on behalf of freedom and against dictatorship, as going to war not for primordial or particularistic values but for those of a civil and universalistic kind. He portrays his suffering inside military prisons as leading him to value political freedom even more strongly.[29] In the years following his release, McCain cultivated a maverick image, presenting himself as a rebel vis-à-vis the powers that be. Nonetheless, the public markers of McCain's mythic identity were warrior ones, the wounds to his public and immortal body inflicted on the field of battle. The military can be a noble field of prowess, and from ancient Athens right up until today the civil sphere's survival has, in critical historic moments, depended upon battlefield success. However, military prowess depends on violence and promotes primal hatred, actions and values that are antithetical to the civil behavior and the more universal forms of incorporation that define democratic life:

> My grandfather, as combatants often do, needed to work up a powerful hate for his enemy. He once recommended of the Japanese "killing them all—painfully." This is an understandable reaction to the losses and atrocities suffered at the hands of the enemy. But hate also sustains the fighter in his devotion to the complete destruction of his enemy and helps to overcome the virtuous human impulse to recoil in disgust from what must be done by your hand.[30]

When the *New York Times* writes that McCain's memoir demonstrates why he deserves to be a hero, the reviewer describes the book as a "testament to the *martial* values of honor and patriotism." The *Christian Science Monitor* observed that the memoir "gets to the core of those ineffable qualities of *wartime brotherhood and self-sacrifice."* While these qualities undoubtedly reach "far beyond common notions of 'patriotism,'" as the *Monitor* suggests, they are still values of a decidedly noncivil, if not anticivil, kind.[31]

Danger and McCain's Military Hero

Candidate Obama periodically reminds his supporters that his Republican opponent is a genuine American hero and that he has "worn the uniform of our country with bravery and distinction, and for that we owe him our gratitude and our respect."[32] Why, as he struggles mightily to defeat him, does the Democrat seem so sanguine in offering this acknowledgment, so willing to confer on McCain a laurel wreath? It is, after all, precisely in the military field that the Obama character is most vulnerable, the very arena in which McCain has made his heroic name.[33] To answer this question, we must consider the social setting for military heroism and how it can change.

It was because the hinge of history had become a matter of military valor—of defending territory and the saving and taking of human life—that in the years after September 11 the heroic character of John McCain was able to move back onto center stage. Danger in the physical sense seemed close at hand. From the Afghan invasion onward, the American nation was deeply involved not in a metaphorical twilight war but in violence and killing on a significant scale. It was because grave physical danger became imminent that the McCain hero, forged decades earlier in the century before, no longer seemed so long ago or far away. For a military hero to be compelling, the world must be dangerous right now. For the military hero to put himself on the hinge of history, the enemy must be at the gates. For seven years preceding the presidential election campaign, the American nation had been, in the words of the *Weekly Standard,* "obsessed with national security." As the conservative journal rightly notes, "the *New York Times* carried more extensive coverage of the Iraqi elections in 2005 than statewide contexts in the United States," and "Khalid Sheikh Mohammad became a household name."[34] From the very beginning, this sense of imminent foreign danger deeply affected the Republican's primary campaign:

> It is September, 2007, a Republican "town hall meeting" in a small white church in New Hampshire during the primary campaign in that state. Before a crowd of some 250 persons, John McCain walks briskly through an honor guard of saluting veterans. Returning their salute, the military veteran climbs briskly onto the stage. Behind him, wall-sized videos project scenes from his days as a prisoner of war. Grainy images follow one upon

the other, of American fighter planes dropping bombs amidst dark clouds of anti-aircraft fire, of Vietnamese in bamboo hats pointing their rifles at the captured McCain, of newspaper headlines announcing the heroic American prisoner's long awaited release. Here is McCain, as a prisoner of war, in the infamous Vietnamese propaganda film, looking up at his interrogators, prone on a table, bound in his cast, slowly and grimly responding to questions from his Communist captors. Today, in this political rally in a New England church four decades later, there is an atmosphere of military struggle, glory and sacrifice, suffering and redemption, solidarity, heroism, and the hierarchy of command. The Republican presidential candidate stalks stiffly around the stage. Shoulders hunched, fists clenched, brows furrowed, McCain announces to his audience that "the main issue, the single most important issue of the 21st century, is the war against radical Islam." He declares that "the question that must be decided in this primary, and this election, is who the best man is to be commander-in-chief!"[35]

Six months after this rally in New Hampshire, the narrative of martial heroism has carried McCain to victory in his fight for the Republican nomination. The *Weekly Standard* recalls his "remarks to an enthusiastic crowd in Dallas, Texas, on the March night he passed the 1,191 delegate mark needed to make him the GOP nominee."[36] It recounts how "McCain expected—or, perhaps, hoped—that national security issues would play a major role in determining the next president." In his speech that early spring night, "McCain defended the decision to remove Saddam Hussein, where 'our most vital security interests' are involved." He declared that "a mismanaged exit could result in sectarian conflict, even genocide" and "warned about terrorist attacks with 'weapons we are not to allow' terrorists to possess." The hinge of history was a military one, the nation's survival a physical matter. From such considerations, there could be only one, ineluctable conclusion: The next president needs to be a military hero. First and foremost, the next president must be a powerful commander in chief. Here is what McCain told the assembled crowd that day:

> Presidential candidates are judged on their records, their character, and the whole of their life experience. But we are also expected to concentrate our efforts on the challenges that will confront Americans on our watch and explain how we intend to address them. America is at war in two countries and involved in a long and difficult struggle with violent extremists who despise us, our values, and modernity itself.... The next president must lead an effort to restructure our military, our intelligence, our diplomacy, and all relevant branches of government to combat Islamic extremism.

Six months later, the *Weekly Standard* remains enthusiastic that narrating heroism in a military manner will bring victory for the Republican side. Five weeks after the risky nomination of Sarah Palin as vice president and three weeks into a dangerous financial crisis, the influential conservative journal reconstructs McCain's success vis-à-vis Obama in a distinctively martial way:

John McCain, restless and emotional, couldn't resist the temptation to join the battle to rescue our financial markets and save the economy. It was the biggest and most important fight around.... Being engaged in the action—in the arena—is where McCain always wants to be.... Obama, placid and professorial, had a different reaction to the fight over the bailout. [He] rejected the idea of putting his campaign on hold.... He returned to Washington reluctantly.... The contrast here is not only dramatic. It's unusually revealing about the two candidates and how they might act as president. There's an analogy here that captures the difference: the warrior and the priest. McCain the warrior, Obama the priest. (If "priest" seems confusing, substitute "professor.") McCain has been a player in every major fight, in war and in Washington, for more than four decades. As far back as 1962, he waited in Florida as a Navy pilot for the order to attack during the Cuban missile crisis. (The order never came.) As a senator, he's never stayed on the sidelines. As a candidate, he likes the rough-and-tumble and unpredictable turns of town hall meetings.... McCain, like a general changing his tactics on the fly, picked Alaska governor Sarah Palin as his running mate. The surprise move unnerved Obama and his campaign staff, and they spent several unproductive weeks taking potshots at Palin. McCain likes surprises and gambles. When his campaign was at its low point in 2007, he rebuffed the advice of his senior advisers and went on what he called a "no surrender tour," defending the unpopular war in Iraq.... In his acceptance speech at the Republican convention in August, McCain stressed that he's a fighter. "I don't mind a good fight," he said. "I fight for Americans, I fight for you."... "Fighting for you" fits perfectly with McCain's pugnacious persona. It's a warrior's message.[37]

In early October 2008, Senator Joe Lieberman, one of the Republican candidate's closest political and personal friends, rallies a crowd at a "McCain for President" storefront headquarters on Philadelphia's Main Line. "This is an extremely dangerous world we live in, the worst in my memory," Lieberman confides to the crowd. It is because "we are standing on the precipice" that Lieberman—once a Democrat and now nominally an independent—has decided to support John McCain for president:

I knew there was only one man I could support, somebody who has proved himself already in the worst conditions, proven his courage. We have stood together in every national security crisis, every challenge to our beloved country over the last forty years.[38]

Lieberman draws a direct analogy between McCain's Vietnam-era suffering and the nation's condition in 2008. He defines the past as a prelude to the extreme physical dangers of the present and suggests that only a military hero can lead the American people into the future.

From Danger to Obama's Hope

By late summer 2008, polling indicated that the representations of military and civil hero were neatly distributed between the respective Republican and Democratic sides. John McCain has succeeded in inhabiting the collective representation of military leader in the unfolding campaign. According to a *Wall Street Journal/ NBC News* national telephone survey, when Americans were asked, "Who do you think would be better when it comes to being commander in chief," only 25 percent answered Obama, and more than twice that number, 53 percent, named McCain. Republican and Democratic candidates were given about equal marks for being "honest" and "straightforward," but a sharp contrast emerged in representations associated with civil repair and internal change. Barack Obama received twice the support of Americans (46 percent to 22 percent) responding to the question "Who do you think would be better when it comes to being compassionate enough to understand average people?" Almost three times the number of Americans (54 percent to 19 percent) identified Obama with "offering hope" and "optimism for the future," and four times as many were more likely to see the Democratic candidate as "likeable" than were those who responded with affection to McCain.[39] Two weeks later, a *New York Times*/CBS poll indicated an equally large Obama advantage (65 percent to 37 percent) in response to a question about which candidate was more likely "to bring change."[40]

The problem for McCain is that, as the campaign progresses, Americans' sense of the nation being in imminent danger declines. In early August, in response to a question about the crisis in Iran, an analyst at the Eisenhower Institute tells the *Wall Street Journal*, "I can't imagine very many Americans would support any kind of military role for the U.S."[41] One month later, as the Republican nominating convention gets under way, nearly two-thirds of Americans (66 percent) report themselves "bored" with the Iraq problem. Writing about McCain's criticisms of Obama's timetable for an Iraq withdrawal, the *New York Times* observes that "the political debate over Iraq with Senator Barack Obama has become more about the past than about the way forward there" and that "neither Mr. Obama's aides nor Mr. McCain's expect the timetable for that withdrawal to be a major issue of disagreement as it was in the spring."[42] Feelings of external danger are on the decline. It has been years since terrorism actually intruded into the American homeland, and domestic concerns outweigh foreign ones. In late August, Americans were asked what single issue "would be most important to your vote." More than 40 percent answered "the economy," more than Iraq (15 percent) and terrorism (9 percent) combined. Health care (11 percent) and energy, especially gas prices (14 percent), rounded out the five top American concerns.[43] War and violence are perceived as issues of the past, not the present. Characters can become heroes only if they stand at the hinge of history. Only if they solve immense problems in contemporary time can their victory provide a pathway to the future.

Conservative media express anxiety. "What John McCain is trying to do," the *Wall Street Journal* reports in mid-August, "is to remind people of what he's been telling them all along: 'It's a dangerous world out there.'"[44] Democrats express hope. In his speech accepting the vice-presidential nomination, Senator Joe Biden suggests "the choice is clear." The nation needs "more than a good soldier." It requires a "wise leader" who "can deliver the change everybody knows we need."[45] Three weeks later Biden feels confident enough of the shifting tide to assert that paying taxes is "patriotic," linking nationalism to the civil rather than the military scene. McCain resists, replying that "raising taxes isn't patriotic" and that it is "not a badge of honor" but "just plain dumb."[46] Badges of honor should be reserved for military heroes, for real patriots, not handed out to champions of civil repair in mundane domestic life.

Conservatives sense that the background undergirding their decade-long electoral success is fading away. They cannot choose a different kind of hero candidate, but perhaps if they rewrite their nominee's script, they can transform the manner in which their figure will be seen. Strategists had already begun to throw out suggestions for a midcourse correction in springtime and early summer. After McCain had secured the nomination and begun to direct his performances to general election audiences, some conservative commentators noticed that the story of the warrior hero was playing to less effect. In response, suggestions were offered that McCain representation should return to the maverick image that had helped balance his military character with domestic concerns in earlier days. McCain and his advisers resisted these suggestions. During the summer months, they tried to combat the Obama hero by deflating him as a celebrity. It was only as the summer turned into fall that they realized the extent of their mistake.

In early September, during the first days of the national convention, Republican political leaders continue to extol their nominee as a military hero. President

Bush reminds the convention's layered audiences that "we live in a dangerous world." From the "lessons of September 11th" Americans have learned that "to protect America we must stay on offense." Senator Lieberman declares that "when others wanted to retreat in defeat from the field of battle...McCain had the courage" not to accept defeat. McCain's former primary opponent Mike Huckabee recounts the Republican nominee's suffering as a prisoner of war and links his war injuries and sacrifice to the convention theme emblazoned behind the speaker's podium—"Country First." Former New York mayor Rudy Giuliani, the hero of 9/11, praises McCain as "a *Top Gun* kind of guy." Declaring that McCain had "proved his commitment with his blood," Giuliani promises the Republican audience and the television viewers that "we will be safe in his hands." Vice-presidential nominee Sarah Palin looks back to the Vietnam confrontation and recalls how McCain had been there "at a crucial hour for our country." Praising "the caliber of the man" and "his sheer guts," she contrasts him with Obama, "a man who can give an entire speech about our wars and never mention the word 'victory' except when he's talking about his own campaign." There's "only one man in this election who has ever actually fought for you, in places where winning means survival and losing means death."[47]

McCain begins his acceptance speech by placing his character inside these martial themes. He declares "I fell in love with my country when I was a prisoner in someone else's," adding, "I wasn't my own man anymore, I was my country's." The Republican candidate soon segues from war to civil matters, though he does not surrender military metaphors and heroic themes. Describing himself not as a bad-boy maverick but a "restless reformer," McCain proclaims that he and Sarah Palin are the "true agents of change." He issues a "warning" to the "old big-spending, do-nothing, me-first, country-second Washington crowd." He will "drain that swamp," he promises, and he calls on "insurgents seeking to topple the establishment" to follow his lead.[48]

The Republican's narrative shift from military to domestic heroism does not go unnoticed. In its coverage of McCain's acceptance speech, the *Times'* subhead describes "A Bid to Seize Change Theme from Rival."[49] Even as the *Wall Street Journal* maintains that "Sen. McCain has always cast himself as a different kind of politician," the conservative paper acknowledges that "only since his convention has he embraced the word 'change'" and that only now do "McCain and his running mate, Alaska Gov. Sarah Palin, regularly talk about change on the stump."[50] The *Journal* claims that "challenging his own party" has always been a "piece of McCain's story," but it acknowledges that after the convention the "campaign is putting it at the center of its message."

This fundamental shift in narrative framing is too little because it is too late. What has been central to the Republican candidate's message is neither civil challenge nor social change. John McCain is Achilles, not Hector. It is as a military warrior that he has won his fame and also how, two months from now, he will lose the campaign.

The Hero's Shadow

Being the right kind of hero when the struggle for power reaches its dramatic zenith is a matter of planning and performative power. It is also a matter of contingency—of just plain dumb luck. Once a political figure's hero character is formed, it is history that decides whether it will fit with that particular time. But there is also a more universal problem that heroes face regardless of the specifics of their situation. It's the problem of hubris. All heroes have their shadow, a negative other whose inverted attributes the bright light of their glory keeps hidden in the shade.

Heroes must be modest. They cannot be seen as overreaching, as trying to be a hero instead of simply and naturally being one, as wanting to be glorious instead of simply wanting to be the (heroic) person they really are. For the Greeks, this was a matter of distinguishing heroes from gods. When heroes try to become gods, they are destroyed. Hubris is the stuff of tragedy. It reveals a fundamental character flaw, one that triggers an action that brings the hero down from the heady heights of victory to the numbing depths of defeat. "Do you see how it is the living things that exceed others in size that the god strikes with lightning and will not let them show their grandeur, while the little ones do not itch the god to action?" Artabanus warns the Persian king in Herodotus' *History*: "Do you see how it is always the greatest houses and the tallest trees that that the god hurls his bolts upon? For the god loves to thwart whatever is greater than the rest. [He] does not suffer pride in anyone but himself."[51]

Modesty is a most civil quality, one that can allow even the military hero to play a constructive role in building the cooperative ties that mark a democratic life. Conceit and arrogance endanger the civil sphere, encouraging superiority rather than equality, secrecy rather than openness, domination rather than reciprocity. So in the struggle for democratic power, when hubris brings heroes to their knees, it also makes them unqualified to represent the civil sphere. Hubristic heroes would be a distinct danger if they were allowed to take power inside the state.

Just before the outbreak of the financial crisis, with the outcome of the democratic struggle for power still very much in doubt, an influential editorial writer for the *Wall Street Journal* compares the heroic characters of the competitors in precisely this way. Reaching back to their published autobiographies, he narrates the modesty of the Republican candidate. He asserts that McCain's imprisonment gives him a cultural advantage because it suggests humility and equality:

Authority that is pre-humbled, as it were, has the tactical edge. John McCain's ordeal in Hanoi doesn't only demonstrate his heroism and patriotism. It portrays his humiliation and the shattering of his ego, as Sen. McCain himself has stressed. The terrible image of Sen. McCain being beaten without mercy in some filthy torture chamber is an image of powerful authority—a national politician, a United States Senator—being made to bend to the higher power of malevolent necessity. It is an image that feeds contemporary democracy's leveling maw.[52]

The conservative essayist attacks the Obama character, by contrast, as the very embodiment of elitist conceit:

Sen. McCain is not above us, [his] carefully crafted story tells us, he is not on the elevated level of [such] articulate, intellectually aloof, Ivy-education politicians [as] Sen. Obama…whose equally crafted autobiography tells us a tale of youthful indecision, wandering, mild drug use and eventual redemption as a privileged young man working among the poor and disenfranchised.… Sen. Obama still struggles with the sin of pride, he tell us with his confident grin and his air of perfect poise. You could be forgiven for thinking that he is proudly displaying his scorn for his own oversized pride. Sen. McCain, on the other hand, confesses, with his lean, Bogartian mouth set in a near-grimace, that "I've been an imperfect servant of my country for many years."

Liberal critics turn the shadow of the hero back upon the Republican candidate himself. They accuse McCain of anticivil hubris, describing his virtuously modest self-narration as a put-on, a deceptive manifestation of barely camouflaged conceit. One month after the *Wall Street Journal's* effort to deflate the Obama hero, a lengthy *New York Times* profile of McCain picks apart the Republican's presentation in exactly this way:

For 25 years after his release from a North Vietnamese prison, Senator John McCain tried to build a reputation as more than a famous former captive. "I never want to be a professional P.O.W.," he often told friends. He refused to let his campaigns use pictures from his incarceration, and he never mentioned his torture. "When somebody introduces me like, 'Here is our great war hero,' I don't like it," Mr. McCain complained in a 1998 interview with *Esquire* magazine. "Jesus," he said, "it can make your skin crawl." Mr. McCain's impatience with his war story soon changed, however, when he become not only its protagonist but also its author. His 1999 memoir, *Faith of My Fathers,* for the first time put his camp ordeal at the center of his public persona. In its pages, he recalled the experience as…the origin of a drive "to serve a cause" larger than himself.... In interviews and speeches, Mr. McCain has increasingly described his life in the book's language and themes, and never more so than during his current campaign. [Some] friends say they marvel at how heavily the McCain campaign relies on the chastened-hero image created by *Faith of My Fathers*.... Robert Timberg, a marine wounded in Vietnam who became Mr. McCain's biographer and admired his memoir, said the John McCain he knew 15 years ago would never have suggested that he was more patriotic than a rival the way the senator has in attacking his Democratic opponent, Senator Barack Obama. "Political campaigns have a way of distorting reality and turning political candidates into caricatures of themselves."[53]

A liberal columnist for the *Times* claims that, while candidate McCain put the "spirit of the warrior on full display," he "never considered the huge costs of war," the down-to-earth civil and human side as compared to the glory that elevates the military hero and state. The *Journal* worries that the McCain hero errs on the military side. It quotes a warning from one academic that "you can overplay your hand and come across as too bellicose for your own good." The newspaper interviews another expert on the Republican's insistent emphasis on military danger, quoting his observation that "probably, for a lot of voters, it would reinforce the idea that some people already have that perhaps McCain is a little bit too eager" for a fight.

Achilles loved war for its own sake; Hector fought for the sake of defending civic life. However, the shadow of hubris is hardly confined to military heroes. As the *Journal*'s critique demonstrates, civil heroes, too, can fall victim to immodesty and conceit. Indeed, as they come closer to the ideal of the democratic hero, they become ever more vulnerable to the melodramatic tension between virtue and vice. As Obama comes so powerfully to occupy the hero character during the heat of the campaign, pushing the threat of military danger off to the side, his shadow became a critical preoccupation. He is continually represented as barely control-ling a bulging hubris not only for his conservative critics but also for those who root for his candidacy from the liberal side. In early profiles on Obama in the summer of 2007, the *Times* quotes a former Republican state senator from Illinois, who observes, "He is a very bright but very ambitious person who has always had his eyes on the prize, and it wasn't Springfield."[54] Obama's principal mentor during his time in the Illinois legislature reveals something similar:

"He said to me, 'You're now the Senate president,'" Mr. Jones recalled. "'You have a lot of power.' I said, 'I do?' He said, 'Yes.' I said, 'Tell me what kind of power I have.' He said, 'You have the power to make a U.S. sena-tor.' I said, 'I do?' He said, 'You do.' I said, 'If I've got that kind of power, do you know of anyone that I can make?' he said, 'Yeah. Me.'"

Bobby Rush, Obama's former opponent, describes Obama as "blinded by his ambition": "Obama has never suffered from a lack of believing that he can accomplish whatever it is he decides to try. Obama believes in Obama."[55] One year later, a *Times* reporter observes that, while Obama projects "a message in keeping with the humility he tries to emphasize," the candidate's "uncanny self-assurance and seemingly smooth glide upward have stoked complaints from his critics and his opponents…that he has not spent enough time earning and learning, that his main project in life has been his own ascent."[56] While Obama "tries to assure" working-class white audiences he and they "have much in common," the reporter caustically comments that "his comparing himself to Joshua and Lincoln can belie his point."

It is the decreasing relevance of the military hero, not so much its hubris, that threatens John McCain's 2008 presidential campaign, compelling the belated effort to shift the Republican's narrative over to the more civil side. As a Democratic civil hero Obama does not face this problem; his character is much more attuned with the national domestic narrative in 2008. What endangers Obama is the hero's shadow, which I have just described. In the summer of 2008, the Republicans managed to frame the Obama character as a celebrity, an arrogant *would-be* hero who is famous not for having accomplished anything but merely for fame itself. Obama's extraordinary performance during the Democratic convention at the end of August, as well as the emergence of the "Palin effect," brought an end to the Republicans' hubris-celebrity campaign. McCain tried to repackage himself as a maverick hero, an antiestablishment agent of change who could also win a good fight. Maverick and military coexisted, but they did not mix. McCain's failed performance at civil heroics during the financial crisis was the icing on the cake.[57]

In the end, what most deflates McCain's heroic character is the bitter fact of defeat itself. If it is true that one must be a hero to be successful in the struggle for power, it is also the case that victory in that struggle makes one a hero indeed. By late October, when McCain begins to seem destined for defeat, the *Weekly Standard* warns against the imminent logic that defines hero stories, regretting how "in search of a narrative, the press constantly seeks to reveal the ending and name the hero before the story has reached its climax."[58] The conservative journal warns that entertaining the possibility of McCain's eventual defeat will powerfully undermine the symbolic power of the Republican campaign. For the result of "a losing campaign" is that "heroes [are] transformed by fickle voters into forgotten minor characters."

CHAPTER FIVE

Working the Binaries

MEANING IS DIFFERENCE, AND POLITICAL LEGITIMACY MUST BE understood in exactly this way. Making oneself pure, polluting one's opponent—this is the stuff of which political victory is made.

Democracy rests upon the viability of a distinctive and independent social sphere, one defined—not by money, power, religion, intelligence, ethnicity, or family—but by broader solidarity of a more civil kind. Insofar as social solidarity is civil, political victory cannot be won by appealing to bigotry, dogma, or family ties. Insofar as such broad solidarity is institutionalized, state power cannot be gained by force or fraud, violence or coercion.

If democracy puts such aggression beyond the pale, however, it does so in a subtly contradictory way. The nonviolent character of democratic conflict is harshly agonistic. This is the irony that sits at the center of democratic society. Only people who are deeply believed to be civil can generate the trust and respect upon which democratic cooperation depends. Only these kinds of persons deserve to win electoral campaigns. Those who contend for power and are not believed to be civil deserve to lose. If they seem dishonest or irrational, domineering or deferential, then they might support institutions of an authoritarian kind. We know ahead of time that we cannot allow such persons to gain control over the state.

As Republican staffers prepare Sarah Palin's unveiling at the party's convention, they know that her daughter is carrying an illegitimate child. Public knowledge might undermine the vice-presidential nominee's clarion call for responsibility and independence, not to mention her more narrowly constructed case for religion and "family values." The Republican campaign team decides to keep the information secret, delaying the revelation until after Palin's acceptance speech. Explaining to reporters that "we are going to flush the toilet" on Labor Day, a senior adviser to Palin reveals the symbolic power of moral impurity on the political scene.[1] When, in the weeks following, Palin's civil stature does become subject to relentless attack, Republicans respond by raining polluting attacks on the other side. A former chief strategist to President Bush explains, "McCain folks realize if they can get this thing down in the mud, drag Obama into the mud, that's where they have the best advantage to win."[2] For those who struggle for power, symbolic pollution must at all costs be avoided, yet it must energetically be attributed to the other side.

As campaigns work the binaries, they try to simplify the meaning of every issue that comes up, bringing it into semiotic alignment with one side or the other of the great divide. Candidates are purified so that their characters can be folded into heroic narrative arcs of a democratic kind. Hillary Clinton comes to symbolize equality and mobility, wisdom and maturity, a modern enlightened woman breaking the glass ceiling. Barack Obama becomes the great emancipator. Calm and reasonable, he is a black Abraham Lincoln promising a more profound and expansive solidarity. John McCain is the wounded prisoner of war who breaks the bonds of enslavement and comes back as a corruption-fighting maverick. He bucks social pressures and material party inducement to do what he believes is moral and right.

There is obviously a paradox here. While democratic citizens are united in the binary logic of such symbolic thinking, they never can agree on which ideology, which party, and which candidate actually belongs to the civil or the anticivil side. Yet, by election time, this is exactly what they must decide. With a plurality or majority of their votes, citizens say one candidate is "civil enough" to be trusted with state power. To convince enough people of this truth is the aim of every political campaign.

The Presumptively Rational Voter

Citizen voters make the crucial decision about the civil and uncivil qualities of candidates. Yet this voting public as such is not physically active in the democratic struggle for power. Democracy is representative not only in the exercise of power but also in the struggle for it. It is a few individuals and parties who vie for power, and their campaigns are directed by political staffs, energized by organizations and associations, and fueled by enormous flows of money. Citizen voters participate in the struggle for power as viewers. They play an essential role as the democratic performance unfolds, for it is directed at them. As the audience for the struggle for power, citizens are culturally constructed, imagined as possessing great intelligence and unquestioned integrity. Such idealized citizens constitute the virtuous public that every candidate must engage. It is difficult to gain approval from this flinty and demanding audience. Its emergent preferences are monitored continuously throughout political campaigns and possess extraordinary subjective power. Collective sentiment is not visible in itself. It becomes visible in the form of attributions. In newspapers and blogs and on television there are continuous reports about what the public is thinking. In opinion polls, samples are published that represent opinion in the civil sphere—the "will of the people"—through statistical techniques. By these rhetorical and technical means, voters become imaginatively central to the struggle for power even if they are not physically copresent. Voter sentiment is projected by media of communication, and it becomes a central driving force in political campaigns.

Social critics of every ideological stripe have for centuries laid into the voting public in ferocious ways, accusing them of being lazy, prejudiced, conformist, or just plain dumb. If the voter audience were consistently portrayed in such a pejorative manner, democracy would be in a difficult fix. Rather than being consulted about their opinions, such insipid, biased, and unreliable creatures would have to be controlled—for their own good and the good of others—by powerful and coercive states.[3] Looking empirically at how contemporary voters are imagined during political campaigns makes it clear, however, that those who struggle for power rarely speak publicly of voters in such disparaging ways. Voters are projected as rational, honest, independent, and capable of decisions that are wise. Like the candidates themselves, they are discursively constructed in terms of the binary discourse that sustains the civil sphere. Unlike the candidates, however, voters are primarily conceptualized in positive terms.

Voters are imagined in terms of the discourse of liberty. If this is myth, it is a fiction upon which democratic truth depends. Because voters are conceived as enlightened citizens, it becomes inconceivable that they can make mistakes of an egregious, antidemocratic kind. In any particular campaign season, voters might be said to be angry, depressed, happy with the status quo, or anxious about the future. However, such passions are taken as expressions of their autonomy, of their rock-solid sense of reality, of their commitment to the public interest upon which American democracy rests. Sometimes voters do elect demagogues and liars. It is believed, however, that they have done so not because they are themselves weak or dishonest. It must have been the case, rather, that they were knowingly and irresponsibly misled by the "other" side. Provided with false or inadequate information, voters have been unable to act on their best instincts and unable to perceive the general will, to act upon what Tocqueville called their "self-interest rightly understood."[4]

In the fervid days after Sarah Palin's debut on the American political stage, the situation begins to look grim for the Democratic side. The self-described hockey mom is a fresh new face; she presents herself as an independent reformer, a champion of civil repair who stands up for the average, undaunted American person in every political fight. Polls show Palin gaining surprisingly wide and enthusiastic support beyond her conservative base—from working mothers, conservative white men, and independents alike. Worried Democrats demanded that Obama do difference better, that he go after his opponents more "aggressively," not be so "mild-mannered," and find a tone less "professor" than "prosecution."[5] Eventually Obama does change, and the media become engaged with Palin as well. However, the Democrat's initial reaction to Palin's rise is to argue that the shifting poll numbers do not actually indicate what American voters feel or believe. Against Palin's claims for her civil achievements, Obama declares, "[Y]ou can't just make stuff up" and that "you can't just recreate yourself." The reason that candidates can't do these things, he explains, is that "the American people aren't stupid." A few days later, a *Times* editorial seconds this expression of rock-bottom belief in the virtue of American voters. In choosing Palin, McCain has demonstrated himself to be "shockingly irresponsible," but, even worse, the Republican candidate's choice "shows a contempt for voters."[6] After Palin's polls go south, the *Times* attributes these shifting numbers to the voters' intrinsic rationality and good sense—the polling "indicates that the number of Americans who think she is not fit [has] increased."[7] Palin has bungled her television interviews and her vice-presidential debate. "Voters have been guided by" these facts, the *Times* explains, and their opinions have changed accordingly; they now express their civil virtue in a more anti-Palin way.[8]

Primary Myth

There is no better illustration of this cultural trope of the American voter than the rhetoric-framing presidential primary campaigns. Primaries are intraparty contests that unfold state by state during the first six months of every election year. Their outcomes largely decide which candidates are allowed to represent their political party in the general election in November. Whether delegates are distributed by winner-take-all or more proportionally, each primary contributes to the overall delegate count.

Every fourth year, "seven days or more," according to New Hampshire law, before any "similar election" can be held in any other state, Democrats and Republicans compete in the first primary of the presidential campaign. The New Hampshire primary is as much myth as math. On Park Street in New Hampshire's capital city of Concord, the New Hampshire Political Library memorializes the rhetoric and iconography of the state's democratic rite. The library's website describes the special exhibit mounted at the shrine for the critical months of the 2007–2008 primary season.

New Hampshire: A Proven Primary Tradition
The Tuck Library, 30 Park Street, Concord, NH Saturday, September 8,
2007—Saturday, May 24, 2008

A new exhibition presented by the New Hampshire Political Library and the
New Hampshire Historical Society titled *New Hampshire: A Proven Primary
Tradition* explores the impact New Hampshire's primary has on the national
presidential nominating process and examines how the state's political culture and traditions have shaped its first-in-the-nation role. Including more
than 260 objects, photographs, and archival materials, the exhibit will
engage visitors of all ages through stories, videos, and interactives.

Those who physically show up at the special exhibit receive an elegantly format-
ted, thickly papered, five-color pamphlet, *New Hampshire: The Time-tested Presidential
Primary Proving Ground.* Every four years, those who would be president must campaign up and down the state of New Hampshire, speaking in homes, schools, shopping centers, storefronts, small groups, and on street corners as well. *Proving Ground*
explains why. It puts a discursive sheen on the so-called retail politics that unfolds over
the hectic quadrennial rite. Offering testimony to America's faith in the rationality,
honesty, independence, and vigor of the democratic voter, the pamphlet serves double
duty as a public relations effort to keep New Hampshire's pole position in the primary
campaign. *Proving Ground* codes New Hampshire voters in the most idealized terms
and raises the specter that anticivil disaster would ensue if the state's privileged primary
position were ever to be pushed aside. New Hampshire voters challenge authority, do
their homework, and demand to be informed. From the time of the American revolution, democracy in America has always depended upon their stewardship, virtue, and
discerning power. Passages from the *Proving Ground* pamphlet are reproduced here.

New Hampshire

*The Presidential candidate stands before a crowded room, nervously antici-
pating tough questions on his newly unveiled economic plan. His plan is
apparently familiar to some in the audience, as he sees copies dog-eared from
close readings. The questions, he knows, will be pointed—and the questioners
will expect real answers, not political spin. He takes a deep breath.*

(continued)

A press conference in Washington, D.C.? A meeting of the candidate's economic advisors? No: It's a living room in New Hampshire, six months before the first Presidential primary.

And the Presidential selection process is just beginning.

EVERY FOUR YEARS, prospective candidates and informed citizens across America look to New Hampshire, home of the first primary in the Presidential electoral process.... Before going national, campaigners must prove themselves here, face-to-face with knowledgeable, dedicated, and discerning voters.

Is this the best process? Are the nation's interests served by having New Hampshire go first in the primary lineup?... The compelling case for New Hampshire derives from this state's well-established conditions and proven credentials that no other state can replicate.

A HIGHLY INFORMED ELECTORATE

Knowledgeable voters: That's what Presidential hopefuls encounter in New Hampshire. Months before the primary, the state's voters are attending meetings with the candidates, listening to speeches, reading reports, and sorting through the issues they believe important.

Consider these representative statistics: Polls taken during the primary season show that 50% of New Hampshire voters actively seek out information on one or more of the candidates. More than 25% say they have attended a candidate's rally or information session. And an amazing 25% report that they have met at least one of the candidates *in person.*

The local media in New Hampshire do their part as well. Newspaper, radio, and television coverage of Presidential candidates is thorough, energetic, and equitable—just as New Hampshire's informed citizenry expects.

It's the last chance we, and the American public, get to see true hand-to-hand politics. I can drive from town to town and watch candidates go to local halls and answer questions from citizens for an hour. From now on [in the election], access will be drastically reduced. The candidates enter a bubble. They land on airport tarmacs, in tight scenarios controlled by the campaign. It's such a richer story when they interact with real people, not an audience constructed by the campaign. It's a great process to watch, and it works.

—Tim Russert, NBC News

That's the thing I loved about New Hampshire. They owed the country a good decision and they were determined to give everybody a listen.

—President Bill Clinton

I am of the firm belief that New Hampshire is and always will be first in this process.... The voters up here...they ask tough questions. These are serious times and people are expecting the candidates to talk in a serious way with them, and those that don't are going to be shuffled out very quickly.

—David Broder, *The Washington Post*

New Hampshire is a bastion of independent thinking. Nobody tells them what to do. They make up their own minds.

—Sen. Bill Bradley, 2000 candidate

AN UNUSUALLY ENGAGED CITIZENRY

Record Turnout. Twice the national average. Phrases like these tellingly describe the voting in New Hampshire. The state consistently records greater participation in both primary and general elections than most other states. One expert calls this "the active stewardship of New Hampshire voters."...Some observers depict New Hampshire as "a hyperpolitical state," where being engaged is an ingrained civic duty. No other state can match New Hampshire's *per capita voter engagement.*

A UNIQUE POLITICAL CULTURE AND TRADITION

More than two centuries ago, England's King George III learned the hard way about the political involvement of New Hampshire colonists. From the tough-minded revolutionaries who declared "live free or die"—and then backed it up on the battlefield of Bunker Hill—to the unpaid citizen legislature of today, New Hampshire has a long tradition of political activism. This tradition translates into a style of participatory democracy unrivaled elsewhere in the United States.

A LEVEL PLAYING FIELD

... Thanks to the state's modest size—it's just 100 miles at its widest point and only 200 miles from north to south—the 234 independent communities that

(continued)

make up New Hampshire are accessible to candidates. This proximity puts candidates in touch with a wide range of voters. Because these new voters are already informed and engaged, candidates readily find willing audiences.

AN IDEAL MILIEU FOR ASSESSING CANDIDATE READINESS

Over the years, many candidates, including sitting Presidents in both parties, have said much the same thing. For these candidates, New Hampshire has presented an invaluable learning opportunity.

What do they learn? How to speak directly to real people. How to listen to citizens. How to convince and energize discerning voters in everyday venues. Manufactured images and slick pre-packaged messages don't play well in New Hampshire.... Answering questions on a Saturday morning at the town hall takes you much further than dispensing sound bites at the airport.... For Presidential hopefuls, it's not just about winning in New Hampshire. It's about *listening and learning* in New Hampshire.

With the New Hampshire Presidential Primary receiving thorough national—and now global—coverage, the Granite State has become an essential proving ground for Presidential hopefuls. Citizens across the country watch as candidates meet with individual voters on the street, in town halls, and on college campuses.

Those who struggle for democratic power must show themselves to be studiously respectful of voters such as these. A candidate can never be seen as insulting or talking down to them. To engage in the former is to be elitist; to engage in the latter is to pander. Elitism and pandering are qualities that disqualify a candidate from representing the civil sphere. Those who fail to garner the electoral support of these mythic voters are constructed in a post-hoc manner as having not been sufficiently civil and thus of having deserved their fate. Their character, campaign, and stance on issues have been rejected by that idealized figure John Q. Public. Regardless of their earlier, preelection days of respect and glory, they are now polluted, having fallen on the wrong side of the civil, anticivil divide. Listen to New Mexico governor Bill Richardson's postprimary indictment of the Hillary Clinton campaign. This former Clinton supporter had switched sides to endorse Barack Obama during the heat of the primary campaign. He now opines that "what hurt them [the Clintons] was their sense of entitlement that the presidency was theirs and all the acolytes should fall in line."[9] Because Hillary Clinton was rejected by the voters, she must now be situated as outside the civil sphere or at least as peripheral to its cultural core. Richardson suggests the Clintons have lost because they deserved to. They were not democratic but arrogant, demanding subservience rather than facilitating autonomy. They put themselves above the voters, taking them for granted until it was too late. As we have seen in chapter 2, even when the putatively arrogant Hillary Clinton finally does energetically court Democratic voters late in her campaign, she is accused of pandering, of deceptively posing as a "working-class hero" rather than speaking truth to stereotype. She is also framed as being overly dependent on her husband, subordinating herself to his pettiness and temper and his insidious, if seemingly implicit, racial slurs against Obama.

Voters have the last word in the struggle for political power. On voting day, by pulling a magical lever whose working parts are, like those of the Wizard of Oz, hidden behind a screen, the secret votes of interested citizens are transformed into the publicly proclaimed general will. The beneficent force of civil solidarity reemerges to calm the passions and interests of divisive partisan struggle.[10] Until that ritual action allows purging catharsis, however, politics is about creating difference, not overcoming it.

Obama Moves to the Center

When they struggle for votes, candidates try to project themselves as worthy vessels of democratic myth. The problem is that political action must be practical and down to earth. Good politicians are strategic and tactical, their speech and action continuously changing. Yet, they must align their shifting behavior with the sacred side of the sharply dichotomous morality—the binary discourse—that defines American democratic life. That discourse is rock solid and relatively unchanging regardless of the vagaries of practical political life.

After winning enough delegates to secure the Democratic nomination, Obama pivots from left to center, announcing positions and policies that, for many of his liberal supporters, seem to undermine the authenticity of his heroic performance and the democratic character of his campaign. "I'm disgusted with him," a young environmentally conscious woman remarks to the *New York Times*. "This is the first time I've ever seen him lie to us," a 27 year old video engineer complains, confessing "it turns out he's another politician."[11] The longtime New York liberal Nat Hentoff publicly announces his feelings of betrayal in a florid and sentimental guest column for the conservative *Washington Times*:

> I was among the millions of Americans to whom such faded words as "change" and "hope" in political campaigns began to brighten as Barack

Obama was energizing both new voters while tempering the hardened skepticism of those of us who had been gulled by glowing politicians who wound up like the enticing con man played by Robert Preston in the classic movie, "The Music Man." Now, more of Mr. Obama's followers are feeling newly gulled by him.... Like millions of Americans, I, for a time, was buoyed—by the real-time prospect of our first black president and much more by the likelihood that Mr. Obama would pierce the dense hypocrisy and insatiable power-grabbing of current American politics. [But] Mr. Obama has decided he can come closer to securing the Oval Office by softening his starlight enough to change some of his principles...Instead of the ennobling clarion trombones of change we have been promised, this "adjusting" of one's principles has long been the common juggling of our common politicians.... I remember the surge of hope for a national change as a child, during the Great Depression, when, while my mother would walk blocks to save a few cents on food, there came Franklin Delano Roosevelt! I haven't seen such a surge since Mr. Obama's first chorus, but I can no longer believe in this messenger of such tidings.[12]

The media seem to agree. According to the *Wall Street Journal,* "the disillusionment has been palpable."[13] The *Washington Times* observes that Obama's "glaring flip-flops have led voters to question his sincerity and his competence."[14] The *New York Times* reports "what some view as a shameless play to a general election audience."[15] The left-wing blog *Daily Kos* announces that Obama's "veneer as a transformative politician has faded."[16]

Flexible Scripts, Fixed Binaries

These are dangerous accusations, challenging Obama's democratic standing as a hero in civil society. Yet, political actors, even those who would be heroes, have flexibility. It is not the broad, highly structured, and long-standing discourse of civil society that determines political performances but narrowly focused, relatively ad hoc scripts. Scripts mediate between deep cultural background and action in the here and now. In political campaigns, arguments over scripting are where the binaries are worked and played.[17]

A major scripting challenge emerges when Obama announces, during the postprimary weeks, that he will withdraw from the public financing system designed for presidential campaigns. The most significant effort at post-Watergate civil repair, public financing represented a serious, if not terribly effective, effort to neutralize the distorting effect of economic inequality on the struggle for democratic power. Not only had presidential candidate Obama always publicly embraced public financing, but as a state legislator in Illinois he had also proudly cosponsored similar reform. His Republican opponent in the presidential campaign was strongly associated with such public financing as well. The "McCain-Feingold" public financing bill was not warmly welcomed in conservative circles.

Obama had adumbrated his doubts about public financing from the time his online fundraising capacity became evident, yet he had promised not to abandon it. He had seemed to draw a line in the sand, demarcating civil pure from civil impure with regard to campaign financing in an implacable way. It is no wonder that, when his new position becomes known, Obama's aides publicly acknowledge their concern that it "might tarnish" him.[18] In a seething report, the *Times* complains that Obama's shift will "likely transform the landscape of presidential elections, injecting hundreds of millions" of dollars of private money into what should be a public and civil electoral campaign. "The decision means that Mr. Obama will have to spend considerably more time raising money," the news story continues, "at the expense of spending time meeting with voters." In its lead editorial that same day, "Public Funding on the Ropes," the *Times* portrays Obama as going against the principles of civil society and as betraying "his evocative vows to depart from self-interested politics."[19] In a tart and bitter column, the paper's in-house conservative David Brooks begins, "God, Republicans are saps."[20] Here they had "thought they were campaigning against Mr. Rogers," when in fact they are up against "Fast Eddie Obama." Obama is not "a naïve Stevenson type," Brooks warns his fellow Republicans, but a "hardball Chicago politician." Obama is a "hidden schizo," an "idealist in public but in private is…the promise-breaking, tough-minded Chicago pol who'd throw you under the truck for votes." By abandoning public financing, "Fast Eddie didn't just sell out the primary cause of his life," but he did it with style, "so risibly insincere" that "he makes Lee Atwater's ghost gape and applaud." It is shocking, Brooks declares, that "the media and activists won't care" about such "cut-throat political calculation."

Faced with these threats to his character as a civil hero, Obama works the binaries. He offers the counterintuitive claim that abandoning public financing actually brings him more closely into alignment with the positive side of democratic discourse. If he has abandoned his earlier promise, it has been to better defend civil society against the secretive and manipulative forces of his Republican opponents, who are "masters at gaming the system and will spend millions smearing" him whether he accepts public funds or not.[21] He has decided to maximize private gift giving, Obama explains, to better defend himself against such Republican attacks. Obama also points out that the Republican Party's war chest stands at $50 million against the paltry $10 million gathered by the Democratic

National Committee, highlighting the anomaly that public funding fails to regulate spending by political parties. Obama gestures, as well, to the ultraconservative nonparty groups—the so-called 527s—that are lining up to run anti-Obama TV ads on behalf of McCain. Their funding is not regulated either, Obama points out. Then, working the binaries even more audaciously, the Democrat insists that his unregulated, online fundraising actually represents "a new kind of politics." Because it multiplies millions of relatively small donations, Obama claims, this new web-based approach is actually the most civil possible way for a candidate to raise money. It should not be classified with the polluted financing the public system was erected to thwart.

McCain tries to prevent the Obama hero from working the binaries in this way. The Republican leader scripts his opponent's action in terms of antidemocratic discourse and accuses him of lying and manipulation. Obama has completely reversed himself and betrayed the American people. As evidence, McCain points to the *Times*' concern that having unlimited access to campaign funding will allow Obama to buy television ads outside "the traditional battleground states." A Republican strategist points out that the Obama campaign had just purchased a raft of television time for advertising in Georgia. "I think the last guy to buy Georgia was General Sherman," the strategist sarcastically remarks, describing it as "a very aggressive election strategy." William Tecumseh Sherman, the Union general who laid waste a wide swath through Georgia during the waning days of the Civil War, became a mythical representation of sectarian, anticivil aggression.

Another controversy erupts when Obama seems to endorse a much-anticipated Supreme Court ruling confirming that the Constitution gives private citizens the right to keep handguns in their homes. Once again, this move seems to challenge Obama's scripted character as heroic civil protagonist. Is Obama's reaction to the Court's ruling courageous and responsible, or is it pandering to the gun lobby and socially conservative voters? In the guise of purely factual observation, *Times* reporter Michael Powell reminds readers that Obama "has executed several policy pirouettes in recent weeks, each time landing more toward the center."[22] Powell describes Obama as stealthily Machiavellian, writing how "this most observant of politicians" has shown throughout his career "an appreciation for the virtues of political ambiguity." Noting "Obama has taken calibrated positions" on a number of issues in recent weeks, Powell characterizes the Democrat's response to the Supreme Court decision as "Delphic." Far from dignifying Obama with this classical metaphor, Powell is suggesting he has been evasive. Though not directly deceitful, Obama's response to criticism has been slippery—like those once issued from the oracle at Delphi, it can be proven neither right nor wrong.

The question really boils down to a philosophical dispute. It pits Immanuel Kant against William James and sits at the core of American political culture: Is public action ethical only if it consistently follows a principled, categorical imperative of universal morality? Or can morality guide action in a more practical manner by taking account of the differentiating details of each situation? How does a practical politician follow principle in a down-and-dirty political fight? According to transcendental morality, Obama must be lying. According to the American philosophical tradition, he is simply being pragmatic. If action is deemed pragmatic, virtue can still be upheld.

To adjudicate this question, Michael Powell, the *Times* reporter, turns to an academic, the American historian Robert Dallek. Dallek assures readers that presidential candidates want to "be seen as pragmatic." When politicians shift positions on an issue, this should not be taken as evidence that "they are utterly insincere." When Franklin Delano Roosevelt ran for president, he "slipped and slid his way through the 1932 election," so much so that Herbert Hoover, the incumbent president and Roosevelt's opponent, "called him a 'chameleon on plaid.'" Roosevelt went on to win this electoral fight and three more after that and today is regarded as a great man. According to pragmatism, politically motivated policy shifts can be signs of flexibility, not the abandonment of principle. They are evidence of intelligence, of rationality rather than dogmatism—not deceit and flip-flops.

PRAGMATIC SHIFTS	DECEITFUL FLIP-FLOPS
Flexible	Rigid
Reasonable	Ideological
Sincere	Calculated
Principled	Evasive

Obama expresses his reaction to the Court's gun decision in an extraordinarily careful way. He suggests the Court has itself been pragmatic and that its protection of handguns "is not *absolute*."[23] The ruling can be seen as supporting not violence but civility, for the Court has stipulated, Obama claims, that gun control remains "subject to *reasonable* regulations enacted by communities to keep their streets safe." Obama reaches for the ideal that is most fundamental to the civil sphere, the belief that individual autonomy and communal obligations are intertwined in principle even if, in practical life, they often restlessly collide. He urges the citizen audience to get beyond the headlines to the small print of the Court's decision. Because the Court does allow gun control laws under certain conditions, the decision "reinforces that if we act *responsibly*," we can protect individuals' rights and the community at the same time.[24] Cities and states can still make laws against "*unscrupulous* gun deals" and pass legislation to keep "*illegal* handguns off the streets."

Against accusations that their candidate has deceitfully flip-flopped, Obama's aides work the binaries with a flourish. They supply extenuating context, reaching for a reality that they claim reveals Obama's larger truth. "Flippers are important," a staffer tells the *Times*' John Harwood, only "when they reinforce a larger narrative about a candidate's negative attributes."[25] In other words, changing one's position may or may not be seen as a polluted flip-flop. Because the expression of this changing of position is open and contingent, it can be aligned with either a democratic or an antidemocratic position. By way of illustration, Harwood reports that "operatives in both parties" agree that former presidential candidate John Kerry's "apparent equivocation on the Iraq war damaged his 2004 campaign"—his shifting positions were seen not as reasoned and pragmatic but as evasive and weak. McCain staffers insist that Obama's reaction to the Supreme Court—which could be seen as nuanced and rational—must be framed in a similarly negative, Kerry-like way. They argue that the new scripting of his actions shows that Obama "is not a change agent but just a typical politician," one who is "stereotypically two faced." Harwood himself refuses to take sides. In the last lines of his political analysis, he implicitly acknowledges the flexible relation between action and frame and reminds his readers that, despite much ado about policy shifting, Republican and Democratic voters alike give both candidates high marks "for being honest and straightforward." As the third-party mediator who represents the civil sphere, Harwood stands back from the struggle for power. Candidates paint their opponents' scripts as dark and dangerous; Harwood assures the national audience that civil rules are still in place.

During this same early summer adjustment from left to center, Obama suggests that he will "refine" his Iraq policies after meeting with military commanders later in the summer.[26] From the days when Obama first emerged on the national scene in his run for the Senate, his character had been tied to an antiwar theme. He had affirmed this position when he began his struggle for presidential power, promising to pull out U.S. forces, and identifying the Republican president's Iraq invasion as a disastrous mistake. In Obama's long primary contest with his more hawkish opponent, Hillary Clinton, he had offered that some U.S. military "support personnel" might remain in Iraq for several years but insisted that they would engage only in defensive missions and that withdrawal would still take place.

That Obama might now be hedging his antiwar position further sets off a firestorm of charges, a flurry of anxious accusations of betrayal from the Left and gleeful exclamations of "I-told-you-sos" from the Right. On both sides, critics demand to know what is behind the Democratic candidate's decision to "refine." What has caused his new policy? To what new conditions, if any, can it be ascribed? One explanation is that the Bush administration's "surge" tactic has worked, that America is now winning the war, and that, to consolidate this change of fortune, a higher military profile must be maintained. The problem with this explanation is that it would mean that Obama's earlier, more unequivocal anti-Iraq position had been either dogmatic or confused. McCain as warrior hero would be vindicated. Such a new configuration of meaning might undermine the coding and narrative of the Democratic side.

Once again, Obama works the binaries to avoid being polluted as flip-flopping, and the *New York Times* helps him in this task. Refusing to empirically acknowledge that the surge has actually worked, the paper limits itself to the minimalist observation that violence in Iraq has declined. This allows Obama space. By itself, declining violence is not enough. For the surge to have worked and John McCain to be vindicated, there would have to be political "reconciliation" as well. It is on the failure to ensure this other civil quality that Obama now rests his case. Though violence has declined, Iraq is still, he insists, not at all a democratic place after the surge, as the Republicans Bush and McCain both had promised it would be. Obama also argues that withdrawing U.S. troops would allow the vast sums currently spent on military operations in Iraq to be invested in tasks such as improving schools and expanding health care at home. Here he connects military withdrawal to civil repair and to his heroic fight against inequality on behalf of more inclusive solidarity.

Yet, even as Obama insists on the failure of the Bush-McCain plan and the continuity of his anti-Iraq War bona fides, he promises to "consult" with military commanders on what exactly the timing for withdrawal will be. If he cannot become a military hero himself, he can engage such heroes in democratic deliberation. At the same time, Obama offers only to consult, not bend to the commanders' will. He engages the military leaders, moreover, not only in order to be cooperative but also to be rational, to garner every piece of "information" possible about the real situation in Iraq. With these facts in hand, Obama pledges that on his first day in office he would give the Joint Chiefs a new military mission. He will order them to end the war but in a civil way—"responsibly, deliberately, but decisively." As Obama puts it later in the summer, he is rejecting the false choice between a rigid timetable for withdrawal that ignored changing conditions and "completely deferring" to the recommendations of the military.[27]

So Obama maintains that his policy on Iraq has not really changed after all. In the United States, heroes do not do flip-flops; they can, however, be pragmatic in the extreme.

McCain Moves to the Center and Then to the Right

In the early days of the postprimary campaign, as Obama faces the danger of being interpreted as flip-flopping, his Republican opponent confronts an even graver danger, that of not being able to do difference at all. On the domestic front, as compared with the foreign stage, John McCain has often had a relatively hard time. Having inscribed himself inside the myth of the warrior hero, it is difficult for him to connect with the hopes for emancipation of a civil kind.

Still, as McCain pursued his ambition to become president, he pushed hard to cut a figure on the domestic scene. In his 2000 primary campaign, McCain certainly put front and center his war hero image, newly burnished by *Faith of My Fathers*. At the same time, he defined his difference vis-à-vis the younger Bush in a domestic way, working the civil binaries and folding them into the narrative arc of an American prodigal son. Scripting himself as standing up against authority and dogma, the emerging McCain character denounced religious fundamentalism and its arbitrary intervention into the political scene. At one point, he publicly criticized Bob Jones University for its ban on interracial dating and its anti-Catholic policies; at another, he confronted the founder of the Moral Majority, minister Jerry Falwell himself. McCain denounced George Bush for pandering to the new religious Right on issues such as abortion and federal funding for religious schools. He unfavorably compared Bush's dependence on his father's legacy with his own fierce independence from his illustrious forebears, as witnessed by his decision to leave the military for politics and the East Coast establishment for the freewheeling Southwest. Unlike many big-time campaigners, McCain did not seem to script his performances either for citizen audiences or for the media. He answered reporters' questions directly, sitting side by side with them on the campaign bus, which quickly became labeled the "Straight-talk Express."

What emerged from McCain's 2000 staging was a collective representation of compelling authenticity embedded in a narrative of potentially significant civil power. The qualities that most distinguished McCain's character in this first phase of his struggle for presidential power were honesty, independence, and transparency. His humiliating loss to Bush and the religious Right seemed to make McCain only more determined to sculpt his own character inside the civil sphere. Certainly, in the wake of the September 11 attacks, McCain did everything he could to project his military image and to stress the imminent danger to American society from outside.[28] Yet, in the years of war following, he also vigorously challenged the abuses at Abu Ghraib, forcefully criticizing the torture of war prisoners as violating international law. McCain also helped sponsor domestically progressive efforts at civil repair. He wrote campaign financing reforms, sponsored immigration laws that laid out a path to citizenship, opposed congressional earmarks, supported cap-and-trade emission controls, and worked to expand health care to those without means.[29] McCain opened up a wide space between his character and the president's, to the point of fanning speculation during this post-2000 period that he might actually switch political sides. In 2004, John Kerry openly solicited McCain as his vice-presidential running mate, though he did not succeed.

With the reelection of George W. Bush in 2004 and neoconservative hegemony in the Republican ranks apparently cemented in place, McCain began moving rightward. While he still pressed to outlaw torture in 2005, by the year following McCain was bowing deeply to the neoconservative side. He announced he would be willing to accept an invitation to Bob Jones University, renounced his earlier criticisms of religious fundamentalism, and sought minister Falwell's blessing, which he duly received. He criticized President Bush for not being tough enough in Iraq, withdrew his support for immigration reform, equivocated on torture, closed the distance between himself and the Republican president, and presented himself as a loyal party man. At the Republican convention, Rudolph Giuliani lauds McCain as "a proud foot soldier in the Reagan revolution," and the new John McCain easily gained his party's presidential nomination.[30] This time around, what distinguishes him from his Republican opponents has nothing to do with domestic issues and everything to do with his earlier martial exploits, and his militant calls for even more aggression to be shown in the nation's foreign policy today.[31]

The Republican Stall

In the meantime, however, the pendulum of American politics is swinging leftward, and the neoconservative lock on the future became unhinged. McCain's sharp movement right, while clearly effective with bedrock conservative audiences, now poses a serious threat to the coding of the McCain character in the broader civil sphere. It muddies the waters of the general election campaign. McCain secures the majority of Republican convention delegates in early March 2008, long before Obama is able to do so in his party. Yet, after succeeding brilliantly in securing the party nomination, McCain's campaign for national office stalls. After tacking so publicly to the right, it is hard to change directions—to move back to his previous path of civil repair. With the danger of terrorism eroding and interest in Iraq fading, McCain cannot convince general campaign audiences of imminent danger outside the United States, but neither can he work the civil binaries in a sharply etched, powerfully delineating way.

With the Republican drive for power spinning its wheels, political partisans and observers rush to code the situation in a manner favorable to their own side. Democrats are quick to credit Obama for the McCain impasse. Not only has the Democrat been able to project his own positive and inspiring story, but he has also "proved defter and more fleet-footed at counterpunching" than either of the party's two earlier candidates, refusing to be "cowed" into submission by the Republican side.[32] While Republican supporters are unlikely to credit Obama, neither are they inclined publicly to blame McCain. If McCain cannot do difference, this is because Obama has not been in office long enough to offer a real target. Also, it is difficult to make negatives stick to "a movement candidate." Another problem seems to be that, in working the boundaries in earlier elections, "conservatives have overstepped," and Republican candidates have "been sharply criticized for racially tinged remarks." McCain promises to be more civil and not to run a nasty, negative campaign. Presenting himself as "respectful" of his African American opponent, he feels compelled to distance himself from some intemperate, racially tinged political advertisements that have been created and financed in his name, as well as from some Republicans' openly racist remarks. Since Nixon, Republican candidates have couched anticivil accusations in racial terms. McCain makes public statements forbidding references to race in his effort to paint Obama in anticivil terms.

It speaks well of McCain the man that he refuses publicly to evoke primordial divisions, but it speaks badly of McCain the politician that he is not adroit enough to work the binaries in some other way. McCain's problems postnomination are the mirror image of his achievements in securing it. David Kirkpatrick, a *Times* reporter who often writes sympathetically of the conservative movement, surveys McCain's difficulties. While the Republican's "heroism as a prisoner of war in Vietnam has given Mr. McCain a special prestige," the reporter observes, "partisans on either side" find the Republican's recent political path "puzzling" and "even infuriating."[33] For his Democratic Senate colleagues, McCain is "a fickle gadfly who ultimately traded his independence to pander to the right." Undermining his earlier identification with civil repair, McCain now is constructed as neither trustworthy nor autonomous and as playing to party politics rather than principle. Yet, despite his movement to the right, McCain's fellow Republicans attribute to him equally anticivil qualities. Calling McCain "a serial turncoat," they accuse him of having a "truculent nature" and of being "aloof" and describe him as "aggressive, brusque, and abrasive." These constructions violate the demand that those who would be president cooperate with others in a civil way. A political scientist acknowledges that McCain has certainly demonstrated a talent for "political reinvention" but frames this ability pejoratively as "the art of political triangulation," recalling President Bill Clinton's decidedly slippery side. Even McCain's own pollster damns with faint praise. He testifies that his boss has been "very astute" in bucking both his own and the other political party, painting McCain as intelligent but calculating. So McCain can't be seen as pragmatic. His flip-flopping is understood to be driven by a desire for glory, for the nomination, not by altruistic concerns for justice. He has no principles to return to, no meaning there to be made.

Summing up McCain's difficulties vis-à-vis the civil sphere, the *Wall Street Journal* observes that "rarely has a party pick made so many enemies along the way."[34] Making enemies and defeating them are qualities that befit warrior heroes, and this is what McCain still seems to be in the postprimary season. "Chief among the strengths of the Republican nominee-in-waiting," the *Journal* writes in response to poll results later that spring, "is his experience with national-security issues, as a naval aviator and longtime senator."[35] The problem is that, in order to become heroes inside civil society, those who struggle for power must create a sense not only of external but also of internal crisis and offer a pathway to civil repair by thematizing change. Here, the *Journal* laments, McCain is failing indeed:

> In an election in which most voters say they seek change, one in five says he [McCain] could deliver it. Likewise, the senator who first emerged nationally as George W. Bush's chief nemesis in the 2000 campaign now represents to many voters a continuation of the unpopular president's policies.

Maverick to the Rescue?

It was to find a way out of this impasse that McCain returned to the "maverick" metaphor that had identified him during his earlier, more independent, less rightward-tilting days. The metaphor had allowed McCain to connect his military narrative with an emerging identity inside the civil scene. The *Washington Post* first dubbed McCain a "maverick" in 1993. A few years later, when he published *Faith of My Fathers*, McCain carefully noted his pranks and troublemaking as a boy, as well as his rebellious impatience with military and political bureaucracies and traditions as a young man. This narrative arc could easily be extended to the qualities of independence and honesty that became attached to the McCain character before and after the 2000 presidential campaign.[36]

"Maverick" is a multivalent symbol, signifying cowboys and cattle rustling, bad-boy pranks, and independence and integrity all at the same time. On the wide open range of the Old West, "maverick" first was descriptive, denoting unbranded cattle. Soon, however, the term became more metaphorical and connotative. It jumped species and, according to the *Cowboy Encyclopedia*, "took on the connotation of extreme individualism." In the late 1950s, this metaphorical meaning was featured in the popular television serial *Maverick,* starring James Garner as a poker-playing cowboy and gambler, a role that launched his career. Adorned in fancy black suits usually reserved for villains, Garner played maverick as a half-comic character, casually cheating his adversaries while being scrupulously honest with friends, famously reluctant to fight but never losing once he started. Thirty years later, Tom Cruise inhabited this trickster character as Pete "Maverick" Mitchell, the naval fighter pilot hero of *Top Gun,* a film that entered American folk culture and crystallized the military and nationalist revival of the late Reagan years.

As McCain moved to the right, this metaphoric moniker of his civility withers. Declaring the obvious in 2007, *Time* magazine headlined "John McCain, Maverick No More."[37] The problem for this maverick-less McCain was that the pendulum of American politics had started swinging back from right to left. In 2006, Democrats had regained their majorities in the House and the Senate. Less than a year after *Time*'s eulogy for Maverick, as McCain's postprimary campaign stalls, he is strongly advised to again brand himself as a maverick. Claiming that media coverage of the Republican campaign is "dead," the image-shaping conservative wizard and former Reagan speechwriter Peggy Noonan blames the performative deficits of the candidate, not the press. "You know McCain's problems," she confides in her *Wall Street Journal* column, "He never seems to mean it. His stands seem like positions. He bebops from issue to issue and never seems fully engaged."[38] The only way "for him to become interesting again," Noonan concludes, is for McCain to "refind his inner rebel, the famous irreverent maverick." At a time when the incumbent president and his neoconservative positions are deeply unpopular, the extreme individualism of the maverick metaphor might allow McCain to work the binaries outside of narrow party lines and to finally emerge as a civil hero. Because McCain "is a maverick," the *Journal* had predicted hopefully that spring, he has "cross-over appeal to independents and some Democrats."[39] A leading congressional Democrat reluctantly agrees: "McCain has appeal beyond his party."[40]

However, as the months go on, the McCain character continues to struggle and disappoint. He is bound too closely to the Right to allow the maverick metaphor to fly. "McCain has argued that he is a different kind of Republican," the *Wall Street Journal* writes in early May but immediately seeks to reassure its readers that, while McCain "courted a maverick image of moderation, he has made clear that his policy agenda will contour to conservative thought"[41]:

> On the stump, Senator McCain is laying out a string of conservative positions. He is proposing hundreds of billions of dollars in annual tax cuts, a deregulated health care system, and judicial nominees who will "strictly interpret the constitution," code for overturning Roe v. Wade...Next week, he addresses the National Rifle Association's annual meeting.[42]

> "I'm a conservative Republican," Senator McCain says over and over again on the trail, belying his frequent image as a moderate or a maverick.[43]

If McCain is a maverick, then he cannot be a warrior hero, a foot soldier for Reagan, and the representative of neoconservative and loyal Republicans today. The metaphor that evokes "extreme individualism" does not compute. It cannot gather up the strands of his reality and excite the public's imagination about him in a new way. "Imagining how John McCain, the navy war hero, would play the role of commander in chief has been easy," the *Journal* observes, "but imagining how John McCain, the policy maverick, would lead as chief executive of the U.S. economy has been tougher."[44] If he is not a true-blue, neoconservative but actually a maverick, the conservative newspaper asks, what exactly would his position in civil society be? "Americans can visualize John McCain behind the desk in the Oval Office. The difficulty is where his policies are, and is he going to take the country where it wants to head." Metaphors work if they crystallize new meanings, but a maverick "McCain presidency would be hard to categorize." Not only for conservatives but also for independents and liberals, McCain is a military hero and deferential to the Right. It is difficult to symbolically change such a character into a new thing.

As spring turns into summer, and the effort at positive image construction fails, the Republican campaign begins to go negative, shifting its metaphorical ambitions to the Democratic side. At the end of July, McCain and his staff launch against Obama a clever "celebrity" campaign. The *Times* headlines, "McCain Is Trying to Define Obama as Out of Touch."[45] Conservative strategists are relieved to see how immediately this metaphor sticks. McCain is finally able to work the binaries not by contrasting himself as domestically civil but by polluting the other side. In the battle over image, this marks a turning point. "After spending much of the summer searching for an effective line of attack," the *Times* explains, McCain "is beginning a newly aggressive campaign to define Mr. Obama." His campaign "will define Mr. Obama as arrogant, out of touch and unprepared for the presidency." Confronting this symbolic surge, Obama works the binaries. He dismisses the Republican campaign as "misleading," calls McCain "McNasty," and criticizes him as "cranky" and "negative." He falls back on the mythical assurance of the rational voter, assuring his supporters that voters "don't have much tolerance for Big Spin." Voters do tolerate the celebrity campaign, however, because they see it not as spin but as saying something real about the character who is leading the Democratic side.

Even so, by summer's end, as Barack Obama prepares for his spectacular performance in Mile High Stadium, it becomes clear that even the spectacularly polluting celebrity metaphor will not be able to stem the Democratic tide. In order to win the struggle for power, McCain will have to positively define himself as a civil hero. Conservative image guru Karl Rove warns that McCain "must achieve…a greater public awareness of the character that makes him worthy of the Oval

Office." Suggesting that "McCain's warrior ethic makes it difficult," Rove argues that "to win, McCain will have to show more." He will have "to persuade Americans he can tackle domestic challenges." While "voters trust him as commander in chief," they still have "doubts" about "whether he understands" them, "their concerns about their jobs, their family's health care, their children's education, the culture's coarseness, and their neighborhood's safety." To evince such understanding and insert himself into domestic life, McCain "must show the voters he remains a maverick who will, as president, work across party lines."[46] The day after Rove's statement, in a widely distributed television ad, McCain calls himself "the Original Maverick."[47] In case anybody misses the point, campaign spokesman Rick Gorka asserts, after McCain visits Nevada to woo its Republicans, "He's independent. He's a maverick. That has tremendous appeal."[48] It would, but McCain isn't. Two weeks later, during the Republican convention, the *Times'* headline says it all: "Party in Power, Running as If It Weren't."[49]

CHAPTER SIX

Walking the Boundaries

I N JOHN MCCAIN'S SECOND AND FINALLY SUCCESSFUL PURSUIT OF the Republican nomination, he cuts a dashing figure as a powerful military hero on the world stage even as he is deferential on the domestic stage to conservative authority and tradition. After securing the nomination, the Republican candidate needs dramatically to reverse course. For one thing, the nation's fear of terrorism has lessened. For another, regardless of the international context, those struggling for democratic power must become heroes on the domestic scene. So John McCain dresses himself back up in the garments of maverick. He finds that the clothing no longer fits. It is harder for him now to embody civil repair in a heroic way.

From this crisis of recognition follow the central turning points of the campaign. Because he is not in shape to become a liberating civic hero, McCain begins working the binaries in a less idealistic way, spinning his Democratic opponent as a celebrity. When this negative effort loses traction, he tries to pull a Republican civil hero out of his hat, tying his fading star to the tail of Palin's comet. When the Palin effect fizzles, McCain seizes upon the financial crisis, his final chance to become a maverick hero on the domestic scene.

Before examining these turning points in part III, I explore a strategy that seems to offer Republicans an alternative pathway to victory. Rather than working the binaries, McCain will walk the boundaries. If he has difficulty navigating ideals inside the civil sphere, perhaps he can focus on themes outside it, evoking noncivil ideals to make difference, to sacralize himself, and to label Obama in a negative way. The Republican candidate has long focused on the foreign policy environment of civil society, suggesting that Obama should not be elected because he cannot lead the

state's military struggle against dangerous anti-American forces outside. The civil sphere is bounded not only by the state, however. It is also surrounded by spheres that focus on religion, family, ethnicity, race, economics, and gender. McCain works to broaden his focus from the state to the other boundaries of the civil sphere. Walking these boundaries is a delicate task, but it must and will be tried.

Noncivil Qualities

Democracy rests upon the viability of a distinctive and relatively autonomous social sphere, one defined not by money, power, religion, intelligence, ethnicity, or family but by liberty, equality, and justice of a broad and universal kind. Insofar as social solidarity is civil, political victory cannot be won by narrow appeals to family connection or ethnic loyalty, to racial preference, to the quality of religious faith or the superiority of ideological dogma, or to the superiority of a gender or sexual tie. Instead, those who struggle for democratic power must prove they possess capacities of a purely civil kind. To win control of the state, the collective political representation must symbolize hopes for broad solidarity and disinterested representation. To make this demonstration, candidates dive deeply into the discourse of civil society. Performing the binaries, they struggle to associate themselves with stirring and uplifting utopian hopes just as they make every effort, and with equal determination, to represent their opponents in terms of those dark and anticivil qualities that identify those from whom democracy must be saved.

The civil sphere is one social sphere among many. Inside it, the rules of democracy are intended to hold sway. Outside it, other conditions rule. In a pluralistic society, all sorts of nondemocratic values and institutions are deemed as important as civil ones and sometimes more. Parents love their children and often believe them to be virtuous no matter what crime they have committed against civil ideals. Believers fervently hew to the glory of their religion even as they acknowledge civil guarantees of religious freedom for all. Ethnic groups remain fiercely loyal to one another, giving preference and deference to their members above those of other groups. Those who struggle for power must be responsive to these noncivil discourses and institutions. They need to evince not just understanding but also sympathy and sometimes even identification with values and institutions that are more particularistic than those that sustain democracy but that provide the struggle for democratic power with energy and resources. Precisely because they strive to represent society collectively, they are compelled to address these other spheres as well. Even as they work the boundaries inside the civil sphere, they walk the boundaries that separate the civil sphere from—and intertwine it with—its external environments.

Candidates must become collective representations not only of civil ideals but also of family values, of ideals about sexuality and gender, religion, ethnicity and race, economy and class, and the military face of the nation-state. They must show themselves to be real men and real women; to be good fathers and mothers; to be people of faith, not atheists; to be good Christians, not Muslims or Jews; to be economically self-sufficient rather than impoverished, skilled businesspeople, not bankrupts; to be fighters for the working class, efficient executives, and good soldiers. During political campaigns, candidates kiss babies, throw out baseballs, go bowling, eat tacos, sport emblems, visit fraternal societies, milk cows, peer through microscopes, visit factories, shake hands with beauty contest winners, don yarmulkes, and admire country music.

Yet, even as they reach over civil boundaries, candidates must assure citizen audiences that they can reconcile such noncivil enthusiasms with the discourse of liberty and that, if they do win control of the state, they will mediate such loyalties in a manner that is disinterested, solidaristic, and democratic. Civil society does not elect people simply because they are good mothers or fathers, real men or women, faithful Christians, working-class heroes, loyal ethnics, efficient executives, or whiz-bang entrepreneurs. To gain democratic power, candidates must combine these sympathies with demonstrations of civil capacity. They must show that their sympathies actually make them more civil and allow them to become better collective representations of democracy itself.

Those who struggle for democratic power cultivate noncivil groups in an open way. Campaigns have outreach coordinators for every different sort of community—athletes, accountants, trial lawyers, Mexican and Japanese Americans, fishermen, farmers, the corporate world, and trade unions. They want these constituencies to see the candidate as favorable to their particular cause, as willing to help them out. Courting support from particular communities, campaigns aim to project the excitement and energy from their candidate to these groups and to channel the energy circulating inside them back again to the campaign. All the while, they must carefully maintain the separation between these communities' particular interests and values and their own, more expansive struggle for civil power. This double consciousness is what makes walking the boundaries perilous. In early August, the *Wall Street Journal* highlights this peril as it describes Obama's challenge as he walks the civil-religion boundary:

The Muslim-outreach coordinator to the presidential campaign of Barack Obama has resigned amid questions about his involvement in an Islamic investment fund and various Islamic groups. Chicago lawyer Mazen Asbahi, who was appointed volunteer national coordinator for Muslim American affairs by the Obama campaign on July 26, stepped down Monday after an internet newsletter wrote about his brief stint on the fund's board, which also included a fundamentalist imam.... The Obama campaign is trying to strike a balance between courting Muslim American voters and dispelling rumors intended by some to link the candidate to radical Islam. Sen. Obama is a Christian. Until Mr. Asbahi joined the campaign, Sen. Obama did not have a Muslim-outreach coordinator and had relied on the Democratic National Committee's efforts. The campaign has long had its own outreach efforts to Catholic, evangelical Christian and Jewish voters. Some Muslim voters have complained about the disparity. An Obama aide says Mr. Asbahi was brought on in part to bridge that perceived gap and to reach out to Muslim communities in Florida, Michigan, Ohio, Pennsylvania and Virginia, states seen as among the most competitive this fall. "We need Muslim Americans to get excited about the Campaign, and there's a lot to get excited about!" Mr. Asbahi wrote in a statement posted on a blog when he was appointed.[1]

To become a collective representation, one must become not only a symbol of the civil sphere but also, to one degree or another, a symbol of the spheres that form its boundaries—despite the paradoxical fact that these other spheres confine civil society's most democratic aspirations.

Left and Right

Candidates of every ideological stripe walk the boundaries, but Left and Right—in the United States, liberals and conservatives—balance civil and noncivil boundaries in markedly different ways. The Left dedicates itself to expanding civil solidarity and championing equality and inclusion. This means opposing divisions inside the civil sphere that are legitimated by arguments about the differential capacities of classes, faiths, ethnicities, regions, races, genders, and sexualities. It also means enlarging government so it can better intervene on behalf of such civil claims. The Right emphasizes liberty over equality, warning of the dangers that big state efforts to undermine divisions in civil society might create. Reacting with alarm to the effervescence of egalitarian social movements and the reformist powers of liberal states, conservatives champion checks and balances, incremental change, and the wisdom of respecting boundaries rather than breaking them down. For the Left, exclusion from full civil participation seems unmerited on its face. For the Right, unequal status in the civil sphere can be justified and sometimes even—on ostensibly civil grounds—reasoned away. Conservatives tend to view inclusion less as an abstract right than as depending on qualification. They often describe ethnicity, class, religion, gender, sexuality, and even intelligence as qualifying or disqualifying virtues, as qualities that may legitimately affect the positions of individuals and groups in civil society in unequal ways.[2] For the Right, the status quo is not necessarily seen as quid pro quo; for the Left, it almost always is.

The *Wall Street Journal* aggressively pursues rumors of Obama's ties to the Islamic religion. When it discovers evidence of them, the conservative newspaper amplifies accusations about the compromising nature of these links. Seeming to exonerate the candidate with its declaration, "Sen. Obama is a Christian," there remains the clear implication that being Muslim might indeed disqualify a candidate from representing the civil sphere in the state. Indeed, from the very beginning of the campaign the *Journal's* conservative editorial pages have placed the Democratic campaign's noncivil boundaries—Obama's "background"—front and center in its coverage of the campaign:

> Midway through the election year, the presidential campaign looks less like a race between two candidates than a referendum on one of them—Sen. Barack Obama. With the nominations of both parties effectively settled for more than a month, the key question in the contest isn't over any single issue being debated between the Democrats' Sen. Obama or the Republicans' Sen. John McCain. The focus has turned to the Democratic candidate himself: Can Americans get comfortable with the background and experience level of Sen. Obama? This dynamic is underscored in a new Wall Street Journal/NBC news poll....More than four in 10 said the Democratic contender doesn't have values and a background they can identify with. Those findings suggest voters' views of Sen. Obama are more fluid than his relatively steady lead indicates.... "Obama is going to be the point person in this election," says pollster Peter Hart, a Democrat who conducts the Wall Street Journal/NBC News poll along with Republican Neil Newhouse. "Voters want to answer a simple question: Is Barack Obama safe?"[3]

Identifying the issues threatening this safety zone, the *Journal* mentions Obama's mixed race, his territorial associations with exotic and foreign climes, his elite status, his religious affiliation, and his family ties:

> The uncertainties about the Obama campaign flow from his unusual personal profile. Not only is he the first African-American to win a major party's nomination: he also was raised by a single white mother, spent his formative years in Hawaii and Indonesia, got an Ivy League law degree, has been in the Senate less than four years, attended a controversial African-American church, and is married to a strong professional woman who

has stirred up some controversy herself. Interviews with voters suggest that while many who seek change in the White House are excited by that profile, others will need time to digest it—and some may never do so.[4]

Six weeks later, it is becoming evident that the referendum on Obama's background may not turn out as conservatives expect. *Journal* editorial writers express concern that the balance between the civil sphere and its boundaries may have changed. "Starting with Ronald Reagan's election as president in 1980," the conservative newspaper explains, "Republicans began campaigning successfully on a formula emphasizing tough military and national-security views, cutting marginal tax rates, reforming the welfare bureaucracy, fighting crime and resisting affirmative action."[5] While such primordial anxieties about racial and military security may have propelled earlier victories, however, such extracivil issues may not be taking hold this time around. The explanation offered by the *Journal* seems more than slightly self-interested. It is that "the goals embodied in that formula have been achieved in the last generation." Whatever the reason, it is now the case that the GOP "may be losing their advantage with the very set of new voters they drew in along the way."

The Left sharply contests such efforts to link the struggle for democratic power to qualities outside the civil sphere, condemning them as particularistic and illegitimate. As its conservative counterpart devotes itself to Obama's nontraditional background, the *New York Times,* the nation's leading liberal newspaper, begins ringing an alarm bell of its own:

> Mr. Obama has been dogged by potent, fast-moving rumors about his religion, his birthplace and his patriotism, to name a few, for more than a year. More recently his campaign has confronted persistent but unsubstantiated reports about Mrs. Obama using angry and derogatory language about white people.[6]

One week later, the *Times* again cries foul. In a story headlined "Campaign Flashpoint: Patriotism and Service," the paper reports on Obama's efforts "to defuse attacks on his own background," describing them as "the latest attempt by the campaign to fight back against incorrect assertions that Mr. Obama will not recite the Pledge of Allegiance, place his hand over his heart during the national anthem or wear a flag pin on his lapel."[7]

The target for these conservative aspersions is a man of the Left, and he strenuously demands that such noncivil considerations be set aside. Obama defends himself by insisting on the breadth of civil solidarity: "We can't afford to be divided by race.... We can't afford to be divided by region or by class and we can't afford to be divided by gender."[8] In making this assertion that civil ties are controlling,

Obama echoes a widely publicized riposte he had made to Hillary Clinton during the primary campaign. Accusing his Democratic opponent of employing "the politics of fear," Obama expressed outrage that Clinton was reaching over the civil sphere boundary in such flagrant ways. He demanded to be judged on the basis of his intelligence and rationality. At the same time, he walked the boundaries himself, evoking patriotic icons and family ties:

> As Obama supporters worked to drum up support, they said they were still hearing rumors that Mr. Obama was Muslim and questions about his patriotism. At an evening campaign stop, a voter asked Mr. Obama how he could allay such concerns. "It frustrates me that people would even have a question about something like that because they don't ask the same questions of some of the other candidates," said Mr. Obama, who told a story about an American flag he received at the funeral of his grandfather, a World War II veteran. "If they don't vote for me, it should be because they think Senator Clinton or Senator McCain have better ideas. It shouldn't be because they think that I am less patriotic or because they question what my religious faith is."[9]

When the general campaign begins, conservative strategists and media trod the path that Hillary Clinton laid out, highlighting anticivil innuendoes she first had raised. Yet, as Republicans aggressively walk the boundaries, the Left pushes back. By summer's end, one of the campaign's most inflammatory mainstream media articles appears in the *Times*. Nicholas Kristof, a regular op-ed writer, accuses Republicans of trying to undermine the civil sphere's democratic authority. The column is titled "The Push to 'Otherize' Obama." Kristof proclaims that, while "nobody needs to point out that he's black," there's been "a persistent effort to exaggerate other differences" about the Democratic candidate in order "to de-Americanize him." Condemning these tactics as a "toxic" threat to democracy, the outraged liberal writer and two-time Pulitzer prize winner protests what he describes as the persistent "sleaziness" of the Republican campaign.[10]

The Left thinks of itself as purely civil and responds with sharp indignation to conservatives' arguments that the civil sphere might be fragmented in a beneficial way. But the Left is not pristine. It sometimes also champions the identities and interests of particular groups—of good-hearted workers over selfish businesspeople, striving immigrants over bigoted rednecks, downtrodden women over domineering men, heroic "people of color" over self-satisfied whites, open-minded gays and lesbians over narrow-minded straights. The Left holds in special esteem groups in the vanguard of movements for equality and civil repair. These favored groups provide compelling identities, and liberal candidates often walk the boundaries looking their way.

There is another reason the Left is not as purely civil as it might like to be. Civil spheres are real, not ideal. Dreams of freedom and equality come down to earth in actual societies, not utopias. Because real societies are stratified and complex, real civil societies are always and everywhere faced with resistance and strain. As they take institutional shape at a particular time in a particular place, real civil societies are distorted by compromise formations. According to the utopian discourse of civil society, human beings are equal, but for centuries, in real civil societies, men without property, women, and slaves were not allowed to vote. Religious exclusion flourishes in real, existing civil societies. There is continuing discrimination against immigrants, and ethnic conflicts are rife.[11] Candidates on the Left, even as they champion expanding civil society in principle, cannot overcome all of these restrictions on solidarity at the same time. No matter how utopian the conviction and ideology, to challenge every compromise formation would be electoral suicide. If the pluralism of society is to be respected and the autonomy of the civil sphere maintained, even left-wing candidates for power must pick and choose which compromise formations to fight. Modern societies are complex and stratified. Struggles for power cannot challenge the fragmentations of real existing civil societies in overly demanding and radical ways.

Economic Boundary

The civil sphere's elected representatives depend on the economic sphere to generate funds for state power. Conservatives might siphon financing from the economy indirectly, via user fees, value-added tariffs, or sales taxes. Liberals often do so more overtly, from steeply graduated income taxes to outright nationalization. Yet, even if intertwined, the relations between economic and civil spheres is never easy, and the boundary between them constitutes a minefield for candidates struggling for power. It certainly makes sense, for example, for political candidates to bring economic experts and authorities on board their campaigns, but when they do so there is often hell to pay. Inside private companies and markets, unequal rewards are confidently embraced as merit based and motivating. In the civil sphere, by contrast, they are viewed with suspicion and often as cause for alarm. Not only liberals but also conservatives who struggle for power in the civil sphere feel compelled to take umbrage at "excessive" compensation packages despite their being viewed on the other, economic side of the boundary as appropriate and routine. From the perspective of the civil sphere, greed is always opposed to public service. Businesspeople offer one another gifts and trade favors; building particularistic ties of loyalty and trust is good for business. In the civil sphere, connections based on loyalty and trading often seem dangerous, suggesting corruption. The *Wall Street Journal* writes about these strains in the early summer of 2008:

> The presidential campaign-attack machines have taken aim at corporate executives advising the candidates, by using the executives' past business activities as fodder. Both Democratic presidential contender Barack Obama and his Republican counterpart, John McCain, rely on former business executives for help on everything from fund raising to economic policy. At the same time, each has railed against corporate greed and vowed to root out corruption. The clash has already led to the resignation of one Obama adviser. On Wednesday, Democratic Party stalwart James Johnson quit as a screener of potential running mates for Sen. Obama after new details emerged about loans that Mr. Johnson had received from mortgage lender Countrywide Financial Corp. Shortly after, Democratic operatives began pushing research on Carly Fiorina, a close adviser to Sen. McCain, related to the business dealings of Hewlett-Packard Co. while she led the tech titan, and to her compensation package after her ouster in 2005. Republicans have fought back with punches for Penny Pritzker, a Chicago billionaire and member of the family dynasty that owns the Hyatt hotel chain, who is Sen. Obama's national campaign chairwoman.[12]

Dynasty and democracy do not go easily together. Walking the economic boundary is always risky; it is not simply a danger for one side, a matter of the Left-versus-Right divide. Each side continually accuses the other of undermining democracy even if they are only walking the economic boundary in between:

> None of the executives named in the attacks have been accused of illegal activity. But even the appearance of backroom deals or favors is enough to raise eyebrows among voters in a campaign where both candidates have cast themselves as reformers. What might be normal operating procedure for an executive, including the terms of a compensation package or favors exchanged in the course of a business deal, could appear as egregious offenses under the political-morality microscope.[13]

As the struggle for democratic power gains traction, the candidates themselves can hardly afford such an Olympian view of the civil/economic divide. They need to do difference, to walk the boundaries in a manner that purifies their own case and pollutes the opposing side. How to walk the boundary becomes central ideologically, creating the difference between Left and Right. In principle, the Right stands for laissez-faire, respecting market decisions and allowing as much independence as possible for private property vis-à-vis civil society and state. The Left is more outspokenly interventionist, more benign about public control of market decisions, and more enthusiastic about challenging private wealth and repairing what it construes as the irresponsible and anticivil elements of economic life.

In times of stability and prosperity, it becomes more difficult for the Left to walk the boundary in this way. When times are tougher and seem to demand reform and change, when economic instability looms and losses rather than profits are on the rise, the conservative manner of walking comes under fire. The soft underbelly of laissez-faire is inequality. Economies are not only markets but also classes, not only contractual agreements and horizontal exchanges but also vertical hierarchies and coercive controls. In times of prosperity and growth, when all boats seem to be rising, the verticality of economic life passes by without as much fuss. In times of trouble, its anticivil quality is harshly brought to light.

This was certainly the case in 2008, when allowing the economy to do its own thing increasingly seemed like not caring about the state of the economy at all. Three years earlier, McCain had famously admitted to the *Wall Street Journal*, "I know a lot less about economics than I know about military and foreign policy issues." The Republican scored a point for honesty, one of his most esteemed civil traits, and implicitly promoted conservative laissez-faire. For conservatives, politicians' not knowing economics can seem like the other side of wisdom, ensuring that the state will not intervene. Now, in 2008, the economic context is changing. The remark is thrown back into McCain's face during the Republican primaries in early 2008 and has haunted him since.[14] The country is sliding slowly into recession, unemployment is beginning to rise, homes are being foreclosed, and people in the economic middle are starting to feel pain.

Responding to worsening economic news, Republican senator Phil Gramm tells the editorial board of the *Washington Times* that "we have sort of become a nation of whiners," that "you just hear this constant whining, complaining America is in decline." The country is in a "mental recession," Gramm suggests, more a "mental depression" than a real economic one.[15] Gramm is candidate McCain's close friend and principal economic advisor, described by the *Washington Times* as "the towering intellectual figure in the McCain campaign."[16] His disparaging remarks make McCain's self-professed ignorance seem dangerous and his hands-off policy less studied than callous. Patronizing the masses of economic have-nots, Gramm has brazenly cut across the very grain of social solidarity, of humane concern for the suffering of others in troubled times. His remarks touch off an explosion inside the civil sphere and become a big issue in Republican circles. Gramm, McCain's chief economic advisor and national cochairman, has walked the civil/economic boundary not just awkwardly but, it seems to many, in a grossly antidemocratic way. Despite their close personal and political friendship, McCain publicly pollutes Gramm's remarks, declaring they have distorted the true Republican economic message. McCain avers that the economy is faltering, that it endangers civil solidarity, and that voters' perceptions of the danger are rational and real. "Let's face it, my friends," McCain tells a town meeting in Michigan, "America is hurting today, and it's hurting badly"[17]:

> "I believe the mother here in Michigan and around America who is trying to get money to educate their [sic] children isn't whining," Sen. McCain told reporters in Belleville, Mich. "America is in great difficulty, and we are experiencing enormous economic challenges. Phil Gramm does not speak for me. I speak for me. So, I strongly disagree."

Trying to protect himself from further pollution, McCain summarily fires Gramm, stressing that Gramm no longer has any formal or informal association with the campaign.

But the damage is done. On August 21, Obama's production team launches a TV ad that depicts McCain as out of touch with everyday people. The day before, McCain has been asked by the *Politico* website how many houses he and his wife own, and he responds, "I think—I'll have my staff get to you."[18] The ad is called "Seven," and it depicts McCain walking the economic boundary in a noblesse oblige, antidemocratic way: "Maybe you're struggling just to pay the mortgage on your home," the voiceover intones, as images of foreclosure signs pass across the screen. "When asked how many houses he owns, McCain lost count. He couldn't remember. Well, it's seven. Seven!" The video becomes one of the top 20 most-viewed videos at BarackObamadotcom, with more than one million hits.[19] The very next day, "Out of Touch," another TV spot, goes on the air. "Call it 'country club economics,'" the video suggests. Then, asking "How many houses *does* he own?" the ad concludes, "Maybe McCain thinks this economy is working for folks like him, but how are things going for you?"[20]

As the Labor Day break approaches, the *Wall Street Journal* complains "there's a perception that Republicans are rich, stereotypical people who don't care about modest-income folk."[21] The reality, it suggests, is altogether different, pointing to millions of "blue-collar" Republicans who are "more comfortable in a big-box store than a country club." Whatever the empirical accuracy of this "Sam's Club Republicans" trope, it cannot balance the moral perception that Republicans are walking the economic boundary in the wrong way. Considered once to be "an icon of traditional conservatives," Phil Gramm himself has passed from the campaign scene.[22] His words about America whining remain, alongside his friend John McCain's remarkable professions of economic ignorance and his inability to recall the extent of his householding. These difficulties are enshrined in American folk memory not as pearls of conservative wisdom but as iconic representations of antidemocratic indifference. Wringing its hands a week after Labor Day, the

Journal disconsolately worries that "the campaign issue of middle-class economic anxiety is central."[23] And news about the financial meltdown on Wall Street is still one week way.

Religious Boundary

The civil sphere promises freedom and equality and demands autonomy, criticism, and rationality. Religion suggests something rather different: spiritual enthrall-ment and intellectual entrainment, a binding to faith, deference rather than ques-tioning of traditional and authoritative wisdom. Religious and civil spheres are, in principle at least, at odds. Inside the American civil sphere, this principled antago-nism is enshrined in a particularly forceful manner by the demand for religious disestablishment, which frees citizens from adhering to any particular religion and even from being subject to any test of religiosity at all. In practice, however, in real civil societies, civil practices have always been religiously inspired and restricted, sometimes by a state church, at other times by prohibition against any church at all. Founded by Puritans who fused religious and civil freedom, the United States has been mostly a democracy of believers. No matter what the Constitution says and no matter how, in recent years, its disestablishment provisions have become ever more strictly applied, being religiously faithful has been construed as essential for civil capacity. Children not only pledge allegiance to the flag and the Republic for which it stands, but they also must do so "under God." Presidents conclude major speeches by asking God to "bless America." Even the most mundane and common coin of the civil realm, the dollar bill, declares that "in God we trust." In contemporary America, nonbelievers certainly are not persecuted, but they are made politically irrelevant. Not only has the American civil sphere not ever been a religion-free zone, it has never been Christian free. Until the Catholic John Kennedy became president, only Protestant Christians were considered worthy to assume this highest of civil positions. No Jewish person has yet gained the nomi-nation for president, let alone been elected, and Muslim qualification is not under consideration. Historically, Islam has been the millennia-long enemy of Western Christendom and, if perhaps less so, of Judaism besides.

It is hardly surprising, then, that Barack Obama, already closely scrutinized for otherness, is constantly asked to prove not only religiosity but also faithfulness of a particular kind. The Democratic candidate is more than prepared. He seem-ingly willed himself into religiosity as his political ambitions spread. He was not raised as a religious person. His white mother was a searcher, agnostic if not athe-ist. His Kenyan father and stepfather were of Muslim background if indeterminate faith. Only when Obama enters politics as a community organizer, after finishing his undergraduate education at Columbia, does his carefully constructed autobiography mention religion. The young man discovers that only those spiritually ministering to Chicago's African American underclass possess the moral authority and material resources upon which community organizing depends. After leaving Chicago for Harvard Law School, Obama returns filled to brimming with political ambition. Only then does he enter deeply into the American black community, and only then does he record his first spiritual encounter with faith. He accepts Jesus Christ as his redeemer and joins Chicago's most prestigious and progressive African American church.

From that time on, Obama assiduously asserts his Christian identity. He announces periodically to the public world that he is not only a citizen and Democrat, a lawyer, teacher, second-generation immigrant, black man, father and husband but also a member of the particular religious community that takes Jesus Christ as savior and its distinguishing token and totem of faith. This man of the Left embraces civil ideals in a radical way, but he insists that the audacity of hope complements an anchoring religious faith. Candidate Obama establishes all sorts of outreach groups to religious communities, but he displays particularly close ties with clergy who are fighting against fundamentalism and espousing a reformist, forward-looking Christianity.

Even as Obama carefully navigates the boundaries between religious and civil sphere, it is the Right that walks the boundary in a particularly aggressive and stigmatizing way. *Insight* is a conservative online periodical owned by the same company as the *Washington Times*. In January 2007, at about the same time that Obama throws his hat into the Democratic primary, *Insight* alleges that, during his Indonesian boyhood, Obama had attended a hyperreligious Islamic madrassa, which indoctrinated him with fundamentalist beliefs.[24] The revelation is taken up by two different FOX news shows. While almost immediately debunked by CNN—its Beijing correspondent pays a fact-finding visit to the Jakarta school—the story fans anticivil fears that begin ricocheting among the private conversations and public media of conservative religious and political groups. One circulating factoid concerns a statement Obama makes in an interview with the *Times*. In a remark intended as sincere praise and revealing of his cosmopolitan disposition—but undoubtedly later much regretted—Obama describes the Muslim call to prayer, which rings out five times each day in most Arabic countries, as "one of the prettiest sounds on earth at sunset," and he repeats its opening lines from memory.[25] There is also pronounced interest in the true meaning of the Democrat's full name, Barack Hussein Obama. The middle word is Arabic for "blessed," but it is also the last name of the man who, throughout the 1990s, was America's most hated foreign enemy. In winter 2008, the Tennessee Republican party features this middle name in its news release attacking Obama for allegedly anti-Israeli views, a report that features a photo from the Democrat's trip to Africa, where he is dressed in a traditional Somali tribal costume. The Republican Party captions it "Muslim" clothing.[26] The Republican National Committee soon forces Tennessee to recant, but speakers at the Republican national convention in late August carefully pronounce every word and syllable of the Democratic candidate's full name. Obama's full name is also juxtaposed with al-Qaeda's Islamic terrorist leader, who has now displaced Saddam Hussein as public enemy number one. Under the headline "Rhymes with…Obama," the *Times* reports that the once-celebrated CBS news journalist Dan Rather, now a producer for HDTV, mistakenly calls the Democrat "Osama Bin Laden."[27] It is not only because Rather is an outspoken liberal that this verbal slip is considered newsworthy. The verbal error has often been jeeringly repeated in conservative circles.

Early that summer, a conservative ideologist and publicist-for-hire named James Corsi writes *The Obama Nation,* which reproduces many of these anticivil shibboleths and other fictitious accusations about the background of the Democratic candidate. Corsi made his name four years earlier by authoring a book that slandered John Kerry as a military coward, laying the foundations for the Swift Boat scandal, which did grave injury to the Democratic presidential campaign. While Corsi feels compelled to acknowledge that Obama never attended an Indonesian madrassa, he manages to raise the Islamic specter in an even more speculative way. He quotes Obama's paternal uncle, Sayid: "I did not see my brother practice Islam, especially after he returned from his studies in the U.S. I did not consider him to be very religious." From this statement Corsi draws the perplexing conclusion that "listening to Sayid there is little doubt Obama senior was a Muslim by birth and upbringing, even if his devotion as a Muslim remained in doubt."[28] The initial printing of *Obama Nation* numbers in the hundreds of thousands, thanks to preordering by conservative political and religious book clubs. The book enters the *Times* best-seller list at number two.

It does not help rebut these festering suspicions when the *Wall Street Journal* confirms, as I mentioned earlier, that the Democratic campaign's "volunteer national coordinator for Muslim American affairs" once served a "brief stint" on the board of an "Islamic investment fund." The fund had been investigated for complicity with terrorist organizations, and it had included a "fundamentalist imam" as a member.[29] The *Journal* reports that, only days after his appointment, Obama's volunteer Islamic coordinator has resigned his formal position, explaining that he does not wish to be a "distraction" to the Democratic campaign.

During the same period in July, the liberal *New Yorker* magazine publishes a cover drawing of Barack and Michelle Obama as fist-bumping terrorists, the latter in Black Panther costume, the former in full Islamic dress. The magazine's editors view the cover as parody, as pushback against conservatives who are walking the religion/civil society boundary in an increasingly anti-Islamic way. The cover is widely viewed, however, as critical realism, not rhetorical trope. Liberals shudder that Obama's putative non-Christian identity is being confirmed by the nation's most sophisticated and liberal weekly magazine. Conservatives scold liberals for not being able to take a joke. Obama's principal spokesman feels compelled to make the line between his candidate's fictional Islamism and his actual Christian identity as clear and clean as possible. "The New Yorker may think...that their cover is a satirical lampoon of the caricature Senator Obama's right-wing critics have tried to create," Bill Burton remarks, "but most readers will see it as tasteless and offensive. And we agree."[30] Obama must pollute those who might be seen as his polluters even if they were making a quirky if failed aesthetic effort to disarm his real polluters themselves. We are reminded once again of how fraught walking the boundaries can be, especially when audiences and candidates deeply believe in the polluting capacity of the values on the other, noncivil side.

By August, the Right's fervid insistence on Obama's religious disqualification becomes full blown and threatens to enter fully into the mainstream. Inserted into the good and evil binary of apocalyptic thinking, Obama becomes constructed as the demonic, world-and-god-threatening Antichrist. The *Wall Street Journal* reports "suggestions that Sen. Obama is the antichrist have been circulating for months."[31] Conservative Christian circles are abuzz with news about Obama's secret religious identity, which is also circulating on Christian radio stations throughout the country. The Red State Shop, a nationally popular, right-wing Internet store, advertises anti-Obama T-shirts, mugs, and stickers that display the Democratic candidate's iconic "O" symbol with horns coming out of the top, above a caption reading "The Anti-Christ."

At the beginning of August, John McCain's in-house advertising staff, Foxhole Productions, creates an Internet ad that implants itself at the heart of this apocalyptic construction of Obama as satanic enemy.[32] Generating a million hits its first week, the polluting message is amplified by favorable and critical television commentary alike. The *Journal* does not fail to take note, while ostentatiously keeping tongue in cheek:

> An Internet ad launched last week by the McCain presidential campaign...mock[s] Barack Obama for presenting himself as a kind of prophetic figure. The ad has also generated criticism from Democrats and religious scholars who see a hidden message linking Sen. Obama to the apocalyptic Biblical figure of the antichrist. The spot, called "the One," opens with the line: "It shall be known that in 2008 the world will be blessed." Images follow of Moses parting the Red Sea and Sen. Obama telling a crowd, "We are the change we've been waiting for."... The End

Times, a New Testament reference to the period surrounding the return of Christ, were popularized in recent years by the "Left Behind" series of books that sold more than 63 million copies. The Rev. Tim LaHaye, co-author of the series, said in an interview that he recognized allusions to his work in the ad....Those ideas are chiefly shared by fundamentalist Protestants and some other evangelical Christians. Among their expectations: the ascension of a false prophet, a one-world government and the Second Coming of Jesus Christ....In some swings states with concentrated pockets of fundamentalists and evangelical Christians, like Ohio, Pennsylvania, Colorado and Virginia, the ads could have particular impact....Some images in the ad very closely resemble the cover art and type font used in the latest "Left Behind" novel. The title of the ad, "The One," also echoes the series; the antichrist figure in the books, Nicolae Carpathia, sets up "the One World Religion."[33]

McCain never refers to, much less endorses, anticivil accusations about Obama's religiosity, the very charges that his campaign staff (and conservative supporters more generally) are projecting into the civil sphere. The Obama campaign declines official comment, but Democratic officials and consultants express both outrage and fear. McCain's spokesman responds, distancing his candidate from possible pollution. He claims humor as the ad's intent and asserts that it is no more than "a light-hearted ad that pokes fun" at Obama.

Obama responds in two ways to the dangerously polluting manner in which conservatives were walking the religious boundary of civil life. As a man of the Left and a domestic hero, Obama energetically reiterates the democratic principle that the struggle for democratic power should be free of entanglements other than those centering on the civil sphere and its qualities. As a practical politician, Obama pays obeisance to real civil society and its compromise formations. He reassures citizen audiences that his personal faith conforms to the dominant religious commitments of the American people. In midsummer, in a widely publicized event, he reminds parishioners at the African Methodist Church in St. Louis, Missouri, that as a community organizer "I let Jesus Christ into my life" and "I dedicated myself to discovering his truth and carrying out his works."[34]

Just six weeks before the election, a Pew poll reveals that almost one-third of American voters either "know" that Obama is a Muslim or believe he might be.[35] And the numbers are increasing. From March to September, those who were certain of his Islamic identity have swelled from 10 to 13 percent. Those who declare themselves uncertain about his religion have risen to 16 percent, and they attribute their doubt to hearing "different things." A liberal New York Times columnist warns that "the political campaign to transform

Mr. Obama into a Muslim is succeeding."[36] That in the end it fails is not for want of trying.

Gender Boundary

If noncivil qualities are always made relevant to struggles for democratic power, there is usually a good deal of hemming and hawing about how and by whom they should be introduced. Walking the boundaries is so delicate precisely because democratic struggles are not supposed to be decided in such ways. Accusations of disqualifying otherness often become shrouded in ambiguity, as do attestations about those qualities that qualify. Candidates preserve deniability and moral purity by wrapping anticivil accusations in camouflage and inserting them via surrogates. Despite the public's explosive indignation over Phil Gramm's elitist remarks, that John McCain had married rich and was either unable or unwilling to offer a full accounting of the couple's seven-plus luxury homes, Democrats only occasionally made issues of them during the heat of the campaign. Despite repeated conservative accusations about Obama's religion, McCain himself never repeats them; when his campaign staff narrate anticivil slanders about Obama, they claim to be doing so only in a joking way.

This is not the case with the boundary that divides civil sphere from family and gender. Gender and family are so deeply inscribed that they still seem perfectly natural settings for the performance of civil sphere qualities on the political stage. Being a real man, a man of proven courage, a handsome man, even a sexy one—these noncivil qualities have always been spoken easily about during the course of America's presidential campaigns. That a candidate is also a family man, a devoted husband, a doting and proud father—these, too, are familiar themes that stretch all the way back to George Washington, the first American president, fondly remembered for centuries as the "father of our country." Neither were women absent from the public stage. They have very much been seen, if only occasionally heard. Their presence underscores the family attachment of the men who struggle for civil power and confers on them male authority. When candidates are elected, their wives perform the role of "first lady."

Hillary Clinton

With contemporary feminism challenging the ways in which struggles for power walk these gendered boundaries, Hillary Clinton becomes subject and object of this change. Emerging on the national scene in 1992, Clinton refuses to perform the role of deferential wife. "I suppose I could have stayed home and baked cookies and had teas," she declares proudly on *Nightline,* "but what I decided to do was to fulfill my profession, which I entered before my husband in public life." During a critical *60 Minutes* interview about her husband's infidelity, she makes the incendiary assertion "I'm not sitting here as some little woman standing by my man like Tammy Wynette." When Bill Clinton becomes president, Hillary Clinton tries to carve out for herself a position of independence, authority, and power. These efforts prove controversial, particularly after her 1994 health care initiative goes down in flames.

The opportunities for performing gender on the presidential stage are narrow indeed. Even as feminism broadly transforms mores and institutions, as a social movement it remains closely associated with the Left. Those struggling for presidential power must thread a needle that stands at the very middle of the political spectrum, where undecided and independent voters always hold sway. As Clinton runs up against these restrictions, she tacks back to the center. Rather than defiant feminism, she displays more traditional virtues of wisdom, common sense, and generosity as first mother and first wife. Only in 2000, when Hillary Clinton moves out from under the shadow of her president husband and the White House, can she present herself as a woman of her own, independent and self-governing, largely separated from the domestic scene. As a senator from one of the nation's most liberal states, New York, she builds an image of autonomy and strength without eschewing a feminine style that reaches from her coiffure to her fashions, from her smile to her signature "listening" campaigns.

When Hillary Clinton enters into the struggle for presidential power, she is once again required to thread the eye of the needle, and her earlier senatorial juggling of gender proves difficult to sustain. Anticipating that stereotypes about female weakness would translate into accusations that she lacks moral judgment and political strength, Clinton and her advisors decided that she should display "toughness," staking her claim that, in contrast with the neophyte Obama, it is she who will be able to make the "hard decisions" required of a commander in chief. Once again, however, doing difference against the grain of traditional gender stereotypes proves to be of limited appeal, especially in contrast with the charismatically charged performance of an attractive African American family man. Surprised and humiliated by her loss to Obama in the Iowa caucuses, Clinton concludes she cannot make meaning in this more feminist way. Appearing before a small, mostly female audience in New Hampshire, she is asked how she manages to juggle everything as a female presidential candidate. "How do you go out the door every day? I mean, as a woman, I know how hard it is to get out of the door and get ready."[37] Clinton responds "It's not easy... as tired as I am," tearfully revealing that "it's very painful for me." Her throat catches and her eyes well up. This insertion of traditional "womanly" emotions into hardball politics electrifies the national media and brings a wave of sympathy to Clinton's struggling campaign. She wins the New Hampshire primary. By displaying a new vulnerability, she finally is able to fuse with her audience in an effective way:

> Hillary Clinton conceded today that a rare moment of public emotion in a New Hampshire coffee shop had helped bring her back from the political dead. The usually stoic former first lady said that the incident, in which she became teary as she discussed what drove her to keep fighting for the presidency, had afforded her a "connection" with New Hampshire voters that had propelled her to a 3 point victory in the state's primary over favourite Barack Obama. "I had this incredible moment of connection with the voters of New Hampshire and they saw it and they heard it. And they gave me this incredible victory last night," she said during an interview with CBS....Stunned aides savouring Mrs. Clinton's victory credited the "humanizing" effect of the coffee shop incident....Bill Clinton too credited the brief glimpse of his wife's vulnerable side for her unexpected win. "People saw who she was," he said. Mrs. Clinton's tough professional exterior has earned her a reputation in some quarters for being a cold and calculating politico, an image she has been trying to soften in recent weeks.[38]

Narrowly traditional constructions of gender still rule from the center of the civil sphere during presidential campaigns. Women may become candidates, but they cannot prove their civil capacity by taking on attributes associated with men. They need to make civil meaning in a female way:

> It was not that Senator Hillary Rodham Clinton teared up. It was the times she did not. Even in low moments, Mrs. Clinton has been a picture of steely public composure. She has rarely, if ever, seemed to let herself go. Not when her health care initiative failed. Not the first time the world found out about her husband's marital misconduct. Not the second time either....Mrs. Clinton has meted out her inner life one teaspoon at a time: a suggestive line in an interview here, a hearty laugh there. So on Monday, when she choked up during an appearance at a New Hampshire coffee shop, making a nakedly emotional plea for her candidacy, Mrs. Clinton prompted one of the most fiercely debated moments of the presidential campaign to date.[39]

What Americans debate is whether such "typically female" behavior—which citizen audiences demand and which Clinton finally supplies—is sincere and authentic or calculated and fake. Only the former can make Clinton qualified to represent the civil sphere in the state:

Americans from across the political spectrum played and replayed the clip, pausing on every flicker of expression on Mrs. Clinton's face, and asking questions like: After a political lifetime of keeping her emotions secret, why was Mrs. Clinton finally letting her guard down? Was it a spontaneous outburst or a calculated show? Was Mrs. Clinton using her gender to win sympathy?...After a year's worth of speeches and debates, several new biographies and reams of journalism, the truth about what sort of person Hillary Clinton is—how genuine, how altruistic—seemed to come down to a few minutes of tape for some voters.[40]

It is extraordinarily difficult to get civil society's gender boundaries right. After winning in New Hampshire, Clinton goes on to lose a string of eight consecutive primaries and, even as her campaign recovers, her supporters argue that sexist media stereotypes are to blame. Certainly there is sexism enough to justify such a claim. In the critical final weeks of her campaign, CNN's Mike Barnicle cracks that Hillary Clinton is "looking like everyone's first wife standing outside of probate court" and Chris Matthews suggests that "the reason she's a candidate for president, the reason she may be a front-runner, is her husband messed around."[41] A Fox News commentator describes Clinton as "looking like 92 years old," suggesting, "if that's the face of experience, I think it's going to scare away a lot of those independent votes."[42] In question is whether such gender stereotyping is the fault of the media or its audience. If gendered perceptions are lodged deeply inside members of the civil sphere, women can win the struggle for power only by demonstrating that they can still thrive in a civil way. Were these attacks being made "because she was a woman," CNN's veteran political correspondent Candy Crowley pointedly asks, "or because she was this woman?"[43]

Michelle Obama

Michelle Obama is a product of the feminist revolution, professionally ambitious, successful, Princeton and Harvard trained, and black. A generation younger than Hillary Clinton, when she enters the national civil stage, she will not repeat Clinton's mistakes. Michelle Obama does not struggle to bring her feminist self into the narrow center of the civil sphere but walks the gender boundary in a more traditional way. Describing her effort to play "the trickiest of political performances," the *Times* observes early on that despite Michelle Obama's "propensity for bluntness and a fierce competitive drive," the woman "who has said she dislikes politics is assuming a starring role in her husband's campaign."[44] Obama makes her ambition to be first mother and first wife evident at every opportunity:

Last week, in Windham, N.H., Mrs. Obama charmed a houseful of Democratic voters, speaking of her romance with the candidate and kneeling next to two little boys and their sister to inquire, "Which one of you is the troublemaker?"

As the female complement to Barack Obama, she performs the difference that makes him more than a civil hero: a traditional husband and a manly man:

> She was still a bit irreverent: "I'm sure this guy is weird," she said, describing her initial reaction to her husband's name. But she turned earnest when talking of the presidency. "I know Barack is something special," she said. "If I didn't, I wouldn't be here."

Michelle Obama reassures skeptics worried about her husband's noncivil differences and fuses with citizen audiences in deeply traditional ways:

> While her husband's story is singular—how many other Hawaiian-Indonesian-African-Midwestern sensations are there?—Mrs. Obama is his more down-to-earth counterpart, drawing parallels between the voters' daily balancing acts and her own. The role suits her natural frankness—she has gone so far as to talk about how she had to cope with an overflowing toilet—and yet confines it safely to the domestic sphere.

Six months later, as Obama starts winning primaries, Michelle Obama walks the gender and family boundaries in a less steady way. Scattered remarks give the impression she wishes to be more independent from her husband, less the gendered helpmeet than the democratic critic. She is heard describing and deploring divisions inside American society: "Our souls are broken.... The problem is with us." She is heard as questioning the sincerity of her fellow citizens and the altruism of their beliefs: "We're too cynical. And we are still a nation that is too mean—just downright mean to one another. We don't talk to each other in civil tones." She is heard rejecting the sacred myth of voter rationality upon which a democratic civil sphere is based: "Barack will never allow you to go back to your lives as usual—uninvolved, uninformed."[45]

The possibility that Michelle Obama's orientation to American civil society is not what it seemed at first is crystallized in remarks she makes in February 2008, when she tells a Wisconsin crowd that "for the first time in my adult lifetime, I am really proud of my country."[46] Conservatives react to these remarks as if they demonstrate Mrs. Obama's frightening anticivil otherness. Announcing "Thunder on the Right," the website of McClatchy newspapers reports that Michelle Obama's remarks "hit critical mass on conservative cable TV, talk radio, and the Internet."[47] The *Times* later recalls that "cable news programs replayed those 15 words in an endless loop of outrage."[48] Racial reactions imputing racist motives to Mrs. Obama bubbled to the surface, but they can gain traction only by working the binaries: They are wrapped inside accusations that she has finally revealed her deeply and truly anticivil ways. Rush Limbaugh accuses her of being "unhinged."[49] A conservative blogger expatiates about "the bitter, anti-American, ungrateful, rude, crude, ghetto, angry Michelle Obama."[50] Christopher Hitchens finds in Obama's Princeton undergraduate thesis signs that, even then, she embraced black "separationism."[51] The *National Review* puts a sneering Michelle Obama on its cover alongside the words "Mrs. Grievance," its vitriolic account describing her "narcissism and self-absorption."[52]

Underlying these criticisms is the suggestion that Michelle Obama is no longer behaving in a traditional, ladylike way. In the *New York Post,* a columnist and blogger declares that "until Obama's 'proud' remark, she was the new, glamorous Jackie O, and most stories focused on her pearls and wardrobe," declaring that her critics should no longer "treat her with kid gloves." *Time* magazine reports Michelle's speeches have become "stark and stern." Calling her "strikingly ungracious," the *National Review* plays on an old Beatles' song to argue that Americans should be afraid[53]:

"MRS. OBAMA'S AMERICA"

Michelle, *ma belle*: These are words that go together well. She looks fabulous, like a presidential spouse out of some dream movie—glossy hair, triple strand of pearls, vaguely retro suits that subtly remind you she'd be the most glamorous first lady since Jackie Kennedy. Michelle, "fear," "cynicism": These are words that go together more problematically.[54]

When the general election campaign begins in June, campaign advisors decide Michelle Obama needs a makeover. Invited by Times reporters "to consider her complicated public image," Mrs. Obama engages in an effort at political-cum-civil contestation: "You are amazed sometimes at how deep the lies can be."[55] That same day, she appears as cohost on *The View,* where she moves to identify herself more firmly with gender than with political divides. Barbara Walters holds up the front page of the *Times* and reads the headline aloud as the camera tracks in on it: "After attacks, Michelle Obama looks for a new introduction." Walters asks Mrs. Obama whether the *Times'* suggestion that she is cohosting the show "with an eye towards softening her reputation" is correct, implying that she need not agree. After Mrs. Obama does agree, Whoopi Goldberg says she wants to "clear up that quote" about Mrs. Obama's not having pride in her country. Playing the actual clip, Goldberg suggests it "has a different feel when you hear it." Elizabeth Hasselbeck points out that Laura Bush chastised the media for playing up Mrs. Obama's pride statement, and discussion then turns to Mrs. Obama's having written Mrs. Bush a note of appreciation. Saying she was "touched by it," Mrs. Obama gives a decidedly civil spin to Laura Bush's gesture of gender solidarity: "And that's what I like about Laura Bush, you know, just a calm, rational approach to these issues. I'm taking some cues—I mean there's a balance. There's a reason people like her, because she doesn't fuel the fires."[56]

These are the last public efforts at purely civil discourse the Democratic candidate's wife will be allowed to make. As presaged by her *View* appearance, Mrs. Obama returns henceforth to the role of mother and wife. "Her husband's presidential campaign is giving her image a subtle makeover," the *Times* reports. Mrs. Obama remains central to the campaign's performance, but the binaries of gender, not those of civil society, are now firmly structuring her performance on the public stage. The campaign assigns to Mrs. Obama a "tough new chief of staff," whose main task will be "softening her reputation."[57]

Michelle Obama's makeover story is splashed across the cover of *US Weekly*.[58] She and her husband are dressed to the hilt, their heads just touching, smiling proudly and brightly. His hands are clasped around her waist, her right arm rests lightly on his shoulder. Inserted on the cover's lower right corner is their wedding photo. To the left, a headline in large yellow script reads "Why Barack Loves Her." A passage just below, in smaller white script, explains: "She shops at Target, loved *Sex and the City,* and never misses the girls' recitals. The untold romance between a down-to-earth mom and the man who calls her 'my rock.'" The inside story overflows with encomium. "She's warm, funny, and off-the-cuff," avers a campaign fundraiser. "Michelle really wanted to be a mom," warrants Valerie Jarrett, recounting that "she talked about kids when I first met her" in the early 1990s. While the rigors of campaigning mean Mrs. Obama "certainly has found her smart-mom shortcuts," the fact is that "making time for the children is always the priority." *US Weekly* reports details of the couple's courtship. On their first date, Barack "took her to the movies . . . got ice cream . . . and strolled along Lake Michigan." Michelle testifies, "He swept me off my feet." A former mentor informs readers that Mrs. Obama has "always had a classic style, and attracts attention in a room because she's tall and attractive with a good bearing about her." On her wedding day, a friend recalls, "her dress was beautiful" and "she was happy" because "she was marrying the man she loves." The difference from Hillary Clinton could not be more clearly drawn, right down to the question of tea:

> To some, her character is being attacked as Hillary Clinton's was when her husband first ran. The difference? "She's not in the least bit interested in being a co-president," says Michelle's pal of 15 years, Valerie Jarrett, "or participating in policy decisions. That's not her cup of tea. Her first

priority as first lady would be that the girls are OK, and to continue to be the outstanding mother that she is." Barack couldn't agree more. "Michelle is an extraordinary mother to our two girls," the candidate, 46, tells *US*. "When we started out on this campaign, we wanted to make sure that life for our girls would remain as normal as possible, and it is because of Michelle that they are so grounded. Nothing is more important to Michelle than being a good mother, and she works every day to instill in our girls the same values we were raised with."

Michelle Obama's makeover is successful. The *Times* explains that Mrs. Obama has reverted to "a softer, smoother, presence on the trail."[59] No longer a lightning rod for conservative rhetoric and retort, she "continue[s] to refashion her own occasionally harsh public image in warmer tones": "Instead of laying down challenges to her audiences, she solicits their concerns and showers them with empathy. She used to appear on news programs; now she gives interviews to *The View* and *Ladies Home Journal*."[60] Campaign strategists scheduled Mrs. Obama for the role of opening speaker at the Democratic National Convention, placing her "at the center of a multimedia charm offensive that may be the most closely managed spousal rollout in presidential campaign history." The speech is widely and wildly hailed.[61] It is an object lesson in walking civil sphere boundaries in a gendered way. Not putting too fine a point on it, the *Times* observes that Mrs. Obama "touched just a bit on her own career, as a lawyer, community organizer and hospital executive, concentrating instead on her roles as a daughter, a mother, a sister and a wife." It is an extraordinarily gendered role indeed:

> I come here tonight as a sister, blessed with a brother who is my mentor, my protector and my lifelong friend. I come here as a wife who loves my husband and believes he will be an extraordinary president. I come here as a mom whose girls are the heart of my heart and the center of my world—they're the first thing I think about when I wake up in the morning, and the last thing I think about when I go to bed at night. Their future—and all our children's future—is my stake in this election. And I come here as a daughter—raised on the South Side of Chicago by a father who was a blue-collar city worker and a mother who stayed at home with my brother and me. My mother's love has always been a sustaining force for our family, and one of my greatest joys is seeing her integrity, her compassion, and her intelligence reflected in my own daughters.[62]

The master stroke of the speech is Michelle's smooth intertwining of her gendered domestic position with her husband's utopian ambitions for civil repair:

All of us are driven by a simple belief that the world as it is just won't do—that we have an obligation to fight for the world as it should be. That is the thread that connects our hearts. That is the thread that runs through my journey and Barack's journey and so many other improbable journeys that have brought us here tonight, where the current of history meets this new tide of hope. That is why I love this country.... Each of us has something to contribute to the life of this nation. It's a belief Barack shares—a belief at the heart of his life's work.... He'll achieve these goals the same way he always has—by bringing us together and reminding us how much we share and how alike we really are...

The Barack Obama I know today is the same man I fell in love with 19 years ago. He's the same man who drove me and our new baby daughter home from the hospital ten years ago this summer, inching along at a snail's pace, peering anxiously at us in the rearview mirror, feeling the whole weight of her future in his hands, determined to give her everything he'd struggled so hard for himself, determined to give her what he never had: the affirming embrace of a father's love. And as I tuck that little girl and her little sister into bed at night, I think about how one day they'll have families of their own. And one day, they—and your sons and daughters—will tell their own children about what we did together in this election. They'll tell them how this time we listened to our hopes instead of our fears. How this time...we committed ourselves to building the world as it should be. Thank you, God bless you, and God bless America.

Sarah Palin

As Republicans and Democrats head into the final two months of the campaign, the gender-family boundary of the civil sphere become singularly significant. "Both Sides Seeking What Women Want," the *Times* headlines in mid-September, describing a "fierce and complicated competition for the female vote."[63] The distribution of money follows the distribution of cultural interest. As the most diverse and widely watched factual construction of the civil sphere, network nightly news remains the largest recipient of campaign advertising dollars. *Oprah* has now become the second most favored outlet, and for the last month McCain has been buying more time there than the Obama campaign. Oprah Winfrey is America's most popular woman entertainer. Her opinions have great influence, and her daily show is watched religiously by millions of female fans. In recent elections, Democrats have had a decided advantage among female voters. The 2008 contest may well be decided, the *Times* reports, by "how much Democrats can maximize the gender difference and how much Republicans can hold it down."

McCain chooses Sarah Palin "because of her image as a reformer."[64] She can work the binaries of civil society and play the domestic hero that McCain himself has struggled to be. She will also help him walk the boundaries by providing a second path along which McCain might walk in a positive rather than a negative way. The boundary McCain powerfully controls is military, but Palin has considered the Iraq War primarily "as a task that is from God."[65] What the head of the Republican ticket wants from his vice-presidential pick is not foreign credentials but something on the domestic side. He wants to be able to stroll confidently along the gender boundary with Sarah Palin arm in arm at his side. Palin's function is female fusion. She will allow the Republican presidential performance finally to connect with the female citizen audience. "When Gov. Sarah Palin of Alaska was introduced as a vice-presidential pick," the *Times* reports, "she was presented as a magnet for female voters."[66]

Palin's fusion potential resides in her potential to combine Hillary Clinton and Michelle Obama, to bring feminist and feminine together at the same time. She governs the nation's largest territory and has made the giant leap from small-town mayor by running a populist campaign. She is also superwife and mom. "Five children…appeal to soccer moms and the hockey moms. She eats mooseburgers…lots of color…a good personal story…and she's also a bit of a libertarian," reads NBC correspondent Andrea Mitchell from the list she compiled after the Republicans' announcement of Palin's name.[67] In his first reaction, Obama feels compelled to observe that "She will help make the case for the Republicans" and acknowledges her "terrific personal story."[68] Palin's striking physical appearance enhances her extracivil power. Once a genuine beauty queen, she has kept herself up. Her husband, Todd, is sexy and good looking, and she saucily celebrates him as "first dude." The *Times* is right: "No one has ever tried to combine presidential politics and motherhood in quite the way Ms. Palin is doing."[69]

On the third day of the Republican convention, Sarah Palin delivers her much-anticipated acceptance speech.[70] Toward the middle of it she reels off her civil qualifications, her legislation to take back part of big oil's windfall Alaskan profits, and her campaign against the office corruption of local and statewide politicians on both ideological sides. Presenting herself as a force for civil repair, she assures her audience that, while there is "much to like about our opponent, this is a man who has authored two memoirs but never a major piece of reform, not even in the Senate." However, Palin prefers approaching civil sphere issues by connecting them to boundaries, most notably in a gendered way. About energy and environment she speaks as a woman of experience. "Take it from a gal who knows the north coast of Alaska" is how she sassily assures voters there is lots of oil left to be drilled. She addresses war from the more somber perspective of motherhood. "As the mother of one of those troops," she avows, "I'm just one of many moms who will say a prayer every night for our sons and daughters, our men in uniform." She assesses McCain's qualifications as a steadfast woman: "That is exactly the kind of man I want as commander-in-chief."

Highly scripted and many times rehearsed, Palin's performance comes off as natural and spontaneous. Television cameras move between her grinning, hyper-alert, almost mischievous intensity and her adoring audience, whose faces are by turns excited and awestruck. The speech is interrupted frequently by frenzied applause, the energy flowing back and forth between performer and audience as a strikingly successful political ritual is made. It is a prime-time hit, the viewing audience just shy of the record-breaking numbers who witnessed Barack Obama's own performance the week before. Some liberal MSNBC commentators have their doubts, but Chris Matthews, a seasoned veteran of the political wars, says otherwise. He admonishes his colleagues to put their sophisticated prejudices aside. "This is Norma Rae's America," Matthew muses, and in this world "she was very affecting, very appealing"—"she's like that." It is her ability to personify the folk image of the spunky, sassy, earthy American woman that makes the Palin character so dangerous. "She is a torpedo aimed at Barack Obama and Michelle," Matthews proclaims.[71]

When the performance concludes, television correspondents, mostly female, fan out to gauge firsthand audience reaction. Andrea Mitchell asks a middle-aged Midwestern woman why she has responded in such an enthusiastic way. The woman stumbles a few times before finally telling Mitchell why. It is because Palin is "an American woman." Mitchell isn't satisfied and asks her what she means. "She is an American woman," the delegate repeats until Mitchell finally seems to get the point.[72] The next day's newspapers are filled with testimonials about how well Palin walks the gender/civil boundary. "I admire her intelligence and I admire her integrity," confides one woman, pointing to Palin's civil capacities, "but first and foremost she's a mom."[73] She supports her because Palin "has an understanding of what being a mom is." After allowing that "I am not into politics," another woman explains "I'm just going to vote for Trig Van Palin's mom," referring to Mrs. Palin's baby son with Down syndrome. Another woman describes Palin as "a devout Christian with a husband who supports her, who's not afraid to show her baby at her hip." Simply put, "she is everywoman," as still another woman explains.

The danger for Palin and the Republican campaign is that the vice-presidential candidate will be hoisted by her own petard. Planting her feet on each side of the gender/civil sphere boundary, she must be careful not to lose her footing. Yet from the moment she appears on the national scene, she finds herself on shaky grounds—on both sides of the divide. "When Gov. Sarah Palin of Alaska was introduced as a vice-presidential pick," the *Times* observes, she was presented as "the epitome of everymom appeal."[74] Since then, however, "Ms. Palin has set off a fierce argument among women":

> As mothers across the country supervise the season's final water fights and pack book bags, some have voiced the kind of doubts that few male pundits have dared raise on television. With five children, including an infant with Down syndrome and, as the country learned Monday, a pregnant 17-year-old…women [are asking] about whether there are enough hours in the day for her to take on the vice presidency, and whether she is right to try.

"It's the Mommy Wars: Special Campaign Edition," unfolding inside the world of women with virtually no input at all from men. "Within minutes of Friday's announcement that Ms. Palin was joining the Republican ticket, women across the country started flooding blogs devoted to motherhood issues. Throughout the [Labor Day] holiday weekend, at scrapbooking sessions, on hikes and at barbecues, women talked over the candidacy and the issues it raised." Just as older women treated Hillary Clinton's run for the presidency "as a mirror in which to examine their lives," so "with Ms. Palin's entry into the field, a younger generation of women have picked up that mirror, using her candidacy to address the question of just how demanding a job a mother with such intense family obligations should tackle."

Some charge that Palin is not being a good mother, that she is not qualified within the very noncivil field of which she is most proud:

> Plenty of working mothers worry that she is taking on too much. "How is this really going to work?" said Karen Shopoff Rooff, an independent voter, personal trainer and mother of two in Austin, Tex. "I don't care if she's the mother or father; it's a lot to handle," she said, adding that Ms. Palin's lack of national experience would only make her road more difficult. "When I first heard about Palin, I was impressed," said Pamela Moore, a mother of two from Birmingham, Ala. But when Mrs. Moore read that Ms. Palin's special-needs child was three days old when she went back to work, she began questioning the governor's judgment. Partly as a result, she plans to vote for Senator Barack Obama.[75]

Others in this all-female conversation feel that, while Palin may be doing a fine job as mother, she should not take on the additional challenge of high national office:

> Many women, citing their own difficulties with less demanding jobs, said it would be impossible for Ms. Palin to succeed both at motherhood

and in the nation's second-highest-elected position at once. "You can juggle a BlackBerry and a breast pump in a lot of jobs, but not in the vice presidency," said Christina Henry de Tessan, a mother of two in Portland, Ore., who supports Mr. Obama. Her thoughts were echoed by some Republicans, including Anne Faircloth, daughter of former Senator Lauch Faircloth of North Carolina. Being a governor is one thing, Ms. Faircloth said, and Ms. Palin's husband, Todd, seems like a supportive spouse. "But running for the second-highest office in the land is a very different kettle of fish," she said. Many women expressed incredulity— some of it polite, some of it angry—that Ms. Palin would pursue the vice presidency given her youngest son's age and medical condition.... Sarah Robertson, a mother of four from Kennebunk, Me., who was one of the few evangelical Christians interviewed to criticize Ms. Palin, said: "A mother of a 4-month-old infant with Down syndrome taking up full-time campaigning? Not my value set." Ms. Palin is "essentially out-sourcing her duties as a mother for the sake of personal political ambition," said Ms. Robertson, gazing down at her own 6-month old daughter, snuggled against her chest.[76]

A more partisan and cutting charge focuses less on Palin as mother than on her qualifications inside the civil sphere. *US Weekly*, which had rallied in support of Michelle Obama's traditionalism, now splashes a smiling Sarah Palin holding newborn Trig on its cover. In sharp contrast with the Obama cover, however, the caption on the Palin cover is harshly critical. Its giant yellow headline reads, "Babies, Lies, and Scandal," and three charges are bulleted on the cover's upper right side[77]:

- Under attack, admits daughter, 17, is pregnant
- Investigated for firing of sister's ex-husband
- Mom of five: New embarrassing surprises

John McCain and his campaign strategists assert that such criticisms are not a good sample, that most American women feel otherwise, and that Palin will become a powerful collective representation. It is sexist, they charge, to suggest Palin cannot walk the boundaries in a confident and competent way. At the beginning of Palin's performance, most influential conservative commentators agree. For *Times* conservative columnist David Brooks, who describes Palin as "the rarest of creatures," her convention speech is "smart and sassy."[78] The Republican strategist William Kristol, also writing for the *Times*, discloses that he has "followed her career pretty closely" and asserts, "I think she can pull it off."[79] Kristol reminds his readers of Margaret Thatcher's famous advice: "In politics if you want anything said, ask a man. If you want anything done, ask a woman." Whether Sarah Palin can get the job done becomes a turning point in the campaign.

Race Boundary

In the struggle for power, not all boundaries are treated alike. Gender can be explicitly embraced without stigma, and so can the boundary relating to military force. Religion must be approached sideways and economic status mentioned only obliquely. It is hardest of all to mention race. In the mainstream of contemporary American politics, race can just about never be talked about at all.

This is not entirely a bad thing—the nation has a long and shameful history of overt racism—yet it is perplexing. In the world of popular expression, Americans have cast "race free" aside in favor of a benign, often positively charged race consciousness in standards of beauty, movie making, book reading, eating, dressing, singing, and other arenas of expressive life. The movie *White Men Can't Jump* captured this multicultural spirit more than a decade and a half ago. In this multicultural version of civility, Americans talk openly about the particular virtues of different races and even speak freely about their putative vices in joking and ironic ways. Being a fully qualified, paid-up member of the civil sphere, in other words, no longer demands radical assimilation. Difference does not need to be shed as incorporation is achieved but can work as positive evaluation. Civil capacities are expressed in living color, not just in shades of gray.[80] It seems quite another thing when race connects to struggles for democratic control over the state. The needle for threading civil power stands at the dead center of the civil sphere. It cannot be threaded in a multicultural way. Controversy is avoided at all costs. Right-leaning undecided and independent voters can easily be offended. Many continue to harbor uneasy feelings about races that are not colored white.

For a century after the Civil War, the Republican party presented itself as the party of Lincoln, aligning itself with the legacy of the North's decisive battle against Southern "slave power" and the aspirations for racial inclusion encouraged by the Reconstruction that followed in its wake. The Democratic Party's power depended on support from the white South, which meant complicity with Jim Crow and black disenfranchisement. These racial alignments reversed themselves with the emergence of the modern movement for civil rights. Democrats identified with racial inclusion, Republicans more with racial backlash. From the 1960s on, Republicans employed Nixon's "Southern strategy"—antivoting rights, antibusing, antiwelfare, anti-affirmative action, anti-immigration, and pro-white. The strategy largely succeeded. As the white South turned Republican, the GOP increasingly took control of national state power.

Despite Republican government, however, the movement for racial justice continued to gather in strength, and the racial climate in the United States profoundly changed. Civil solidarity broadened. Millions of African Americans experienced dramatic improvement in employment, education, health care, and housing even as a substantial black minority continued to be consigned to the ravages of the underclass. The impact of the majority's transformed social condition was palpable. Working-, middle-, and upper-class African Americans began to seem, in most significant aspects, not so different from whites. A new, more interracial meritocracy emerged from prestigious private and public schools, from elite military academies, and from the Ivy League. Barack and Michelle Obama, and their affluent, postracial world of high-achieving friends, children, and colleagues embodied this change.[81] Deracialization became the goal of American higher education, inside and outside school. Less convinced of white superiority and sensitive to strong moral and legal sanctions against it, conservative Americans became less comfortable with public expressions of racism even if racial feeling lingered in private life. In offices and schools, in businesses and in public places, zero-tolerance signs were posted everywhere. This new racial cultural climate was bolstered by postsixties' immigration flows of Hispanics and Asians that not only shifted racial demographics but also fueled multicultural symbols of cross-racial interest.[82]

Conservatives can no longer play the Southern strategy. Claims on behalf of whiteness no longer appeal to the political center. In 2008 a midsummer *New York Times*/CBS poll reports that 70 percent of whites "are ready to elect a black president."[83] However, the real "news" revealed by the poll, according to the *Times*, is that "racial discord" persists—"even as the nation crosses a racial threshold when it comes to politics." The racial sensibilities of many white Americans remain tender, and conservatives often try to touch them in politically expedient ways:

> Americans are sharply divided by race heading into the first election in which an African-American will be a major-party presidential nominee, with blacks and whites holding vastly different views of Senator Barack Obama, the state of race relations and how black Americans are treated by society. After years of growing racial polarization, much of the divide in American politics is [now] partisan. More than 80 percent of black voters said they had a favorable opinion of Mr. Obama; about 30 percent of white voters said they had a favorable opinion of him.[84]

When Los Angeles Mayor Tom Bradley ran for governor of California in 1982, a significant majority of the city's white voters told pollsters the African American candidate would be getting their vote. Behind the curtain of the voting booth, it turned out that Bradley did not in fact receive them. He lost the race, and the "Bradley effect" was born. In the years since, election experts have debated whether it still holds. Does the new race-free public order mean that race has stopped being a factor in struggles for political power? When white citizens cast secret ballots, will the racial feelings that linger in their private lives have a public effect, or will they vote in a race-free way?

> Political strategists once assumed that polls might well overstate sup-
> port for black candidates, since white voters might be reluctant to admit
> racially tinged sentiments to a pollster. New research has cast doubt on
> that assumption. Either way, the situation is confounding aides on both
> sides, who like everyone else are waiting to see what role race will play in
> the privacy of the voting booth.
> Harold Ickes, a Democrat who was the Rev. Jesse Jackson's senior
> adviser when he ran for president—and who worked in the civil rights
> movement in the 1960s and for Senator Hillary Rodham Clinton in her
> race against Mr. Obama this year—said that when he looked at the polls
> now, he routinely shaved off a point or two from Mr. Obama's number to
> account for hidden racial prejudices. That is no small factor, considering
> that Mr. Obama and Mr. McCain are separated by very thin margins in
> many polls in battleground states....Saul Anuzis, the Republican chair-
> man in Michigan, said he had become accustomed to whispered asides
> from voters suggesting they would not vote for Mr. Obama because he is
> black. "We honestly don't know how big an issue it is," Mr. Anuzis said.[85]

Conservatives Attack

Conservatives know that the version of "civil society'08" is supposed to be race free, but they tried walking its racial boundaries all the same. Publicly, McCain discourages them from doing so, pledging that he will "run a 'respectful' campaign."[86] On occasion, he even intervenes: "Mr. McCain felt forced to distance himself from conservatives who sought to damage his opponent...by running a commercial that played up his ties to his former pastor, who has been criticized as making racially inflammatory remarks." But for years conservative bigwigs have forced McCain to kowtow to gain the nomination, and they are undermining his effort to reclaim his maverick image during the general election campaign. On the matter of race, too, they will have their way.

At the end of June, in a thinly disguised effort to give hope to the struggling Republicans, the *Wall Street Journal* reminds its readers that during the primary season Obama had "suffered a big defeat" at the hands of Ohio voters, where "a large number of voters said race helped drive their vote."[87] The story concludes on the upbeat note that Obama's expected "gains among black voters could be offset by a loss among whites." Still facing discouraging polls a month later, the *Journal* reminds its readers, in what seems a tone of reassurance, that Obama's "lead could prove to be tenuous."[88] The reason is that "the McCain campaign is working each day to nurture doubts about Sen. Obama." One of the Republicans' "overriding themes" is that "Sen. Obama's election would represent too big a risk for voters to take." The biggest risk is Obama's race. Acknowledging that, for now, "only a small fraction of voters say race is a dominant factor in their choice," the *Journal* predicts this percentage will grow higher. True, only "10% said race is the most important factor" in the most recent poll, but that is "up from 6% a month ago." The critical question is just "how much voter uncertainty about Sen. Obama's background involves his race?" The *Journal* answers that "it's an explicit factor for some voters" and presents interviews to back up its opinion:

> Riki Frank, 44, a graphic artist and stay-at-home dad from Auburn, Wash., leans toward Sen. Obama, but hesitates because of his personal background. "I'm a white-bread American. I was raised in Iowa. I got the Midwestern work ethic," says Mr. Frank. "He's a black man. His name— is unique. It's definitely not a Catholic name. He's kind of way off the pattern of the norm of what I grew up with. That's not necessarily a bad thing. Just because I can't relate to the person doesn't mean it's a bad thing."

A 62-year old retired credit clerk, a woman from Oshkosh, Wisconsin, agrees. "I just don't think we're ready for a black president," says Donna Bender, frankly explaining, "I'm prejudiced."

Days later, the *Weekly Standard* writes sympathetically of Geraldine Ferraro's effort to walk the boundaries in a racial way. Once the first female vice-presidential candidate and today a fervent Hillary Clinton supporter, Ferraro trashes Obama's political qualifications: "If Obama were a white man, he would not be in this position." The *Standard* sarcastically praises Ferraro's bitter remark as "this year's most spectacular example of the truth offense," suggesting reverse racism as the only way that "Obama's amazing rise in presidential politics" can be explained.[89]

Weeks after, the *New York Post* headlines: "Barack Brother in Shack Shock— Living in Kenya on $1 a Month and Ashamed to Reveal Who He Is."[90] The story, first published by the Italian *Vanity Fair*, aligns Obama with racial stereotypes about black poverty and degradation and with antidemocratic behavior besides:

> Barack Obama's long-lost half brother has surfaced in Kenya—living like a recluse on less than $1 a day and hiding his family ties. George Hussein Onyango Obama, 25, said he's embarrassed to reveal his

identity—because he makes his home in a 6-by-9-foot hut on the out-
skirts of Nairobi while his world-famous brother is hoping to move into
the White House.... Barack Obama, 47, wrote warmly about his youngest
half brother in his autobiography, describing him as a "beautiful boy with
a rounded head."... Italy's Vanity Fair tracked George Obama down to
the violent Kenyan town of Huruma.... He said he was homeless for 10
years.... His home now, the shanty town of Huruma, is "a tough place,"
he said. "I have seen two of my friends killed," he added. "I have scars
from defending myself with my fists. I am good with my fists."

Days later, the *Washington Times* complains that this story is being "virtually
ignored by the American press."[91] Drawing on the same polluting racial frame, the
account begins "Sen. Barack Obama has a problem: It lives in a hut." Unabashedly,
the right-wing paper expresses its hope that this racial-guilt-by-association will
undermine Barack Obama's performance in the campaign and predicts that "the
inconvenient George Obama could emerge as a compelling character in the freshman senator's carefully edited road-to-the-White-House narrative."

As Labor Day approaches, the conservative media walk the racial boundary to Michigan, where McCain has declared a victory absolutely critical to his
campaign. The *Weekly Standard* begins its account by stressing the racial identity
Obama shares with the story's putative subject, the mayor of Detroit:

He is African American, charismatic, and controversial. Barack Obama's
campaign would prefer that he not attend the Democratic National
Convention. And he is not the Rev. Jeremiah Wright. Meet Detroit mayor
Kwame Kilpatrick [who] has helped turn Democratic-leaning Michigan
into something approaching a tossup state.[92]

Mayor Kilpatrick is then framed as anticivil in the extreme:

The mayor faces eight charges of perjury, misconduct in office, and
obstruction of justice related to his testimony in a Detroit police whistle-
blower lawsuit. Complicating matters, Kilpatrick also faces two charges
of assault for allegedly attacking a detective who was delivering a summons to the house of the mayor's sister.

The *Weekly Standard* lays out two pathways for guilt by association:

Obama praised him as a "great mayor" during a May 2007 appearance
at the Detroit Economic Club. "I'm grateful to call him a friend and
colleague," Obama said. Later, Kilpatrick lauded the Rev. Wright while
introducing him for an April keynote address to the Detroit NAACP
annual dinner. Just a few days later, Wright had a raucous appearance

at the National Press Club in Washington—after which Obama finally disowned his longtime pastor."

A conservative expert tells the *Weekly Standard* that Obama will be mortally wounded by this guilt. "'The fact that Kilpatrick can be linked to Obama/Wright at a time when Kilpatrick has a 2 percent favorable rating outside of Detroit makes the link devastating,' says Michigan GOP pollster Steve Mitchell." The state's voters have not forgotten, according to Mitchell, that "during the primaries, Obama dismissed some white voters by saying they 'cling to their guns or religion.'" The racial feelings of Michigan citizens remain tender, Mitchell states: "Democrats must now worry that white voters in Michigan may well cling to their enormous antipathy toward Kwame Kilpatrick and take it out on Barack Obama." An African American political consultant agrees that "Kilpatrick scares white mainstream voters and could cost Obama Michigan and thus the presidency in a tight election."[93]

Three weeks later, the *Wall Street Journal* elaborates on this upbeat conservative account of Michigan's racial divide. The focus is Macomb County, the blue-collar northern Detroit metro area that has proven hugely important to the outcome of recent presidential campaigns. The publisher of an influential newsletter, *Inside Michigan Politics,* frames Obama's supposed difficulties in Michigan in racial terms: "Obama is still an exotic candidate to this heavily white, socially conservative electorate."[94] For perspective, the *Journal* turns to the reliable Steve Mitchell. The GOP pollster declares his faith in the Bradley effect:

> Will race be a factor in the election? Mr. Mitchell suspects it might be. He points out that in 2006 a ballot initiative to ban racial quotas trailed by substantial margins in polls until Election Day, when it won by a landslide 16%. Support for Mr. Obama may be overstated. If it is, the slim lead he holds in the polls is very tenuous.

Whether the conservatives' decision to walk the racial boundary is "resonating in the national polls" is not entirely clear, according to the *New York Times*. What is clear is that, with less than three weeks left in the campaign, "the McCain campaign's depiction of Barack Obama as a mysterious 'other' with an impenetrable background has found a receptive audience with many white Southern voters."[95] Drawing on extensive interviews, the *Times* finds that "white voters made it clear that they remain deeply uneasy with Mr. Obama—with his politics, his personality and his biracial background":

> "He's neither-nor," said Ricky Thompson, a pipe fitter who works at a factory north of Mobile, while standing in the parking lot of a Wal-Mart store just north of here. "He's other. It's in the Bible. Come as one. Don't create other breeds." Whether Mr. Obama is black, half-black or half-white

often seemed to overshadow the question of his exact stand on particular issues, and rough-edged comments on the subject flowed easily even from voters who said race should not be an issue in the campaign. Many voters seemed to have no difficulty criticizing the mixing of the races—and thus the product of such mixtures—even as they indignantly said a candidate's color held no importance for them. "I would think of him as I would of another of mixed race," said Glenn Reynolds, 74, a retired textile worker in Martinsdale, Va., and a former supervisor at a Goodyear plant. "God taught the children of Israel not to intermarry. You should be proud of what you are, and not intermarry."...Other voters swept past such ambiguities into old-fashioned racist gibes. "He's going to tear up the rose bushes and plant a watermelon patch," said James Halsey, chuckling, while standing in the Wal-Mart parking lot with fellow workers in the environmental cleanup business. "I just don't think we'll ever have a black president."

Conservative efforts to define civil qualities in racial terms also resonate outside the South:

On a recent evening here in eastern Nevada, Cathy Vance, a volunteer for the presidential campaign of Senator Barack Obama, went knocking on doors of voters who had been identified as potential Obama supporters. Elko County is largely rural, with few black residents, located in a state with a dearth of black elected officials. Among the people she found that night was Veronica Mendive, who seemed cautiously warming to Mr. Obama's candidacy. But she had a thought. "I don't want to sound like I'm prejudiced," Ms. Mendive said. "I've never been around a lot of black people before. I just worry that they're nice to your face but then when they get around their own people you must have to worry about they're going to do to you.[96]

Encountering such prejudice, liberal volunteers sometimes feel compelled to equivocate about race and to distance Obama from blackness so he will not be polluted in an anticivil way:

Ms. Vance responded: "One thing you have to remember is that Obama, he's half white and he was raised by his white mother. So his views are more white than black really." She went on to assure Ms. Mendive that she was so impressed with Mr. Obama the person, that she failed to notice the color of his skin anymore.

Another volunteer organizer acknowledges similar encounters:

I'm canvassing for Obama. If this issue comes up, even if obliquely, I emphasize that Obama is from a multiracial background and that his father was an African intellectual, not an American from the inner city. I explain that Obama has never aligned himself solely with African-American interests—not on any issue—but rather has always sought to find a middle ground.

Liberals become increasingly anxious as conservatives persisted in walking the race boundary. By the Fourth of July the *Times* is reporting that "Republicans have been criticized for racially tinged remarks."[97] A month later, the paper acknowledges that "many of the culturally conservative swing voters that Mr. Obama needs...do not get squeamish at the specter of racial polarization."[98] In August, writing in *Slate,* the liberal online magazine, Jacob Weisberg asserts, "If Obama Loses: Racism Is the Only Reason McCain Might Beat Him."[99] In late September, Nicholas Kristof suggests that, because "it's not acceptable to express reservations about a candidate's skin color...discomfort about race is sublimated into concerns about whether Mr. Obama is sufficiently Christian."[100] The next day, Brent Staples, an influential African American member of the *Times* editorial staff, mounts a scathing assault on what the newspaper headlines as the "Language of Race."[101] In the old South, Staples points out, civil qualities "viewed as laudable among whites were seen as positively mutinous when practiced by people of color." For example, blacks "who looked white people squarely in the eye—and argued with them about things that mattered—were declared a threat to the racial order." Today, while "no sane person would openly express" such "obsession with black subservience," it has emerged as "a persistent theme in the public discourse since Barack Obama became a plausible candidate for the presidency." A Georgia Republican, Representative Lynn Westmoreland, has called the Obamas "uppity," and a Republican from Kentucky, Representative Geoff Davis, warned "that boy's finger does not need to be on the button." A McCain commercial accuses Obama of being "disrespectful" to the white female candidate, Sarah Palin:

> The throwback references that have surfaced in the campaign suggest that Republicans are fighting on racial grounds, even when express references to race are not evident. In a replay of elections past, the G.O.P. will try to leverage racial ghosts and fears without getting its hands visibly dirty.

The danger for Democrats is that the civil capacities of their candidate—the very qualities that have made him into a collective representation of democracy—will be undermined by their association with his still stigmatized race. Obama "is always an utterance away from a statement—or a phrase—that could transform him in a campaign ad from the affable, rational and racially ambiguous candidate into the archetypical angry black man who scares off the white vote."

Obama's Answer

Race marks the most difficult boundary of Obama's civil sphere campaign. "In Obama's campaign for the Presidency," observes David Remnick, the most assiduous and insightful of Obama's biographers, this "most persistent of all American problems was a matter of intricate complexity from the first day."[102] Christopher Edley, an African-American friend of Obama's who had been one of his law school professors, remarks that "race isn't rocket science, it's harder."[103]

Conservatives regard Obama's campaign for civil power as a cipher for race politics, and some white and black leftists see it in the same way. In an influential cover story at the very beginning of Obama's candidacy, *Rolling Stone* locates his "radical roots" in an angry racial consciousness: "This is as openly radical a background as any significant American political figure ever emerged from, as much Malcolm X as Martin Luther King Jr."[104] Black leftists also often insist on seeing him racially, but for them Obama is playing white. An African American politician in Chicago tells the *Times* that Obama is nothing more than a "white man in black face."[105] Jesse Jackson publicly urges Obama to "stop acting like he's white"[106] and, in what he thought was a private conversation preceding a news interview at Fox television, accuses him of "talking down to black people." He adds, "I want to cut his nuts off."[107] Black columnist Stanley Crouch's remarks are less physical but equally acerbic: "When black Americans refer to Obama as 'one of us,' . . . I do not know what they are talking about."[108]

Obama pushes back against such racial identification not only from the beginning of his campaign for the presidency but also from the moment, long before, when he first begins thinking about a public career. His white mother raises him outside the African American community while instructing him, as he recalls in his autobiography, that "to be black was to be the beneficiary of a great inheritance, a special destiny, [of] glorious burdens that only we were strong enough to bear."[109] Obama flirts with racial militancy during his freshman and sophomore years at Occidental College in Los Angeles. However, in the first political speech of his life, the young activist issues a ringing call for cross-racial solidarity in the name of universal claims:

> There's a struggle going on [and] it's happening an ocean away. But it's a struggle that touches each and every one of us. Whether we know it or not. Whether we want it or not. A struggle that demands we choose sides. Not between black and white. Not between rich and poor. No—it's

a harder choice than that. It's a choice between dignity and servitude. Between fairness and injustice. Between commitment and indifference. A choice between right and wrong.[110]

As a community organizer in Chicago, Obama turns profoundly against racial categorization both as public principle and political strategy. "My identity might begin with the fact of my race, but it didn't, couldn't, end there," he writes in *Dreams from My Father*.[111] The communities he sees himself fighting for "had to be created, fought for, tended like gardens," and "they expanded or contracted with the dreams of men." The "community I imagined was still in the making," and it was "built on the promise that the larger American community, black, white, and brown, could somehow redefine itself."[112]

As an adult, Obama follows the well-trodden pathway of hyphenated Americanism. Privately, he explores race as an ethnic identity, joining an African American church and marrying Michelle Robinson, whom he later praises, at a critical moment in his political life, as having "the blood of slaves and slave-holders" in her veins.[113] Yet even this private world is mixed race—extended family, friends, and integrated neighborhoods—and Obama works in white-dominated law firms and universities:

> As the child of a black man and a white woman, someone who was born
> in the racial melting pot of Hawaii, with a sister who's half Indonesian
> but who's usually mistaken for Mexican or Puerto Rican, and brother-
> in-law and niece of Chinese descent, with some blood relatives who
> resemble Margaret Thatcher and others who could pass for Bernie Mac,
> so that family get-togethers over Christmas take on the appearance of a
> UN General Assembly meeting, I've never had the option of restricting
> my loyalties on the basis of race, or measuring my worth on the basis
> of tribe.[114]

In his emerging public life in politics, moreover, Obama strongly opposes identity politics, insisting progressive politics demands that racial, religious, and class differences be subsumed under broader democratic solidarities. He attacks the politics of difference as anticivil, whether on the left or the right, advocating "reconciliation over rancor."[115]

It is in this spirit that Obama defuses the Reverend Wright crisis, which threatens to overwhelm his primary campaign. In March 2008, conservatives finally manage to get snippets from Wright's angry, often antiwhite speeches into the media mainstream, and the video creates an explosion of racial outrage. "In the past week," the *Times* reported, "videotaped snippets of the incendiary race rhetoric of Mr. Obama's longtime pastor, the Rev. Jeremiah A. Wright Jr., seemed on the verge of tainting Mr. Obama with the stereotype he had carefully avoided: angry black politician." Declaring that "race is an issue that I believe this nation cannot afford to ignore right now," Obama addresses the race issue head-on in a nationally televised speech, also viewed online in its entirety (37+ minutes) more than 6.2 million times:[116]

> Mr. Obama's address came more than a year into a campaign conceived and conducted to appear to transcend the issue of race, to try to build a broad coalition of racial and ethnic groups favoring change. In the issues he has emphasized and the language he has used, as well as in the way he has presented himself, he has worked to elude pigeonholing as a black politician. He has been criticized as "not black enough" and "too black."[117]

The "anger and bitterness" expressed by "the men and women of Reverend Wright's generation," Obama explains, must be placed into the context of painful memories of racial "humiliation." Understanding the reasons for their bitterness and anger, however, is very different from justifying it. Obama condemns Wright's remarks as divisive and anticivil. He states that they are contrary to the idea that is "seared directly into my genetic makeup—the idea that this nation is more than the sum of its parts—that out of many, we are truly one." When we face severe challenges, he tells his mixed-race audience, we must not "retreat into our respective corners." Instead, we must "be able to come together and solve challenges like health care, or education, or the need to find good jobs for every American":[118]

> The speech was…hopeful, patriotic, quintessentially American—delivered against a blue backdrop and a phalanx of stars and stripes. Mr. Obama invoked the fundamental values of equality of opportunity, fairness, social justice. He confronted race head-on, then reached beyond it to talk sympathetically about the experiences of the white working class and the plight of workers stripped of jobs and pensions.[119]

Once bewitched by the eloquent and fervent race consciousness of Malcolm X, in this defining moment of his public adulthood Obama will not walk the racial boundary in this bitter way. He follows in the footsteps of Malcolm's nemesis, Martin Luther King Jr., endorsing the martyred preacher's "vision of an America where we are united not by the color of our skin but by the content of our character." King had fused with the democratic aspirations of Northern white citizens by fighting for a more purely civil society. Forty years later, Obama wishes to do the same.

Throughout the general election that follows, Obama insists the struggle for democratic power must be race free. In the face of Republican innuendo, he condemns "slice-and-dice politics"[120] and insists that "low-road politics distract voters from real issues."[121] Such interventions, however, are offered up only occasionally. As conservatives venture carefully along the racial boundary of civil society, Obama must be cautious not to protest too much. He pushes back, but if he does so adamantly conservatives will accuse him of inserting race into the campaign. During a difficult period in late June, Obama tells a fundraiser: "We know what kind of campaign they're going to run. They're going to try to make you afraid. They're going to try to make you afraid of me. 'He's young and inexperienced and he's got a funny name. And did I mention he's black?'"[122] Conservative politicians and the media jump on these remarks. Rather than acknowledging they are themselves walking the boundary, they accuse Obama himself of "playing the race card." The *Wall Street Journal* declares that "at no time" has McCain "said anything remotely touching on his opponent's race."[123] If true, this declaration remains disingenuous, for McCain's conservative supporters have raised the flag in every conceivable way. Six weeks after this incident, facing the onslaught of McCain's anticelebrity campaign, Obama once again asserts that Republicans are walking the race boundary: "So what they're going to try to do is make you scared of me. You know, 'He's not patriotic enough, he's got a funny name,' you know, 'He doesn't look like all those other presidents on the dollar bills." Once again, Republicans are furious and self-righteous, and once again they condemn Obama for injecting race into what they claim is a perfectly civil campaign. The *New York Post* laments that, up until now, Obama had always "talked of the goodness he sees in people—even in whites" and that unlike so many other black public figures, Obama had "refused to allow race to define him."[124] Now he has engaged in "racial calumny" and "committed the worst blunder of the campaign." He is violating the basic rules of the civil sphere; what he says is "completely unfair." Scrambling to defend himself, Obama denies accusing McCain of racism. Lindsey Graham then takes civil umbrage. The southern senator, a McCain confidant, denounces Obama's denial as a lie, and Republicans demand an apology. Obama feels compelled to offer one. He publicly declares he does not believe McCain to be racist.[125] Obama is boxed in. Because he is African American, he is an object of persistent racial questioning from the Republican side. Because he is African American, he cannot make an issue out of it. He cannot fight his way of this box, but he can still win the game.

Foreign Boundary

There is a boundary of the civil sphere that seems physical. The territory of the nation-state separates those inside, who may become full members of civil society, from those outside, for whom citizenship is never on offer. Because of its physicality, this boundary must be materially marked and defended by force if necessary. Even the most democratic society sustains military might by organizing and financing armies that guard its borders, prevent invasion, and project the threat of violence, if possible, far and wide. Whoever wins the democratic struggle for power represents not only the civil sphere but also the nation and the state. The winner sits atop not only a civil bureaucracy but also a command structure that monopolizes violence and organizes military attack. If John Locke is the patron saint of democracy, offering lessons on civil tolerance, Thomas Hobbes describes the "war of all against all," which characterizes relations between states, where might too often makes right and where Leviathans usually rule.

On McCain's Watch

At a defining moment of McCain's candidacy, when he first secures the Republican nomination in March 2008, the Republican deploys a military metaphor to define the presidency, vowing he will "concentrate our efforts on the challenges that will confront America on our watch."[126] His message is clear: The principal threat to civil society is foreign violence, and presidents must first and foremost be able to make war. We are in a "long and difficult fight with violent extremists who despise us," the Republican candidate warns. Because these extremists possess "weapons we dare not allow," he explains, "our most vital security interests" are at stake, which is why America is "at war in two countries." The job of "the next president," he concludes, is to "lead an effort to restructure our military, our intelligence, our diplomacy and all relevant branches of government to combat Islamic extremism." In reporting on this speech, the *Weekly Standard* notes that "McCain did mention the economy and health care and jobs," but "it was clear...he saw a president's duties as commander in chief as more important than any other role."

If the president's duties are not primarily civil but military, then McCain's road to power is clear, for he is more qualified for this job. The Republican candidate makes difference in this way time and again during the campaign. His opponent, he asserts, "does not have the experience or judgment to be commander in chief."[127] Obama seems to think the whole world is a civil society, McCain complains, ignoring the Hobbesian brutality that rules the world outside the United States. "He continues to state his desire and mission to sit down and negotiate with some of the most despotic and cruel dictators in the world."[128] Obama has fallen for the idea that civil negotiation can replace military force. Such an inward focus—on the prospects for domestic reform—will weaken the nation's physical boundaries and ultimately bring military defeat. Acknowledging that "both candidates pledge to end to the war and bring our troops home," McCain declares that "the great difference—the great difference—is that I intend to win it first."[129]

Obama has promised to withdraw U.S. troops from Iraq 16 months after his election, but this "would be an act of surrender in a war we are winning."[130] On the first day of the Republican convention, President Bush walks the military boundary in a similar way. A president's biggest job is "protecting our country," and on this issue "the American people are going to have a clear choice." Americans should support McCain because "he knows what it takes to defeat our enemies."[131] Later in the convention, Sarah Palin warns her listeners about McCain's Democratic opponent: "This is a man who can give an entire speech about the wars America is fighting and never use the word 'victory,' except when he's talking about his own campaign."[132]

Obama Antiwar

When Obama begins his campaign for the presidency, he separates himself from the military boundary in a radical way. It is not only that he presents himself as a domestic hero. He also defines himself as a peace candidate vehemently opposed to the Iraq War, the military conflict that brought the Republican administration to its knees. Obama's antiwar position rests on civil principle. Invading Iraq violates ideas about honesty and truth because Republican leaders lied about WMDs. They violated other constraints of civil society as well by torturing military prisoners and flaunting domestic liberties in the name of "the war on terror." Obama commits himself to fighting terrorism, but he rejects the "war" on terrorism as overly military and as a dangerously antidemocratic ploy. Besides, cutting the defense budget will free up more funds for domestic issues.

This antiwar position proves a winning strategy in a nation exhausted by years of fighting and thousands of military deaths—with no end in sight. Hillary Clinton tries to walk the military boundary against Obama by warning he will not be prepared for the "3 A.M. phone call" announcing a military crisis in the dark of night. Obama accuses her of the "politics of fear" and pounds her for having supported an invasion based on lies.[133] Later, when McCain reiterates Clinton's accusations, Obama replays the tape. The former professor of constitutional law, wrapping himself in the mantle of nonviolence and civil rights, concentrates on calling for domestic change. After 9/11, he chose not to wear an American flag pin,[134] and he stands accused—wrongly but revealingly—of not putting his hand over his heart for the national anthem and the Pledge of Allegiance.[135] In response to such accusations, Obama publicly rejects "the use of patriotism as a political sword or a political shield."[136] An advisor on national security, the former general and NATO commander Wesley Clark, makes a case for separating civil and military qualifications in a sarcastic, cutting, and controversial way: "I don't think riding in a fighter plane and getting shot down is a qualification to be president."[137]

Obama Reconsiders

By June, when Obama is confident he has secured the nomination, he takes a deep breath and looks ahead to his next five months of campaigning against McCain. He is ahead on points, but the chances he will score a knockout are slight. Can he really afford to let his opponent walk the military boundary all by himself and in an unfettered way? There is also the concern that the once-unhappy situation in Iraq is changing. The "surge" of U.S. troops has calmed the conflict and taken imminent danger off the campaign table, but it also cuts the other way. Obama wanted to withdraw from Iraq long before and has always maintained that Iraq is doomed to be a losing fight. The surge is McCain's idea. Might centrist Americans conclude that McCain, not Obama, got the war right? Does Iraq's new calm make it more reasonable to stay, to remove troops more slowly, or even to leave some significant presence behind? General David Petraeus, freshly appointed as Iraq commander, devises and implements the surge. He is now widely represented as a great military leader. Can Obama, the quintessential civilian, go head to head with the nation's newest military hero in an argument over strategy in Iraq?

As Obama contemplates the future, he seems to realize that his antiwar position cannot be sustained. Carefully but unmistakably he alters the public perception of his ideas about foreign policy and military affairs, just as he does, during that postprimary season, on a number of other issues besides. The Democrat makes it plain that he is not against war and that it is sometimes what civil societies must wage. He reminds Americans of what he actually said at the antiwar rally in Chicago in October 2002, when he had first warned against invading Iraq:

> [A]lthough this has been billed as an anti-war rally, I stand before you as someone who is not opposed to war in all circumstances.... What I am opposed to is a dumb war. What I am opposed to is a rash war.... That's what I'm opposed to. A dumb war. A rash war. A war based not on reason but on passion, not on principle but on politics.[138]

Obama continues to criticize McCain's military policies, but his grounds for doing so shift. The problem with Iraq is that this "war of choice...has not made the nation safer."[139] Rather than being wrong in principle, the Iraq War was stupidly conceived. He has never believed that all troops should be withdrawn, Obama now insists, and he offers what is largely a pragmatic reason for the troops he wants to withdraw. They should be removed so that the United States can wage more war in another place. During an Obama presidency, the candidate promises, the military will rev up its Afghanistan fight, not wind it down, as the Bush administration had wrongly done. Affixing the flag pin firmly to his label and placing his hand firmly over his heart, the man who would be president declares in a widely reported television ad that he has "a deep and abiding faith in the country I love."[140]

Obama's Excellent Adventure

Obama cannot actually become a military hero, but he can create a drama that will allow him to walk on a military stage and perform the role of foreign policy leader to audiences inside and outside the territorial boundaries of the state. The campaign staff announce that their candidate is planning a major foreign trip. He will visit Iraq, Kuwait, and Afghanistan, where he will meet with troops and consult with U.S. military commanders and political leaders. Then, after visiting Israel and Jordan, Obama will travel to Europe, engaging with America's most powerful allies in Berlin, Paris, and London. "The trip is intended," the New York Times declares in its front-page coverage of Obama's first day in Afghanistan, "to build impressions...about his ability to serve on the world stage in a time of war."[141]

On Saturday, July 19, the candidate, his campaign staff, foreign policy team, and hundreds of trailing news reporters arrive in Afghanistan. Obama is entering into a new space, one that, he hopes, will allow him to become a mythical hero in another way. He may not be the warrior Achilles, but he can still audition for other strong man roles. Declaring that Obama will have to "swiftly and convincingly perform the political equivalent of the Labors of Hercules," New York Times columnist Maureen Dowd exclaims that "cleaning the Augean stables in a single day seems like a cinch compared with navigating the complexities of Afghanistan, Iraq, Israel, Palestine and Jordan in a few short days."[142] This next stage of Obama's "amazing presidential Odyssey," Dowd continues, confronts the Democrat with a "perilous quest." It is not only physically dangerous, but it is extremely risky in a political sense as well. The trip will be highly public, and the candidate's performance cannot be scripted in advance. Writing that "His every move is receiving intensive attention at home and abroad," the Times evokes an audience raptly watching a high wire act performed without a safety net underneath.[143] Obama is walking the foreign boundary for the first time, and there are many chances for him to misstep along the way. "It carries political risk," the Times explains. "[I]f Mr. Obama makes a mistake," it will be visible for every audience far and wide, for "the three broadcast network news anchors will be along."[144] If Obama stumbles, his bid for the presidency will be at stake. From such dangerous quests are heroes made.

Obama pulls off a series of deft performances, acting in meaningful and coherent roles, and thoroughly fusing with his foreign and local audiences at every step along the way. In Iraq, he is photographed in a helicopter beside General Petraeus, who provides him with an aerial tour. The civil and the military leader appear deeply engaged as they look down on the war-torn but possibly hopeful urban scene below. Beneath this front-page photo, the *Times* headlines "For Obama, the First Step Is Not a Misstep," reporting "it is difficult to find a picture of Mr. Obama not surrounded by American commanders or troops."[145] Offering a progress report on the Democrat's quest, the *Times* reports that, "after a day spent meeting with Iraqi leaders and American military commanders, Mr. Obama seemed to have navigated one of the riskiest parts of a weeklong international trip without a noticeable hitch." The meetings provide Obama "a new opportunity to blunt attacks," for they offer the Democrat "a measure of credibility" on the world stage. The big news is that after "a weekend of dispute about precisely what Mr. Maliki was suggesting," the Iraqi government finally "left little doubt" that it favors Obama's own Iraq war plan over President Bush's. A quest is determined as much by fate as effort. "Whether by chance or by design," the *Times* explains, Prime Minister Maliki transforms Obama into a far-sighted foreign policy leader, for his policy on Iraq is "suddenly aligned with what the Iraqis themselves now increasingly seem to want." Theater more than fate is at play when Obama seizes the moment by declaring that he rejects "a rigid timetable for withdrawal that ignore[s] changing conditions." He is now a man who can walk the military boundary. He is creating an effective drama indeed.

When Obama arrives in Israel, the *Times* continues to employ the framework of quest. Visiting the Jewish-Palestinian conflict is "a perilous challenge," and it will be immensely difficult "to avoid missteps."[146] Yet Obama is greeted "with a fanfare typically orchestrated for a visiting head of state." The paper reports that, "flanked by a large retinue of advisers [and] tailed by camera crews, Mr. Obama created something of a spectacle on local television, in newspapers and even among the government ministers who jockeyed to join in the attention."[147] Israel's most revered living political figure, President Shimon Peres, declares that his fondest wish is for a "great president of the United States—that is the greatest promise for the U.S. and the rest of the world." The *Times* assigns Alessandra Stanley, its renowned television critic, the job of evaluating Obama's adventure as its Middle Eastern phase comes to an end. She sees a dramatic aesthetic creation, concluding that a powerful symbolic impression of presidential power has been made:

> In the shadow of the ancient Temple of Hercules in Amman, Jordan, Mr. Obama solemnly described his vision for peace in the region while standing at a lectern, the Middle East sprawling out behind him. Reporters were cordoned in front of him like the White House press corps.... All three cable news networks carried Mr. Obama's news conference live and in full.... It's not pro-Obama bias in the news media that's driving the effusion of coverage, it's the news: Mr. Obama's weeklong tour of war zones and foreign capitals is noteworthy because it is so unusual to see a presidential

candidate act so presidential overseas. Mr. Obama looks supremely confident and at home talking to generals and heads of state...

Mr. Obama's stops in Afghanistan, Iraq and Jordan provided arresting video of the candidate being mobbed by American troops, surveying terrain by helicopter alongside Gen. David H. Petraeus and holding talks with Prime Minister Nuri Kamal al-Maliki of Iraq and King Abdullah of Jordan. When posing for an official photograph with a foreign leader, Mr. Obama often places his hand paternally on the other man's arm, subliminally signaling that though a visitor, he is the real host of the meeting. Touring ruins of the Citadel in Amman, Mr. Obama strode confidently with his jacket crooked over his shoulder in classic Kennedy style. He also practiced statesmanly restraint, telling reporters in Amman that he wouldn't criticize his opponent while abroad.... It's a very short trip by diplomatic standards, but it's a long one for television.[148]

Obama's quest takes him next to Europe. In Berlin, "on a perch steeped in history,"[149] he "delivered a tone poem to American and European ideals and shared history," and the response is "emotional, responsive, replete with the sense of hope." A 65-year-old man from the former East Germany relates that this American reminds him of Martin Luther King Jr., whom he had seen on his visit 45 years before: "I thought, here is someone coming from the same place." In a story titled "In Berlin, Oratory with Echoes," the *Times* offers detailed illustrations of how Obama's speech iterates iconic passages from great rhetorical performances of yore:

Any presidential hopeful introducing himself to a German-speaking crowd might be tempted to draw on the eloquence of Shakespeare, the wisdom of Lincoln, the idealism of Franklin D. Roosevelt, the youthful energy of John F. Kennedy or the grit of Ronald Reagan. Better yet: why not invoke them all? This is what Senator Barack Obama seems to have done in the speech he gave on Thursday before a crowd of 200,000 in the Tiergarten.[150]

Flying on to Paris, Obama is "warmly embraced" at the Elysée Palace by President Nicolas Sarkozy, who asserts that the Obama candidacy presents "a bold moment to change the United States' image around the world":[151]

"The America that France loves is an America that's farsighted, that has ambitions, great debates, strong personalities," Mr. Sarkozy told reporters. "We need an America that is present, not absent."... The newspaper Le Monde published the speech Mr. Obama gave one night earlier in Berlin. "The French love the Americans," Mr. Sarkozy said with a grin, praising Mr. Obama, and added, "the French have been following him with passion."

As the curtain comes down on Obama's excellent adventure, his performative ambition by now plain to see, the liberal media judged the dramatic trip a success. *The Week* magazine describes how "Obama visited Afghanistan and the Middle East, using the cinematic backdrop of war zones and grand diplomatic venues to create a presidential aura."[152] In the Sunday *New York Times'* "The Week in Review," Frank Rich, drama reviewer turned op-ed columnist, writes of "Obama's magical mystery tour through Old Europe and two war zones" as a "media-made fairy tale" that "was perfectly timed to reap the whirlwind."[153] The *New York Post* had predicted as the tour began that it was "not going to be all rousing cheers and adoring accolades."[154] But it was. One of the media's favorite political scientists, Larry Sabato, declared Obama "absolutely has to avoid any major gaffes that will haunt him in November," and the Democrat had. Obama rarely stumbled as he walked the foreign boundary, his acting partners were enthusiastic, and the press coverage respectful and often admiring. For performances to be successful, however, good acting and favorable mass mediation are not enough. There remains the matter of reception. "Despite a private series of dawn-to-dusk meetings," the *Times* reminds its readers, "the audience for the trip...clearly was the American electorate as much as the foreign leaders," with Obama seeking "to reassure voters of his capacity to serve on the international stage."[155] In the end, it is not whether Obama's performance has been extraordinary that counts, but how it is received back home. Foreign audiences adore him. Have his performances fused with American audiences at the same time?

Republicans' Plight

Republicans try to block this fusion with their well-rehearsed but by now rather tired accusation that Obama simply is not qualified to walk the foreign boundary in a competent way. When Obama decides not to visit U.S. troops in Germany—after the Pentagon, supposedly fearing "politicization," places restrictions on what he might do and say—McCain accuses him of exhibiting more concern for photo ops than patriotism. The Republican's staff create an Internet ad: "He made time to go to the gym, but canceled a visit with wounded troops. Seems the Pentagon wouldn't allow him to bring cameras."[156] McCain tells ABC, "If I had been told by the Pentagon that I couldn't visit these troops, and I was there and wanted to be there, I guarantee you, there would have been a seismic event." Conservative pundits make an issue of Obama's "adoring post-national hosts."[157] Rather than defending America's interests, they complain, Obama has presented himself as a "citizen of the world." He has used the pronoun "we," pretending that Americans and Europeans share some higher, supranational ties. This misguided internationalism "could prove fatal to our national sovereignty," the *Washington Times* opines. These complaints fall on deaf ears. Whatever Obama's lack of actual experience, he embarked on a remarkable quest that symbolically demonstrated his foreign and military bona fides in a powerful and dramatic performance.

When Obama is away, McCain tries attracting the attention of America's citizen audience to his program for domestic change. With the stage to himself for the first time, he intends to show himself hard at work on local American needs. He tells reporters he will be "campaigning across the heartland of America and talking about the issues" that make life difficult for the average American today. "That, at least, was the plan," quips one of the reporters accompanying McCain.[158] It's not a problem with the script but with making it walk and talk. The Republican's performance cannot take flight from domestic ground. If the McCain action figure is powerful, the McCain domestic figure cannot inflate. "As his Democratic rival" soared in Europe, "Mr. McCain went on an awkward grocery-shopping trip with a mother and two children in a Pennsylvania market and held a news conference at a dairy case." As Obama "spoke to a rousing crowd of more than 200,000 in Berlin on Thursday, Mr. McCain had a bratwurst lunch with the owner of a car dealership and other local business people in Columbus." The emerging contrast is not what the Republican campaign has intended to make:

> At every stop that was supposed to be about the economy, energy or health care, Mr. McCain faced questions about Mr. Obama's foreign trip, and spent as much time reacting to his opponent as pushing his own domestic plans. [He] did not hide his frustration.... "I am again deeply disappointed that Senator Obama would not recognize the fact that the surge has succeeded," Mr. McCain said in typical, now-daily comments before the refrigerated case of shredded cheese in Bethlehem, Pa.

The old navy flyboy is brought to ground by the dreary ordinariness of the domestic scene. McCain is "like the wallflower at an international political dance," the *Times* records, but he is resigned—"'It is what it is,' Mr. McCain said with a hint of exasperation." However, "Mr. McCain's comments were mild compared with the bleak mood and frustration on the part of his advisers."[159] "It is safe to say that Mr. McCain... is not having a spectacular week," the *Times* notes, adding "the mood is not good at [Republican] headquarters in Arlington, Va."[160] In response, McCain's close advisor Mark Salter professes "he was not alarmed," suggesting "that Mr. McCain had spent the week in battleground states meeting with people who actually vote in American elections." Salter sees fused performance: "I think he's getting his message out.... It's John McCain on energy and the economy." Ed

Rollins, the conservative strategist and cable pundit who organized Mike Hucka-bee's nomination campaign, sharply disagrees. Rollins has been around Republi-can politics since the Reagan salad days:

> McCain is having a disastrous week. It would have been better if he had just kept a low profile and stayed out of the limelight. He got dragged into making a lot of stupid comments about Obama, and there's been this tremendous contrast with the visuals, which is what a lot of people pay attention to.

Hero's Shadow

Even as McCain fails miserably to mount his counterperformance, the media report what seems at first an inexplicable fact. The polls do not indicate any bounce, any shift of opinion to the Democratic side. "There has been no detectable flurry of swing voters rushing to Obama," according to the *Times*. If the civil sphere's center has not been moved by Obama's foreign trip and the Republicans can figure out why, it may allow them finally to parry Obama's thrusts and to seize the lead in the final phase of the campaign. The *Times* reports that there is "one area where Republicans [do] see an opportunity, if only a glimmer of one."[161] The opportunity is the other side of their opponent's success. Insofar as Obama achieves heroic stature in his foreign perfor-mance, to that degree he casts a shadow that haunts his success. The taint of hubris is on everybody's mind as the Obama odyssey proceeds. "Mr. Obama said he knew the risks of 'flying too close to the sun,'" the *Times* reports, recording the Democrat's allu-sion to the mythological Icarus, whose wax wings melted when he soared higher in the sky than the gods allowed. Obama's "confidence has swelled since he claimed the Democratic nomination early last month," and it is certainly on display as he blithely, almost preternaturally sweeps past the obstacles that mark his quest. The question is, Does he "cross a political line" by "coming across as too presumptuous?" This, the *Times* reveals, is something that "he and his advisors quietly feared."

In his radio address at week's end, McCain feigns to confess that "with all the breathless coverage from abroad, and with Senator Obama now addressing his speeches to 'the people of the world,' I'm starting to feel a little left out." He suggests, "maybe you are too."[162] If, despite the foreign trip's dramatic pyrotechnics, many critical swing voters maintain their distance from Obama, it will be his hubris that is to blame. By suggesting he has been put off, too, McCain hopes to gain the cen-ter's sympathy and identification. If Republicans attack Obama's hubris, they might be able to roll out a new and improved performance even if McCain's maverick and military images are splintered and neutralized and must ultimately be left behind. Republicans can still work the binaries in a negative way.

PART III

Victory and Defeat

CHAPTER SEVEN

Celebrity Metaphor

IN LATE JUNE, PEGGY NOONAN MAKES THIS PREDICTION: "THE campaign will grind along until a series of sharp moments…Things will move along, Mr. Obama in the lead. And then, just a few weeks out from the election, something will happen."[1] The wily wordsmith of Reagan's presidency knows the democratic struggle for power is not determined by structures. Only after it's all over do social scientists and pundits claim the contest was predetermined to come out in this or that way. While certainly oriented to economic situations and cultural traditions, the struggle for power is not directed by them. It is a flow, a stream of meaning making. Rather than grinding along, this coursing river hurtles steeply downward from the mountaintop of the contest's beginning to the finish line in the valley below. Candidates feverishly ply their campaign ships along this fiercely churning current, struggling to keep direction, sometimes just to stay afloat. As they navigate the rushing water, giant boulders suddenly emerge, seemingly at random, blocking their path. The political skippers try desperately to maneuver around these looming impediments. Their efforts to do so mark the turning points of campaigns. The electoral stream divides, one branch gushes onward to triumphant victory, the other peters out to deflating defeat.

Three boulders emerge as the turning points in 2008: celebrity metaphor, Palin effect, and financial crisis. The first emerges at the end of July and showers radioactive dust over the Democratic campaign until, five weeks later, Obama demonstrates his hero bona fides at his convention speech. Immediately afterward, the newly hopeful Democratic campaign is knocked off balance again by the energy burst of Sarah Palin as she explodes on the national scene. Then, even as ship Obama succeeds in righting itself—the half-life of the Palin effect is shorter than celebrity metaphor—the financial crisis looms suddenly like a giant iceberg threatening to capsize both campaigns. The Republican craft lists dangerously, the Democrats' hardly founders. By early October, the rushing stream of the election has divided, marking the effective end of the 2008 campaign.

The next three chapters explain these turning points as struggles over meaning, revealing their complex symbolic structuring, the twists and turns of each side's agonistic performance, and the continuously shifting prospects for political success. While working through this thicket of qualitative interpretation, it is helpful to have a condensed overview of changing public opinion over the course of the entire general election campaign. This is a quantitative, not a qualitative, task, one that depends on asking statistically representative samples of Americans the same simple and repeated yes-and-no questions, correlating their answers mathematically, and spreading the results over some extended time. By this means, national polls propose to represent the voice of the civil sphere, and they do so in an influential, if relatively thin and restrictive way. There are many national

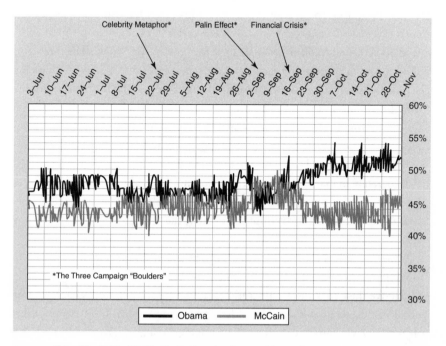

FIGURE 7.1. The Poll of Polls, Daily Results, June 3–November 4

polling organizations, however, and each asks slightly different questions, samples at different intervals, and weights their samples in different ways. The "poll of polls" brings together what I consider the best measurements of national public opinion from June until Election Day. The findings can be illustrated graphically in different ways (see figures 7.1, 7.2, and 7.3).[2]

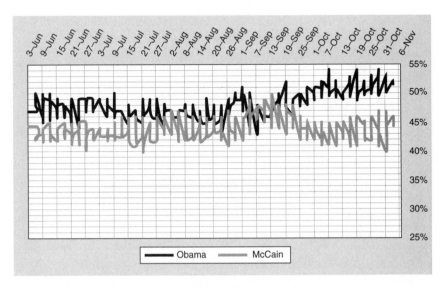

FIGURE 7.2. The Poll of Polls, 3-day Intervals, June 3–November 4

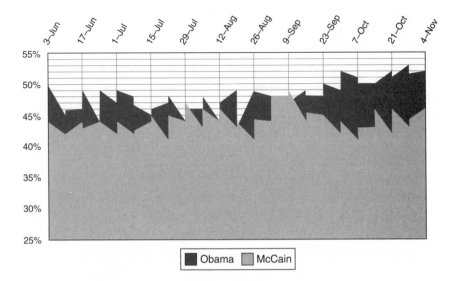

FIGURE 7.3. The Poll of Polls, 7-day Intervals

Factors and Performances

In late September, as McCain confronts the financial iceberg, the *Wall Street Journal* puts the best face on his struggle, suggesting that "the fundamentals of the race"—the structural "factors"—have always been stacked against him:

> The economy is weak. The president is unpopular. It's a change, not a status quo, election. The surge has worked, but the war in Iraq is hardly a campaign plus. The political cycle points to a Democratic takeover. Democratic voter registration is up. Republican registration is down. Republicans trail Democrats in party identification.[3]

Such preexisting factors do affect the outcome of a political race, but contingent performances are what determine victory and defeat. Candidates win power by connecting and fusing with a citizen audience that is not narrow but broad. To fuse they must become powerful collective representations who sculpt an image and control it in what citizens believe to be an authentic and civil way. Three months before the *Journal* cites preexisting conditions to explain McCain's maladies, the conservative daily has actually handicapped the Obama campaign in a similar way:

> Barack Obama has claimed the Democratic nomination, but he limped rather than sprinted to the end of the long primary season. Now his campaign must overcome the vulnerabilities....The Illinois senator moves forward from the primaries after a string of losses, a rocky breakup with his longtime church, and an apparent weakness in attracting the white, working-class demographic seen as crucial to a democratic victory in November. Unlike Hillary Clinton, who based her campaign around winning key swing states, the Obama campaign focused on picking up delegates wherever they could. A string of wins in small states and caucus states helped Sen. Obama solidify a lead. But it also left him hobbling toward the finish line....Sen. Obama's losses in Ohio and Pennsylvania have some people wondering if the candidate will face difficulty in connecting to voters in these key states in November....A Quinnipiac University poll of likely voters released May 20 shows Sen. McCain defeating Sen. Obama in two of the three major swing states: Florida, Ohio and Pennsylvania.[4]

In the months following this prediction that conditions are stacked against Obama, the Democratic candidate performs in a masterly political manner. He works the binaries more subtly, walks the boundaries more agilely, and continues to present himself as a hero for his time. By contrast, McCain stumbles badly. Only one month after the *Journal* describes Obama's imposing post-primary hurdles, the paper reports with alarm "the blurry, often-conflicting signals Sen. McCain had been sending voters."[5] Acknowledging that "controlling the message of a candidate is tricky for any campaign," the *Journal* suggests, nonetheless, "it seems to be a particular challenge for Sen. McCain." The Republican's "message is fractured,"[6] his campaign events "thrown together with little more than a flag and a microphone."[7] When he tries reading from teleprompters, he seems wooden and fake.[8] When he tries for spontaneity, he seems confused—when he "speaks off the cuff and strays from his script," the campaign veers dangerously "off-message":[9]

> Carly Fiorina, the Republican National Committee's "victory chair" and the former chief executive of the Hewlett-Packard Co.... met with reporters Monday morning and suggested women should be able to choose a health-insurance plan that covers birth control but not Viagra. "Those women would like a choice," she said. On the campaign bus, Sen. McCain was then asked about his support of insurance coverage of birth control and immediately seemed uncomfortable. The awkwardness of the exchange was magnified on cable television, with Sen. McCain's fidgeting and sighing replayed over and over. CNN featured the exchange Friday on its American Morning program. Armstrong Williams, a conservative talk radio host, called it a "sad and ridiculous moment."[10]

Here is the paradox of performative politics. To avoid seeming ridiculous and to regain authenticity, McCain must become more self-conscious and skillful in presenting his image. William Kristol observes that so far—in June and early July—"Obama has achieved the important feat of seeming an increasingly plausible president," while McCain has managed to seem "less plausible."[11] The problem is not with the actual candidate but with the symbolic framework containing him. Kristol bemoans the fact that the "campaign has failed to develop an overarching message." For McCain to regain his authority and popularity, the Republican campaign "desperately needs a message and a narrative," one that is "appropriate for the candidate and for the times." It has become overwhelmingly clear that McCain cannot be left to his own devices. He must be taken in hand. Kristol suggests that Republicans bring back Mike Murphy, describing the veteran conservative consultant as a "creative" tactician and an "imaginative ad maker." Murphy's "great skill has always been an ability to find a clear theme for his candidates." The title for Kristol's column is "Where's Murphy?"

The McCain campaign knows it needs a makeover, but the job of directing the operation is given to someone else. As the *Wall Street Journal* reports,

Steven Schmidt will be in charge of sculpting and controlling the image of John McCain:

> Steven Schmidt, who worked on crafting the campaign message for Bush-Cheney 2004 and ran California Gov. Arnold Schwarzenegger's re-election campaign, has been placed in charge of daily operations. He will run Sen. McCain's day-to-day messaging and handle the travel calendar as well as oversee the campaign's political team. "It's a recognition that we need to be tighter on doing what we're doing," said a McCain senior adviser. "There's not a lot of room for error and we need a very tight operation that executes perfectly every day.[12]

The nation's leading conservative newspaper is obviously relieved. Promising readers that "change will be evident as soon as next week," the *Journal* reports that the Republican campaign's "retooled, focused messaging machine" will now be "pushing a carefully crafted and consistent message." Explaining that "Mr. Schmidt runs his teams with an almost military style of discipline," the paper offers anecdotal reassurance: "He thinks in bullet points, McCain senior adviser Mark Salter once quipped, and is impossible to move off message." One week later, both the *Journal* and the Republican campaign team are ready to declare the new performance a success:

> After a rocky three months, John McCain's presidential campaign embarked this week on a clear mission....Everything the campaign could plan for was carefully choreographed. Events...were thoughtfully staged, including a rug with the campaign logo and soft lighting on the candidate. The Arizona Republican, not known for his oratorical skills, delivered his scripted speeches with confidence and accuracy....McCain spokesman Tucker Bounds said Friday the campaign deemed the week a success[,] saying the campaign had, overall, managed to keep a "focused, targeted, and disciplined message on the economy."... The week was framed around town-hall meetings in Colorado, Ohio, Michigan and Wisconsin. Each of these events began with a scripted speech or bulleted talking points. Sen. McCain, typically rusty as a public speaker, made peace with the teleprompter and enthusiastically delivered his ideas.[13]

It is with this newfound discipline and creativity that the Republican performance team navigates the swiftly flowing power struggle, confronting the boulders that loom up to threaten its campaign.

Glimmer from the Dark Side

As August approaches, the McCain campaign is still struggling. The figure of military hero is blocked by events. The significance of the Iraq War is fading, terrorism fast becoming a horrific memory. The success of Obama's excursion takes foreign affairs entirely off the table. Yet for McCain to shift directions and become a civil hero seems difficult indeed. He tries floating the maverick persona, but it's shot down not simply by liberals and moderates but also by the conservatives, whose support has secured his nomination. If McCain cannot construct a heroic narrative and engage the civil binary in a liberating way, he will have to go negative. The sliver of hope that Republicans find in Obama's triumphant odyssey is a glimmer from the dark side. Every hero has a shadow. If Obama can be convicted of hubris, of being arrogant and aloof, Republicans may still block his heroic ascent and make him seem antidemocratic besides:

> "Gentlemen, let me put a few things on the table for observation and discussion," Steve Schmidt said to his fellow strategists while sitting in a conference room in the Phoenix Ritz-Carlton. "Would anyone here disagree with the premise that we are not winning this campaign?"
>
> No one disagreed. It was Sunday, July 27, and Obama had just concluded an eight-day swing through the Middle East and Europe that received practically round-the-clock media coverage. "Would anyone disagree with the premise," Schmidt went on, "that Mr. Obama has scored the most successful week in this entire campaign? I mean, they treated him like he was a head of state! So tell me, gentlemen: how do we turn this negative into a positive?"
>
> "It's third and nine," Bill McInturff, a pollster, observed. "Time to start throwing the ball down field."
>
> Eventually, it was Schmidt who blurted out the epiphany concerning Obama. "Face it, gentlemen," he said. "He's being treated like a celebrity."
>
> The others grasped the concept—a celebrity like J-Lo! Or Britney!— and exultation overtook the room.[14]

Schmidt's revelation marks an extraordinary moment of aesthetic discovery, creating a trope that threatens to upend the Obama campaign. When metaphors work, they clarify conflicting feeling and understanding. The liberal press admires Obama's foreign adventure, and European crowds love him, but for conservatives convinced of his anticivil qualities and for moderates who still worry about them, this adulation seems undeserved. The unease is palpable, and many seem unnerved. On Fox afternoon news, after observing "Barack Obama looking like a rock star in Germany today," David Asman, former editorial writer for the *Wall Street Journal*, asks a rhetorical question: "Is the fact that they loved him there a red flag for Americans here?"[15] The next day, on the same television show, a conservative journalist exclaims: "When Americans look at their televisions and see these waves of adulations washing across Obama, they say, 'Wait a minute. If they like him so much, there's something wrong here. I think that's why you haven't seen a bump in the poll.'"[16]

As Obama's foreign quest unfolds, conservative media and pundits move to separate his heroic image from his mundane person, making the person seem fake and the performance staged. The Democrat frames his foreign visit as a "fact-finding" tour, but his critics call this a ruse. As Obama meets with military and political leaders in the Middle East, conservative politico and former UN ambassador John Bolton asserts on Fox that Obama "had his mind made up on Afghanistan and Iraq before he went" and that rather than being independent and open-minded, "he's simply repeating the mantra of the last few years."[17] The next day the *New York Post* agrees, informing its readers that Obama has "already made his decisions" and that it is his intention "to flash through" hotspots so he can make a show of solving problems "that have stymied peace-makers for years."[18] Sean Hannity describes the trip as a "photo-op," giving it high marks only for being "well choreographed."[19] The veteran conservative journalist Fred Barnes lauds Obama's "stagecraft" as "tremendous," sarcastically acknowledging that the "TV shots...and some of the newspaper pictures—with Obama in the helicopter—looked great."[20]

If Obama's foreign trip is merely an outrageously staged performance, why is it hailed on all sides as a powerful success? For Obama's conservative opponents, it can only be the messengers, not the members of the citizen audience, who are to blame. With the trip still in its early days, an analyst for the conservative Media Research Center lashes out at "Obama's magical media tour."[21] In a website video titled "Obama Love 3.0," the McCain campaign replays enthralled comments by reporters against the background music, "Can't Take My Eyes Off of You,"[22] and a Fox pundit later explains that "the campaign is going with the Frankie Valli song" because "of how much the media loved Obama."[23] The *Washington Times* complains of "adoring press coverage Elvis would envy" and of the press having "crowned" Obama "as the permanent American Idol."[24]

Not only is the message fake but the messenger is colluding in the deception. "There was more worship of Obama on this trip than occurs in an average church on Sunday morning," conservative columnist Cal Thomas fulminates on Fox at the end of Obama's trip. "I've never seen anything like it," Thomas exclaims. It was "more than Kennedy....It was messianic and unbelievable."[25] Fred Barnes marks down Obama's conservative scorecard in the same way, declaring "the trip was entirely over the top" and calling it "breathtakingly presumptuous."[26] On *Fox News on Sunday* with Chris Wallace, the conservative guru Karl Rove agrees that Obama displayed "a hint of arrogance" and that the foreign adventure "bespoke a little bit of brashness and arrogance."[27] Far from being pure and heroic, the Obama image is shadowed and threatening. The Democratic candidate stands accused of hubris on a grand scale. Is he guilty as accused?

The Advertisement

This question is answered symbolically, not factually, two days after Obama returns from Europe, on July 29. That evening, McCain's campaign places a 30-second advertisement on its website that calls out Obama as a "celebrity." The next day the advertisement runs nationally on cable and locally in 11 battleground states, and over the next week it's "played endlessly on news channels" and draws "millions of hits on YouTube."[28] The ad begins with a powerful, slightly blurred tracking shot of the enormous German crowd that gathers for Obama's speech in Berlin. Seconds later, muffled chants of "O-ba-ma! O-ba-ma! O-ba-ma!" roll rather ominously from the screen. With the chanting in the background, flashbulbs pop brightly, Britney Spears and Paris Hilton are glimpsed in famous poses, and a grinning Barack Obama appears on the screen addressing the massive crowd. He stands before a tilting Victory Arch in Berlin, his image grainy as if in an old newsreel. A baritone voiceover intones gravely, "He's the biggest celebrity in the world, but is he ready to lead?"[29]

At first, skeptical observers on both sides of the ideological spectrum reject out of hand the idea that this most serious, ambitious, and moralistic of contemporary political figures is a celebrity. Evaluating it empirically, they declare it to be false, an outrageous distortion of factual reality. One contributor to ABC's *Good Morning America* advises, "You wanna [*sic*] draw contrasts between yourself and your opponent, but you want voters to see that as valuable contrasting information rather than simply as name calling."[30] That same day, NPR interviews an academic expert on negative campaigning and asks, "What do you make of this McCain ad which aims to draw a comparison between Obama and Paris Hilton and Britney Spears? Will people buy that?"[31] The professor answers, "I suspect not," and explains that "I don't think it's a very good ad" because, while not "incorrect or factually inaccurate, per se...it strikes me as a stretch." A few days later, NBC luminary Tom Brokaw confronts McCain friend and campaign surrogate Senator Joseph Lieberman with the same factual query: "What does [Obama] have to do with Paris Hilton or Britney Spears?"[32] Even the entertainment journalists on

Showbiz Tonight are having nothing to do with it. "It first broke on Wednesday," comments cohost A. J. Hammer, and "quite frankly, it was just plain ridiculous."³³ Guest Jane Velez-Mitchell immediately agrees:

> It's so shocking....John McCain should not be comparing Obama to any actors whatsoever, but especially not Britney Spears. That is so over the top. Let's remember, Britney Spears is a woman who was rushed on a stretcher into a psych ward and committed for several days until her father was given conservatorship over her affairs because she was deemed to be incompetent of [*sic*] taking care of herself. And that's the person that McCain is comparing Obama to? This is absolutely outrageous.

In response to such moralistic criticism of factual content, McCain protests that the celebrity ad should not be taken so seriously. "We're having some fun," the Republican protests, chiding his overly literal critics.³⁴ His communication director tells another reporter that it is just "a very fun, light-hearted ad."³⁵

Taking such empiricist criticism to its logical conclusion, the *Wall Street Journal* reports, on August 1, that "the celebrity link was a leap that fell flat."³⁶ But it did nothing of the kind. Months later, in mid-October, the *Journal* will implicitly acknowledge its error: "A deft negative ad, like McCain's spot questioning the substance behind Obama's extraordinary celebrity, still can send an opponent reeling."³⁷ The paper now places the celebrity campaign into the pantheon of political advertising alongside LBJ's 1964 "daisy ad" against Goldwater's nuclear policies and George H. W. Bush's Willie Horton campaign against Dukakis.

It is the symbolic power of the celebrity advertisement that matters, not its factual accuracy. Its authority is performative, and its cultural power immediately felt. Up to this point, accusations about Obama's hubris have been suggestive, general, and atmospheric, offering analogies such as Obama is "*looking like* a rock star." With its newly confident and sober verbal identification of Obama as a celebrity, as well as its iconic visualization, the new advertisement makes these atmospherics concrete. The idea of hubris is no longer a matter of making two different things seem similar. It becomes, instead, a statement about one thing. Obama is not *like* a celebrity; he *is* one. In place of simile, there is metaphor. Prescription becomes description, and an admixture of qualities becomes a single compound. The *Washington Times* describes the ad as "stark, harsh and groundbreaking."³⁸ This gets its metaphoric power just right.

Celebrity metaphor creates a new cultural playing field. "Do the American people want to elect the world's biggest celebrity or do they want to elect an American hero?" Steve Schmidt asks reporters as he announces the rollout of the ad campaign. The Republicans' brilliant and cunning new image maker presents Obama's celebrity as if it were an indisputable fact, one that, on its face, disqualifies the Democrat from occupying the hero position in the campaign. While Obama protests that the ad is inaccurate, Republicans rise above the factual level to narrative reality. "Like most celebrities," a campaign spokesman suggests, Obama "reacts to fair criticisms with a mix of fussiness and hysteria." Campaign manager Rick Davis responds to questions about the advertisement's accuracy in the same way: "Only celebrities like Barack Obama go to the gym three times a day, demand 'MET-RX chocolate roasted-peanut protein bars and bottles of hard-to-find organic brew—Black Forest Berry Honest Tea'—and worry about the price of arugula."[39] Karl Rove suggests that, "in politics, when you get that kind of hubris," you must expect such criticism. He portrays Obama's fall as caused by the natural laws of politics, not by partisan feeling: "[Y]ou know, those whom the gods destroy, they first make prideful, and he's getting a little prideful."[40] *Today Show* host Matt Lauer asks Republican senior strategist Nicolle Wallace, Steven Schmidt's partner, whether the celebrity advertisement is "demeaning."[41] Wallace declares it was not a matter of moral judgment but objective fact:

> This ad is in some ways a celebration of his celebrity. I mean, I don't think there's much to debate this morning about whether he is or is not a celebrity. The ad…makes a very serious and sober point.…We've never made jokes about Paris Hilton…and look, I don't think we're making a joke of Senator Obama and neither were the 200,000 Germans who were there to celebrate his celebrity.…No one can forget or overlook or obscure the fact that Barack Obama is the celebrity in this contest and Senator John McCain, an American hero, is the underdog.

While the pleasures derived from this metaphorical eruption are partisan, the symbolic reality of the new playing field cannot easily be disputed by the Democratic side. Celebrity metaphor clarifies conflicting lines of conjecture and emotion by reducing anxiety, eliminating confusion, and seeming to offer new hope not only to frustrated conservatives but also to muddling citizens in the middle of the fight. "It has attention value," explains Annenberg's independent media scholar Kathleen Hall Jamieson, who attests that it "breaks through the clutter."[42] On the evening it is posted on the Republican campaign website—before its nationwide distribution the next day—the ad's attention-getting power reveals itself when long-time Democratic advisor Susan Estrich refers to the *already* "widely talked about McCain ad that blasts Obama."[43] The day after it is placed in circulation, CBS evening news anchor Katie Couric highlights what she already describes as "the now-infamous McCain ad."[44] Celebrity metaphor has finger-snapping, clutter-reducing, breathtaking impact. It is a matter of experience, not cogitation, providing an "ahaa!" moment for many. The morning after its circulation, an ABC reporter on *Good Morning America* is already asking, "Could the charge stick?"[45] That evening, on *World News,* ABC anchor Charles Gibson observes that "some think McCain may have struck a cord [*sic*]."[46] The next day, on National Public Radio's *Morning Edition,* Mara Liasson, apologizing that her question may seem "a bit silly," asks whether the new ad might not be "hitting home?"[47] As the celebrity metaphor moves from mundane fact to dizzying symbol, a panelist on CNN's *Showbiz Tonight* observes, "[T]his is one of those moments that's taking on a life of its own."[48] The airwaves are filled with hints of fusion, and the sense of performative success is great. One week after the ad's introduction, former senate majority leader Tom Daschle, political mentor to Obama, reluctantly acknowledges to the *Financial Times* that "the ad looks like it's working."[49]

Celebrity Pollution

Celebrity metaphor has such impact that it can retrospectively alter the media's narration of a campaign. On the day the ad circulates, Mara Liasson of liberal National Public Radio reports, "[T]hat certainly has been the narrative this week, that Obama is getting too big for his britches, that he's too presumptuous."[50] Not long after, the conservative *Washington Times* writes about "the continuing week-long drive to define Obama as an empty pop-culture creation."[51] No wonder that George Stephanopoulos, the former Clinton aide who is now a leading ABC political journalist, reports that the McCain camp is "certainly confident about this," that it's "feeling good," and that, despite criticism, "they're not backing off—at all."[52] John Broder covered the campaign for the *New York Times*. He remembers the "celebrity effect" as a "pretty good trick": "It certainly seemed to succeed in taking the gloss off" of Obama's foreign trip:[53]

> All of us sort of [were] swept up in the idea that [Obama] could draw 200, 300,000 people in a foreign capital—this was Kennedy-esque in the extreme, and they, the McCain people, were quickly able to turn that into a negative. That trip suddenly became sort of cancelled out. It was supposed to show his *moda vitas* and his ability to represent the country in the Middle East and Europe, and suddenly it was something that was no longer talked about.

The symbolic pollution of celebrity metaphor enters into the media mainstream. On July 30, number 10 on late-night talk show host David Letterman's famous top-ten list is a "proposed bill to change Oklahoma to Okla-bama."[54] Brit

Hume of Fox News reports the incident: "When the late-night comics start talking about something, you know it's getting in the bloodstream."[55] ABC's celebrated journalist Diane Sawyer describes the Republican evocation of Britney Spears and Paris Hilton as having the force of a "political nuclear attack."[56] Journalist Jake Tapper of ABC fulsomely elaborates upon the advertisement's claims: "Well, the McCain campaign thinks they have an effective line of attack against Senator Barack Obama, that he is an arrogant, arugula-eating, fancy berry tea drinking celebrity…akin to Britney Spears and Paris Hilton, pretty, pampered, not up for being president."[57] Senior ABC editor Michelle Cottle lends veracity to her colleague's observation: "Americans don't like presidents who think they're better than the average guy."[58] On the Republican campaign website, staffers set up an "audacity watch."

In their democratic role as carriers of civic virtue, Americans are deeply suspicious of celebrity, comparing its anticivil publicity with true public spiritedness and polluting its pseudofame as selfish and manipulative. For the Left, celebrity is the dangerous product of an unbridled capitalism in which, as Andy Warhol once remarked, "Everybody is entitled to their fifteen minutes of fame." For the Right, celebrity is the product of a degenerate modernity where, as one conservative columnist puts it, "America's stoic traditional culture" is being replaced by "hedonism, relativism, and self-indulgence."[59] This shared conviction serves as cultural background for celebrity metaphor. What triggers the epiphany is connecting this signifier to Obama at a heated, anxious, and confusing moment in the campaign. For a statistically significant segment of the American electorate's muddling middle, the metaphor defines, retrospectively, Obama's foreign adventure and also, prospectively, the content of his character. On the day after the ad begins circulating, a man from Clintonville, Wisconsin, makes this declaration to NPR's call-in show, *Talk of the Nation*:

> I would just like to speak particularly to John McCain's most recent ad. But I have found this to be a characteristic of other negative ads. His is just, perhaps, the finest example that I have ever heard. And when I speak of hear, I mean that the particular chant in the background of the ad—the Obama! Obama! Obama!—sort of smacks of chants that we have heard when we've seen images of dictators in a variety of foreign countries.…It's extremely disquieting, and unnerving, and really almost oppressive.[60]

As the virus attaches itself to Obama's political DNA, celebrity emerges as one of the most damaging epithets of the campaign. A guest host on the liberal MSNBC declares: "Fifty years ago, the charge being hurled around that would hurt any candidate was, you know, 'communist sympathizer.' There's another 'C' word out there today, celebrity…He's a celebrity!"[61] To which the veteran NBC reporter Andrea Mitchell replies, "[I]f they can succeed in categorizing him, in painting him as someone who is a lightweight, quote, unquote, who doesn't have substance, who is young, inexperienced, is part of pop culture but not a serious leader, then they have accomplished something."[62] One week after the celebrity metaphor emerges, Fox News interviewed Republican and former House Speaker Dennis Hastert. After professing, perhaps disingenuously, that he knows nothing about the ad campaign, Hastert launches into a riff that demonstrates he certainly knows everything there is to know about politics and celebrity. Promising to "tell you what I think the American people want," Hastert suggests his fellow citizens want "somebody who is willing not to be a celebrity, somebody who is willing to roll up their sleeves and work and make this country better." That the other party's nominee is not such a man Hastert is certain: "Barack Obama has kind of been dancing with the stars."[63]

Reality Redefined

Less than a week after the launch of the celebrity metaphor, seven out of ten Americans have seen the original ad, and a slew of related children-of-celebrity ads, videos, counterattacks, press releases, and campaign statements have appeared in the meantime.[64] This statistic of 70 percent records more than merely passive exposure. It suggests the energy that the celebrity coding is generating, how rapidly the narrative image is circulating, and how Americans have been drawn into the ad's symbolic meaning and are seeking it out. The ad cost less than $15,000 to produce and no more than $200,000 to air in the 11 battleground states nationwide.[65] It is poetics, not money, that makes its performative success great.

SPEARS AND HILTON RAISE MCCAIN COVERAGE EVEN WITH OBAMA

For the first time since this general election campaign began in early June, Republican John McCain attracted virtually as much media attention as his Democratic rival last week. Barack Obama was a significant or dominant factor in 81% of the campaign stories compared with 78% for McCain.…That was a high water mark for McCain in the general election season (his previous best was 62% from June 30–July 6). And the virtual dead heat in the race for exposure between the two candidates also marked the first time his weekly coverage had even been within 10 percentage points of Obama's total. Indeed, in the eight weeks since early June when the general election context began, 79% of the stories have significantly featured Obama, compared with 55% for his Republican rival. The spike in press attention to the McCain campaign came a week after Obama's tour of the Middle East and Europe commandeered the headlines, accounting for half the election coverage for July 21–27....Last week, the McCain campaign...drove the narrative...in a controversial ad. It described Obama as "the biggest celebrity in the world" and featured images of Britney Spears and Paris Hilton—two tabloid favorites known more for hard-partying lifestyles than any other achievements....As soon as McCain's new ad was released on July 30, it triggered a torrent of commentary.[66]

For the first time, McCain pulls even with Obama in the Gallup daily national tracking poll.[67] Both candidates now register 44 percent, when just the week before Obama had a nine-point lead.[68] A critical segment of the citizen audience is not only watching but also connecting with celebrity message, sensing verisimilitude, not construction, seeing its claim not as fiction but as truth. The *New York Post* reports the celebrity onslaught is having "far-reaching effect," allowing McCain "to claw his way back."[69] The *Sunday Times* describes the Democrats' "suddenly vulnerable presidential campaign."[70] According to the *Washington Times,* the "brutal yet entertaining attack ads and web videos" are the sixth most watched YouTubes of the week, McCain edging out Obama for seven straight days and eleven out of the last fourteen.[71] The conservative newspaper trumpets that the celebrity attack has "transformed" McCain's campaign and "stumped" Obama's.[72] It is because independents and Reagan Democrats are moving back toward McCain that, "as celebrity ads went viral on the Internet, national polls tightened to show the race neck and neck."[73] Three weeks into August, the *New York Post* headlines: "Poll Roll Blows Away O Lead; McCain Juggernaut Wipes Out O's Lead in Prez Polls":

> Barack Obama's lead over John McCain has collapsed, according to the latest polls, including a Wall Street Journal/NBC survey that last night showed the race in a statistical dead heat. Obama held a mere 3-point edge over McCain, 45 percent to 42 percent—down from the 6-point margin he'd had a month ago and within the 3.1 point margin of error....Other polls, too, have detected a dramatic tightening of the presidential context....An LA Times/Bloomberg news poll, along with a Zogby poll and a Quinnipiac University survey, all show Obama sliding from the position of strength he held....The most recent Reuters/Zogby poll, released yesterday, actually shows McCain taking a 5-point lead over Obama—erasing the 7-point edge the Illinois Senator held just last month.[74]

At the end of August, the *Washington Times* sees a turning point: "Mr. Obama has been pummeled by Republican ads painting him as an inexperienced celebrity, as his poll lead evaporated and the race became tied."[75] Chuck Todd, NBC's chief political correspondent, reports on the mood of the image makers who created the campaign. "[T]he current people running the McCain campaign," Todd confides, "they have swagger right now."[76] The strategists confess to Todd that "[E]verybody told us we were going to be down double digits this summer going into the conventions" and that "everybody said this guy was going to overwhelm us." They now brag, "[W]e've brought this race even":

> They are borderline cocky right now.... They feel like they have brought Obama down a notch. They feel that this celebrity stuff has been so effective against Obama that they've already...beaten down the hype.... They already feel as if they've lightened up his persona and, and really softened him up."

Democrats' Response

Obama and the Democrats initially present themselves as utterly unworried about the celebrity campaign, as taking the high road, certain of its lack of effect. They are talking the talk, but, as veteran Republican consultant Ed Rollins observes, they are not walking the walk. Obama "thinks that the ads must have been effective," Rollins tells CBS news, since "he's basically out there responding already."[77] When Republicans first launch the celebrity trope against him, Obama tries repelling the weapon by denying its metaphorical status. At one campaign stop he offers a seemingly casual, winking response: "They got me in an ad with Paris Hilton, you know, I've never met the woman."[78] In this mundane and empirical manner, Obama is rejecting the symbolic logic of association upon which metaphor is based. On the following day, Obama works the binaries, suggesting that to brandish symbols is to flee the rigors of democratic struggle: "You'd think we'd be having a serious debate. But so far, all we've been hearing about is Paris Hilton and Britney Spears. I do have to ask my opponent, is that the best you can come up with?"[79]

That morning on the *Today Show* Obama spokesman Robert Gibbs squares off against Nicolle Wallace, challenging the already-burgeoning celebrity metaphor in exactly the same way. According to the *Wall Street Journal*, Gibbs has emerged as "Obama's advocate-in-chief with the media," the person "in charge of shaping his message, responding to the 24/7 news cycle, schmoozing with the press and fighting back when he disagrees with its reporting." Gibbs describes himself more simply: "I'm a protector of the image."[80] Gibbs begins with the standard of empirical truth. "Independent observers," he asserts, say the celebrity claim is "false and baseless" and that it rests on "absolutely no evidence."[81] Obama is not a celebrity,

Gibbs avers, but "one of the most down-to-earth people that I've ever met." From empirical truth claim, Gibbs moves to the rhetoric of truthfulness itself. Evoking a value at the core of democratic discourse, Gibbs asserts that "We've responded with what we think is the truth, which is the truth." And he continues working the binaries. While "McCain is an honorable man," the celebrity advertisement demonstrates he is "running an increasingly dishonorable campaign." Rather than sticking to principle and maintaining civility, "the McCain campaign has very clearly decided that the only way to win this election is to become very personal and very negative." If he does not engage the liberating discourse of civil society, he cannot be a democratic hero. The Republican is practicing the "same old, tired politics," Gibbs suggests. Electing him would not transport citizens from the sullied past and troubled present into a bright new future.

A Democratic advertisement that responds immediately to the emergence of the celebrity campaign lays out a similar line of attack: McCain is playing "the same old politics of the past."[82] Obama campaign manager David Plouffe sends out a mass email saying that the McCain campaign has taken a "nasty turn" into the gutter.[83] The campaign sets up a website called lowroadexpress.com, inverting the valence of McCain's 2000 campaign bus, the Straight Talk Express.[84]

None of these efforts to work the binaries gains traction as the celebrity metaphor continues to explode into the scene. In its frustration, the Democratic campaign tries walking the boundaries. Obama suggests that accusing him of celebrity amounts to playing the race card: "Since they don't have any new ideas, the only strategy they've got in this election is to try to scare you about me...to try to say I'm a risky guy...to try to say, 'Well, you know, he's got a funny name, and he doesn't look like all the presidents on the dollar bills and the five-dollar bills."[85] This tortured logic, while supported by some African American commentators, is less than compelling for the broader mainstream. The effort boomerangs, allowing Obama himself to be polluted as anticivil in turn. "Barack Obama has played the race card," McCain campaign manager Rick Davis indignantly complains: "He played it from the bottom of the deck. It's divisive, negative, shameful and wrong." Backed into a corner, Democrats recant their charges, insisting they have never suggested anything of the kind. McCain adviser Lindsey Graham self-righteously tells Fox News that "to say that Barack Obama did not intentionally inject the idea of his name and his race is a lie."[86] Unfortunately, he is right.

Democrats can barely contain their consternation. The performative ascendancy of celebrity cannot be denied. It is the right trope at the right time. Celebrity has become a highly charged, dangerously menacing symbol at the heart of late summer's campaign. Playing the hand he has been dealt, Obama and his allies accept celebrity as a redolent political evil, hoping now merely to deflect the symbol's fallout away from the Democratic to the Republican side. The real Paris Hilton steps out of Republican metaphor and into the Democrats' campaign. In a breezy style, the *New York Post* calls the play:

> Professional airhead Paris Hilton yesterday slapped down president wannabe John McCain with a spoof of the GOP senator's recent ad depicting her as a celebrity bimbo. "He's the oldest celebrity in the world, like, super old…but is he ready to lead?" begins the snarky ad, created by the comedy Web site funnyordie.com. Hilton then appears in a sexy leopard-print swimsuit lounging on a chair. "Hey America, I'm Paris Hilton, and I'm a celebrity, too, only I'm not from the olden days, and I'm not promising change like that other guy. I'm just hot," she smirks. "But then that wrinkly, white-haired guy used me in his campaign ad, which I guess means I'm running for president. So thanks for the endorsement, white-haired dude."[87]

Days after Hilton's cameo campaign appearance, the Democrats try their own hand at turning celebrity metaphor against McCain. The *New York Daily News* finds the feeble effort infantile but amusing:

> WHO YOU CALLIN' A CELEB, MAC?
> You're a CELEBRITY! No, you're a celebrity! Nearly two weeks after John McCain unleashed a series of ads tarring Barack Obama as a silly celebrity akin to Paris Hilton and Britney Spears, the Illinois senator counterattacked with a 30-second spot labeling McCain as, um, a celebrity. It's the presidential politics version of that old school playground adage: I'm rubber, you're glue—your words bounce off me and stick to you. "For decades, he's been Washington's biggest celebrity," an announcer in Obama's ad intones as images of McCain with late-night comics Jay Leno and David Letterman, and on "The View" and "Saturday Night Live" flash across the screen. "Lurching to the right, then to the left, the old Washington dance, whatever it takes," the announcer continues. "A Washington celebrity playing the same old Washington games." The ad accuses McCain of running a "low road campaign" and notably shows McCain in various embraces with President Bush.[88]

While McCain ignores the ad, the Republican National Committee responds by suggesting that the celebrity charge appears to "have gotten under Obama's skin." It has. A month later, the *New York Post* reports that "Obama advisers last week began to admit privately that this European Idol tour was a mistake."[89] They may have been right.

Stretching the Metaphor

McCain's new image makers appear to have pulled victory from the jaws of what once seemed looming defeat. The question is whether this momentum can be maintained. "The key thing here," Ed Rollins observes, "is it's building on the celebrity…that's their message…That's the message you want to drive."[90] As August unfolds, Republicans deploy the celebrity metaphor to walk the boundaries of family, economy, and race:

> Eager to seize on any opening, McCain released another television ad yesterday zinging Obama over his celebrity. Paris Hilton and Britney Spears were left on the cutting-room floor for this one, which features Obama standing before an adoring crowd in Berlin. "Is the biggest celebrity in the world ready to help your family?" a female narrator asks. The ad then portrays Obama as a pol who will raise taxes and run jobs out of the country.[91]

> John McCain released a blistering TV attack yesterday portraying Barack Obama as a tax hiker who would be an "economic disaster" for America. The 30-second spot, appearing in 11 states, comes a day after Obama put the final touches on his economic plan. It plays off a prior ad linking Obama to bimbo celebrities Paris Hilton and Britney Spears. Obama is shown addressing rapturous supporters chanting "Obama, Obama." Flashbulbs from photographers go off. "Celebrity? Yes. Ready to lead? No," the narrator says. "Obama's new taxes could break your family budget.…Obama's taxes mean 'higher prices at the pump' and is [sic] a 'recipe for economic disaster,'" the announcer says, quoting from newspaper clippings. "Higher taxes. Higher gas prices. Economic disaster," the narrator charges.[92]

> Since Barack Obama became a celebrity, several relatives have shared in his fame, including half-brother Bernard, a Kenyan auto-parts dealer who was front-page news when he visited England last month. But until now, almost nothing was known about George, who was born to Barack's father, Barack Sr., and his fourth wife.…Italy's *Vanity Fair* tracked George Obama down to the violent Kenyan town of Huruma, where he lives alone in a shack adorned with soccer posters, a calendar depicting beaches around the world, and a frontpage newspaper photo of the

Democratic presidential nominee-to-be. George Obama said he has no contact with his brother, and apparently has cut himself off from the rest of the family.[93]

McCain, in a 30-second TV spot, again likened Obama to a Hollywood celebrity and cast him as a pol who would raise taxes....."Celebrities don't have to worry about family budgets, but we sure do," the voice in the new McCain ad says, as supporters chant, "Obama!" It adds: "We're paying more for food and gas, making it harder to save for college, retirement. Obama's solution? Higher taxes, called 'a recipe for economic disaster.' He's ready to raise your taxes but not ready to lead."[94]

Republican momentum depends on keeping the celebrity metaphor alive. The real test is the Democratic convention, which comes at month's end. Can Republicans evoke the celebrity trope to frame Obama's nomination? This is their aim. The Democrats are "on the verge of nominating the first celebrity presidential candidate in U.S. history," announces the *Washington Times*.[95]

Party conventions no longer function as arenas for actually contesting nominations. Instead, they have emerged in the television era as extraordinary performative occasions. They create a liminal time by symbolically dividing the usually more languid politics of summer from the final fierce months of campaigns. Conventions provide candidates an immense audience free of charge, before which they struggle to inflate themselves as collective representations, to fuse, connect, and persuade. As the Democratic convention approaches, the Republicans try connecting Denver with Berlin. If they can paint Obama as a celebrity when he accepts the nomination, he can be separated from his audience, not from those actually sitting in the hall but from the layers outside, the tens of millions who receive Obama representation in a mass-mediated way. If Obama fails to fuse with these faraway members of his citizen audience, his convention performance will fail, and his campaign will continue to slide against a rising McCain.

Fighting over the Stage

For Democratic activists in the trenches, according to the *New York Times*, the "convention they had once anticipated would be a breezy celebration of Mr. Obama, had turned into a more sober and consequential event."[96] As a former national Democratic chairman confides, "Back in June and July, I truly thought he was going to blow McCain out of the water and carry 30 or 40 states," but "what has happened is that Republicans—McCain specifically—have really twisted his great charisma and this electric personality, to discredit his ability, his experience, his capacity, his judgment....I fear [what] they are about to do to him." Montana's Democratic Party chairman underscores the free-floating anxiety: "Normally I might say these conventions are not so important, but I don't think that's the case this year." He explains that "there seems to be a sense of urgency....We have had a couple of weeks that were not so good."

In the days leading up to the Monday of the convention, liberal *Times* columnists worry that Obama has misplaced his finely tuned talent for theatrics. They want to revise the script and pump up the acting. On Saturday, Bob Herbert indicts Obama for running a campaign whose message "has seemed directionless, uninspired and addicted to the empty calories of generalities." He declares that "the candidate himself has seemed flat. No fire. No passion." To regain his leading position, "Obama needs a first-rate crackling-with-excitement populist message," and "he needs to show a lot more fire." Warning that "there is nothing genteel" about "the struggle for the ultimate power of the presidency," Herbert wonders out loud whether Obama really has "the right stuff" to "take the fight to his opponent."[97] When his turn comes on Sunday, Frank Rich strongly advises Obama to find "an effective story."[98] Walking the foreign boundary has put him in danger. If he is to recover his destiny as civil hero, his narrative must explain "how we dig out of this quagmire." Rather than "a story of endless conflicts abroad," the script should be an "inspiring tale of serious economic, educational, energy and health-care mobilization at home." Only "a story that is more about America and the future" will allow Obama to "rekindle the 'fierce urgency of now.'" Three days later, in the midst of the Denver convention, Maureen Dowd titles her column "High Anxiety in the Mile-high City."[99] Finding a "weird and jittery" vibe completely at odds "with the early thrilling, fairy dust feel of the Obama revolution," she attributes this symbolic deflation to the Republican celebrity campaign:

> Democrats have begun internalizing the criticisms [by] John McCain about Obama's rock-star prowess, worrying that the Invesco Field extravaganza Thursday, with Bruce Springsteen and Bon Jovi, will just add to the celebrity cachet that Democrats have somehow been shamed into seeing as a negative...."We're seeing a train wreck all over again," said one top Democrat.

As the convention becomes imminent, conservative efforts to extend the celebrity metaphor focus like a laser beam on Obama's Thursday-night acceptance speech. Republicans know what is at stake. When Obama chooses to turn on the rhetorical throttle, he can display extraordinary dramatic force. His short speech at the 2004 convention triggered a frenzy of excitement that catapulted him to national fame even before his actual election to the Senate. During his drive for the presidency, crowds have flocked to his speeches, seeming to become larger and more passionate with each passing week. The Republicans, then, have good reason to be afraid. But they also have cause for hope. If they can metaphorically frame Obama's acceptance speech as celebrity, none of his rhetorical skills will matter. The enormous crowd, the millions of television viewers, the frenzy, the transcendence, the passion—all of it will be polluted as hubris and artifice on the celebrity stage.

It is not so much the impending speech that draws Republican attention. It is the physical setting—the actual stage upon which Obama will stand. In preparing his orations, Obama is a careful wordsmith, his rhetoric drawn from the civil religion's time-honored phrases and themes. The jerry-built stage upon which he will deliver his convention speech is another matter entirely. It will be easier to interpret harshly, to place its meaning at an oblique angle to the earnest intentions of an idealistic African American politician. So it is the means of symbolic production, not the rhetorical symbols themselves, about which the Republicans choose to fight. Two months earlier, when celebrity was still a metaphor confined to Hollywood stars, the Obama campaign decided to move the acceptance speech—the convention's most dramatic moment—away from the indoor intimacies of the convention hall to a giant outdoor football stadium seating upward of 80,000 people. It seemed like a good idea at the time. When the day arrives actually to deliver the speech, things have changed:

> Denver—When Senator Barack Obama announced in early July that he would give his nomination address in an outdoor stadium in front of 75,000 people, he wowed members of both parties who saw it as an inspired stroke of campaign image making. But as he landed here on Wednesday and prepared to become the first presidential candidate in nearly 50 years to accept his party's nomination on such a big stage, the plan seemed as much risky as bold. With daunting challenges of logistics, style and substance, the plan was hatched before the Republicans began a concerted drive to paint Mr. Obama as a media sensation lacking the résumé to be president.[100]

Democrats insist that the fluted columns, classical backdrop, and elevated dais are designed to evoke the White House and the Lincoln Memorial. Conservative critics are having none of it. They declare the stage setting pretentious and artificial—totally celebrity. The *Wall Street Journal* exposes the feverish construction upon which Obama's performance will depend:

In a blur of 20-hour workdays, a crew nearly 300 strong is stringing cable, laying walkways and building the dais that will transform an open-air football stadium into the launching pad for the final stage of Sen. Barack Obama's presidential campaign. Staging experts plan a striking backdrop for Sen. Obama to accept the Democratic Party's nomination Thursday night at the 50-yard-line of Invesco Field at Mile High, the home of the Denver Broncos football team.... The campaign chose to stage the event at Invesco Field, rather than in the Pepsi Center indoor arena where the rest of the convention is being held, so they could accommodate bigger crowds. Tens of thousands of everyday voters will pack the stands, in addition to delegates and donors. The potential upside: A made-for-TV moment in front of a revved-up crowd of 80,000. The potential downside: The larger-than-life scale could aid Republicans in their quest to portray Sen. Obama as a celebrity candidate more suited to drawing adoring throngs than governing.[101]

Other conservative media make the charge of hubris more explicit and biting. On Fox, Bill O'Reilly speaks of "the Zeus factor": "According to Reuters, the set of Barack Obama's speech Thursday night will feature a Greek Temple background. Wow…First it was 'The Chosen One,' and now the Democrats are calling on the Greek gods?"[102]

The Washington Times reminds its readers that "for weeks, John McCain has been pounding Barack Obama in TV ads that depict him as an inexperienced, in-over-his-head celebrity candidate."[103] Reporting that the latest Zogby poll shows "Mr. McCain edging ahead by a 46 percent to 41 percent margin," the paper claims that this statistic, along with another "slew of polls," has "stunned Mr. Obama's high command":

Thus, there is much riding on this week's convention and the political image Barack Obama and the Democrats present to the nation over four successive nights, culminating with his mega-rally extravaganza.… The closing act on Thursday night will be Barack Obama delivering his acceptance speech before a monster, outdoor rock-concert-style rally that favors his kind of promise-them-anything oratory. It will be like that gigantic outdoor rally in Berlin, where hundreds of thousands of frenzied Germans turned him into a global celebrity that has backfired on his candidacy.

On the morning of the speech, the *New York Post* predicts that "Democrats will kneel before the 'Temple of Obama' tonight," evoking the celebrity ghosts haunting the Obama campaign in a concrete way:

As if a Rocky Mountain coronation were not lofty enough, Barack Obama will aim for Mount Olympus when he accepts his party's nomination atop an enormous, Greek-columned stage—built by the same cheesy set team that put together Britney Spears' last tour. John McCain's campaign mocked the massive neoclassical set created for Obama's speech at [the] 75,000-seat Invesco Field. Some Republicans have dubbed it the "Barackopolis," while others suggested the delegates should wear togas to fit in among the same Doric columns the ancient Greeks believed would stroke the egos of Zeus and Athena. "It's only appropriate that Barack Obama would descend down from the heavens and spend a little time with us mere mortals when accepting the Democratic nomination," said Republican National Committee spokesman Danny Diaz. The McCain campaign quickly dispatched a memo calling the stage the "Temple of Obama."...The structure has an aluminum frame, and the faux-stone walls and columns are made of wood....Democratic delegates defended the grandiosity as fitting with the monumental importance of this election.[104]

New York Post Washington Bureau chief Charles Hurt suggests that the Republicans' "lampooning of Obama's acceptance-speech stage as the 'Barackopolis' has created a genuine trap."[105] He predicts that it "may turn out to be one of the most fatal political mistakes in modern history."[106]

Democrats labor mightily to resist this metaphorical frame. On the day of the speech, the *New York Times* reports that Obama's aides are "feeling all the more pressure to bring a lofty candidate to ground level, showing Mr. Obama grasps the concerns of everyday Americans."[107] Obama insists his acceptance speech will be human, not transcendental: "'I'm not aiming for a lot of high rhetoric,' Mr. Obama said Wednesday as he made his way to Denver. 'I am much more concerned with communicating how I intend to help middle-class families live their lives.'"

Workers struggle up to the last minute to alter the physical setting of the speech. If they can tweak this material construction, its symbolic construction by critics and audiences might be more likely to go the Democrats' way:

On Wednesday, workers were still making changes to Invesco Field, home to the Denver Broncos, so it would feel more intimate, less like the boisterous rallies that served Mr. Obama so well early in the primaries, but also created the celebrity image that dogs him. They were still testing camera angles, so Mr. Obama would appear among the giant crowd, not above it. They took steps to reduce the echo effect, familiar to football fans, of speaking in such a cavernous space....Workers put the finishing touches on the backdrop—faux columns intended to suggest a federal building in Washington and create an air of stateliness....Mr. Obama's family will sit on seats on the floor before him, along with voters from swing states. The goal is to highlight ordinary people.

Despite all their efforts, Democrats remain deeply anxious that Obama's performance might fail:

> Dee Dee Myers, a former press secretary to President Clinton, said that delegates in the hall were excited about the stadium event but that it was the party's senior strategists who were more wary of the setting. "There's a concern in the campaign about how do you pull this off in a way that makes it about the economic themes they want to hit," Ms. Myers said. "He needs to get from the stadium to the diner, and it's a hard thing to pull off."

On the day of Obama's acceptance speech, the *New York Times* "Man in the News" features "Barack Hussein Obama." The story is written by the newspaper's most assiduous campaign biographer, Jodi Kantor, and it is placed inside a four-column box plunked in the middle of the front page. While hailing this "self-made man" as the symbol "for a new political age," Kantor describes Obama's connection with citizen audiences as far from being fused tight.[108] "There is little about him that feels spontaneous or unpolished," she writes, suggesting that audiences often experience his performance as rehearsed and artificial. "Even after two books, thousands of campaign events and countless hours on television, many Americans say they do not feel they know him." Describing what she calls Obama's "uncanny self-assurance," his "seemingly smooth glide upward," and his "aura of specialness," Kantor reports that "Mr. Obama can seem far removed from the troubles of some voters." If this is true, then the shoe may be on the other foot, with Obama facing troubles indeed.

Obama's Drama

The Republicans' fervent hopes are frustrated, and the Democrats' fearful anxieties assuaged. The staged events and audience reactions that fill up the afternoon and early evening at Invesco Field project sincere feelings and deeply patriotic principles, not artifice and celebrity. They create an expressive festival of community, belying the impression of a top-down, rehearsed, directed-from-the-top event.[109]

In its preconvention issue, *Time* magazine has laid out the objectives that Obama the performer must fulfill:

> A stadium's size is its message: it is the (literal) arena in which the audience connects individually to the man onstage and communally with the rest of the crowd. Like an arena rocker, Obama must make all listeners think he is speaking to each of them personally. And he has to reach a broad crowd, from the hipsters who think his early stuff was better to the mainstreamers just discovering him.[110]

This is, in fact, exactly what he achieves. Directly challenging his metaphorical construction, Obama proclaimes "I don't know what kind of lives John McCain thinks celebrities lead, but this is mine." As he speaks about what he insists are his real life and his true values, television cameras scan whites, blacks, old folks, and youngsters nodding in earnest affirmation. Offering ambitious proposals to repair the nation's torn social fabric, Obama moves seamlessly from the practical and mundane to the inspiring promises of civil repair and solidarity—because "that's the idea of America, the promise that we rise and fall together, than I am my brother's keeper, my sister's keeper."

As we've seen already, the response of liberal journalists to Obama's performance is gushing. Declaring "To hell with my critics," Chris Matthews switches back and forth between the first persons singular and plural as he underscores the intensity of the personal-cum-civil connection Obama achieves: "I think what he said was about us, and that's why we care…He said, 'Our strength is not in our money or our military…[but in] the American promise.'" Obama has asked, "Was my upbringing a celebrity's upbringing?!" Declaring "Enough!" Obama demonstrates that, far from being a flighty celebrity, he is tough. He lands "four direct punches to George Bush and four more to the Republican party. No shots are left unthrown. There has been an extraordinary laying down of the glove." Chuck Todd agrees that Obama "is saying I'm going to fight," asserting that "the toughness of the speech is what's…going to stand out." Todd predicts McCain won't "know how to react to this speech," declaring, "I don't know how the Republican Party is going to be able to go against this show." Tom Brokaw admiringly remarks, "This guy is just a step above no matter what you think of him or his politics."

After the speech, even some of Obama's most implacable conservative critics are persuaded that the Democrat might become a compelling collective representation of American democracy. Charles Hurt, the *New York Post*'s Washington Bureau chief, who suggests the staging for Obama's speech might prove a fatal political mistake, declares himself deeply impressed. "However the campaign turns out," Hurt tells his conservative readers, "something very significant happened last night." His account is a hymn to democracy, the sentimental prose redolent with myth:

> Thousands of people—far more than just the delegates to the convention—marched in lines stretching for miles under the searing Colorado sun to get here. They filled the arena from its grassy field to the mountain-top bleachers of Mile High Stadium. Awaiting each of them at their seats were small American flags, fluttering in the dry, mile-high breeze. Respectfully, they picked them up and held them. Or waved them. But they didn't lay them down. Spontaneously, the crowd broke into chants of "U-S-A! U-S-A!," a refrain uncommon in most Democratic rallies. And when Obama mentioned Republican John McCain's military service the crowd bled into applause and cheers. These were not the usual liberals who normally populate Democratic political events. They were some 85,000 Americans, many attending their first-ever campaign event. They were young black kids with doo rags and very old white men. Men in suits with ties and teen girls wildly whipping little flags in the air. Hispanics in garishly sequined jeans and well-fed union guys. They were a mom who trudged up the impossibly vertical metal steps to the very tippy top of the stadium with a big baby strapped to her chest, a milk bottle in her hand and a backpack on her back. And for hours, they were transfixed. At times, it was a rock concern. At other times, it seemed like a great final sporting event. Or a religious revival. Yet what drew them all here was a political figure.[111]

The fusion Obama hero has created causes the celebrity metaphor to die:

> Help from Hollywood is usually far more curse than blessing in American politics. But to dismiss last night as just so much celebrity would be very dangerous for Republicans. There was something else going on... [and] it is mighty powerful, and John McCain could easily wind up on the losing end of it.

The morning after Obama's speech, *Today Show* host Matt Lauer asks Peggy Noonan, "So how did Barack Obama do?"[112] The former speechwriter is in Denver, observing firsthand. Lauer reminds Noonan: "Before the speech you wrote in the *Wall Street Journal* that you were unimpressed with the staging, the Greek-column look, the hugeness of the arena." He then asks: "You were there with some 80,000 other people last night. Did you change your mind?"

NOONAN: I did a little bit. It—you could look at that staging, at the Athenian columns and—at the specific look of it, and you could think, "Man, that's odd looking," and you couldn't figure out how it connected to Obama. But by the end of that speech, I think I broke the code. At the end of the speech, Barack Obama spoke about Martin Luther King, 45 years before, speaking in front of the Lincoln Memorial with the beautiful columns behind him. And suddenly I realized that whole set was meant to be an evocation of Martin Luther King and his great speech that day...and I think the set by the end had a certain glow to it. So I think at the end of the day it worked...

LAUER: Let's talk a little bit more about content. Here's what you write in your column this morning..."The speech itself lacked lift but had heft. It wasn't precisely long on hope, but I think it showed audacity. This was not smiling O. He was not the charmer or the celebrity, and he didn't try much humor. Mr. Obama often looked stern, and somewhat indignant." So if you were one of those people who's come to love those lofty hope-filled speeches, were you disappointed by this?

NOONAN: No, I don't think so. I think there was a certain science behind what Mr. Obama was doing. I think he was thinking, "Look, I'm going to have 30, 35, maybe even 40 million people watching me tonight. A lot of them have never seen me before. They've seen me from out of the side of their eye when they walk by a television, but they haven't really focused on me. I'm going to make them focus on me tonight but in a different way. I'm not going to be charming, lovely, vaguely humorous, interesting and expansive on the issues. I'm going to be a very serious, seriously adult person talking thoughtfully..."...Now in the past few weeks, John McCain's been giving him a few hard wallops. Obama has been holding his fire. All of a sudden in that speech last night he was not holding his fire. He was tough, he smacked him [McCain] around....He was trying to...steady the field there and even things up.

LAUER:...Let me end with history...Did the speech, in your terms, live up to its historical significance?

NOONAN: They asked themselves to live up—to a lot when they put it in that big place. Did it live up to it? I think it was distinguished and memorable.

The half-life of celebrity metaphor was extraordinary, but it could not be stretched as far as the Republicans knew it must be. Still, even if it came up short for conservatives, it was a nightmare for the Democrats that seemed to last a lifetime. Defeating the metaphor represented a lifeline for the Democratic campaign (figures 7.4 and 7.5).

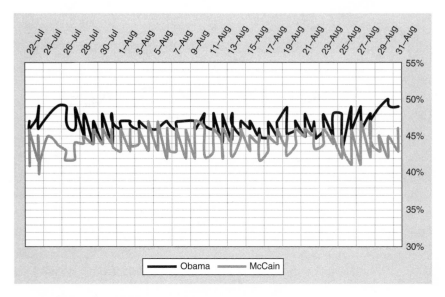

FIGURE 7.4. The Celebrity Metaphor, July 22–August 31

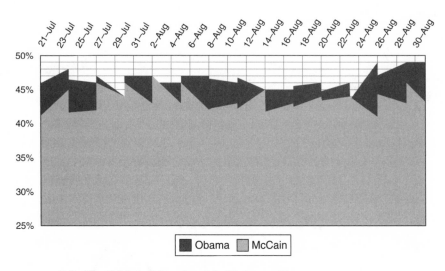

FIGURE 7.5. The Celebrity Metaphor, July 22–August 31

CHAPTER EIGHT

Palin Effect

I N THE BOTTOM OF THE NINTH INNING, WITH HIS DEMOCRATIC TEAM
trailing, Barack Obama faces off against a newly energized Republican pit-
cher now throwing wicked strikes. With the game on the line, the Democrat
slams a 3–2 pitch into the bleachers between center and left field. It is a contingent
but deeply ritualized moment, and its performative power immediate and devastating to the Republican side. "Thursday night, after Obama's well-orchestrated,
well-conceived, and well-delivered acceptance speech, Republicans were demoral-
ized," writes the influential conservative strategist William Kristol in his weekly
New York Times column.[1] After weeks of deflation as a fake celebrity, Obama has
reinflated his image and become a collective representation of the American civil
sphere once again. The evening before the speech, a news analysis in the *Times*
reports "concern" among Republicans that Obama's "command of such a large
crowd on the last night of the Democratic convention would give him the aura of
a president"—and not just to those immediately attending at Invesco Field but
also to citizen audiences and media interpreters far removed from the performative scene.[2] Their worries were justified. Taking back his role as protagonist in the
dramatic struggle for democratic power, Obama has thrown down the gauntlet to
John McCain. For the Republican, the cultural danger is now grave. From being
the Democrat's principal and principled antagonist, he risks being thrown off the
stage. As Kristol puts it, McCain faces the prospect of being forced into "accepting
a role as a bit player in The Barack Obama Story."[3]

At no point during the 2008 campaign has the McCain image generated
much dramatic force. When Steven Schmidt assumes control over image making
in early summer, even he cannot liven up the image. Schmidt tries redressing the

deficit of excitement by attacking the image on the other side. With the celebrity campaign running out of gas, Republicans must now generate performative power from their own side. Because their standard bearer cannot symbolize, they need to choose a running mate who can. When McCain names Sarah Palin his choice for vice president, she officially assumes the junior partner position. Symbolically, however, the reverse is the case. The dimly lit McCain figure is plugged into the high-wattage image from Alaska. Palin has the dramatic power and the prospective political glory. As Kristol suggests, "she is, in a way, now the central figure in this fall's electoral drama."[4]

On July 25 a *Wall Street Journal* headline reads, "Who'll Be McCain's Veep? Who Cares?"[5] The choice will be routine, the paper confidently predicts, and "today's anticipation, excitement and obsession about vice-presidential running mates [soon] will be a distant memory." Events falsify this prediction both ways. The choice of Sarah Palin is unexpected, even shocking, for she is largely unknown and untried on the national stage, and the choice generates extraordinary excitement and passion. Aware that even celebrity metaphor has a sell-by date, Republican image makers have prepared for its demise. Palin's nomination is announced just the morning after Obama made his speech. It has been in the works for weeks. "Despite recent polls showing a close race," a GOP strategist observes after the nomination is announced, "the campaign clearly felt they needed to shake this race up and go for broke."[6] Well before Obama's performance let the air out of the celebrity metaphor, Schmidt and McCain were preparing to send a new Republican image into the political ether, shaping the Palin image for public release.

The GOP strategists and politicians present their vice-presidential pick with the fanfare automobile makers reserve for next year's models. Palin's paint job sparkles, and she is clearly built for power and speed. This new Republican model projects the right image, and she has many of the special features the public desires. However, before plunking their money down for the Republican brand one more time, citizens and reporters want to kick the tires. They want to take the Palin model out for a trial spin and see how she handles on the road. Before they get their chance, the Palin image is out of the gate.

Mavericky Palin Works the Binaries

The beauty of the Palin choice is that her image promises to resolve the slowly burning performative crisis threatening the Republican campaign. As a military hero McCain is not in step with the times. The alternative is to become a civil hero, but his maverick moniker won't fly. Looking back on the Palin effect, *Newsweek*'s Richard Wolffe writes of "a maverick brand that needed rebuilding," the *New York*

Times of "a way to re-establish the maverick persona McCain had lost while wedding himself to Bush's war."[7] Palin's nomination allows McCain to don the maverick image vicariously and to seem as if he, too, can work the binaries of civil
society in a democratic way. In choosing Palin, according to the *Washington Times*,
"the Arizona Republican showed himself to be the maverick, reform-minded
leader he always has been."[8] What's most notable about this conservative paper's
endorsement is its insistence on reform. In his earlier, maverick days, McCain had
seemed to embody the quality of independence, sharply challenging the powers
that be on the American domestic scene. In the years since, as he primped for the
political and religious Right, he could no longer convincingly make such a claim.
Palin allows him to do so again. McCain introduces her to the American public for
the first time at a rally in Dayton, Ohio, on Friday, August 29. "I found someone
with an outstanding reputation for standing up to special interests and entrenched
bureaucracies," McCain declares, "someone who has fought against corruption
and the failed policies of the past."[9]

In its coverage the next day, the *Wall Street Journal* reports that Palin "revels
in her reformer role." Providing factual support for her maverick claim, the paper
aligns Palin's political record with the liberating discourse of civil society. Attesting to
"her reputation as a reformer in Alaska," the *Journal* documents courage and integrity: "As a small-town mayor, she took on her own party elders to run for governor
in 2006, as an FBI corruption probe rocked the state's political establishment." Her
conservatism makes her independent, not subservient, feisty rather than docile:

> As mayor of Wasilla, which is 45 miles north of Anchorage, Gov. Palin
> tried to slim down the size of the city's government and dropped three
> property taxes. And the future governor showed her independent flair—
> attending a campaign event for conservative insurgent Pat Buchanan in
> 1999 and brandishing a "Buchanan" button.

Elected governor, Palin continues standing up for the common folk against political and economic power. Her citizen audiences respond in kind:

> Gov. Palin portrays herself as a crusading government reformer…Her
> popularity in Alaska has soared as high as 83% as she has sacked political
> appointees with close ties to industry lobbyists and shelved pork projects
> by fellow Republicans. In her remarks Friday, Gov. Palin singled out the
> congressional earmark that Sen. McCain loves to hate. "I told Congress
> 'thanks but no thanks' on that bridge to nowhere," she said, referring to
> a controversial proposal for a $400-million link to a sparsely populated

area in southeastern Alaska that had been championed by Alaska's congressional delegation.

Palin is a self-reliant, down-to-earth reformer, virtuous and frugal, upholding the morality of office, abhorring the luxurious trappings of power:

> In office, Gov. Palin set an earthier style than her predecessors. She sold the private jet [former governor] Mr. Murkowski used to get around Alaska, relying instead on commercial airlines and her family's Jetta and a state-issued black Suburban. "I love to drive," she says. She also waved off a security escort, driving herself to and from work every day from Wasilla.

Until Palin's unveiling, Republicans have presented their candidate's domestic qualifications in terms of experience, the theme drawing together McCain's long Senate tenure with his readiness to defend the nation's boundaries in a crisis. The new Republican story of Palin as domestic reformer presents "a jolting narrative shift," according to the *New York Times*.[10] Stephen Schmidt informs campaign staffers that "the story line [is] now Change." Such narrative discontinuity opens the Republicans to charges of opportunism, but the gains it promises up front outweigh any possible later pain. Palin-as-maverick offers Republicans a script that can neutralize the Obama hero on the domestic stage. "The spunky hockey mom that America beheld the next morning," according to the *Times'* Robert Draper, "instantly hijacked Obama's narrative of newness." When he introduces Palin the Friday morning after Obama's speech, McCain hollers "Change is coming!" with such exuberance that he almost seems to surprise himself. Ten days later, at a spirited campaign rally with Palin standing beside him, McCain shouts "Change is coming! Change is coming! Change is coming!"[11]

Palin images civil reformer by pushing back against "failed policies of the past." The vigorous and attractive candidate is untried but she is also heretofore unknown. She stirs up Republican hope because, despite her party loyalty, she puts space between herself and the party's recent and troubled past. Her youthful presence promises a future that will be different and bright. With Palin in the lead, the Republicans can get back into the business of secular salvation. "From the outset," writes the *Weekly Standard*, "McCain was determined to make a bold, transformative pick":

> McCain's selection of Palin ended a long and gut-wrenching selection process driven by the senator's desire to do something unconventional. For weeks, McCain advisers said that the pick would be "transformative"…Neither [governors] Romney nor Pawlenty…was the transformative pick McCain wanted. McCain thought that Palin might be.[12]

Promising transformation lifts the Republicans up onto the hinge of history. The conservatives are relieved:

> Mrs. Palin is history in a dress. And her script is straight out of Hollywood—like those teen movies with the clichéd ending featuring the female valedictorian delivering the speech of a lifetime projecting a bold and transformative future with an independent-minded woman in charge. That future is now.[13]

Palin has the trappings of a civil hero, and with this feisty and forward-looking political figure at his side McCain performs as if he might finally be able to become one too. "I've been called a maverick," he brightly proclaims in his acceptance speech at the Republican convention, "someone who marches to the beat of his own drum." Describing himself as a "restless reformer," he issues a "warning" to the "old big-spending, do-nothing, me-first, country-second Washington crowd."[14] He promises to "drain that swamp," calling upon "insurgents seeking to topple the establishment" to join him and become "true agents of change." David Brooks responds enthusiastically to the call. The Palin pick, writes the conservative *Times* columnist, allows McCain to present himself publicly as he sees himself privately, not "as the old goat running against the fresh upstart. but as the crusader for virtue against the forces of selfishness…[as] cleaning out the Augean stables of Washington."[15] The Palin transfusion is working. It gives McCain the virtue of a crusader and the strength of Hercules. He is becoming a hero again, this time on the domestic scene.

Mavericky Palin Struts the Boundaries

It is not only that Palin works the civil binaries in an energetic way. She walks the boundaries boldly as well. A determined and outspoken born-again Christian, something McCain can never be, the party's vice-presidential nominee "drew raves from the conservative evangelical community," which McCain can never receive.[16] Palin secures the Republicans' religious boundary by reaching out to the troublingly large minority of American citizens who worry about the authenticity of Obama's religious belief. "Here is the thing about Gov. Sarah Palin," the *Times* explains, reporting on a rousing campaign stop she made to conservative enclaves in Ohio and Virginia:

> She Loves America. Really loves it. She loves the smell of cut grass and hay, as she told Ohio voters Sunday. She loves Navy bases, she

said in Virginia Beach on Monday morning. She loves America's "most beautiful national anthem," she told a crowd here a few hours later. Apparently there are people who do not feel the same way about America as Ms. Palin does, she said at campaign rallies over the last two days. Those people just do not get it. "Man, I love small-town U.S.A.," Ms Palin told several thousand people on a field in Ohio, "and I don't care what anyone else says about small-town U.S.A. You guys, you just get it."[17]

Representing the real America against some putatively other one, reaching out to those in small towns with cut grass and hay and not to those in big and crowded urban spaces—all this implicitly connects Palin not only to the civil sphere's religious but its racial boundary, reaffirming the Republican ticket's identification not only with outspoken Christianity but with native ethnicity and the skin color of white.

These promenades bring joy and energy to the devoted Republican base, but neither race nor religion has constituted a vulnerable boundary for the Republican campaign. McCain needs to expand his appeal beyond the conservative base to the center. The boundaries that matter are class and gender.

Three decades ago, the conservative movement in the United States moved beyond the privileged elites by building a big tent and bringing "Reagan Democrats" inside. In recent years, the Republicans' insistence on tax cuts for rich Americans and its effort to privatize Social Security have pushed working-class Americans back toward the Democrats once again. Minnesota governor Tim Pawlenty complains, "[T]here's a perception that Republicans are rich, stereotypical people who don't care about modest-income folks," but he asserts, "It's not true."[18] It was Pawlenty who had early coined the term "Sam's Club Republicans," identifying working-class Americans who shop at discount chains and never set foot in country clubs but who have often supported the Republican side. The *Wall Street Journal* frames the choice of Palin in precisely this way:

PALIN PITCHES SAM'S CLUB TENT
Republican reformers have been crying out for the party to do more for the ranks of "Sam's Club Republicans"—that is, working-class GOP voters more comfortable in a big-box store than a country club. With Gov. Sarah Palin of Alaska as John McCain's running mate, the party now has a new national leader whose personal story resonates precisely with those Sam's Club Republicans....."I'm sure this is partly why the McCain people picked her, she is the prototypical figure for working-class Republicans," says Ross Douthat, author of a new book entitled, "Grand New Party:

How Republicans Can Win the Working Class and Save the American Dream."

When McCain introduces Palin to the American people at the rally in Dayton, Ohio, he identifies her husband, Todd, as a card-carrying union member. Responding to Palin's performance at the rally that day, MSNBC's Chris Matthews says "She's Norma Rae's America," alluding to the legendary assembly-line worker turned union organizer that Sally Field made famous in her academy award performance in 1979.[19] The *Journal* more prosaically confirms that "Gov. Palin's husband is a production operator in an Alaskan oil field and a member of the United Steelworkers union."[20] The next day, the newspaper provides its assiduously pro-business readers with the peculiarly reassuring news that Palin "appealed to populist sensitivities."[21] What they mean is that she blurs the class line.

The boundary along which Palin promenades most proudly and seemingly even more effortlessly is the one that marks the gender divide. And it is here that the greatest cache of still undecided voters resides. In its first report on Palin, the *Wall Street Journal* describes her nomination as "a surprise stroke aimed at attracting Hillary Clinton supporters":[22]

> The move is the most dramatic in a series of efforts to appeal to Clinton backers. Some of those voters have shown a willingness to change party allegiance: A Wall Street Journal/NBC poll taken before this week's Democratic Convention in Denver showed that only about half of the people who had voted for Sen. Clinton in the primaries were planning to vote for Sen. Obama in the general election. About 20% said they would vote for Sen. McCain, and the rest said they were undecided.

In her first public performance after her nomination is revealed, Palin presents herself as walking along the same pathway that Hillary Clinton and other feminist reformers tread, the one that simultaneously separates and connects the civil sphere to gender and family. She claims that her nomination is adumbrated by these feminist achievements and that her election will fulfill the movement's utopian impulse for civil expansion and the perfection of democracy:

> During her speech in Dayton Friday, Gov. Palin went out of her way to appeal directly to the Clinton refugees. Noting the historic nature of her own bid for the vice presidency, she paid homage first to Geraldine Ferraro, who ran on the Democratic ticket in 1984, and then to Sen. Clinton, "who showed such determination and grace in her presidential campaign." She repeated Sen. Clinton's line that she had "left 18 million

cracks" in the glass ceiling that keeps women from only rising so far, a reference to the Clinton vote total in the Democratic primaries. "It turns out the women in America aren't finished yet, and we can shatter that glass ceiling once and for all," Gov. Palin said.

There is no doubt this boundary-shaping performance calls out a powerful response:

> Amy Siskind, a big Democratic fundraiser from Westchester, N.Y., and a proud backer of Ms. Clinton, said she would now make a switch after voting Democratic "up and down the ticket," all her life. She had decided there was no way she would vote for Sen. Obama after the bruising primary campaign. Sen. McCain's announcement Friday sealed her decision, she said, even though she disagrees with his party's opposition to abortion rights: "I'm voting Republican."

The day after, when a male MSNBC commentator disses Palin as merely rehearsing for the role of "cheerleader-in-chief," a female colleague tartly retorts that "Moms feel her story."[23] It seems indeed to be the case, as the *New York Times* reports, that "images of Ms. Palin's smiling family" present a "tableau" that constitutes a "potential counterpoint to the young families of the Democratic ticket."[24]

The next evening at the Republican convention, Palin delivers a remarkably poised, slashingly aggressive, and deftly worded acceptance speech. The *Times'* David Brooks is smitten, lauding Palin as a new kind of feminist hero. It is "stupendous to see a young woman emerge from nowhere to give a smart and assertive speech," he gushes.[25] Brooks grades Palin as scoring 10 on the fusion scale: "She embodies the spirit of the moment." Many female viewers intertwine binaries and gender boundaries in the same way. "I admire her intelligence and I admire her integrity," a woman tells the *Times,* "but first and foremost she's a mom, she has an understanding of what being a mom is."[26] Another woman, referring to Palin's infant with Down syndrome, declares, "I'm not that into politics," but "I'm just going to vote for Trig Van Palin's mom." It is about who Palin is, about her gender and her family, not what her achievements in politics or her civil qualifications might be. It's that she's a "devout Christian with a husband who supports her," somebody who's "not afraid to show up in public with her baby on her hip." The bottom line: "She is everywoman."

In response to Palin's belated and potentially polluting acknowledgment of her unmarried daughter's pregnancy, the *New York Post* reports that GOP strategists are admonishing journalists "that candidates' families are off limits" in the campaign.[27] The reality is that they are anything but. Families and the women who are central to them are a major GOP concern. For years, Democrats have benefited from a gender gap on the female side. The challenge for Republicans is to find a candidate who can narrow if not reverse it. Sarah Palin is the collective representation about whom conservatives have dreamed. During her convention speech, as she endorses the U.S. presence in Iraq and McCain's military judgment, Palin finesses her utter lack of foreign policy experience with a blushingly old-fashioned and sentimental affirmation of female identity: "As the mother of one of those troops, that is exactly the kind of man I want as commander-in-chief. I'm just one of many moms who will say a prayer every night for our sons and daughters, our men in uniform." The *Times* observes that, in "making motherhood an explicit part of her appeal," nobody "has ever tried to combine presidential politics and motherhood in quite the way Ms. Palin is doing."[28] Looking back on the first week of Palin's performance, *Time* magazine declares that "a front-row view of Sarah Palin's campaign debut reveals why her grip on women voters is likely to last."[29]

Moose Hunting on the Last Frontier

There is no doubt about Palin's performative effect. Liberal observers speak about the "freshness" of her image.[30] Conservatives confess to being "thrilled,"[31] and an astute neoconservative strategist asks: "A Star Is Born?"[32] Palin is a wizard at working the binaries and struts along boundaries with the greatest of ease, and she is even more besides. She is not just a "hockey mom" from some Northern state but also a "moose hunter" from Alaska, a figure, as the usually skeptical *Times* puts it, who "comes from a place in the West that embodies…myths…metaphor… [and] a state of mind."[33] Even if Palin cannot walk the nation's military boundary, she is deeply rooted in its land. In the American imagination, as the *Times* reminds its liberal, urban, and cosmopolitan readers, the West is a "distant and exotic" place, an "untamed wilderness brought to heel by fiercely independent souls." Alaska is the American West's last frontier. Back in the nineteenth century, the maverick metaphor signaled the rugged independence and extreme individualism that emerged from the language of cattle rustlers and cowboys. McCain hails from that Western cowboy land, but he has been in Washington too long. He is tamed and civilized. Alaska is the new frontier. A photograph of Sarah Palin in Teddy Roosevelt pose, rifle dangling from bent arm and boot resting on a dead moose, circulates through news media and blogosphere. Maverick migrates to Alaska and becomes Palin property. She uses this highly charged symbol to light up the image of McCain. Palin "seemed to confer not only valor but virility on a 72-year-old politician who only weeks ago barely registered with the party faithful," the *Times* muses. "If not suddenly younger," McCain now certainly appears "freshly boisterous as he crowed 'Change is coming, my friends.' "[34] One fresh maverick makes the worn-out one come alive. Together they are the once and future king and queen, a "team of Mavericks coming to lay waste the Beltway power alleys."

After being presented to the American public in Dayton, Ohio, on Friday, August 29, Palin withdraws into a liminal space hidden from public view, where she is ministered to by strategists, speechwriters, acting coaches, and fashionistas. She emerges from this chrysalis transformed, a beautiful butterfly whose sweeping wings launch a majestic political flight. Looking up to the sky, Republican conventioneers crane their necks for a glimpse. They are enthralled. The fusion is recorded by an observer from the *Times*:

> [F]ive days later [i.e., after the Dayton rally], in the hours after Palin's stunningly self-assured acceptance speech at the G.O.P. convention, I watched as the Republicans in the bar of the Minneapolis Hilton rejoiced as Republicans had not rejoiced since Inauguration Night three and a half long years ago. Jubilant choruses of "She knocked it out of the park" and "One of the greatest speeches ever" were heard throughout the room, and some people gave, yes, Obama-style fist bumps. When the tall, unassuming figure of Palin's speechwriter, Matthew Scully, shuffled into the bar, he was treated to the first standing ovation of his life. Nicolle Wallace confessed to another staff member that she had cried throughout Palin's speech. Allowing his feelings to burst out of his composed eggshell of a face, Schmidt bellowed to someone, "Game on!"...A commotion erupted, followed by outright hysteria. It was 11:45, and the Palins had entered the bar. Dozens of staff members and delegates flocked to the governor, cellphone cameras outstretched. Todd and Sarah Palin posed, shook hands and extended their gracious appreciation for 15 minutes. Then, no doubt realizing that they would never be able to enjoy a drink in peace, they withdrew for the evening, again to raucous applause.[35]

The Republican vice-presidential candidate enters into myth, her person and accessories achieving iconic form. "Palin's Style Sparks Buying Frenzy," headlines the front page of the *Wall Street Journal*.[36] Her red high heels become visual icons:

> Jay Randhawa, a brand director at House of Brands Inc. in San Diego, says he was surprised to learn that Gov. Palin was introduced as Mr. McCain's vice-presidential choice wearing a red pair of peep-toe pumps with 3½ inch heels. The shoes, marked by his company's Naughty Monkey line, generally are geared to women in their early to mid-20s who go clubbing, he

says. "The age bracket we target is a little younger. It's a very edgy, very hip, very street brand," adds Mr. Randhawa. Celebrities like Paris Hilton had been photographed in the brand's shoes, but seldom, if ever, a 40-some-thing politician. Mr. Randhawa says he realized that Gov. Palin's footwear choice offered the chance to pitch the Naughty Monkey line to a new demographic. The company quickly sent out emails to its retailers with a photo of the Alaska governor wearing the shoes and the slogan "I vote for Naughty Monkey!" At Amazon.com Inc.'s Endless.com shoe unit, sales of the red Naughty Monkey shoes shot up 50%, to thousands of pairs, says Mr. Randhawa. A spokeswoman for endless.com declined to provide specific sales data but says the unit "saw definite spikes in sales after Sarah Palin wore the shoes" and sold out in four sizes. Other retailers reported similar increases.

Palin's elegant and trendy Italian eyeglass frames are similarly celebrated. The *Journal* reports that the Kazuo Kawasaki rimless frames sell for $375. They are now on backorder. "To keep up with orders, which have more than quadrupled since the Republican National Convention, manufacturing has shifted to a 24-hour produc-tion cycle." On ABC's *Good Morning America*, the spectacles are shown on and off Sarah Palin, as journalists and everyday folk express iconic admiration:[37]

> GIGI STONE (voiceover): They're calling them the new pantsuit, vice-presiden-tial candidate Sarah Palin's rimless eyeglasses. Whether you're a Democrat or Republican, they're the latest bipartisan must-have fashion accessory.

> SHOPPER (female): I may not totally agree with her political views. But I have to say the glasses make her look very put together, smart, and sophisticated.

> GIGI STONE (voiceover): The company that manufactures them says their phones have been ringing off the hook.

> AMY HAHN (vice president): We began hearing from our authorized dealers, and they wanted to stock multiple pairs of the exact same frame and style and color she had.

> GIGI STONE (off camera): At glasses stores everywhere, women are asking for similar styles. They wanna [*sic*] capture that Palin look.

Headlining "Back Off, GI Joe," the *New York Times* reports that "hot out of the mold come a series of Sarah Palin Action Figures."[38] In "The Upshot on Palin and Her Updo," the paper addresses Palin's unusual hairstyle, the "much-discussed updo."[39] Relentlessly pursuing the secret of how "how Palin toned her image," Amer-ica's highbrow newspaper tracks down Palin's Wasilla hairdresser, who acknowledges the startling news that her longtime client is "very involved in her look and how she's perceived." Confiding "we would talk a lot about how if she looked too pretty or too sexy, people wouldn't listen to her," the hairdresser recalls how she and the Alaska governor had persisted—"we just kept polishing her look." Their hard work has not gone for naught, according to the *Wall Street Journal*: "John Barrett, whose salon sits in the penthouse of tony New York retailer Bergdorf Goodman, says that in the past week he has given five clients the loosely tied-back hairstyle Gov. Palin wore during the convention. 'People are requesting it—it shows off the cheekbones.'"[40]

Getting Back to Even—and Beyond

Pat Buchanan, the conservative strategist turned MSNBC commentator, declares after Palin's Republican convention speech, "You've got an almost even race in terms of enthusiasm, energy, and fire."[41] Will this ritual energy also make the race even in terms of prospective votes? Does "Palin electrification" reach to the center, or does it circulate only within the circuits of the Right? The audience for Palin's acceptance speech is massive, just under the record-breaking crowd that watched Obama six days before. How do those looking in from the undecided center perceive it? Palin's performance is immensely affecting, but is it narrow or wide? She has become a collective representation, but does she symbolize broad and civil solidarity or a connection more particular and confined?

In the struggle for power, meaning is difference. The law of gravity in politics is clear: For every powerful dramatic action there is an equal and opposite reaction. As Palin becomes a bright and powerful star, according to the *Times*, she is "drawing the spotlight away from Obama," dimming his light.[42] Without a spotlight, you cannot have performative power, no matter how fine your virtue or extraordinary your gift. "For one of the few times in his candidacy," the *Times* reports, "Obama is suddenly not the freshest and most telegenic figure on the ballot."

Palin effect is a performative tsunami overwhelming Obama and his team. "The jolt of energy among Republican voters," the *Times* attests, "has caught Mr. Obama and his advisers by surprise."[43] While Obama later protests "it's amazing that it worked," he acknowledges the overwhelming power of the symbolic wave: "I've never seen it before. Just the degree to which everybody got sucked up into this weird vortex."[44] But Palin effect is not at all weird. It is perfectly sensible in a symbolic way, and it reaches well beyond Republican voters. From the moment of Palin's emergence, Democrats worry that responsiveness from female audiences will extend way beyond the ideological divide:

> Obama's aides felt constrained by their recent battles with Hillary Clinton and were unsure how women would react to their new opponent.

The campaign issued two press statements: one belittling her experience, the other congratulating her on breaking a political barrier for
women...When the candidate and his own running mate stopped for
questions in Pennsylvania...they kept their comments respectful and
even positive..."She seems like a compelling person," Obama said, "obviously a terrific personal story."

When "the Obama camp watched her rousing performance at the Republican
convention," the *Wall Street Journal* reports, "focus groups assembled to test the
voter reaction" and Obama "advisers couldn't believe what they were hearing:
'Sarah Palin is one of us.'"[45] The *Washington Times* confirms that the Palin effect
has "confused" the Democrats, throwing the Obama camp "on the defensive" and
turning "the race for the White House upside down."[46] The "Democrats panicked,"
writes Wolffe.[47]

Just days after he has apparently stemmed the resurgent Republican tide,
Barack Obama is in trouble again. As the Democratic campaign craft races downstream, a giant boulder named Palin emerges in its path. On September 7, the
New York Times headlines "Rival Tickets Redrawing Battlegrounds," reporting that
Palin's rise "is energizing conservatives in the battleground of Ohio while improving [the ticket's] chances in Pennsylvania and several Western states."[48] Two days
later, crowing that "it all worked," David Brooks triumphantly announces that
"McCain got a huge postconvention bounce in the polls."[49] This is not just a conservative's fond hope but as near to objective truth as the art of social statistics can
be. According to the *Wall Street Journal,* after the Republican convention "independents broke for McCain by a 15-point margin and he surged in swing state
polls."[50] Wolffe, who had been reporting for *Newsweek,* writes that for two weeks
after Palin's emergence "a half-dozen polls showed McCain taking his first sustained lead of the election."[51] This astonishing reversal of fortune is confirmed
by my own reconstruction in the Poll of Polls (pp. 164–65), the relevant dates of
which are featured in figures 8.1 and 8.2.

Polls help constitute the civil sphere. The public's opinion is sacred, and its
shifting shape a source of immense authority. Polling gives this symbolic power
precision, and its increasing ubiquity gives voice to citizen audiences in real
time. As the new polling about the Palin effect becomes known, Democrats face
the prospect of a shocking reversal of fortune. They make their dissatisfaction
known in short order, and, this close to election time, there is ferocity to their
complaint:

On his weekly strategy call with Democratic senators after the Republican
convention in early September, Obama Chief of Staff Jim Messina began,

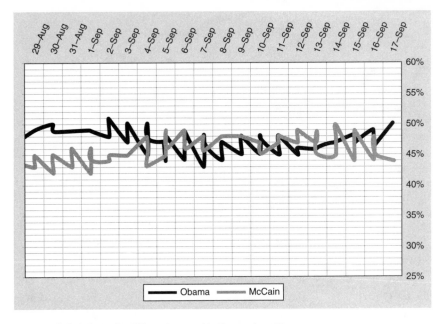

FIGURE 8.1. The Palin Effect, August 29–September 17

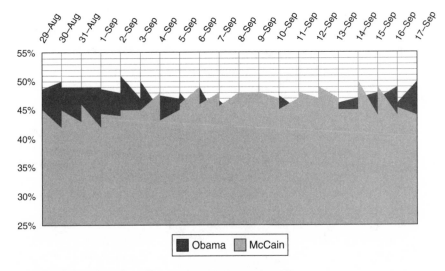

FIGURE 8.2. The Palin Effect, August 29–September 17

"Let me walk you through this week's events." He was cut off by angry senators calling for a more aggressive response to the Republican running-mate pick: "Go after Palin." "Define Palin." "Make the race about Palin." Mr. Messina was startled by the new nervousness in the party ranks.

In a Sept. 11 meeting in Chicago, Mr. Axelrod [Obama's major strategist] addressed his staff. They were worrying about a budding "Palin phenomenon."[52]

The *Times* headlines "Obama Plans Sharper Tone as Party Frets,"[53] and in a separate article records "cries of alarm" from party leaders "after a week in which Ms. Palin has dominated the stage."[54] Obama's performative power is weakened. A Democratic congressman from Alabama declares that "the Obama message has been disrupted in the last week."[55] The *Times* reports that Democrats outside the campaign are demanding that Obama "be urgently working to regain control of the message." Hillary Clinton's former press secretary says the campaign "needs to reboot." Obama is accused of being "too mild mannered" and urged to go after McCain "more aggressively."[56] According to the *Washington Post*'s liberal columnist E. J. Dionne, "it's clear that Obama has lost control of this campaign," and "he will not seize back the initiative with the sometimes halting, conversational and sadly reluctant sound bites he has been producing."[57] Obama needs "crisp, punchy language to force the media and the voters to pay attention," Dionne asserts, and he quotes a North Carolina Democratic congressman, who has observed that "there has not been the direct personal connection." Obama "needs people to feel angry," the congressman argues, "he needs to get people to feel something is at stake."

In a column titled "From the Gut," bestselling author and *Times* columnist Thomas Friedman exclaims, "whoever slipped that valium into Barack Obama's coffee needs to be found and arrested."[58] Delivering a pointed primer in performance studies, Friedman explains that politicians "must connect with voters on a gut level." Earlier in the campaign, Obama had demonstrated this ability "like no other politician since Ronald Reagan," but now he has gone "from cool to cold." If Obama "wants to rally his base, he must be more passionate about his own ideas," delivering positions "clearly, crisply, and passionately." That's what Palin is doing, which explains her giant effect. "I don't know how long or high the 'Sarah Palin bounce' will go," Friedman writes, "but I would take her very seriously as a politician." It's not about policy but aesthetic form: "She may not know nuclear deterrence theory, but she can deliver a line." A political consultant tells Friedman: "Sarah Palin is Roseanne from the 'Roseanne' show." 'Roseanne' was the No. 1 comedy five years in a row and seven out of nine in the top 10." It is because Palin performs like a TV star that "she is connecting at a gut level," Friedman confides.

As the Democratic poll numbers go down and the advice pours in, the nation's most influential newspaper provides a forceful statement about what's at stake politically, about the ferocity of the struggle, and about how victory and defeat depend on symbolic shape. There is "now an intense war between the campaigns to define Ms. Palin in the public mind, a battle that both campaigns consider potentially critical to the election outcome."[59] On one side of the political stage there are script and actor; on the other side is audience. Between them are the space of interpretation and the media. Inside this space a battle is being waged to reshape Palin's image in more and less favorable ways. "The fight is over how she is going to be defined in the eyes of the American public." The fight is strenuously sincere and utterly manipulative at the same time.

Media v. Palin

In fact, the battle to deflate the Palin image is already well under way, but it's not launched by the Democrats, much less by the Obama campaign. It unfolds as a battle between the Republican campaign team and the mass media, mostly but not entirely its news side. "The McCain campaign is regularly battling reports from news organizations that have the potential to undermine the image that it has presented of Palin as reformer."[60] So writes the *New York Times*. The first part of this sentence is observational; there is indeed a battle. The second part is evaluative; it suggests Palin is a constructed image rather than a reformer in fact. What connects the second part to the first—what makes the accusation seem less objectionable, more fact than critique—is the reference in the middle to "reports from news organizations." Information with the potential to undermine Palin's image is not coming from liberals and Democratic politicians but from those who practice the profession of journalism. This particular assessment of Palin's situation is issued by the nation's most authoritative news outlet, which is decidedly liberal, yet few outside the Republican campaign staff and its most deferential media acolytes would disagree.

The McCain team accuses Obama of trying "to destroy" Palin, writes the *Washington Post*'s media critic, Howard Kurtz.[61] He's right about Obama's wishes but wrong about his acts. As the Palin effect unfolds, the Democrat's scope for action is rather restricted, political circumstances making it prohibitive for liberals to act against Palin in an overtly destructive way. As his lead implodes, Obama fears he will seem a bad sport, more partisan than civil, as somebody who believes reform is something only one side can play. Held in check by the delicacy of the gender-family boundary, Obama is afraid that attacking Palin will be seen as anti-woman. For two weeks, as the press exercises what it presents as its simple civic duty, Democratic leaders and their candidate hold back and wait. "For now," ABC reports on *World News Sunday*, "[T]he Obama campaign, fearing a backlash, will not ask its surrogates, including Hillary Clinton, to launch an all-out bashing of Governor Palin."[62] Instead, "the Obama campaign will aim its heaviest artillery at McCain, while waiting and hoping that Sarah Palin makes a mistake." In the face of media criticism, McCain staffers and supporters decry sexism. On Fox cable news, Sean Hannity bemoans "this effort to smear, besmirch, the character assassination and destroy this woman," to which his guest, former senator Fred Thompson, responds, "The media, of course, has gone totally overboard."[63] The conservatives are right to be worried. To the degree the media coverage turns negative, the case against Palin becomes that much easier to make. It seems less spin and more truth. The press supplies facts to the public, the citizen audiences, which always have rationality on their side:

> Speaking to reporters in York, Obama waved off a question about whether media coverage of her has been sexist. "If they want to work the refs, they are free to do so," he said of GOP supporters who have made the allegation. "And I think the public can make their judgments about this." But, he added, "I assume she wants to be treated the same that guys want to be treated, which means that their records are under scrutiny. I've been through this for 19 months. She's been through it, what, four days so far?"[64]

Doubts shadow the public's excitement about Palin's nomination from the moment it's announced. Chuck Todd, NBC's chief political correspondent, responds with caution to the Republican news release on August 29. Speaking on MSNBC, the mainstream network's cable channel, Todd reports that, while McCain's staff is "excited" and "fired up," the Palin nomination "might be a disaster at the end of the day."[65] The reason is that "she's got no real experience," as his colleague puts it. The "biggest downside," Todd observes, "is that this could look like a gimmick." Looking like a gimmick means Palin and McCain would be viewed as performing rather than as acting in an authentic way. It would mean that their symbolic actions would not be believed.

In its coverage of the announcement the next day, the *Wall Street Journal* patterns its reporting in a similar way. The article is authored by three of the conservative paper's leading political reporters, with five other staffers contributing to the lengthy piece. They begin by noting that Palin is "little known on the national stage" and that "McCain passed over many high-profile, more conventional choices for the job."[66] Because of this "thin political résumé," according to the *Journal*, the "campaign's key theme of experience" might now be "undercut." Reporting that "not all Republicans were sanguine about the political dynamics," the story quotes a "GOP strategist" observing "this is a very risky choice." The reporters add, "many Republicans were puzzled because choosing a political newcomer holds special perils."

The danger is that, under the heightened scrutiny of a national stage, something unexpected and potentially polluting about Palin might be revealed. The "classic example" of such "poor vetting," the *Journal* recalls, occurred "when then-Vice President George Bush chose Dan Quayle as his running mate, a decision that appeared to be bold and fresh but wound up widely derided." In making this analogy, the reporters communicate the vulnerability of the Palin image: despite its increasingly positive representation in the binary discourse of civil society, the image might still be shifted to the negative side. The journalists wonder whether McCain's aides are being truthful when attesting that they are "mindful to avoid a similar scenario." They report that "the McCain campaign professed no concern about Gov. Palin's experience." The clear implication is that McCain and his staff might be acting in an anticivil way. The *Journal*'s reporters reveal that "McCain's personal interactions with his new running mate have been sparse." He "first met her just six months ago" at a National Governors Association meeting, and while "they spoke again by phone this past Sunday"—only six days earlier—"campaign officials would not say if there had [been] any interactions in between." Not saying anything seems to validate speculation that Palin's inexperience can be dangerous; reporting that the Republicans are not forthcoming suggests that there is, in the Palin nomination, a faint whiff of political deceit. The implication of secrecy is underscored by the *Journal*'s observation that, even after Palin was chosen, "McCain's decision was closely held." Is there, in fact, something to hide? Shifting its skeptical gaze from McCain to Palin, the *Journal* informs its readers that "while she revels in her reformer role, Ms. Palin has not been free of controversy herself." The controversy is recounted in a she said/he said format that describes the Alaska governor putting narrow family loyalty ahead of the impersonal obligations of office:

> In July, she fired Alaska Department of Public Safety Commissioner Walt Monegan. He later said that Gov. Palin and her husband had pressured him to remove a state trooper who had been married to her sister and feuded with the family. Gov. Palin denied that, saying she removed the commissioner she appointed 18 months earlier because she wanted "a new direction" and offered him a job as liquor board director, which he turned down.

The *Journal* frames this Alaskan drama as an "affair," presenting it as a controversy generated not by partisanship but by principle. Office corruption is, after all, a systemic threat to civil society:

Some legislators have called for an investigation into the affair. "This is going to show people just how vindictive and obsessed the Palins were with this guy," says Andrew Halcro, a rental-car executive in Anchorage and fellow Republican who ran against her in the 2006 gubernatorial contest. "It's not going to be pretty."

That same day, the *Los Angeles Times* also frames Palin's nomination as having the potential to cast doubt on the civil capacity of John McCain:

MCCAIN'S CHOICE OF PALIN IS A RISK
American voters on Friday began learning about Sarah Palin. But the selection of an obscure Alaska governor as the Republican vice presidential nominee also offers clues about the leadership style of the man who placed her on the ticket.... For a candidate known to possess a quick temper and an unpredictable political streak, the decision raises questions about how McCain would lead—whether his decisions would flow from careful deliberations or gut checks in which short-term considerations or feelings outweigh the long view. "Americans like risk-takers, but they also want to know that in times of crisis, you're going to be calm," said Matthew Dowd, who was a senior campaign strategist for President Bush but is neutral in the McCain-Obama race. "Americans don't necessarily want somebody in a time of crisis to be overly emotional," Dowd said. "That's the balance that John McCain's going to have to show the public."..."On its face, it looks like a gut decision," said a Republican strategist who requested anonymity when discussing McCain's judgment...."This is a guy who takes big gambles," said the Republican..."but we're talking about somebody who is 72 running for president, and I don't know if you gamble with those decisions, do you?"[67]

The next day, the *New York Times* takes up the critical themes that the *Wall Street Journal* and the *Los Angeles Times* have raised. In a double-bylined story, reporters stated as fact that "the choice of his running mate said more about Senator John McCain and his image of himself than it did about Sarah Palin."[68] What it says is not all good. After reviewing the briefness of their meetings and the last-minute nature of McCain's decision, the *New York Times* concludes that "at the very least, the process reflects Mr. McCain's history of making fast, instinctive and sometimes risky decisions": "'I make them as quickly as I can, quicker than the other fellow, if I can,' Mr. McCain wrote, with his top adviser Mark Salter, in his 2002 book, 'Worth the Fighting For.' 'Often my haste is a mistake, but I live with the consequences without complaint.'" McCain has insisted that "the last thing he wanted was the kind of rushed decision that President George Bush had made in 1988 in selecting his running mate, Dan Quayle." According to the *New York Times'* reporters, however, this may, in fact, be precisely what characterizes the decision McCain himself has now made. For weeks, the Republican candidate has wanted to name his good friend Senator Joseph Lieberman as his running mate, but the Jewish moderate—once a Democrat, now an independent—supports women's abortion rights, and "the outrage from Christian conservatives [finally] had become too intense to be ignored." At the last minute McCain turns from Lieberman to Palin. She would walk the religious boundary in a more acceptable way. McCain calls her to his home in Sedona, Arizona, for a face-to-face meeting, and "within hours if not minutes after the interview concluded Ms. Palin had the job." The *New York Times* headlines "Selecting Palin, McCain Falls Back on History of Instinctive, Often Risky, Moves." Once again, maverick is checkmated by the Right. If McCain has been forced into submission, his potential for independence is undermined, and he will not be able to reach out to the center in a civil, reformist way.

Roadblock at the Gender Boundary

It is not just a matter of where the Palin nomination sits on the civil binaries—of the thinness of her résumé and the whiffs of scandal wafting from Alaska down to the lower 48. The glow of the Republican representation is also shadowed as she walks the boundaries connecting the civil sphere to the world outside. The Palin image generates its surging performative power not only by presenting the Republican candidate as civil but also by displaying her gender and motherhood. As I discuss briefly in chapter 6, even as Palin is celebrated as a working mom extraordinaire, her image is becoming entangled by what the *New York Times* headlines as "A New Twist in the Debate on Mothers:"[69]

> Within minutes of Friday's announcement that Ms. Palin was joining the Republican ticket, women across the country started flooding blogs devoted to motherhood issues....In interviews, many women, citing their own difficulties with less demanding jobs, said it would be impossible for Ms. Palin to succeed both at motherhood and the nation's second-highest elected position at once....Many women expressed incredulity—some of it polite, some angry—that Ms. Palin would pursue the vice presidency given her younger son's age and condition....Sarah Robertson, a mother of four from Kennebunk, Me., who was one of the

few evangelical Christians interviewed to criticize Ms. Palin, said: "A mother of a 4-month-old infant with Down syndrome taking up full-time campaigning? Not my value set." Ms. Palin is "essentially out-sourc-ing her duties as a mother for the sake of personal political ambition," said Mrs. Robertson, gazing down at her own six-month-old daughter, snuggled against her chest. One detail of Ms. Palin's biography jumped out to many mothers, becoming a subject of instant fixation. "She went back to work as governor of Alaska three days after giving birth," a poster named cafemama marveled on another blog, urbanmamas.com.

On Monday, the possibility of controversy at the gender-family boundary becomes public in a much more vivid, even flagrant way. The McCain campaign reveals that Palin's daughter Bristol, 17 years old and unmarried, is five months pregnant. What the *Times* headlines Palin's "Family Problem" could undermine Palin's boundary-traversing qualities. "It will test…what in these times is consid-ered a normal family life," reports the *Times,* for it "clearly stands as a challenge to the traditional image of a potential first family." In fact, the revelation "could well provide fodder for provocative conversations around kitchen tables or sly refer-ences in the late-night television comic-sphere."[70] Not merely liberal opinion, this is a widely shared media representation of the political difference Palin's revelation might make. Among Republicans at the convention on Monday, the *Times* reports, "Ms. Palin's announcement of her daughter's pregnancy was much of what people were murmuring about inside the halls here [and] at the cocktail hours."[71] Not just the more cosmopolitan *Wall Street Journal* but also the religiously conserva-tive news media frame these revelations as potentially polluting. They press the Republican campaign for more information even if it might block the gender and family boundary in a fatal way:

[O]n Monday, more details seemed to be spilling out. McCain cam-paign officials first confirmed to the Christian Broadcasting Network on Monday that Todd Palin had pleaded guilty to driving while intoxicated in 1986; he had been pulled over, they said, in Dillingham, Alaska, while driving a pickup truck with friends. Mr. Palin has several other minor traffic violations, records show. He pleaded no contest to illegally oper-ating an off-road vehicle in a game refuge in 2002, and that year was charged with failing to stop for a red light.

The Palins eloped on Aug. 29, 1988, and their first son, Track, was born eight months later, a fact that Maria Comella of the McCain cam-paign, declined to elaborate on.

What shapes up is less a battle between liberal and conservative ideology than a war between the mass news media and the Republican presidential campaign. Even as the media continue to document and help constitute Palin's civil celebration and gendered popularity, reporters and columnists sketch out darker and possibly debilitating interpretations. In the *Journal's* report on the first day of the Republican convention, its lead paragraph highlights the "controversy surrounding John McCain's vice-presidential pick."[72] The first sentence describes Palin's problems with the gender-family boundary, the second her difficulties with the civil binaries: "The McCain campaign issued a statement early in the day that said Alaska Gov. Sarah Palin's 17-year-old daughter was pregnant and planned to marry the baby's father. By day's end, the campaign had issued a memo defending Gov. Palin's actions in firing her state police trooper chief." Instead of devoting itself to opening-day speeches and festivities, the nation's leading conservative newspaper is exploring whether Governor Palin acted upon personal interests at the expense of the ethical demands of her office:

> [N]ews spread that Gov. Palin had retained a private attorney to represent her in the firing of her state trooper chief. At issue was her decision in July to fire Department of Public Safety Commissioner Walt Monegan. Mr. Monegan said Gov. Palin and her husband, Todd, had pressured him to remove a state trooper who was a former brother-in-law that Gov. Palin and her family had feuded with. Gov. Palin denies any wrongdoing.

The scandal frame is now set firmly in place. *Journal* reporters next reveal efforts by the Republican campaign to engage in a coverup:

> Meantime, officials with Arizona Sen. McCain's presidential campaign asked Gov. Palin's friends and family to refrain from speaking to the media. And according to one participant, in a conference with friends and local activists, the campaign suggested that all media requests be funneled through the campaign to make sure "we said supportive things."

On the day the Republican convention opens, conservative guru William Kristol, even as he extols Palin's fusing qualities, issues a warning on the op-ed page of the *New York Times.* Yes, the Palin choice allows McCain to replace the image of "crotchety elder" with "fly-boy and gambler," but if the Alaskan "turns out not to be up to the challenge for which McCain has selected her, McCain will pay a heavy price."[73] The Republican leader's "judgment about the most important choice he's had to make this year will have been proved wanting." The representation of McCain's civil capacity is on the line. A front-page headline in the next day's *Los Angeles Times* moves these doubts from future conditional to present tense, seeming to confirm Kristol's worst fears: "Stakes of McCain Bet Are Clearer."[74] The nation's leading West Coast newspaper writes that, "only four days after the nation's voters were asked to accept McCain's reassurances," there are now burgeoning doubts. The ghostly shadowing of Palin representation is here put forward not as interpretation but as empirical fact: "For every piece of the portrait of Palin that the campaign sketches, a far more complicated picture of the Alaskan governor is drawn." Conservative columnist and former Bush speechwriter Robert Scrum tells the *Los Angeles Times* that there is "a growing sense of unease" that McCain didn't "do his homework." Mike Murphy, the veteran conservative strategist, expresses his hope that this is not "a window into the skills of McCain."

On the front page of the *New York Times* the same day, a large-font, two-column headline directly ties Palin's "revelations" to McCain's capacity: "Palin Disclosures Spotlight McCain's Screening Process."[75] The lead reports as fact that "a series of disclosures about Gov. Sarah Palin" has "called into question" how "thoroughly Mr. McCain had examined her." Among "the questions swirling around Ms. Palin" is whether "she abused her power in dismissing the state's public safety commissioner." Whether or not the charges are true, "at the least…it was increasingly apparent that Mrs. Palin had been selected…with more haste than McCain advisers initially described." Republicans are now "worried that Democrats would use the selection of Ms. Palin to question Mr. McCain's judgment and his ability to make crucial decisions." Suggestions of coverup are this time launched from the liberal side. They are presented not as the product of partisan feeing but as a matter of empirical judgment, as a finding lodged in what both sides acknowledge as the emerging struggle "media v. Palin-McCain." Journalists are deeply skeptical about when and how the information about the pregnancy of Palin's daughter is released:

> Mr. McCain's aides disclosed the news at the same time as Hurricane Gustav struck land in what they said was an orchestrated attempt to minimize attention to it.…Mr. McCain's campaign, which has shown itself adept at handling the news media, tried to influence coverage of the disclosure by releasing it as Hurricane Gustav was slamming into the Gulf Coast. (The Palin news was not mentioned on the "CBS Evening News" until 15 minutes into the newscast). It was also by every appearance tucked into a series of problematic tidbits released about Ms. Palin's past, including news that her husband, Todd, was arrested for driving

while impaired in 1986. "We are going to flush the toilet," said Tucker Eskew, who is a senior adviser to Ms. Palin, describing the campaign's plans for Labor Day, when much of the nation was busy with family and social activities.[76]

Despite such energetic efforts at protecting Palin's surging representation, the *Times* suggests that Republicans may not have the symbol-sculpting process fully in hand. "The McCain campaign has moved into unfamiliar—and potentially difficult—territory," reports the paper's chief political correspondent, and "for all the confidence expressed by Republicans here, it is too soon to judge whether this is just a blip—the kind of event that will be forgotten in a news cycle or two—or one of those events that help shape the narrative of the campaign," In the *Times'* op-ed pages that day, conservative columnist David Brooks sketches out what the worst-case scenario might be.[77] Despite his enthusiastic initial support for McCain's choice, Brooks now wonders whether choosing Palin illuminates McCain's "restless, thrill-seeking personality" and whether it confirms McCain's "tendency to personalize issues, a tendency to lead life as a string of virtuous crusades." This is not the kind of candidate, Brooks worries, that members of the civil sphere should choose to represent them inside the state.

Image Alert

Despite Palin's soaring symbolic power, the *Times* observes that at this early point in its rollout, the Palin image is not fully formed, that it remains vulnerable to being shaped in a negative way. Revelations about Bristol's pregnancy are "occurring at a critical moment for Ms. Palin," according to the *Times,* "when a picture of her is just being drawn for the American public."[78] While "Mr. McCain's advisers said they were confident the [pregnancy] story would fade soon," right now its dramatic repercussions are real: "It seemed certain, along with other dribbles of disclosures about Ms. Palin, to interfere with the careful effort by the McCain campaign to portray her as a socially conservative, corruption-fighting hockey mom with five children." In fact, it is conceivable, if only barely, that this challenge to the sculpting of the Palin image might actually disrupt the performance of the entire Republican campaign. On an inside page, just beneath its trailer, "*THE 2008 CAMPAIGN:* A Candidate under Scrutiny," the *Times* splashes a large-font, six-column headline:

Palin Daughter's Pregnancy
Interrupts G.O.P. Convention Script

In the story that follows, the paper reports how "the still-unfolding story of Ms. Palin, 44, and her family eclipsed whatever other message anyone may have hoped to send from the Republican National Convention here on Monday."[79] The *Times* describes the eruption of the counterstory as a "narrative worthy of a Lifetime television drama." Interviews with grassroots members of the Republican convention audience confirm that a performative disruption has occurred:

> Like so many here, Ted Boyatt, 20, a delegate from Maryville, Tenn., seemed stunned by Ms. Palin's announcement and its awkward timing. "It seems like the whole script has just been knocked out of balance," Mr. Boyatt said. "We had it on paper," he said of the convention agenda, "and in the blink of an eye it all went out the window."

Just days after Palin has been introduced with great fanfare and in the very midst of her image fusing on the national scene, the captains of the McCain campaign ship see the outlines of ominous boulders looming downstream. Interpretations challenging their scripting are being widely broadcast even if, for now, they are subdued by the Republican campaign's louder and more resonant themes. Facing the prospect of disruptive messages, the campaign decides to attack the messenger. On the night of Monday, September 1, appearing on Campbell Brown's nightly program, "Election Central," Republican campaign spokesman Tucker Bounds asserts that, because of her job commanding the Alaska National Guard, Governor Palin has more executive experience than Senator Obama. The CNN host expresses incredulity, pressing Bounds sharply:

> "Can you tell me one decision that she made as commander in chief of the Alaska National Guard, just one?" Ms. Brown asked.
> Mr. Bounds responded, "Any decision she has made as the commander of the National Guard that's deployed overseas is more of a decision [than] Barack Obama's been making as he's been running for president for the last two years."
> Mrs. Brown pressed again, saying: "So tell me. Tell me. Give me an example of one of those decisions."
> To which Mr. Bounds said, "Campbell, certainly you don't mean to belittle every experience, every judgment she makes as commander." The argument devolved from there, with no real resolution.[80]

This televised contretemps is widely discussed and reported, and the next day a Republican campaign spokeswoman denounces the "relentless refusal by certain on-air reporters to come to terms with John McCain's selection of

Alaska's sitting governor as our party's nominee for vice president." For the worried Republican campaign team, "to come to terms with" means to accept their own framing of Palin image; the "relentless refusal" of the media paints their resistance as obstinate, irrational, unfair, and anticivil. That evening, McCain is scheduled to be interviewed on CNN by Larry King. In a calibrated demonstration of outrage, the Republican campaign announces McCain will not appear. This disclosure generates extraordinary publicity. The venerable interviewer Larry King is more gossip and free-floating empathizer than journalist, let alone ideologue, and his interview show is widely watched late-night entertainment. Campbell Brown is edgy but not partisan. She is married to a Republican consultant and presents herself as a hard-nosed seeker of unvarnished truth. The television channel employing King and Brown, CNN, is the globe's oldest cable news channel, and it ostentatiously places itself at the political center between MSNBC on the left and Fox on the right. As it confronts CNN and its correspondents, the McCain campaign seems to be moving against the media as a civil institution, not to confront liberal belief:

> Hey, what did Larry King ever do to anybody? Nothing, aides to Senator John McCain said. Still, Mr. McCain will no longer be sitting down with Mr. King on CNN on Tuesday, as punishment for what his aides said was an unfair interview of a McCain campaign spokesman by the network host Campbell Brown on Monday night. Wolf Blitzer, the CNN anchor, announced the news on Tuesday afternoon, saying, "A senior McCain adviser tells CNN the interview has been pulled because of a segment CNN ran last night during Campbell Brown's 'Election Central.'"
> ...
> Mr. Blitzer said, "CNN does not believe that exchange was over the line." It was just one of several arguments the campaign had with news organizations over various reports about Ms. Palin on Tuesday, including with ABC News and the *New York Times*.

The next day on MSNBC television, *Newsweek* correspondent Howard Fineman incredulously relates to audiences on *Hardball* that hostility between Republicans and the news media has become so intense that "McCain operatives are calling out journalists by name!"[81]

These strategic warning shots over the media bow have an equal and opposite effect. The attack on reporters and networks connects the disputation over the Palin image with the issue of media independence. Whether journalism is a civil institution or personal and particularistic is of deep moral interest in a democracy and a matter of the media's institutional self-interest besides. Heels are dug in. Howard Kurtz, the *Washington Post*'s Pulitzer Prize–winning media reporter, reports Steven Schmidt distributing a statement attacking "the efforts of the media and tabloids to destroy this fine and accomplished public servant."[82] Kurtz is outraged and insulted: "By lumping 'media and tabloids' together," Schmidt has "seemed to suggest that all Palin stories bubble up from the same fetid swamp":

PALIN & PRESS: A TESTY START

From the moment Sarah Palin stepped onto the national stage, she was mauled, minimized and manhandled by an openly skeptical media establishment....The uproar handed John McCain's team an opening to declare war on the press...Press-bashing plays well among Republicans. [But] serious journalists have written serious pieces attempting to answer fundamental questions about Palin's record in Alaska and what qualifies her to be, in the endlessly repeated cliché, a heartbeat away from the presidency. That, by the way, is our job. It does not mean that journalists are, as Steve Schmidt, McCain's top strategist, told me last week, "on a mission to destroy Sarah Palin."

In the days after McCain's confrontation with Brown and King and the emerging antimedia complaint of the Republican campaign, expressions of skepticism about the Palin image are broadcast far and wide. A leading *Wall Street Journal* columnist questions whether Palin is really the conservative reformist she and John McCain have proclaimed. He reminds readers that "as governor she has claimed to have resisted 'earmarks,' those congressional appropriations that fund specific projects with federal tax dollars."[83] Pushing back against this assertion—which is central to Palin's reformist image—the conservative opinion writer remonstrates that "news reports from the time indicate she *pushed* for earmarked funds for her city while a mayor." Two days later, in a story headlined "Palin's Pitch to Parents of Disabled Raises Some Doubts," the *Journal* convicts Palin of dishonesty once again:[84]

Little Trig Palin prompted more than delegate coos when he joined his mother on stage at the Republican convention. He also raised new questions among parents whose children have disabilities. Was Alaska Gov. Sarah Palin...exploiting him in a tight presidential campaign?...Republican strategists predicted Gov. Palin could unify the country's 41 million disabled people behind their party...[but] Down syndrome blogs...were filled with questions about Gov. Palin's record on services to the disabled during her two years in state office. This spring, Alaska agreed to almost triple its spending on special-needs children … but Gov. Palin didn't help draft the legislation.

One week later, acknowledging that "Gov. Palin has proven to be extremely popular," the conservative paper observes with barely concealed sarcasm that the vice-presidential candidate has been "ginning up enthusiasm on the trail and helping to lift Sen. McCain's poll numbers."[85] The *Journal* contends that critics' questions about "whether Gov. Palin is experienced enough to step into the Oval Office should she need to" have not yet been answered. The reason is that Palin has not "appeared publicly in anything but scripted settings." To find out the truth about Palin, whether she is an independent figure of virtue or merely a scripted performer, journalists must be allowed to question her directly. Republicans are preventing the media from exercising their civic duty on behalf of the American people.

For two weeks after her nomination, news reporters have not been allowed to meet and question the Republican nominee face to face. The *Times* characterizes the situation as a "news media blackout,"[86] and one of its editorials wittily headlines "In Search of Gov. Palin."[87] But it's no laughing matter. As the *Times* portrays it, the ethical core of American civil society is at stake:

> It is well past time for Sarah Palin, Republican running mate, governor of Alaska and self-proclaimed reformer, to fill in for the voting public the gaping blanks about her record and qualifications to be vice president. The best way to do that would be exactly what the campaign of John McCain is avoiding—an honest news conference. Instead, she has been the bell-jar candidate, barnstorming safe crowds with socko punch lines … But as for talking to reporters … the McCain campaign sniffishly says they must first show "some level of respect and deference." That is a peculiar response for someone who is campaigning as one tough, transparent politician who can take the heat.

A columnist in the *Washington Post* portrays the weight of the conflict in the same way. Observing that Palin "has not opened herself to *any* serious questioning since McCain picked her to be next in line for the presidency" (emphasis in original), E. J. Dionne points to the remark by Republican campaign manager Rick Davis on *Fox News Sunday* that Palin "would not meet with reporters until they showed a willingness to treat her 'with some level of respect and deference.'"[88] This demand, according to Dionne, threatens the core values of democracy:

> Deference? That's a word used in monarchies or aristocracies. Democracies don't give "deference" to politicians. When have McCain, Obama, Biden, or,

for that matter, Hillary Clinton asked for deference? ...A week ago, Elisabeth Bumiller of the New York Times cited McCain sources questioning "how thoroughly Mr. McCain had examined her [Sarah Palin's] background before putting her on the Republican presidential ticket." She reported that Palin had been selected "with more haste than McCain advisers initially described."...McCain's people trashed Bumiller, saying she had opted to "make up her own version of events." Steve Schmidt...said the Times had written "an absolute work of fiction" about the vetting process...It turned out the McCain side misled journalists. Bumiller was right about the vetting. The lesson is that McCain's counselors are not interested in fair treatment, and they are certainly not interested in the truth.

The raging symbolic-cum-institutional confrontation has come to a boil.

Palin Painted

A small army of investigative reporters flies to Alaska searching for the truth about Palin's qualities and McCain's claims. Five days after the vice-presidential announcement, the *Los Angeles Times* writes that "reporters are beginning to work their way across Alaska, reconstructing Palin's personal history."[89] Two days later, an ABC news correspondent, reporting from Palin's hometown of Wasilla, observes that "by our calculations" there is "one national media person for every 130 Wasillians."[90] Three days after that, the *Washington Post* finds reporters "looking under every igloo in Alaska for information that could change perceptions of Palin's record."[91] The reports that media investigators project back to citizen audiences provoke alarm, confirming earlier worries about Palin double-crossing boundaries and violating civil binaries. The most explosive disclosures concern the former, but revelations about the latter are never far away. Maureen Dowd writes that Wasilla is "crawling with ...journalists—from Sydney to Washington—who are here to draw back the curtain on the shiny reformer image that the McCain camp has conjured for their political ingénue and see what's behind it."[92]

There is no doubting how grandly Palin promenades along the gender and family boundary. The question is whether she can walk it in a democratic way. The raft of news stories coming out of Alaska report evidence that Palin's family and gender ties persistently compromised her faithful representation of the civil sphere, first as mayor of the city of Wasilla, later as governor of the state of Alaska. On the first page of its Sunday edition, the *Washington Post* headlines "Palin's Family Has Always Held a Place in Her Politics."[93] That Palin's effort to fire her ex-brother-in-law, Alaska state trooper Mike Wooten, is a genuine scandal is now treated as a fait accompli. Today's revelation concerns the possibility that Palin may also have fired the state police commissioner who stood in her way. This possibility causes a meta-phorically polluting suffix to be added—"gate." As the *Post* explains a day earlier, "the state investigation now dubbed 'Troopergate' is also a family affair":[94]

> Palin is under investigation by the state legislature to determine if she pressured the state police commissioner to fire Wooten and then fired the commissioner because he did not. A senator leading the investigation said Friday that the bipartisan committee moved up the completion date of the report several weeks to Oct. 10. Wooten and the governor's sister divorced in 2005, and the couple have been embroiled in testy child-custody fights. On the same day that [Palin's sister Molly] McCann filed for divorce in April 2005, the governor's father called the state troopers to report allegations of wrongdoing. Complaints filed by McCann, Sarah Palin and her family resulted in more than 20 internal affairs investigations.

That same morning, on NBC's *Saturday Today,* it is reported that "back home in Alaska," just "as Sarah Palin made her campaign trail debut as the official vice presidential nominee," there have been "new turns in the ethics investigation that has dogged her since the summer."[95] Not only will the state legislative committee looking into the matter release its report three weeks ahead of time, but it will "now seek subpoenas after seven witnesses this week reversed course and refused to testify." The "Highlight" lead-in to *CNN Newsroom* that evening proclaims: "Palin is accused of using her political clout to punish the man who wouldn't fire her brother-in-law":[96]

> DREW GRIFFIN, special investigations unit correspondent (on camera): This is an ugly divorce which has blown up into a statewide scandal here in Alaska and is now turning into a national media feeding frenzy involving presidential politics.
>
> VOICE OF WALTER MONEGAN, fmr. Alaska Public Safety Commissioner: I believe I was fired because I did not fire Mike Wooten . . .
>
> MEG STAPLETON, fmr. aide to Gov. Palin: She had nothing to do with the pressure to fire Monegan over Wooten. That is absolutely ridiculous and absurd.
>
> GRIFFIN: But records reveal that staff in her administration, as well as her husband, contacted the Public Safety Commission about Mike Wooten some 20 times since Palin became governor.

VOICE OF MONEGAN: In my heart of hearts, the governor I think did allow her personal feelings to get involved in her professional responsibilities and she ventured where she should have not ventured into, into a personal matter that involved an immediate family member of hers.

Compromising official obligations by pursuing personal interest is the very essence of antidemocratic corruption. If power holders represent themselves instead of the civil sphere, they are not behaving in an ethical way. According to the director of Alaska's Public Safety Employees Association, "the governor's grudge against Wooten clouded her judgment."

This line of boundary criticism is extended when journalists report that Palin's husband, Todd, seems always by her side not only in private life but also in the official business of the state of Alaska. While noting with tongue in cheek that Todd was "a celebrity in his own right as a champion snowmobile racer before becoming known as 'First Dude,'" the *Washington Post* reports that he now "confers with cabinet officials and is copied on the governor's emails":[97]

Guests summoned to the governor's office often find Todd Palin sitting in on the meeting. Tom Whitstine, a fellow Wasilla-based oil worker and friend, recalled raising concerns to Todd Palin about legislation that would impact the oil industry. "I talked to Todd sitting on the couch... there on Safari Lake, in April 2007," said Whitstine, who expresses disappointment with Palin's performance. "It's a known fact Todd was right there when those kind [sic] of policy decisions were being made." Said a Bristol Bay politician who asked not to be named: "He's someone you could call and get the lowdown."

The *Post* later reports on the response to its revelation: "Gov. Sarah Palin is being asked by a local Republican activist to release more than 1,100 emails she withheld from a public records request, including 40 that were copies to her husband, Todd."[98]

An Anchorage attorney speaks frankly to the media about the antidemocratic implications of Palin's actions: "She has allowed Todd Palin—who has not been elected by the people of Alaska, who is not a state employee—to entangle himself apparently as he sees fit in the operations of the executive branch of the state government." A former state employee once close to Todd Palin, who has filed a related ethics complaint against his wife, tells the *Post* that "by withholding these emails, Sarah Palin has broken on her promise of being open, honest and transparent." The governor reneged on commitments basic to civil society. One day earlier, on its front page, a *Post* headline reveals: "Palin Billed State for Nights Spent at

Home; Taxpayers Also Funded Family's Travel."⁹⁹ Reminding its readers that "during her speech at the Republican National Convention last week, Palin cast herself as a crusader for fiscal rectitude as Alaska's governor," the Washington newspaper suggests that, behind the public curtain, Palin is nothing of the kind:

> Alaska Gov. Sarah Palin has billed taxpayers for 312 nights spent in her own home during her first 19 months in office, charging a "per diem" allowance intended to cover meals and incidental expenses while traveling on state business. The governor has also charged the state for travel expenses to take her children on official out-of-town missions. And her husband, Todd, has billed the state for expenses and a daily allowance for trips he makes on official business for his wife.

These polluting declamations are presented as news, not as interpretations, as matters of empirical reality, not ideology. The *Wall Street Journal* sends reporters to dig up dirt in Alaska from the more conservative side. They cover the same bases as journalists at more liberal papers, and they come up with their own, highly damaging scoops besides. Reminding readers that Palin and McCain have portrayed the vice-presidential nominee "as a hard-nosed reformer with unimpeachable integrity," the *Journal's* investigators find that the facts disagree.¹⁰⁰ While state "officials had previously agreed to meet with the independent investigator looking into Gov. Palin's firing of Commissioner Walt Monegan," the governor's lawyer has now "forbidden her staff from any direct contact with the investigator, forcing the lawmakers to consider subpoenas." This may be another sign of a Palin coverup, for it seems to "suggest she bent the rules to her personal interests and used her office for retribution." A *Journal* headline the next day proclaims: "Campaign '08: In Palin's Past, the Personal Got Political; An Aide's Affair May Have Become Grounds for Firing."¹⁰¹ The news today from Wasilla is that Palin fired lifelong friend and political aide John Bitney after learning of Bitney's affair with a close family friend. Allusions are once again made to deception and coverup:

> Gov. Palin's spokesmen have given conflicting explanations for Mr. Bitney's dismissal. At the time, the governor's office cited "personal reasons" for Mr. Bitney's "amicable" departure, according to contemporaneous news reports. Last week, Sharon Leighow, a spokeswoman for the governor's office, said "John Bitney was dismissed because of his poor job performance."…Mr. Bitney said he was shocked to learn that the governor had had any complaints about his performance…."That's the first time I've heard that," he said when told of Ms. Leighow's statement.

In May 2007, less than two months before she fired him, Gov. Palin had publicly declared the legislative session—Mr. Bitney's major responsibility—"wildly successful." After he was fired, Mr. Bitney landed a job as chief of staff to Alaska House Speaker John Harris, another Republican. "I don't think it was fair…," Mr. Harris said of Mr. Bitney's dismissal."

Two days later, the *Journal* headlines: "Ethics Adviser Warned Palin about Trooper Issue; Letter Described Situation as 'Grave,' Called for Apology":[102]

> An informal adviser who has counseled Gov. Sarah Palin on ethics issues urged her in July to apologize for her handling of the dismissal of the state's public safety commissioner and warned that the matter could snowball into a bigger scandal. He also said, in a letter reviewed by The Wall Street Journal, that she should fire many aides who had raised concerns with the chief over a state trooper who was involved in a bitter divorce with the governor's sister. In the letter, written before Sen. John McCain picked the Alaska governor as his running mate, former U.S. Attorney Wevley Shea warned Gov. Palin that "the situation is now grave" and recommended that she and her husband, Todd Palin, apologize for "overreaching or perceived overreaching" for using her position to try to get Trooper Mike Wotten fired from the force.

Mixing seamlessly with these revelations of boundary double-crossing, news spills out that Palin has been working the binaries of civil society in polluting ways. From the media's Alaska investigations emerge a daily drumbeat of facts belying Palin's representation of herself as civil reformer. *Time* magazine's website reports early on that, shortly after being elected mayor, Palin fired Wasilla's librarian for resisting her request to remove controversial books.[103] Reporters debunk one Palin claim after another as pieces of the Palin puzzle, one after the other, are every day put into place. The newly elected governor did not sell her official plane on E-bay. She did not refuse pork-barrel funding from Washington. She did not, at least initially, oppose the infamous "bridge to nowhere." She did not begin construction on a natural gas pipeline that would get cheap energy flowing to the lower 48. The media encases this fuselage of empirical discoveries inside the moralizing language of the civil sphere. By September 6, CNN has this starkly binary framework firmly in place:

> Some Alaskan lawmakers say this hockey mom turned governor is a pit bull—bold, outspoken, gutsy. But critics say she's also stubborn and so aggressive she will step on anyone in her way. Political analysts refer to the body count of Palin's rivals….Alaska Senate President Lydia Green is a Republican like

Palin. Green decided not to run for another term because of differences with the governor. She admits Palin may be charming, but says she governs like a one-way street. Disagree with her and you're done. She takes it personally.[104]

The jigsaw puzzle is completed by a series of television broadcasts from the nation's three leading news networks. Hewing to the model set in place 35 years earlier by the media's framing of the Watergate crisis—a pattern iterated many times since—these televised ritual performances feature serious reporters and worried anchors revealing patterns of antidemocratic deception and scandalous deceit:

NBC NIGHTLY NEWS 6:30 PM EST
SEPTEMBER 9, 2008
WHOLE TRUTH ABOUT SOME CLAIMS MADE BY SARAH PALIN
BRIAN WILLIAMS, anchor: It was just six nights ago, after all, [that] Sarah Palin introduced herself to the GOP convention and to the nation with that speech that made her a star. While it contained several memorable applause lines, it's a lot of what people came to know about her. They remember those stories she told, and Governor Palin has repeated them. But how do they all match up against the truth? Our senior investigative correspondent Lisa Myers takes a closer look tonight.

LISA MYERS reporting: It's one of Governor Palin's biggest applause lines.

GOVERNOR SARAH PALIN: I told Congress thanks, but no thanks on that bridge to nowhere. If our state wanted to build a bridge, we were going to build it ourselves.

MYERS: And featured in McCain's latest ad.
(clip from McCain political advertisement)

MYERS: But that's not the whole story. Here's what the campaign leaves out about the bridge. First, when Palin was running for governor in 2006, she actually supported the project, to build a bridge linking the small town of Ketchikan with sparsely populated Gravina Island.

GOVERNOR PALIN (October 29, 2006): You know, I support these infrastructure projects that will build Alaska, and it's cheaper to do it today than it is tomorrow.

MYERS: Second, Congress had already turned against the project by the time Palin withdrew her support. In November 2005, Congress voted to give Alaska $223 million but no longer required that it be spent on the bridge to nowhere.

STEVE ELLIS (Taxpayers for Common Sense Action): The state could have spent the money on the bridge to nowhere, or they could have spent it on any other project in the state.

MYERS: Last year, citing bloated costs, Palin ended the project, which has brought ridicule on the state, saying, "We are about $329 million short of full funding, and it's clear that Congress has little interest in spending any more money." Some experts say Palin has embellished her role.

ELLIS: The project was already at death's door. She put the final nail in the coffin to end the project.

MYERS: Questions have also been raised about Palin's claims on how she got rid of the governor's jet.

GOVERNOR PALIN (at the Republican convention): The luxury jet, it came with the office, but I put it on eBay.

MYERS: That's accurate, but not quite the whole story. She did put the jet on eBay, but it did not sell. It was eventually sold by a conventional aircraft broker. Her running mate said this:

SENATOR JOHN MCCAIN: She took the luxury jet that was acquired by her predecessor and sold it on eBay and made a profit.

MYERS: That's inaccurate. Not only did it not sell on eBay, the state lost money. A campaign spokesman now says McCain simply misspoke. Finally, there's the governor's private chef.

GOVERNOR PALIN: And as governor, I cut the personal chef position from the budget, which didn't really thrill my kids.

MYERS: That's true. However, earlier this year, the chef was back in the kitchen, cooking for the state legislature.[105]

CBS EVENING NEWS 6:30 PM EST
SEPTEMBER 9, 2008
FACTS BEHIND PALIN'S INVOLVEMENT IN BRIDGE TO NOWHERE
KATIE COURIC, anchor: There's also controversy over the way Governor Palin is trying to attract voters by portraying herself as a reformer opposed to government earmarks, and the example she continues to cite is her opposition to the infamous bridge to nowhere. But she doesn't quite tell the entire story, so tonight Wyatt Andrews fills you in on what the governor leaves out in this reality check.

WYATT ANDREWS reporting: It's one of those claims that gets so much applause....

GOVERNOR SARAH PALIN: I told Congress thanks, but no thanks for that bridge to nowhere.

ANDREWS: ...Governor Sarah Palin just won't let it go.

GOVERNOR PALIN: I told Congress...thanks, but no thanks...to that bridge to nowhere up in Alaska.

ANDREWS: But the truth is, the governor never rebuffed Congress. Here are the facts. After a year of supporting the proposed bridge near Ketchikan, Governor Palin pulled state funds from the project, which killed the bridge for good, but she never said "no thanks" to the federal funds promised by congress, $233 million. In fact...Palin is spending those federal tax dollars on other highway projects around Alaska. As a candidate for governor, she defended every dollar for roads and bridges the state could wrangle from Washington.

GOVERNOR PALIN (from C-SPAN): I'm not going to stand in the way of progress that our congressional delegation—in the position of strength that they have right now—they're making these efforts for the state of Alaska.

ANDREWS: Now, however, Palin is on a Republican ticket that's promising to reform all earmark spending, all of those federal grants aimed at specific local projects. And McCain's credibility here is excellent.

SENATOR JOHN MCCAIN: I have never asked for nor received a single earmark pork barrel project for my state of Arizona.

ANDREWS: Governor Palin's record on earmarks is mixed. Compared to the previous governor, her earmarks are down, 44 percent. But she still requested more than $450 million over two years. By repeating the claim she said no thanks to the bridge, the implication is that Governor Palin confronted a Congress recklessly wasting money. The record shows she wanted that bridge until the end and kept the money.[106]

ABC NEWS TRANSCRIPT
SEPTEMBER 10, 2008
GOOD MORNING AMERICA 7:07 AM EST
PALIN AND THE LIBRARIAN; DID PALIN TRY TO BAN BOOKS?
ROBIN ROBERTS (anchor): No doubt Sarah Palin has a huge following already. So many love her, but many want to know more about her résumé. The details of her tenure as mayor and governor are still coming into focus. And this morning, we have new information on one battle she waged as mayor of Wasilla, a battle that brought her toe-to-toe with a local librarian over which books were appropriate and which were not. Something her critics say crossed

the line into censorship. Our chief investigative correspondent, Brian Ross, has the details. Good morning, Brian.

GRAPHICS: Brian Ross Investigates

GRAPHICS: Palin and the Librarian

GRAPHICS: Did Palin Try to Ban Books?

BRIAN ROSS (voiceover): Sarah Palin was elected the mayor of Wasilla in 1996 with the strong backing of her church, the Wasilla Assembly of God.

REVEREND HOWARD BESS (Church of the Covenant): It wasn't just simply a matter of her using the religious Right to get elected. She was one of them.

BRIAN ROSS (voiceover): Palin has since changed churches. But Assembly of God ministers are well known in Wasilla for taking strong positions on moral issues, including this recent sermon by the current pastor.

REVEREND ED KALNINS (Wasilla Assembly of God): Everybody in the world has a guilty conscience. That's why homosexuals want laws of the land to justify their sin because they have a guilty conscience.

BRIAN ROSS (voiceover): Around the time Palin became mayor, the church and other conservative Christians began to focus on certain books available in local stores and in the town library, including one called "Go Ask Alice" and another written by a local pastor, Howard Bess, called "Pastor, I Am Gay."

HOWARD BESS (Church of the Covenant): This whole thing—of controlling, you know, information, censorship, yeah, that's part of the scene.

BRIAN ROSS (voiceover): Not long after taking office, Palin raised the issue at a city council meeting of how books might be banned, according to news accounts and a local resident, a Democrat who was there.

ANNE KILKENNY (Wasilla resident): Mayor Palin asked the librarian, "What is your response if I ask you to remove some books from the collection of the Wasilla Public Library?"

BRIAN ROSS (voiceover): The Wasilla librarian, Mary Ellen Emmons, the then president of the Alaska Library Association, responded with only a short hesitation.

ANNE KILKENNY (Wasilla resident): The librarian took a deep breath and said, "The books in the collection were purchased—in accordance with national standards and professional guidelines. And I would absolutely not allow you to remove any books from the collection..."

BRIAN ROSS (voiceover): A few weeks after the council meeting, the mayor fired the librarian, although she was reinstated after a community uproar.

JUNE PINNELL-STEPHENS (Alaska Library Association): You'd like to hope that elected officials understand the role of the librarian in a democracy, that is to provide access to information to everybody in the community...

ROBIN ROBERTS: I'm sure, Brian, you know there's so much out there on the— Internet. Much of the information is wrong. In fact, in response to your story right there, the McCain campaign sent out this [sic] three pages to us. And they're trying to shoot down as much as they can...

BRIAN ROSS (voiceover): The mayor did raise the question of how to get books off the shelf...The librarian was offended by that, as were members of the Alaska Library Association who to this day remain very wary of Sarah Palin.

ROBIN ROBERTS (voiceover): All right. Thank you for separating fact from fiction.[107]

These performances of scandal and corruption lend critical support to journalists in the deadly serious contest "Media v. Palin." A two-column story soon appears on the front page of the Sunday New York Times that puts the icing on the media cake. The product of 60 interviews by three veteran reporters, its headline reads: "Once Elected, Palin Hired Friends and Lashed Foes."[108] The subhead announces "Governor's Style of Politics Is Highly Personal." According to the reporters, Palin's image as civil reformer is just that, an image that hides a power-hungry and narrow-minded politician crouching underneath. "Palin walks the national stage as a small-town foe of 'good old boy' politics and champion of ethics reform," the authors write, "but an examination of her swift rise and record as mayor of Wasilla and then governor finds that her visceral style and penchant for attacking critics—she sometimes calls her local opponents 'haters'—contrasts with her carefully crafted image." The investigative journalism inscribes Palin in antidemocratic morality:

Interviews show that Ms. Palin runs an administration that puts a premium on loyalty and secrecy. The governor and her top officials sometimes use personal e-mail accounts for state business; dozens of e-mail messages obtained by The New York Times show that her staff members studied whether that could allow them to circumvent subpoenas seeking public records....Interviews make clear that the Palins draw few distinctions between the personal and the political...Ms. Palin ordered city employees not to talk to the press...Her showman's instincts rarely failed....The administration's e-mail correspondence reveals a siege-like atmosphere. Top aides keep score, demean enemies and gloat over successes. Even some who helped engineer her rise have felt her wrath.

[According to] Dan Fagan, a prominent conservative radio host and longtime friend of Ms. Palin,...[she] characterizes critics as "bad people who are anti-Alaska."

The article is long and deeply reported, but it is also a searing indictment that could be mistaken as a bill of particulars. The *Times'* authority makes the piece explosive. In two weekly columns, the paper's ombudsman, its "public editor," records his and others' misgivings. They complain that the article reports incriminating evaluations without demonstrating the effect that Palin's attitudes have on her actual decisions and policies. The reporters stoutly defend their investigation. Of the three, Michael Powell has the most experience reporting on the presidential campaign. He insists the story's information and its judgments are fully in accordance with professional standards and with journalistic objectivity. They are matters of fact, not ideology:

> The point we made to our own ombudsman [that] was interesting, and what I pointed out to him, and it's still true to this day: neither the McCain campaign nor the governor's office has ever disputed a single fact...never attempted to dispute a single fact in that piece. Every single thing we had in there was on the record. We didn't rely on a single anonymous source.[109]

Revealingly, Powell also justifies the article on the grounds of democratic morality. He portrays himself and his fellow reporters during their weeklong Alaska investigation as standing in for the citizen audience. The average American, Powell is certain, would have agreed with the reporters' own sense that the facts they were uncovering endangered the civil sphere of the United States:

> There were three of us and that helped...We knew what we wanted to do in the sense—you go here, you go here, you go here. It rapidly became clear that, as an editor said, "It's a target-rich environment," and almost everywhere we were calling around and starting to explore, we were finding interesting things....We were coming up with more and more...and we rather rapidly, probably within three days, realized that—that this was kind of disturbing—what we were finding—putting together what I find, what Jo finds, what Peter finds, putting these things together [into a] powerful piece...There is a real sense that this was a candidate who had not been well vetted...I mean, any one of these things taken in isolation would have been perhaps unremarkable. I mean, she hires friends—okay, the argument was certainly made to us, everybody hires friends. She has

a very distant and removed style of governing—well, so did Reagan. You can kind of go around, but when you started to put them all together, it was, I think, and it should be, troubling to anyone who looks at it with a clear eye...I think we did have, all of us, a sense that we were finding things that were very disturbing and that people should know—that people needed to know. Because this—let's face it—in pure actuarial terms...if she becomes vice president—[she] will have the best chance of succeeding to the presidency.

Performing Badly in Public

Palin finally permits herself to be questioned by reporters face to face. However, rather than convincing audiences of her character's authenticity, the interviews confirm the growing sense her public image is hollow and contrived. Before the first interview on September 11, with ABC evening news anchor Charles Gibson, the media suggest that Palin the real person is not up for the task and that she needs coaching and rehearsal beforehand, like an actress preparing for a part. Here is the headline in the morning *Times:* "Squad of G.O.P. Aides Prepares Palin for Interviews":[110]

> Tucker Askew, a veteran of Mr. Bush's primary season campaign against Mr. McCain, has been advising Ms. Palin this week, as she has hopped between S.U.V.s and planes, all the while reading briefing materials or receiving tutorials from policy advisers who have dipped on and off the campaign trail to visit with her. On Wednesday night, three of them were on the plane to Alaska...[including] Steve Biegun, a former staff member of Mr. Bush's National Security Council who has taken leave from his Ford Motors job to advise Ms. Palin...Also accompanying Ms. Palin to Alaska as she prepared for her interview was Nicolle Wallace, a communication director for Mr. Bush's 2004 campaign...and [her] husband, Mark Wallace, Mr. Bush's deputy campaign manager in 2004, is [also] helping prepare Ms. Palin for the debates....Aides have developed a set of presumed questions and answers that they are walking Ms. Palin through. Aides traveling with Ms. Palin have reported back to associates that she is a fast study—asking few questions of her policy briefers but quickly repeating back their main points.

In her column the day before, *Times* columnist Maureen Dowd puts this skepticism in a mocking way:

MY FAIR VEEP

For the first time in American history, we have a "My Fair Lady" moment, as teams of experts bustle around the most famous woman in politics, intensely coaching her for her big moment at the ball—her first unscripted interview this week here with ABC's Charlie Gibson. Eliza, by George, got it and brought off the coup of passing herself off as a Hungarian princess rather than a Covent Garden flower seller. Sarah's challenge is far tougher, and that's why she's pulling the political equivalent of an all-nighter.[111]

With millions watching, Palin flunks the test. In making her replies, she often seems to be controlled by someone—or something—else. When Gibson asks her whether she is confident that she has enough experience, Palin answers, "I'm ready," explaining in a naively revealing manner, "You have to be wired in a way of being so committed to the mission, the mission that we're on, reform of this country and victory in the war."[112] According to the political reporter covering the interview for the *Times,* Palin does indeed seem wired, "appearing to hew so closely to pre-pared answers that she used the exact same phrases repeatedly."[113] Media interpret this first interview negatively not so much on the grounds of substance, about which partisans can disagree, but on the grounds of form. It is because it fails aesthetically—fails to communicate an authentic performer—that the audience's doubts are confirmed. The interview is covered not just by news reporters but also by drama reviewers. The *Times'* TV critic gives the Palin-as-actor a thumbs down. While she "tried to project self-confidence, poise and even expertise," Alessandra Stanley writes, her eyes "looked uncertain and her voice hesitated, and she looked like a student trying to bend prepared answers to fit unexpected questions."[114] Palin "skittered through with general answers, sticking to talking points that flowed out quickly and spiritedly—a little too much by rote to satisfy her interviewer that she was giving his questions serious consideration." What the television critic calls an "unnerving first interview" actually becomes the subject of the lead editorial in next day's *Times,* in which the editorial writers complain of Palin's "befuddlement" and of her being "so visibly scripted and lacking in awareness." And online critics are no less blunt.[115]

While Palin's interviews with CBS news anchor Katie Couric are televised two weeks later, they fuse with the first (ABC) interview in the public's mind. This time critics and audiences focus more on substance than form. Their principal target is Palin's response to a single question. Couric asks what Palin means by suggesting that Alaska's proximity to Russia provides her with foreign policy expertise. While the *Times'* Alessandra Stanley does take note of the how—"Palin's answer was surprisingly wobbly: her words tumbled out fast and choppily, like an outboard motor loosed from the stern"—this time around she is much more concerned with the what:[116]

> "Alaska has a very narrow maritime border between a foreign country, Russia, and on our other side, the land—boundary that we have with—Canada," [Ms. Palin] replied....Ms. Couric pressed her again to explain the geographic point. "Well, it certainly does," Mrs. Palin said, "because our, our next-door neighbors are foreign countries, they're in the state that I am the executive of." Ms. Couric asked the governor if she had ever been involved in negotiations, for example, with her Russian neighbors. "We have trade missions back and forth," Ms. Palin said. "We—we do—it's very important when you consider even national security issues with Russia as Putin rears his head and comes into the airspace of the United States of America, where—where do they go? It's Alaska. It's just right over the border." Ms. Palin, looking at Ms. Couric intently, kept on going. "It is from Alaska that we send those out to make sure that an eye is being kept on this very powerful nation, Russia, because they are right there. They are right next to—to our state."

Stanley writes that this "exchange was so startling that it ricocheted across the Internet several hours before it appeared on CBS and was picked up by rival networks."[117] Conservative interpreters respond in more dramatic and critical ways. *National Review* editor Rich Lowry describes Palin's performance as "dreadful."[118] Beliefnet's Rod Dreher calls it a "train wreck," confessing to being "well and truly embarrassed."[119] CNN's Jack Cafferty damns the interview as "one of the most pathetic pieces of tape I have ever seen from someone aspiring to one of the highest offices in this country" and warns that if Palin's being "one 72-year-old's heartbeat away from being president of the United States...doesn't scare the hell out of you, it should."[120] Acknowledging that "when Palin first emerged as John McCain's running mate, I confess I was delighted," *National Review* and *Washington Post* columnist Kathleen Parker declares that "Palin's recent interviews...have all revealed an attractive, earnest, confident candidate" but one "Who Is Clearly Out of Her League."[121] Parker ends her column by begging Palin to withdraw from the race. She "can save McCain, her party, and the country she loves" if only "she can bow out." David Brooks also overcomes his earlier adulation, now framing Palin as anticivil in the extreme.[122] To believe Sarah Palin "qualified to be vice president," he writes, is to betray conservative values, especially the "prudence" upon which the civil exercise of power most depends. Asserting that "the creation and execution of policy is hard," Brooks reminds his readers that "most of all, it requires prudence":

What is prudence?...It is the ability to absorb the vast flow of information and still discern the essential current of events...to engage in complex deliberations and feel which arguments have the most weight....Sarah Palin has many virtues [but] she...does not have a repertoire of historic patterns and,...[she]...compensate[s] for her lack of experience with brashness and excessive decisiveness.

Saturday Night Live unrolls its fall season premier three days after Palin's ABC interview, on September 14, and Tina Fey, SNL's former star comedienne, takes time off from her hit show, *30 Rock,* to participate in the evening's opening skit. Fey performs Sarah Palin performing herself in the interview with Charles Gibson. The snide parody is so dead on as to be dumbfounding, mimicking the Alaska politician's voice and visuals and highlighting her explanation "I can see Russia from my house." Calling Fey's appearance the "most eagerly anticipated opening in the show's long and storied history," the *Huffington Post* media critic pronounces the performance of a performance "a brilliant interpretation."[123] The SNL fiction has the clear ring of truth. Responding to a poll by CBS's *The Insider,* which asks, "Do you think Tina Fey did a good job playing Sarah Palin?" one respondent comments on Fey's transgressive intertwining of actress and politician: "Politics aside...not only did she sound like her but she looked like her. She was dead on."[124] Another suggests Fey's fictional character is more real than the politician she portrays, inserting SNL's political entertainment into the binary discourse of civil society: "Does anyone here think that these SNL skits are helping educate nondecided voters? It seems that this Tina is so on, and it's all so 'on' that only the hard-core base couldn't see that the GOP has gone flaky, and dangerously so." Visited millions of times on YouTube, the skit becomes the "most watched viral video ever."[125] In the weeks that follow, Fey shows up frequently on SNL, her parody of the Republican's vice-presidential nominee becoming a nationally talked about shadow haunting the real thing. After the Palin-Couric interview, the Fey character provides a devastating commentary simply by channeling the exact wording of Palin's actual replies. Replaying highlights from Fey's performance the next evening on *The Situation Room,* the perpetually dour CNN anchor Wolf Blitzer laughingly remarks to political reporter John King, "This is the first time I've heard a parody on SNL that used the actual words!"[126] King asks whether what they've just seen is a case of art imitating life or life imitating art. Fey's fictional creation presents itself as entertainment, but it quickly becomes a symbolic reference for constructing the empirical reality of the campaign. Fey wins an Emmy for her fusing performance of Palin as merely a performer, somebody who seems incapable of representing the civil sphere in an effective, much less a democratic, way. If the struggle for power is representational, the *Wall Street Journal* explains, such fictional mediation should not surprise us:

> Comedy shows have been an especially vital force in framing the presidential election for a mass audience, cementing caricatures of the candidates…At a time when election coverage and commentary are being pumped out in reams, comedians have managed to break through the clutter by coming up with lasting takes on the election, repeated around water coolers and on Sunday morning political talk shows…."There's just so much to play with here," said Eric Stangel, one of the head writers of CBS's "The Late Show with David Letterman"…"There's been so much media coverage, so many investigative reports, so much out there about this election, and then Tina Fey holds up a flute, and that's what everyone's talking about," Mr. Stangel said, referencing a segment on last week's "Saturday Night Live," in which Ms. Fey spoofed Gov. Palin's performance at the vice-presidential debate….Political comedy has lifted SNL's ratings 50% compared with last year, and the show has added three prime-time political specials…Ms. Fey's impersonation of Gov. Palin became a hit online and served as a reference point in political discussions, including on NBC's "Meet the Press" on Sunday.[127]

Bleeding into Image McCain

The deconstruction of the Palin image casts a darkening shadow over John McCain. Once energized by his association with her symbol, he is now depleted by it. He has lived by Sarah's sword; he now risks dying by it. Up until mid-September, the knock-on effect of painting Palin badly has been relatively restricted. As Palin's performance comes to seem performative, McCain's recommendation letter for her is discredited, his decision making faulted, and his judgment impugned as impulsive. Now, after the interviews and Tina Fey parodies, the damage goes deeper. The descriptions of McCain's anticivil qualities are generalized. The accusation that he is not being honest with the American people spreads from Palin to McCain's broader conduct in the campaign. While the *Times'* lead editorial on September 12 is titled "Gov. Palin's Worldview," its first sentence is not about her but her running mate, John McCain: "As we watched Sarah Palin on TV the last couple of days, we kept wondering what on earth John McCain was thinking."[128] What the newspaper's editors and other Americans wonder about is whether the Republican candidate has a deficit of civil capacity or a callous lack of respect for the same:

If he seriously thought this first-term governor—with less than two years in office—was qualified to be president, if necessary, at such a dangerous time, it raises profound questions about his judgment. If the choice was, as we suspect, a tactical move, then it was shockingly irresponsible.

Being tactical about something so important—about prospectively assuming the presidency in a time of crisis—is shocking because it suggests McCain does not respect citizen audiences and that he would not be responsive to the members of the civil sphere if he held state power. The *Times* concludes that this might well be the case. McCain "shows a contempt for voters," the most grievous sin a candidate struggling for democratic power can display. Holding voters in contempt raises the dark danger of despotism and deceit, gesturing to the polluting discourse that threatens to undermine every effort at building a democratic state. It "raises frightening questions about how Mr. McCain and Ms. Palin plan to run this country."

From this point onward and right up until Election Day, McCain and his campaign are persistently accused by representatives of the American civil sphere of telling "lies." It seems like a simple and unelaborated criticism. Doesn't everybody know that politicians shade the truth? Posed in a certain manner and context, however, the suggestion of political deceit is devastating. If it cannot be dismissed as partisan, it suggests that the powerful do not deserve to have democracy on their side. The media often present this accusation as coming from centrists and conservatives, but just as often they inscribe such Republican scheming in the facts of social life.

The View is a long-running, late-morning talk show that has a devoted following. Recipient of 24 Daytime Emmy awards, including "Outstanding Talk Show," its website describes the entertainment program as a "morning chatfest" conducted by "a team of dynamic women of different ages, experience, and backgrounds discussing the most exciting events of the day." On September 12, the day after Sarah Palin's ABC interview, *The View*'s famous guest is her running mate, John McCain. He is smiling and relaxed, ready for an easy exchange. Sitting on McCain's left, at the center of the cozy half-circle of cohosts, is Joyce Behar. Without warning, the comedienne turns to the Republican candidate and bluntly accuses him of lying. McCain is ambushed and surprised. Here is how the confrontation is related the next day in the *Times*:

On Friday on "The View," generally friendly territory for politicians, one co-host, Joy Behar, criticized his new advertisements. "We know that those two ads are untrue," Ms. Behar said. "They are lies. And yet you, at the end of it, say, 'I approve these messages.' Do you really approve them?"[129]

McCain is defensive and crisply objects that "actually they are not lies." The cohosts rally around their colleague, isolating the leader of the Republican campaign. The *Washington Post* tells the story in a broader way:

> Obama got something of an assist from the hosts of the "The View," who challenged McCain on the integrity and honesty of his campaign. Joy Behar questioned two ads he is running against the Democrat—one accusing him of supporting "comprehensive" sex education for kinder-gartners, the other saying he called Palin a pig when he used the say-ing "lipstick on a pig" in reference to McCain's claims to be an agent of change. "We know that those two ads are untrue," Behar said. "They are lies." When McCain defended them, Barbara Walters noted that McCain had made the same lipstick on a pig comment about Sen. Hillary Rodham Clinton's health-care proposal. "About health care," McCain said. Obama "chooses his words very carefully. He shouldn't have said it." McCain has portrayed Palin as a reformer unwilling to accept pork from Washington, but Walters and Behar pressed. "She also took some earmarks," Walters said. "No, not as governor she didn't," McCain responded, inaccurately. The Obama campaign quickly produced newspaper articles about Palin seeking various earmarks as governor. In February, her office sent Sen. Ted Stevens (R-Alaska) a 70-page memo outlining almost $200 million worth of funding requests for her state.[130]

The confrontation is widely watched and endlessly reported and replayed.[131] It shows how the nose-diving Palin image is polluting McCain's. The pieces from her broken image are falling on the man who chose her. "What is the world coming to," asks the blog *Wonkette: The DC Gossip,* "when the ladies on The View ask John McCain the toughest questions he's gotten in weeks?"[132]

What it has come to is that Republican campaign statements are no longer being given the traditional leeway with facts. Held to the standard of truthful-ness, not truthiness, they do not meet the grade. Those issuing them are broadly accused of lying. On its left-hand column the day after *The View* debacle, the *Times* headlines: "McCain Barbs Stirring Outcry as Distortions."[133] The story quotes nonpartisan authorities and conservative sources to establish McCain's deceit, but it also makes factual judgments on its own:

> Harsh advertisements and negative attacks are a staple of presidential cam-paigns, but Senator John McCain has drawn an avalanche of criticism this week from Democrats, independent groups, and even some Republicans for regularly stretching the truth in attacking Senator Barack Obama's

record and positions....[T]he McCain campaign twisted Mr. Obama's words to suggest that he had compared Gov. Sarah Palin...to a pig after Mr. Obama said, in questioning Mr. McCain's claim to be the change agent in the race, "You can put lipstick on a pig; it's still a pig."...Then he falsely claimed that Mr. Obama supported "comprehensive sex education" for kindergartners...Those attacks followed weeks in which Mr. McCain repeatedly, and incorrectly, asserted that Mr. Obama would raise taxes on the middle class...Indeed, in recent days, Mr. McCain has been increasingly called out by news organizations, editorial boards and independent analysts like FactCheck.org. The group...has cried foul.

McCain is described as embracing pollution as a campaign strategy and as speaking on behalf of the anticivil side:

> Mr. McCain came into the race promoting himself as a truth teller and has long publicly deplored the kinds of negative tactics that helped sink his [own] candidacy in the Republican primaries in 2000. But his strategy now reflects a calculation advisers made this summer—over the strenuous objections of some longtime hands who helped him build his "Straight Talk" image—to shift the campaign more toward disqualifying Mr. Obama in the eyes of voters. "They just keep stirring the pot, and I think the McCain folks realize if they can get this thing down in the mud, drag Obama into the mud, that's where they have the best advantage to win," said Matthew Dowd, who worked with many top McCain campaign advisers when he was President Bush's chief strategist in the 2004 campaign, but who has since had a falling out with the White House....Some who have criticized Mr. McCain have accused him of blatant untruths and of failing to correct himself when errors were pointed out.

On the inside, where this front-page story continues, a large box is inserted at the center of the page:[134]

THE REALITY BEHIND THE CLAIMS
Senator John McCain and his running mate, Gov. Sarah Palin of Alaska, have been criticized for a number of recent false, incomplete, or misleading claims in his commercials and on the stump.

Below run two vertical columns, on the left "McCain campaign" and on the right "Reality check." They are cross-cut by four horizontal strips, each of which concerns issues upon which the Republicans are portrayed has having deceived voters:

TAXES, ENERGY, HEALTH CARE, and EARMARKS. The four boxes that run vertically on the left side are filled with quotations from the Republican candidate, his running mate, or campaign ads. The boxes running vertical on the right side contain statements by nonpartisan research groups, quotations from the media, or statements of fact by the *Times*. At the end of the story, just below the box, the newspaper quotes an academic expert on health policy teaching at a prestigious southern university. He addresses the McCain campaign's claims that Obama's plan will force families into a government-run system. "I would say this is an inaccurate and false characterization of the Obama plan," the academic states, adding, "I don't take these words lightly." Neither, most assuredly, do the American people, much less the *Times*.

Polls Slide, Barack Appears

Although he is in for the highest stakes, Barack Obama does not have his own dog in this ferocious fight. It is the media and civil society against Sarah Palin and John McCain. Obama enters the ring with apparent reluctance, even distaste, and only after his opponents are bloodied and bowed. In the midst of media revelations from Alaska, he carefully echoes their complaint about the bridge to nowhere. To an applauding crowd in Michigan, Obama allows about Palin that "she was for it until everybody starting raising a fuss about it and she started running for governor and then suddenly she was against it." Working the binaries, he accuses her of deception and of insulting voters: "I mean, you can't just re-create yourself. You can't just reinvent yourself. The American people aren't stupid."[135] Only after Palin's ABC interview and *The View*, after internal polls indicated opinion turning back to him,[136] and after public criticism beginning to generalize from Palin to McCain—only now does the Obama campaign ratchet up its criticism:

> [S]ensing an opening in the mounting criticism of Mr. McCain, the Obama campaign released a withering statement after Mr. McCain's appearance on "The View." "In running the sleaziest campaign since South Carolina in 2000 and standing by completely debunked lies on national television, it's clear that John McCain would rather lose his integrity than lose an election," Hari Sevugan, a spokesman for the Obama campaign, said in a statement.[137]

Obama works the binaries, carefully following the emerging civil society line:

At an event in Dover, N.H., a voter asked Mr. Obama when he would start "fighting back." Mr. Obama...said, "Our ads have been pretty tough, but I just have a different philosophy that I'm going to respond with the truth. I'm not going to start making up lies about John McCain."

The next day Obama's campaign releases a scathing ad titled "Honor." It opens by asking "What's happened to McCain?" It then calls McCain's smear ads "sleazy" and "truly vile" and labels the Republican campaign "disgraceful" and "dishonorable." The spot closes with "It seems deception is all he has left."[138]

But Obama does not have to speak out forcefully. By now, the center of the citizen audience has begun to find its voice, speaking out through the polls against Palin-McCain. On September 12, the *Wall Street Journal* headlines "Palin Bump Falls Flat."[139] According to a new Quinnipiac poll, "Sen. John McCain's vice-presidential pick, Sarah Palin, hasn't yet changed his fortunes in some of the largest swing states." Last month Obama was just one point ahead in Ohio, the poll announces, but now he is leading by five. Six days later, in a two-column story on the left side of its front page, the *Times* reports that "the Palin effect" has had only "a limited burst."[140] A *New York Times*/CBS poll, "taken right after Ms. Palin sat down for a series of high-profile interviews with Charles Gibson on ABC News," shows that only 40 percent of Americans now have a favorable impression of Sarah Palin. Before the Republican convention, McCain led Obama 44 to 37 percent among white women, and polls "suggested that Mr. McCain had enjoyed a surge of support...among white women after his selection of Gov. Sarah Palin of Alaska as his running mate." Now, however, white women are evenly divided between the two candidates. A vast majority of the citizen audience tells pollsters they believe McCain chose Palin for calculating and selfish reasons, not because of her actual qualifications. In fact, "75 percent said they thought Mr. McCain had picked Ms. Palin more to help him win the election than because he thought she was well qualified to be president"; only 31 percent feel that Obama chose Biden in this way. Palin's support is still deep, but it is no longer wide. McCain's choice has "excited" supporters, but it has "helped Mr. McCain only among Republican base voters." A *Wall Street Journal*/NBC News poll taken September 19–22 found that nearly half of the respondents believed Palin unqualified to be president, while one in three said they were "not at all" comfortable with the idea of Governor Palin as vice president.[141] Moreover, just days before going into the vice-presidential debate, 32 percent of registered voters polled by ABC/*Washington Post* on September 29 said her selection makes them "less likely" to support John McCain for president, up from 19 percent on September 4. Offering that "Palin looks more like a drag than a boost to the GOP ticket," the poll release went on to say this:

Her basic ratings are weaker still. Just 35 percent say Palin has the experience it takes to serve effectively as president, down a dozen points since early September; 60 percent think not, up 15. And just 46 percent think Palin "understands complex issues," while 49 percent think she doesn't—a poor assessment on this most basic qualification.[142]

The next day's *Times* reports that "a month after Gov. Sarah Palin joined Senator John McCain's ticket to a burst of excitement," there has been a "rapid change in fortunes."[143]

By then, the financial crisis is already well under way.

CHAPTER NINE

Financial Crisis

I N THE SUNDAY *NEW YORK TIMES* ON SEPTEMBER 14, THE LEAD
campaign story stretches across the two columns on the left side of the
front page: "Once Elected, Palin Hired Friends and Lashed Foes." It is the
last of the searing investigations that deflates the Republican candidate for vice
president and her senior partner as well. Beneath this story, a two-column headline in smaller font announces: "A Wall Street Goliath Teeters amid Fears of
Widening Crisis." The story recounts fears that "Lehman Brothers is only days
away from collapse," reporting that government officials and senior Wall Street
officials are meeting "to try to arrest a downward spiral that might imperil other
financial institutions."[1] In that Sunday's "Week in Review" section, most of the
front page is still devoted to Sarah Palin, but one column headlines "A Financial
Drama with No Final Act in Sight," the highlighted insert explaining "Don't
expect the economy to pick up until Wall Street settles down."[2]

The really big news this day is Hurricane Ike. "Damage Extensive as Storm
Batters Texas," the lower case headline splashes across four columns of the *Times'*
front page. Just one day later, news about stormy weather begins focusing primarily on the economic kind. A large-font, all-caps, italic, and bold-faced headline
screams across three front-page columns of the September 15 *New York Times*:

FINANCIAL CRISIS RESHAPES WALL STREET'S LANDSCAPE

The third and final turning point in the struggle for state power has arrived,
even as the second colossal boulder blocking the rushing river of the campaign is
barely past. The river's surface remains murky. The deeper tectonic shifts shaping

its current, so clearly traceable after the race is over, are now becoming sensible, but they are not yet fully visible and perceived. Palin is declining, but is she in free fall, her image about to smash upon the campaign ground? What about the recent "resurgence" of McCain? It remains a vivid topic of conversation, even as it fades from the electoral scene.[3] Obama continues receiving urgent and unsolicited advice from liberal strategists and pundits just as the campaign is turning his way.[4] Sympathetic journalists fret that the media environment is so saturated and audiences so fractured that effective political communication is no longer possible; yet, at this very moment, Obama's message clarifies, and his triumph becomes imminent.[5] Five weeks from now, the conservative congressman turned MSNBC host Joe Scarborough looks back on this moment and ruefully recalls that the GOP was ahead until the financial crisis. Because of the Palin effect, he remembers, they had gone "from 10 points behind to two, three, four points ahead."[6] But this is not at all the case. Scarborough's nostalgically backward glance is deeply misleading. The Palin effect deflated before the financial crisis, and her polluted representation had already brought down McCain. From that point on, the Republican campaign's civil power was in decline.

Setting a New Stage

However misplaced the anxieties and distorted the apperceptions, they do reveal a larger truth. The outcome of the democratic struggle for power is neither inevitable nor determined. Despite their recent misfortunes, the Republicans still have a chance. The looming economic boulder presents grave new dangers, but it also offers opportunity. There seems little doubt that it will be a turning point in the campaign, but how it will direct the rushing river—how the campaign crafts will navigate it—is not yet known, nor can it be. Financial crisis is a cause, but it doesn't trigger an inevitable effect. What it creates is a new stage for the unfolding of political drama, for those struggling for power to perform, and for citizen audiences to decide.

The economic boulder breaks the surface of the rushing river for objective reasons, driven by events and institutional logics that stand outside the cultural structures and meaning struggles of the political campaign. The *New York Times'* screaming headline on September 15 has it right when it depicts events in the driver's seat: *"FINANCIAL CRISIS"* is the doer, the mover, the subject, the force that *"RESHAPES."* And what it reshapes, what it bends to its will, is *"WALL STREET'S LANDSCAPE."* After years of housing bubbles and increasingly esoteric financial instrumentation, impersonal market rationality has been taken to such an extreme that forces, not actors, now seem in control. Events are in the saddle, not human beings. The *Times* describes the "venerable firm" of Lehman Brothers as being "hurtled toward liquidation" and recounts how many "once-proud financial institutions have been brought to their knees."[7] In the days following, front-page headlines in four-column italics, bold-faced and in caps, depict the financial crisis as objective and overwhelming:

WALL ST. IN WORST LOSS SINCE '01
DESPITE REASSURANCES BY BUSH[8]

NEW PHASE IN FINANCE CRISIS
AS INVESTORS RUN TO SAFETY[9]

Yet, while its origins seem objective and impersonal, the financial crisis takes on a decidedly subjective character as it enters the public stage. Up until this point in the struggle for power, the economy has been treated as a boundary of the civil sphere and a secondary one at that. Now it moves to the very center. Civil society in the United States becomes engulfed by an extraordinary sense of precariousness. "A Jittery Road Ahead" proclaims a large and arresting subhead in the *New York Times* on the first day of the financial crisis, and the authors of the story that follow note that "some fear a precipitous decline."[10] Observers speak of the "end of an era," the first sentence of the *Times*' lead story that day describing "one of the most dramatic days in Wall Street's history."[11] A powerful investment banker and former cabinet secretary declares, "I've been in the business 35 years, and these are the most extraordinary events I've ever seen." A deep crack has appeared in time's continuous unfolding, and the hinge of history is swinging again. That same day in the arts section Michiko Kakutani addresses the recent suicide of wunderkind novelist David Foster Wallace. The headline describes Wallace's quirky, avant-garde writings as "Exuberant Riffs on a Land Run Amok," and Kakutani praises the novelist's "keen sense of the metastasizing absurdities of life in America at a precarious hinge moment in time."[12] On another inside page, under the headline "Washington Takes on the Feel of Wartime," the *Times* reports that "the realization [has] settled in that American capitalism is going through something historic—and not in a good way."[13] In the religiously weighted language of apocalypse, the paper ominously warns about the imminence of "judgment day"—the "policy and political choices the two parties make now could weigh heavily on voters when they go to the polls in little more than six weeks."

When the actual day of electoral judgment arrives, journalists, pundits, and academic analysts will evoke demographic determinism and declare that financial crisis made McCain's defeat inevitable. When "the financial panic escalated into a near-meltdown and Americans began to fear for their prosperity," the *Wall Street Journal* laments on November 5, "public support for Republicans fell across the board."[14] This is not, however, how the financial crisis is actually experienced and perceived. A week into the catastrophe, the *Times'* John Harwood reports that, far from deciding Democratic victory and Republican defeat, the financial crisis has "snapped voters' attention back to the alternative visions" the parties offer about government intervention in economic life. Now "each candidate can offer credible arguments rooted in his philosophy and track record," Harwood reports, adding that, if anything, "recent presidential contests suggest the electorate's philosophical instincts lie closer...to those of Republicans."[15]

In these final weeks of struggle, the candidates are presented with dramatic new opportunities, but the scripts for their political teams remain to be written, and their performances await. As the curtain goes up, each is "seeking to gain the upper hand in the newly dominant issue in the presidential campaign," writes the *Wall Street Journal,* reporting that "John McCain and Barack Obama rushed to release new proposals to address the financial crisis."[16] To Americans frightened that the center will not hold, both Republican and Democrat promise that order will be restored. Yet such a restoration will not come via economic rationality. The market has failed. The promise of crisis resolution must be articulated not within the language of capitalism but inside the discourse of civil society. The challenge for candidates is to bring the moral ethos of democracy to bear on this raging economic storm.

McCain Blunders

McCain, anxious for civil restoration, intervenes first, on the very morning of Monday, September 15. In a televised rally in Jacksonville, Florida, McCain declares, "Our economy, I think still, the fundamentals of our economy are strong."[17] The remark becomes a major event, exploding over the Internet.[18] The Republican's words might mean several things. Interpreted sympathetically, the remark provides assurance that, no matter what the nation's current troubles, the economy will come back to full health and civil order be restored. However, McCain's factual assertion is not interpreted with such charity. It is regarded, rather, as a fateful, perhaps even a fatal mistake. For many critics and audience members, the remark suggests McCain still sees the economy as a boundary issue rather than something that threatens the core of the civil sphere. The Republican seems both blithely unaware that there is a deep civil crisis and unable to appreciate the world-historical stakes. A lead editorial in the *New York Times* articulates this combustible mixture of outrage and incredulity:

John McCain spent Monday claiming—as he had countless times before—that the economy was fundamentally sound. Had he missed the collapse of Lehman Brothers or the sale of Merrill Lynch, which were announced the day before? Did he not notice the agonies of the American Insurance Group? Was he unaware of the impending layoffs of tens of thousands of Wall Street employees on top of the growing numbers of unemployed workers throughout the United States?[19]

McCain has left the "impression," according to the *Times*, that he "lacks the experience and understanding" to handle the financial crisis, and his advisors are now scrambling "to erase the notion that he is out of touch."

Within hours, McCain strenuously reverses course. Pulling the financial crisis from boundary to center, the Republican issues a declaration of "total crisis." He roundly attacks the "the excess, the greed, and the corruption" of Wall Street, describing what he now declares to be clear and present economic danger in vividly anticivil terms. Positioning himself as a representative of civil society against economic elites, McCain promises to clean up Wall Street, urging the creation of a powerful reform commission.

Despite this new performance, questions remain. How felicitous will this new McCain persona be? Will the citizen audience allow the Republican candidate to become a new character and to narrate his struggle for power as a crusade for civil repair? It's not easy for an actor to erase an impression that his own performance has just made. The difficulty is that much greater because the public is already uncertain about McCain's civil stature. His initial response to the financial crisis underscores growing skepticism about his civil bona fides and his tendency for quick and impulsive action besides.

Obama Gains Traction

When the Palin effect unfolded, Barack Obama hung back, afraid. Not this time, not now. "What are you talking about?" he immediately and very publicly demands of John McCain.[20] Before now, Obama has not exactly been quiet about economic problems. To the contrary, he frequently warned that economic danger threatened the civil sphere, delivering major economic speeches against Republican policies from the beginning of 2008. Back in January, the *Times* headlines "With Economy Slowing, All Speeches Are Turning to It," pointing to the "latest evidence that the campaigns are being reshaped by the slowing economy."[21] The campaigns were not reshaped, however, and five months later, the *Times* reports that Obama is trying again, "moving to focus on the ailing economy as the central theme of the general election campaign."[22] Once again, the Democrat does not succeed. Six weeks later, he tries yet another time. In an effort at "keeping the presidential campaign focused on economic issues," the *Wall Street Journal* reports, "Barack Obama met with Federal Reserve chairman Ben Bernanke [and] discussed the current crisis and his proposals for tougher oversight of financial institutions."[23] Following up on an earlier story titled "Unraveling Reagan,"[24] the *Journal* reminds its readers that as early as the past "March, Sen. Obama proposed broadening government regulation of financial markets and expanding the power of the Federal Reserve to oversee investment banks in certain cases."[25] Yet, despite his best efforts, Barack Obama cannot get the public to pay attention to his economic jeremiads or his calls for institutional change.

The problem is not factual but cultural. Indications of massive economic crisis have long been apparent, and for months, the Democratic candidate has been suggesting in every which way that this dark brew, cooked up during Republican times, has to be confronted and remade. These performances do not fuse with citizen audiences until September 15. "Even his advisers conceded that voters might have not noticed," the *Times* explains—reporting on a well-received economic address by Obama in mid-September—"until he spoke here Tuesday as turmoil rippled through the financial markets."[26] In the weeks immediately preceding the financial crisis, even more of the audience is focusing—"63 percent of voters said they were paying a lot of attention to the campaign, up from 51 percent before the parties held their conventions."[27] With the financial explosion, attention must finally be paid to political performances addressing the nation's economic life. Obama can make political meaning through economic difference for the first time.

Only now, in the new atmosphere of social trembling, with the nation balancing precariously on the hinge of history, can the citizen audience finally imagine Obama-the-civil-hero riding to rescue America's economy. Obama is "urgently working to seize the economic issue," the *Times* reports, to "define his candidacy around the economy."[28] His performative ambition is clear. He wants to be "seen as connecting with the struggles of Americans." In order to create such fusion, he's "striving to boil down the argument ... to make it more applicable to the lives of all voters." Obama is doing difference, "using the nation's worsening economy to draw ever sharpening distinctions with his Republican rivals." These sharp distinctions are the binaries that divide the civil sphere into the democratic sacred and the antidemocratic profane. When market rationality careens out of control, it overflows the economy's boundaries and threatens the core of civil life. Obama explains he's not against the "market being free"; free markets are entirely legitimate outside civil life. What he's against is the market "running wild." Wildness exposes the civil sphere to danger; it is a polluted quality for democratic life.

Adroitly, the Democrat moves to align the market's wild irrationality with the character of John McCain. The trope of impulsivity begins attaching itself to the Republican in the blowback from Palin. Now, Obama earnestly reminds the public of McCain's long interest in privatizing Social Security, which would expose citizens' savings to risky stock markets and to the very "casino culture" that sparked such disastrous Wall Street speculation. So the financial crisis leads back to the character of McCain. "He's the one," Obama warns his fellow citizens, "who wants to gamble with your life savings":[29]

> "If my opponent had his way, the millions of Floridians who rely on it would've had their Social Security tied up in the stock market this week," Mr. Obama told an audience.... "How do you think that would have made folks feel? Millions would've watched as the market tumbled and their nest egg disappeared before their eyes."

Like the speculators on Wall Street, McCain is a gambler. Should such an impulsive man be trusted to represent the civil sphere inside the state?

If working the binaries is one way to make difference, assuming the mantle of hero is another. "Let's be clear," Obama declares to an audience of citizens in Colorado, "What we've seen the last few days is nothing less than the final verdict on an economic philosophy that has completely failed."[30] McCain is a man of the past, a past that poses dire danger to the present. Yesterday's man is hardly fit to lead the nation from the crisis of the present into a bright future day. "Instead of offering up concrete plans to solve these issues," Obama contends, "Senator McCain offered up the oldest Washington stunt in the book: you pass the buck to a commission to study the problem." The nation needs a hero, and it isn't John McCain. "Here's the thing," Obama declares, "we know how we got into this mess. What we need now is leadership that gets us out":

> "It's hard to understand how Senator McCain is going to get us out of this crisis by doing the same things with the same old players," Mr. Obama told a cheering crowd of about 2,000 people. "Make no mistake: my opponent is running for four more years of policies that will throw the economy further out of balance."

In a costly two-minute television advertisement laying out his economic message, Obama insists: "We need change, real change. This is no ordinary time, and it shouldn't be an ordinary election."[31]

The performative contrast is potent and striking. Four days into the crisis, the *Times* headlines "McCain Laboring to Hit Right Note on the Economy," a subhead declaring the Republican to be in a "Struggle for Balance."[32] McCain has "struck a discordant note at a sensitive moment." If political performance is a symphony, the Republican candidate is playing out of key. The Democratic performer, meanwhile, has regained perfect pitch, the *Times* observing that "Obama seems to have the more passionate voice that Democrats nervous about his working-class appeal have listened for."[33]

What makes it even more difficult for McCain to do difference is that his newly populist persona seems to imitate, not contrast with, his Democratic opponent's economic line. As public attention shifts to the economic drama at the nation's center, Treasury Secretary Paulson and Federal Reserve chairman Bernanke huddle desperately with congressional leaders to develop a massive government "bailout package" for the economy. President Bush gives his blessing. The print and television media go into a Washington-watch mode, framing the outcome of these negotiations as determining the nation's fate. The candidates become bystanders. Not only are they forced to sit and wait, which is not a good thing for the plummeting image of John McCain, but they also seem compelled by reason of both exigency and propriety to publicly express support for jaw-dropping government intervention in the economy. Each expresses hope for the bipartisan negotiations to come out right. On September 19, the *Wall Street Journal* reports "emerging consensus among policy makers" on the bailout package, and McCain, warning that government "cannot wait until the system fails," declares that the nation's financial institutions need a "safety and soundness regulator."[34] Four days later, the *Journal* reports both candidates "embracing the general concept" of the bailout. There is a "similarity in rhetoric," according to the conservative paper, and "in many ways the candidates agree on what they want changed."[35]

This might be good social policy, but it is bad meaning making for John McCain. Left and Right both convict the Republican of the sin of performativity. McCain is not himself but merely an empty shell. The *Journal* publishes an "I told you so" op-ed from a former Clinton aide:

> "I'm always for less regulation," John McCain, March 3, 2008. "Casual oversight by regulatory agencies in Washington is responsible for the crisis," John McCain, September 17, 2008. Which is it, Sen. McCain: regulation or deregulation?...Can Mr. McCain now square a circle by calling himself a conservative while favoring increased regulation?[36]

Times columnist Gail Collins says the same thing in a more sarcastic and polluting way:

"The people of Ohio are the most productive in the world!" yelled John McCain at a rally outside of Youngstown on Tuesday...[and] [f]olks were wildly enthusiastic...[W]hen McCain took the center stage, they were itching to cheer the war hero and boo all references to pork-barrel spenders. Nobody had warned them that he had just morphed into a new persona—a raging populist demanding more regulation of the nation's financial system. And since McCain's willingness to make speeches that have nothing to do with his actual beliefs is not matched by an ability to give them, he wound up sounding like Bob Dole impersonating Huey Long....The whole transformation was fascinating in a cheap-thrills kind of way. It's not every day, outside of "Incredible Hulk" movies, that you see somebody make this kind of turnaround in the scope of a few hours....It makes you think that he's trying to impersonate something he's not. Or wasn't. Or might not be. The image is getting fuzzy.[37]

The Play within the Play

In the midst of an objective financial crisis, McCain faces a subjective crisis of symbolic representation. His character is being polluted and his narrative degraded. Can the Republican campaign team regain control of the McCain image? In an effort to do so, they write a play within the play, plotting an opportunity for the Republican candidate to become a hero again. McCain announces he will suspend his campaign, fly to Washington to forge a solution to the financial crisis, and postpone the first of three nationally televised debates.

On September 24, as McCain's "ears were already throbbing with bad news," the Republican meets with his top advisers in his suite at the Hilton Hotel in Midtown Manhattan.[38] Among this group are Mark Salter, McCain's speechwriter and coauthoring alter ego, and Steven Schmidt, the chief image maker of the general election campaign. "The meeting was to focus on how McCain should respond to the crisis," according to a later report in the *Times,* one participant describing it as an effort "to try to see this as a big-picture, leadership thing":

We presented McCain with three options. Continue offering principles from afar. A middle ground of engaging while still campaigning. Then the third option, of going all in. The consensus was that we could stay out or go in—but that if we're going in, we should go in all the way. So the thinking was, do you man up and try to affect the outcome, or do you hold it at arm's length? And no, it was not an easy call.

McCain and his strategists opt for the hard thing. This is what a manly fighter pilot and military hero turned presidential candidate must do:

> Discussion carried on into the afternoon at the Morgan Library and Museum as McCain prepared for the first presidential debate. Schmidt pushed for going all in: suspending the campaign, recommending that the first debate be postponed, parachuting into Washington and forging a legislative solution to the financial crisis for which McCain could then claim credit.... Schmidt evidently saw the financial crisis as a "true character" moment that would advance his candidate's narrative.

The McCain action character will deploy his hero skills to reform civil society, bringing military and civil together in a manner he has found impossible heretofore. The hero will succeed this time not by being a maverick but by being a civil legislator, "forging a legislative solution." He will achieve a domestic *coup de main,* a great and glorious restoration that will repair the financial crisis and mend the rent fabric of civil society all at the same time. It is because he failed earlier to be a civil hero that McCain went negative, framing Obama as a celebrity. When that negative construction failed, McCain introduces Sarah Palin as a Republican hero. With the Palin effect fizzling, the campaign is back to square one. Against the odds, they must try to make McCain a civil hero one last time.

The script is now composed, but will the McCain production team be able to make it walk and talk and to act it out in real time? The *Wall Street Journal* writes of the suspension announcement as a "dramatic gesture" that "draws attention" to McCain and will "help him recast the question as one of leadership, where he is positively viewed."[39] His gesture puts "the roiling U.S. financial crisis" at the center of the Republican campaign. In its postelection analysis six weeks later, the *Journal* recalls how "the economic turmoil then took center stage in the campaign" and highlights the riskiness of this play within the play, triggering "the start of a three-day stretch that proved pivotal."[40] Timing and staging are crucial for McCain's performative gambit to succeed. This is a liminal moment; there is a sense of time temporarily suspended, of an open-ended but still time-bound narrative that begins with the suspension announcement on Wednesday afternoon and ends whenever the legislative bailout is achieved. After McCain's announcement on Wednesday, Schmidt tells reporters "this has to be solved by Monday."[41]

In making their case for suspension, McCain's advisers appeal to soldierly instincts and battlefield bravery. Analogizing from military to civil crisis, Schmidt reminds the candidate that "if Kansas City blew up, you'd stop doing everything else." It is in such a martial spirit that McCain publicly presents his decision later that day:

Barely a week ago, both men had suspended activities to mark the anniversary of the Sept. 11, 2001, terrorist attacks, and Sen. McCain evoked the event again. "Our national leaders came together in a time of crisis," he said in a statement. "We must show that kind of patriotism now."[42]

"A crisis," McCain exclaims, "calls for all hands on deck."[43] As in war, so now in peace. "I do not believe that the plan on the table"—the bailout bill currently being discussed by Congress in Washington, D.C.—"will pass as it currently stands," McCain pronounces.[44] "We are running out of time. We must meet as Americans, not as Democrats or Republicans, and we must meet until this crisis is resolved." It is "a time for leadership," an unidentified senior adviser tells the *Journal*. When McCain parachutes into Washington, he will meet with Senator Obama and other high-ranking lawmakers "for the next 100 hours or however long it is between now and Monday morning," Mark Salter predicts. The *Journal* describes McCain's decision as a "bold" move that has great civil promise, for it can "rise above partisanship" on the domestic scene.

"The story line did not go as scripted," the *Times* will later report.[45] McCain's performance does not succeed. The solider-citizen stumbles right out of the gate. "Belying a crisis situation," the *Times* reports, "McCain didn't leave New York immediately" on Wednesday evening but stayed overnight and "spent Thursday morning at an event for Clinton Global Initiative, the nonprofit foundation run by former President Bill Clinton." The Republican declares an extraordinary crisis that required nothing less than the suspension of his campaign, yet he waits a full 24 hours before parachuting into Washington. And when he finally does sit down for the critical negotiations, the man who would be a legislative hero fails to forge. At the White House meeting convened by Bush and attended by Obama and congressional leaders of both parties, "McCain said almost nothing," the *Times* reports, "even when House Republicans declared that they were not yet willing to sign on to the administration's $700 billion proposal." When a clearly frustrated President Bush asks for his views, according to the *Journal,* McCain responds, "I respect seniority," vowing "he would defer to the Republican congressional leaders who were present."[46] So much for McCain's determination to rise above partisanship:

The sudden objections [by House Republicans] caused agitation among Democrats present, who thought they had the makings of a deal. The group turned to Sen. McCain to ask if he endorsed his party's qualms, but he dodged the question, saying only that the concerns had to be addressed, according to people familiar with the meeting. He wasn't specific about the legislation itself.

So much for independent and courageous leadership.

The "nay" from House Republicans throws a monkey wrench into the progressive arc of the bailout negotiations, threatening to derail the bipartisan proposal and leave the financial crisis aflame. "The unexpected opposition from House Republicans," the *Journal* reports, "had thrown into chaos efforts to craft a rescue package for the financial markets."[47] Thursday has been a day of drama, but it does not unfold John McCain's way. Instead of bipartisan unity and the restoration of civil order, it sows chaos. "The day's drama represented," according to the *Journal*, "a remarkable public display of dissension in a town used to high drama."[48] For both Left and Right, this combustive disruption can be traced back to the self-proclaimed peacemaker, John McCain. The *Journal* reports that "House Republicans see Sen. McCain's arrival as the point that revitalized their rear-guard action." The *Times* confirms that the Republican candidate played exactly such a subversive role. "By keeping his views to himself, McCain kept the House revolt alive," the *Times* reports, which "infuriated the White House and Congressional Democrats" but brought him " accolades from House Republicans."[49]

Despite the fact that "the deal maker had produced no deal," as the *Times* put it, from lemons the McCain campaign tried to make lemonade.[50] The morning after the negotiations break down, the Republican campaign announces success, releasing a statement that McCain is "optimistic that there has been significant progress toward a bipartisan agreement." The suspension is now suspended, and McCain travels down to Mississippi that very afternoon to meet Obama in the first of their three debates. Two days later, on Sunday, on NBC's *Meet the Press,* Steven Schmidt insists that, despite every appearance to the contrary, McCain's leadership has succeeded in bringing "all of the parties to the table" and that "there appears to be a framework completed." The very next day, however, the bailout proposal goes down to legislative defeat. House Republicans proudly take the lion's share of the blame. There is not a framework in place. Progress has not been made toward bipartisanship, but the very opposite. What has McCain being doing all week?

Attributing Incapacity

Only days after it's voted down, the bailout bill is reconsidered. It has been scarcely changed, but this time moderates who care more about the danger to civil society carefully separate themselves from congresspersons who care more about telling the story from their own side. The bill passes, and the machinery of state begins moving into place. This is the first of many steps that the U.S. government will take in the coming months (and years) to repair the economic fabric of civil society, but it is no thanks to the efforts of the Republican presidential candidate,

John McCain. His play within the play has not made the grade. "Scene by scene," the *Times* reports, "McCain failed to deliver the performance that had been promised."[51] The Republican created the staging "to show what kind of president he might be," but he "came off more like a stymied bystander than a leader who could make a difference." The *Journal*'s verdict is the same: "To several McCain advisers, Sen. McCain's public show of dealing with the crisis by trying to broker a bailout deal between the president and Congress had fallen flat. 'We completely blew it,' said one. 'The execution of a potentially great move couldn't have been worse.'"[52] Commander McCain's plane has been shot down again, but this time in a civil, not a military, conflict, and it is his own fault besides.

THE FINANCIAL CRISIS IS MCCAIN'S KATRINA

If John McCain fails…his slow response to the financial hurricane of 2008 will be Exhibit A. The betting here is that when the McCain campaign's black box is recovered it will show he lost altitude during the six days from Sept. 24, when Sen. McCain suspended his campaign, to Sept. 29, when the House GOP defeated the first Paulson Plan to rescue the American financial system. Neither Mr. McCain nor the GOP is likely to recover before Nov. 4 from those six dramatic days, when they did little to deal with Hurricane Fannie's Category 50 financial crisis.[53]

Because of the failure to have performative effect, the McCain character is denounced by critics and audience as fake and artificial. The *Times* now writes that the Republican was only "*pretending* to 'suspend' his campaign so he could ride to the rescue,"[54] and the *Journal* reports that the Republican was simply "*making a show of* involving himself in the shaping of the [bailout] bill."[55] Pretending and making a show of political action suggest not just failed performance but civil incapacity as well. When the play within the play begins, on the Wednesday of McCain's announcement, Obama denounces it as little more than gimmickry. It reveals, Obama declares, an inability to deal with complexity—not being able to multitask. "Presidents are going to have to deal with more than one thing at a time," the Democrat caustically comments; "It's not necessary for us to think we can only do one thing and suspend everything else."[56] The remark recalls Lyndon Johnson's disparagement of Gerald Ford—then House minority leader—as "so dumb he can't walk and chew gum at the same time." Obama's deployment of the rhetorical trope circulates rapidly, further crystallizing suspicions about McCain's fitness to be president.

Anticivil pollution deepens in the wake of the suspension announcement, as McCain's actions begin markedly to diverge from his publicly declared script. On Saturday, the *Wall Street Journal* reports McCain is "widely portrayed in recent days as erratic and angry in his response to the collapse of Wall Street firms and the proposal to rescue them."[57] That same day, the *Times* notes McCain's "unsteady response to the nation's widening fiscal crisis."[58] "McCain was by turns action-oriented and impulsive," the *Times* writes, looking back on McCain's handling of the crisis and noting how the Republican looked "impetuous" and "dive-bombed targets."[59] By contrast, Obama appeared "measured, cool and thoughtful," somebody who "does not tend to take fiery or partisan swipes just for the sake of them."

FINANCIAL CRISIS AND THE DISCOURSE OF CIVIL SOCIETY

CIVIL: OBAMA	UNCIVIL: MCCAIN
Calm	Impulsive
Analytical	Instinctive
Measured	Uneven
Thoughtful	Dramatic

With increasing frequency, the civil-uncivil antinomy is employed to map the difference between the Democratic and Republican candidates for president. It provides a simplified, vivid, and very public schema that seems able to account for their differences. From being an after-the-fact interpretation, the account gradually becomes an empirical description upon which future predictions of behavior can be made. In his *Times* column on September 29, William Kristol regretfully describes McCain's "impetuous decision to go to Washington last week."[60] From this, the neo-conservative strategist concludes that "McCain is on course to lose the presidential election to Obama." In its postelection retrospective, the *Journal* explains the candidates' responses to the financial crisis in binary terms and reasons from there to the result of the election: "How the candidates responded— Sen. McCain's dramatic moves and sometimes-uneven temperament and Sen. Obama's more analytical reaction and calm vibe—was a window into how they made decisions. And voters responded."[61]

The Rational Voters Decide

On September 30, reporting on the fallout from congressional defeat of the rescue package, the *Times* describes how "the McCain campaign worked to contain the potential for damage."[62] But the pollution cannot be contained. Two days later, poll data show Obama for the first time taking a large and commanding lead. "Senator John McCain's image has been damaged," the *Times* writes, reporting on the Republican's struggle to become a collective representation, and "Senator Barack Obama is showing signs of gaining significant support among voters":[63]

> A CBS News poll released Wednesday found that Mr. Obama's favorabil-
> ity rating, at 48 percent, is the highest it has ever been in polls conducted
> by CBS and The New York Times. At the same time, the number of voters
> who hold an unfavorable view of Mr. McCain—42 percent—is as high
> as it has been since CBS News and The Times began asking the question
> about Mr. McCain in 1999, the first time he ran for president. The CBS
> News poll showed that Mr. Obama had a nine-percentage-point lead over
> Mr. McCain—49 percent to 40 percent. It is the first time Mr. Obama has
> held a statistically significant lead over Mr. McCain this year.

The next day's *Wall Street Journal* reports that "polls in competitive states around the country show Sen. Barack Obama with leads in nearly enough states to win the White House" and that "polls also show traditional Republican strong-holds such as Indiana and North Carolina to be tossups."[64] The reason for these disappointing results seems obvious to the conservative side: "Sen. McCain's per-formance as Congress took up a rescue package appears to have undermined his standing with voters." Days later, the *Journal* is reporting that McCain "now trails by a consistent margin in all national polls—six percentage points in a new Wall Street Journal/NBC News survey—and has lost ground in the key battleground states of the upper Midwest, as well as pivotal Florida":[65]

> Voters were much more likely to say they felt good about Sen. Obama's
> handling of the current economic crisis than they were to say the same
> of Sen. McCain. About one in three voters said they were "more reas-
> sured" by Sen. Obama versus just 25% who said that about Sen. McCain.
> Even worse, 38% of poll participants reported being "less reassured"
> by Sen. McCain's approach... Sen. Obama improved his standing with
> voters across the board. Men, for instance, typically favor Republicans,
> and sided with President George W. Bush by 11 percentage points in
> 2004. In the Journal poll two weeks ago, Sen. McCain led among the
> male voters by five points. In this poll, the two candidates were tied
> among men.[66]

Most alarming is the evidence that "independent voters are starting to swing behind Barack Obama and Joe Biden." Less ideologically prescriptive members of the citizen audience are more responsive to shifting performance than straight party-liners:

Independent voters are among the most important voting blocs because many of them would consider voting for either candidate. In the Journal/ NBC poll two weeks ago, independents favored Sen. McCain by 13 points. The new survey finds Sen. Obama leading by four points.

On October 3, the *Times* headlines "McCain Abandons Efforts to Win Michigan," describing the event as "a major blow" to the campaign. Throughout the summer, McCain has returned again and again to this densely populated Midwestern state. In July, he declares to a crowd outside a factory in Belleville, Michigan, that "the state of Michigan, as it has in many elections in the past, will determine who the next president of the United States is."[67] If victory in Michigan is central to the Republican plan for victory, abandoning the state just four weeks before ballots are cast is evidence of imminent defeat. "I think you're seeing a turning point," the chairman of the Michigan Republican party confides to a *Times* reporter. "Our message, the campaign's message, isn't connecting."[68] Connecting has always been McCain's challenge. Performative failure is fatal to him this time. The financial crisis is the last turning point in the general election campaign. Three strikes and you're out at the old ball game.

The new polls broadcast, for the first time in the campaign, that the American voter—the sensible citizen whose mythical common sense sustains the democratic civil sphere—has reached a decision. The withdrawal from Michigan confirms that the Republicans' private polls are telling them the same thing. When the Palin effect fizzles, Obama pulls in front but only barely. He is ahead on points. As the financial crisis unfolds, the pollution of McCain deepens, and Obama considerably lengthens his lead. Time of death is recorded by the *Wall Street Journal* in a laconic way:

> Howard Wolfson, who was never afraid to ruffle feathers when serving as spokesman for Sen. Hillary Clinton's presidential campaign, is again prepared to boldly go where few men have gone before. He says the U.S. presidential race is over, and Sen. Barack Obama will win. Period, no qualifying clauses.... You can agree or not, but that analysis indicates how bad the past two weeks have been for Sen. McCain.[69]

Reaction and Response

John McCain and Sarah Palin stand accused in the court of public opinion. They exercise bad judgment; their thinking is irrational; their emotions are petulant and impulsive; their actions are performative and faked. The public begins to make these accusations as the Palin effect implodes, and its convictions harden as the financial crisis unfolds. There is now a sense of finality, of an immensely important struggle for power being lost by the conservatives, and of an extraordinary opportunity for liberal control of the state being gained.

The Left has long supported Obama, and the Right will always support the Republican side. It is the middle of the political spectrum that now decides. Once this judgment registers, it affects the future performances of the campaigners in a profound way. As the center recuses itself as an audience for Republican messages, the incentive for the GOP to provide broad and expansive performances disappears. What ensues is a pronounced and visible narrowing of the Republican campaign. In the closing weeks of the general election, the party's standard-bearers move back to the type of intraparty representation normally reserved for primaries. They play to the most conservative, convinced-no-matter-what base. The Republican candidates continue to work the binaries and walk the boundaries, but in the eyes of most Americans they do so in far less appealing ways.

This more restricted and ideologically conservative slice of the citizen audience enthusiastically "others" Obama, pushing the Democrat to the noncivil side of boundaries defined in ethnic, religious, racial, and territorial-national terms. This more circumscribed audience is less interested in civil repair and more inclined to build walls that repel calls for change. Rather than expanding solidarity and demanding that obligations to others become more universal, these more partisan conservatives draw the line between inside and outside more starkly, harkening after a national community of a more primordial and less civil kind.

Only after the polls show the center being lost is Obama painted as a radical and a traitor at Republican campaign events. The most conspicuous reality reference for such representation is Bill Ayers. Once a militant leader of the revolutionary Weather Underground, Ayers later became an education activist and university professor in Chicago. Obama served with Ayers on the board of a local educational reform foundation in the mid-1990s, while both were living in Hyde Park on Chicago's south side. Ayers privately hosted one of the many fund-raising "coffees" when Obama first ran for Illinois State Senate in 1995.

Sarah Palin repeatedly attacks Obama for what she characterizes as his revealing association with Ayers. The Democrat who would be president, she proclaims at an airport hangar rally in Englewood, Colorado, on October 4, is "palling around with terrorists," which puts him on the anti-American, antidemocratic side:[70]

> This is not a man who sees America as you see it and how I see America. We see America as the greatest force for good in this world. If we can be that beacon of light and hope for others who seek freedom and democracy and can live in a country that would allow intolerance in the equal

rights that again our military men and women fight for and die for for [*sic*] all of us. Our opponent, though, is someone who sees America it seems as being so imperfect that he's palling around with terrorists who would target their own country?

Three days later, at a rally in Clearwater, Florida, Palin exclaims, "I'm afraid this is someone who sees America as imperfect enough to work with a former domestic terrorist who had targeted his own country."[71] Placing Obama on the other side of the nation's territorial boundary and associating him with violence, Palin works the binaries, aggressively questioning the Democrat's civil qualities:

> She ridiculed [Obama] for his campaign's statement that he did not know Mr. Ayer's full background when they were first acquainted. "He didn't know that he had launched his career in the living room of a domestic terrorist?"... Asked if she was saying Mr. Obama is dishonest, she answered only that the Ayers association raised questions of "judgment and the truthfulness and just being able to answer very candidly a simple question about when did you know him, how did you know him." She added, "I think it's relevant."

While the logic of this guilt by association is far fetched, it appears eminently plausible to the Republicans' now severely restricted citizen audiences, who are of the most partisan, conservative kind.[72] Outraged candidate and angry audience fuse. "Standing before a sea of red T-shirts and homemade signs reading 'No Communists!' and 'Palin's Pitbulls,' Ms. Palin... nestled into her Republican base."[73]

> The Ayers line of attack, indeed, played with the crowds who came to see her during her two days in Florida... [and who] described themselves as staunch Republicans who said they would never consider voting for a Democrat.... Many people said they were still strong supporters of President Bush, part of the 25 percent of Americans in a Gallup Poll released Monday who said they approved of his performance.
>
> On a two-day, five-rally campaign swing through Florida, Ms. Palin was met by an enthusiastic response from audiences who devoured every word of her anti-Democratic pitch. From Jacksonville in the northeast to Pensacola in the Panhandle, the fiery crowds gathered to jeer at any hint of liberalism, boo loudly at the mere mention of Senator Barack Obama's name and heckle the traveling press corps (at a rally in Clearwater, one man hurled a racial epithet at a television cameraman). If there were

undecideds, independents or swing voters among them, they were awfully hard to spot.

Walking determinedly along the territorial boundary of the civil sphere, Palin accuses Obama of, in effect, supporting the nation's wartime enemies against the troops fighting for our side:

> "Our opponent voted to cut off funding for our troops," Ms. Palin said, as she was interrupted by a deep-throated chorus of boos. "He did this even after saying that he wouldn't do such a thing. And he said, too, that our troops in Afghanistan are just, quote, 'air-raiding villages and killing civilians.' I hope Americans know that is not what our brave men and women are doing in Afghanistan."

A conservative radio host later reinforces the message, telling the crowd Obama "hangs around with terrorists." If Obama is outside American boundaries and truly anticivil, he is an enemy of democracy and must be dealt with in kind. "Treason!" one angry member of the audience shouts. Another yells out, "Kill him!"[74]

Despite his occasional calls for moderation, McCain carefully orchestrates his running mate's campaign strategy, often seconding her extreme speech. On October 6, a new TV ad called "Dangerous" is posted on McCain's website.[75] Replete with grainy black-and-white pictures of a strident Obama and brief selections from his speech, a deep baritone voice exclaims, "How dishonorable," "how dangerous," and "too risky for America" over a color picture of a smiling John McCain. The next day, at a campaign event in New Mexico, McCain tells a crowd that "even at this late hour in the campaign, there are essential things we don't know about Sen. Obama or the record that he brings to this campaign."[76] The day after that, at a rally with Palin at his side, McCain demands, "Who is the real Senator Obama?" employing what the *Times* reports as "an increasingly sharp tone":[77]

> These attacks pump up crowds on the campaign trail, where it is the sharp criticism of Mr. Obama…that draw[s] the biggest, loudest response from the conservative and almost all-white crowds…As the crowd booed angrily at each mention of Mr. Obama's name, Mr. McCain threw himself more vigorously into his speech.

Two days later, headlining "McCain Joins Attack on Obama over Radical," the *Times* reports that the Republican has insisted to a raucous Wisconsin crowd: "We need to know the full extent of the relationship" between Ayers and Obama in order to judge whether the Democrat "is telling the truth to the American people or not."[78]

At another campaign stop in Ohio that day, Cindy McCain—"in a departure from her normally mild public remarks"—confesses to the crowd that Obama's politics make her physically afraid: "The day Senator Obama decided to cast a vote to not fund my son while he was serving sent a cold chill through my body, let me tell you." Before the same crowd, the Lehigh County, Ohio, Republican chairman twice refers to the Democratic candidate by using his full name "Barack Hussein Obama."[79] The *Times* reports on the "increasingly hostile atmosphere at Mr. McCain's rallies," in which "voters furiously booed any mention of Mr. Obama."[80]

In their first televised debate, McCain refuses to look at Obama directly, prompting the Obama camp to suggest, according to the *New York Times*, that the Republican lacked "the courtesy of even returning Mr. Obama's gaze", and that "he was being disrespectful or condescending to his rival."[81] A few days later, in an exchange with the editorial board of the *Des Moines Register,* which the paper videotaped and posted on its website, McCain presents what the *Times* styles as a "primer on testiness."[82] In the second debate, McCain refuses to refer to his opponent by name, at one point nodding in his direction and sarcastically referring to "that one."[83] In his closing statement at the third debate, McCain continues employing what the *Times* calls "dark Salteresque" rhetoric, referring to the moody pessimism of Mark Salter, McCain's speechwriting alter ego. Presenting civil repair as if it were war making, McCain looks full face into the camera and declares, "I've been fighting for this country since I was 17 years old and I have the scars to prove it—if you elect me, I will fight to take America in a new direction."[84] In a rally that same day, Sarah Palin testifies that "John McCain is always proud to be an American" and leads the crowd in cheers of "USA! USA! USA! USA! USA!"

These are bravura political performances, but they suffer from a debilitating paradox. Republicans are pitching ever more particularistic performances to an ever more enthusiastic core audience, but in so doing they are separating themselves ever farther from the more moderate voters, upon whom victory ultimately will depend. Struggling to wrestle the binaries in their favor, McCain and Palin's desperate final weeks of of campaigning actually strengthens—for the majority of the citizen audience—their identification with the anticivil side. Condemning the "politics of attack," the *Times'* lead editorial acknowledges the "sorry fact of American political life that campaigns get ugly, often in their final weeks." Yet, the Republicans "have gone far beyond the usual fare," the nation's most influential opinion page charges, entering "into the dark territory of race-baiting and xenophobia." Palin's rallies "have become spectacles of anger and insult," and "her demagoguery has elicited some frightening, intolerable responses."[85]

Liberal columns and news commentaries link this anticivil outpouring to the viscous current that for two decades has polluted the Republican mainstream. In "Tao of Lee Atwater," *Times'* Maureen Dowd accuses Republicans of "running a seamy campaign originally designed by the bad seed of conservative politics, Lee Atwater." Republican strategist for George H. W. Bush's 1988 campaign against Michael Dukakis, Atwater developed an infamous series of television ads associating the Democratic candidate with escaped African American convict and convicted murderer Willie Horton—"Atwater gleefully tried to paint Willie Horton as Dukakis' running mate."[86] "With a black man running," Dowd remarks, now "it's even easier for [the] Atwater's protégé [Steven Schmidt] running McCain's campaign to warn that white Americans should not open the door to the dangerous Other, or 'That One,' as McCain called Obama in Tuesday night's debate." McCain follows Atwater's dark and odiferously anticivil script not only by issuing "slithery character attacks" of his own. Having "cynically picked a running mate with less care than theater directors give to picking a leading actor's understudy," the Republican presidential candidate "unleashed Sarah Palin to slime their opponent" in a manner "that would have made Atwater glow."

A *Times* news analysis reports that the adjective "Rovian" has become a "symbol of evil."[87] Surveying Democratic opinion about the "revered and reviled Republican maestro," a reporter interviews former Georgia senator Max Cleland, against whose reelection Rove organized an effectively nasty and innuendo-ridden campaign. Cleland attests that campaigning against Rove was "like going up against the devil himself." Steven Schmidt and his colleague Nicolle Wallace "worked closely with Mr. Rove in the [Bush] White House," the *Times* reminds its readers, and these two "Rove protégés" are now "two top McCain aides." Even so, McCain's top advisors "shudder at the perception that Mr. Rove is calling the shots" because "his reputation is toxic among swing voters."

Struggles for the presidency are not games. There is too much ultimate power at stake. Struggles to win civil power over the state are as vicious and aggressive as culturally and legally they are allowed to be. This is why participants and observers describe political conflict in the language of war, and why campaigns are plotted and remembered in terms of battles won and lost. It is by reason of this antagonism that "partisanship" becomes the most fraught and ambiguous word in democratic politics. Solidarity is the sine qua non of the civil sphere, yet it is threatened by the political struggles to represent it. In the democratic struggle for power, intense and sharp hostilities are unleashed in the name of a broad, inclusive, and pacific solidarity. Only by promoting such periodic bouts of political agonism can the civil sphere maneuver social complexity, and finesse ideological fragmentation, temporarily reconciling, if never completely eliminating, the deeply opposed material and ideal interests at stake. This paradox is not only abstract and conceptual. It is also experienced as deeply dangerous in real life. Electoral battles challenge the fellow feeling and mutual identification upon which civil society depends. As a result, the invisible line separating "healthy" and "normal" party conflict from pathologically anticivil faction is closely monitored. Crossing this line is what dirty tricks are all about, where offline and under the table funds pay for plumbers' operations and Swift Boat ads. In the face of such dangers, there are continuous demands to maintain decorum and civility. Watergate remains etched into the collective memory of the American civil sphere, recalling how partisanship can turn into anticivil hostility and standing as a warning that even the proudest of democracies can be deceived and almost done in.[88]

One week after the reactionary restriction of the Republican campaign begins, on October 15, a *New York Times*/CBS News poll demonstrates that, far from reversing the Republican plight, the Republicans' new accusations and spluttering aggressiveness actually confirm the mainstream identification of McCain and his running mate with the anticivil side. The critical polling question is this: "Has the candidate spent more time explaining what he would do as president or attacking his rival?"[89] Among all registered voters, twice as many now believe that McCain has spent more time attacking than explaining, a percentage that holds when only independents are asked. Significantly more than twice as many registered voters believe that Obama has conducted himself differently, that he has been explaining rather than attacking, and the difference actually increases among independents. Sixty-two percent of independents believe McCain has spent too much time attacking, and only 24 percent of independents believe this about Obama. The Republicans' narrowband performance has boomeranged in its effect:

> Voters who said their opinions of Mr. Obama had changed recently were twice as likely to say that they had grown more favorable as to say they had worsened. And voters who said that their views of Mr. McCain had changed were three times more likely to say that they had worsened than to say they had improved.

If the struggle for power was effectively over two weeks earlier, it is even more over today: "[T]he poll found that if the election were held today, 53 percent of those determined to be probable voters said they would vote for Mr. Obama and 39 percent said they would vote for Mr. McCain" (see figures 9.1 and 9.2).

Two and a half weeks before the voting ritual closes the curtain on the struggle for power, conservative columnist David Brooks delivers a valedictory on the 2008 campaign.[90] The debates are over, the three great boulders of the campaign have been navigated, the rushing river of the campaigns has parted, and the reaction has passed. The identities of victor and vanquished apparent, Brooks writes a rapturous paean to the civil qualities of the champion representing the Democratic side:

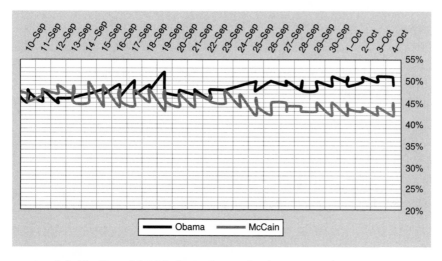

FIGURE 9.1   The Financial Crisis, September 10–October 4

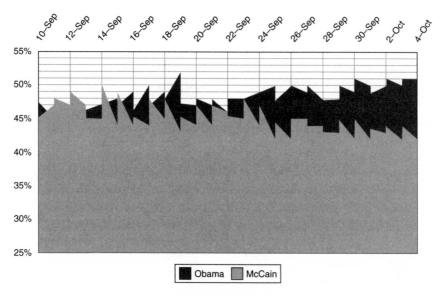

FIGURE 9.2   The Financial Crisis, September 10–October 4

We've been watching Barack Obama for two years now, and in all that time there hasn't been a moment in which he has publicly lost his self-control. This has been a period of tumult, combat, exhaustion and crisis. And yet there hasn't been a moment when he has displayed rage, resentment, fear, anxiety, bitterness, tears, ecstasy, self-pity or impulsiveness. Some candidates are motivated by something they lack... [b]ut other candidates are propelled by what some psychologists call self-efficacy, the placid assumption that they can handle whatever the future throws at them. Candidates in this mold, most heroically F.D.R. and Ronald Reagan, are driven upward by a desire to realize some capacity in their nature. They rise with an unshakable serenity that is inexplicable to their critics and infuriating to their foes.

Placing Obama unequivocally into this august second group, Brooks explains, "That's why this William Ayers business doesn't stick." Obama "may be liberal, but he is never wild." By reason of his character Obama is eminently qualified to represent civil society inside of the state. "It is easy," Brooks believes, "to sketch out a scenario in which he could be a great president":

> He would be untroubled by self-destructive demons or indiscipline. With that cool manner, he would see reality unfiltered. He could gather—already has gathered—some of the smartest minds in public policy, and, untroubled by intellectual insecurity, he could give them free rein. Though he is young, it is easy to imagine him at the cabinet table, leading a subtle discussion of some long-term problem.

On October 15, MSNBC anchor Keith Olbermann announces that "TV's longest-running series comes to an end."[91] The narrative has been classic melodramatically, about good and bad, right and wrong, darkness and light. Like any good readers of melodrama, American voters have the feeling that, in the end, it all came out right.

Epilogue

JUST BEFORE MIDNIGHT ON THE EVENING OF ELECTION DAY, NOVEMBER 4, 2008, in Chicago's Grant Park, Barack Obama acknowledges victory in a speech to the hundred thousand people who gather to consecrate this moment. His win has been decisive. Almost 70 million Americans vote for him, whereas John McCain receives only 60 million of the ballots cast. Winning the popular vote 53 percent to 46 percent, the Democrat trounces the Republican even more decisively in the electoral college, 68 percent to 32 percent. The sway of Obama's performance over swing states, as well as independent, moderate, and Republican-leaning voters, allows Democrats also to gain 8 seats in the Senate and 21 in the House, paving the way to a supermajority in the U.S. Senate for the first time since 1979.

In his speech at Grant Park, Obama places these numbers into the framework of his campaign. He declares that the hinge of history has swung, and he calls upon Americans "to put their hands on the arc of history and bend it once more toward the hope of a better day." The bright future will be restored. The united spirit of a democratic people will be able to breathe freely again:

> This is our moment. This is our time—to put our people back to work and open doors of opportunity for our kids; to restore prosperity and promote the cause of peace; to reclaim the American dream and reaffirm that fundamental truth—that, out of many, we are one; that while we breathe, we hope. And where we are met with cynicism and doubt and those who tell us that we can't, we will respond with that timeless creed that sums up the spirit of a people: Yes, we can.

Americans have elected a civil hero. He will restore the utopian spirit of the nation's revolutionary origins and the promise of its founding fathers to create a more perfect democracy:

> If there is anyone out there who still doubts that America is a place where all things are possible; who still wonders if the dream of our founders is alive in our time; who still questions the power of our democracy, tonight is your answer.

In voting for this new hero, this once and future king, the American people have really been voting for themselves. Obama presents himself as but the expression of the solidarity out of which American democracy is made:

> It's the answer spoken by young and old, rich and poor, Democrat and Republican, black, white, Latino, Asian, Native American, gay, straight, disabled and not disabled—Americans who sent a message to the world that we have never been a collection of Red States and Blue States: we are, and always will be, the United States of America.

Candidate Obama has expanded Democratic support into what once were the exclusively Red States of enemy territory, and he has connected powerfully with nonaligned moderates in the middle as well. President-elect Obama knows his presidency can succeed only if he continues to massage the wavering centrists and continues to earn the respect, or at least discourage the enmity, of people and regions who stayed Republican and Red. Pivoting from the partisan contentiousness of campaigning, the president-elect declares, "while the Democratic Party has won a great victory tonight, we do so with a measure of humility and determination to heal the divides that have held back our progress." After a bruising and heated electoral struggle, Obama calls for the restoration of solidarity. He draws upon the language employed by an earlier, newly elected president when the nation teetered on the brink of a malevolent and violent civil strife, facing real and not merely rhetorical battle: "As Lincoln said to a nation far more divided than ours, 'We are not enemies, but friends...Though passion may have strained, it must not break our bonds of affection.'" Speaking "to those Americans whose support I have yet to earn," Obama declares, "I may not have won your vote, but I hear your voices, I need your help, and I will be your president, too." President-elect Obama hopes that the partisanship of the struggle for power will not carry over to his term in the White House. Will President Obama be able to convince those who resisted his campaign performances that he hears their voices—after the campaign? If they do believe their voices are heard, then McCain voters might yet sustain some affection for Obama, and the two sides, even if not friends, might avoid becoming obdurate enemies. Barack Obama will have to perform the role of president just as felicitously as when he auditioned for it during the campaign, if not more so.

One year after that Grant Park speech, on November 4, 2009, the *New York Times* marks the anniversary of Obama's ascension to power in a story headlined "A Year Later, a Daily Grind: The Glow of Obama's Election Has Long Faded:"

> For a president elevated to power on the back of history, the tears and euphoria of Grant Park feel like a thousand years ago. It has been just one year, of course, since Barack Obama's election, a year since that moment when supporters felt everything was possible amid lofty talk of "remaking this nation" and determined chants of "Yes, we can."...The hope and hubris have given way to the daily grind of governance, the jammed meeting schedule waiting in the morning, the thick briefing books waiting at night, the thousand little compromises that come in between....Mr. Obama has spent the last 12 months learning more about wielding power.[1]

The tone is elegiac, contrasting campaigning and governing, idealism and reality, liminality and everyday routine. It is also about the hinge of history having swung and to what avail. At such moments, even the toughest of real-politic tacticians contemplates the ineffable and disappointing transformation of the sacred into the profane:

> In the White House, the wistfulness for the simpler days is palpable. "The day was just suffused with emotion and hope and warmth," David Axelrod, Mr. Obama's senior adviser, recalled about Election Day last year. "But it is an emotional peak that you can't maintain day to day as you do the business of government. The challenge is to maintain that degree of idealism and optimism as you work through the meat grinder. Everything about the politics of Washington works against hope and optimism and unity. So you have to push against that every day, understanding that it's going to be an imperfect end result." He added: "That night was sublime. And much of what goes on in Washington is prosaic. Or profane."

The election of Barack Obama entitles him to occupy the office of president. When he swore the oath of office before millions standing before him on the Capitol Mall and hundreds of millions more via mass media at home and abroad, he promises to protect and defend the nation's democratic constitution. Now he is legally bound to represent the civil sphere inside the state. President Obama becomes the official symbol of the civil sphere, not somebody fighting to represent it. He is the most potent and visible totem of American democracy, the most powerful civil symbol in this or any other land.

The bridge from struggle and partisanship to this presumption of totemic solidarity is the ritual of voting.[2] When the American voters have spoken, as democratic lore has it, they cannot be wrong. Physically, Election Day means pulling a lever or punching a ballot; metaphysically, it is the laying on of hands. In a democracy, voters are narrated as the ultimate font of wisdom, the ultimate repository of civil authority. After many months of conflict and division, voting restores to the civil sphere a respite of solidarity, and the president-elect promises to represent *all* the people. When voters anoint a candidate, the ritual seems to wash partisanship from his body. The candidate emerges pure as the morning, fresh as the brightly shining sun. In a myth central to American democracy, the best person has won.

Once they have elected and betrothed their newly sacral representative, Americans discharge the old and now deflated symbol who has been governing them, typically with markedly decreasing success. The inflated form of the newly elected president allows the weary spirit of democracy to be revived and once again to become flesh. For some weeks before and after Obama's consecration, his heroic stature is everywhere consecrated in material form: T-shirts, paintings, prints, photographs, sculptures, songs, graffiti, and tattoos—iconic images of Barack Obama flood the public sphere.[3] Obama's immortal body enters remarkably into legend, according to the moral and aesthetic logic of myth, even as he assumes control of the secular state according to the rational rules of the Constitution.

The rites of Inauguration Day dress the private, personal body of the president-elect in the public, impersonal body of the presidency, elevating the civil sphere's current representative into the pantheon of democratic heroes, the solemn, gravely enumerated list of those other ordinary humans who also once occupied the exalted office of president of these United States. A new and indelible historical identity attaches to the person of the president. Henceforth, Barack Hussein Obama is not simply a Democratic politician from Chicago or even the first African American to be elected to the nation's highest office. He is the 44th president of the United States. This is a Roman, even a royal process, not at all Greek. The original founders of democracy drew lots for political leadership, reserving elections for military chiefs, and rarely representing either in an iconic way. Memorials for Greek heroes were modest and impersonal, sculpted images reserved mainly for the gods. The Romans changed everything. They had their Caesars and relentlessly made graven images of them, along with the personalized statuary of patriarchs, matriarchs, aristocrats, and military and athletic heroes of every kind.

It is said of the American presidency that "the office makes the man." Certainly the merely human figure who occupies the office is seen through its lens. To be president is ipso facto to be in some part a mythical hero. A republic demands nothing less. Henceforth, musical "Ruffles and Flourishes" accompany the appearance of Barack Obama in public, and deference is paid to him wherever he goes. In the course of his duties, he is addressed impersonally by the title of his office, never, even by old friends who now serve him, by his given names. Such symbolic bowing and scraping is perceived not as demeaning and undemocratic but as obeisance to democracy, as pride in the civil sphere, not as kowtowing to authority but as exalting the collective representation of democracy.

Despite these ritual flourishes and beneath this putative, symbolic canopy, the United States remains open, diverse, fragmented, and extraordinarily combative. Barack Obama is not elected only as a symbol of the civil sphere but also as a representative of the party. He is, in addition, head of a mind-bogglingly massive organization that is the government of the United States, wielding not only domestic power but also control over the greatest arsenal of physical violence ever known. As the only nationally elected leader and the civil sphere's single most vivid symbol, the president exercises impressive executive power, yet he remains a person of his party and does not possess legislative control. The power to make law belongs to Congress, not to the president. Congress can be, and often is, controlled by the opposing party. Even when it is not and the party controlling the Congress is the president's own, the chief executive exercises only titular control over members of Congress and senators of the president's own side.

Presidents struggle continuously to control divisions inside their own party and to gain influence over members of the opposition. The heart of the campaign staff moves into the West Wing of the White House. The same performance team that has fought and clawed and cleared Obama's pathway to power, that has worked the binaries and walked the boundaries and molded the image and depicted the other fellow and his party as the gravest of dangers to the democratic character of the United States—this same group of men and women now needs to work the old magic and more if Barack Obama is to govern successfully as president of the United States. Yet, even as assuming power demands an expanded audience and enlarged performance, the paradoxical consequence of victory is that the ambition and energy for dramatic action often ebbs. There's a post-hoc sense of naturalism among those who win big in the struggle for great power. Having always been convinced they are worthier than their opponents, they are now tempted to believe that their actual superiority is what allowed them to win. The staff and candidate forget that their campaign persona was symbolically constructed, that their winning character was performed, and that the election could have gone against them if they had not been so skillful or their opponents so clumsy or if the stars had been aligned in a different way.

Whether the newly inaugurated president remains a powerful collective representative is always in doubt. The charisma of the people is only deposited in the person of the president. It is given to him on inspection. The president has taken a loan, and he must pay it back with speech, action, and good works of an impressive kind. His legislation can be blocked, his government paralyzed. The binaries can be worked against him, and he may come to seem distant and autocratic. He can stumble while walking the boundaries, seeming to mishandle the economy or distort race relations or fail powerfully to defend, via arms or diplomacy, the interests of the United States. To the degree that the president is perceived to fail in these tasks—whether symbolic or real—he is constructed as an inadequate representative of the civil sphere in the state. His person is separated from his public body. The image deflates, and his poll ratings nosedive. The nation's leader will not be able to govern or preside. To his small band of still-devoted followers, the chief executive is a fallen hero. To the majority of the citizen audience, he seems incompetent, irrational, or irresponsible, somewhere between being evil and simply being a jerk.

To collectively represent the civil sphere in the state, politically and symbolically, the newly elected president must demonstrate not only integrity and competence but also heroic might. Not only must he possess power putatively but actually exercise it in real time as well. To sustain utopian possibilities for transformation, to be the changer rather than changed, the president must not only move society but be seen to move it, facing down foreign leaders and domestic legislators alike. He must cut the Gordian knot of festering social problems that have bedeviled his predecessors. He must change the world practically and resolve the "crisis of our times" rhetorically constructed during the campaign.

Whether such literal accomplishments are even remotely possible is a matter of fortune, competence, resources, and strategy. But the figurative matters, too. Nothing is more practical than a good performance. The president needs to claim the center of the nation's imagination. Yet, even as he spreads his "manna," the president cannot be seen as mixing too much with mundane figures, or else the aura of sacred charisma will fade.[4] So the president brings in down-and-dirty men and women who are practical and clever and expert at weaving the fabric of the real world, not the fairy wisps of the heroic imaginary that the president himself must seek to sustain. Even as the person of the president busily directs these minions, the president's public body sequesters itself inside the mystery of the White House, wrapped inside the aura of high office. When he steps outside, it is not to make sausage with legislators but to spread symbolic power, to project and rejuvenate his totemic status as civic symbol. The president meets "the people" in cloistered settings and collects their energy and applause before cameras that project an elevated image back to the wider public audience at one remove.

The president does not personally get down and dirty in public. Though a partisan himself, he wishes to be seen as working the moral binaries that define civil society in a nonpartisan manner and as walking the boundaries that relate the civil sphere to the rest of American society in an expansive, dignified, yet high-spirited way. It is as a putatively collective representation that the president visits grade schools and universities; families and ethnic communities; mosques, churches, and synagogues; factories and small businesses; civilian and military hospitals; and foreign lands regardless of their distance from or friendship with the United States. The presidential totem embodies the positive aspirations of the civil sphere. When it makes contact with noncivil spheres and organizations, they become connected with an emblem of a wider, more universal solidarity in a vivid, powerful, often electrifying way. If the president collects enough charismatic authority and successfully conserves it, he can bend the arc of history, creating legislation and organization that will allow the crisis of our times to come out right.

It is a big "if." Despite the powers of office, presidential performances are contingent and fragile. The president is a tightrope walker. Citizen audiences and media interpreters watch the performer's every move, and there is no safety net underneath.

Note on Concept and Method

T HE 2008 PRESIDENTIAL CONTEST SHOWS MEANING MAKING AT THE center of the struggle for power in democratic societies. *The Performance of Politics* interprets and explains this meaning-centered process. This is not a description of social reality but a reconstruction. Reality has far too many working parts simply to be mirrored; it must be refracted and interpreted. Social reality is made first by acting and speaking social actors. When intellectuals try to understand it, we remake it—subject to the constraints of both common sense and disciplinary rationality. Social scientists and journalists, too, are compelled to pick and choose, highlighting a few themes over many others, capturing and reproducing hundreds of statements out of hundreds of thousands, stretching a handful of narrative arcs across plot points while recognizing that other arcs can be drawn. Social scientists do not only observe but also presuppose.[1] During our training as students and our preparation as theorists and researchers, we develop ideas about social reality before we confront the actual objects of our study. What we find is filtered through these conceptual lenses.

Intellectual preconceptions organize themselves into schools of thought as theories and methods. These paradigms are often relatively specific—rational choice theory, media effects models, regression analysis—but they also form broad traditions that stretch back for centuries. Today's academic disagreements over how elections should be studied connect to the arguments about politics in Plato's *Republic*.[2] Thrasymachus sees social actors as cynical egoists; against this sophist philosopher, Socrates defends the possibility that political actors respect one another and that they are motivated by feelings of reciprocity and guided by the ethical power of cultural ideals. A bright line runs from Thrasymachus to philosophers, theorists, and empirical social scientists who see contemporary elections primarily in tersm of tactics, strategy, money, and organization. Against this tradition stand the intellectual descendants of Socrates, who make meaning central and place morality and feeling at the center of struggles for democratic power.

Many social scientists regret that such profound disagreement continues to rend the science of society and long for what they imagine to be the more purely observation-based approach that allows sciences of nature to be more objective and consensual and more able to steadily accumulate verifiable knowledge. But society contrasts with nature because its subjects are moral and because they think and feel. Thinking, feeling, and morally deliberating are impossible to observe and difficult even to operationalize. They must be intuited from fragmentary evidence, and in offering such interpretations, social analysts will disagree. This is the weak argument for the lack of consensus in social science. The strong argument is that, because social analysts experience the same cognitive, emotional, and moral conflicts as the subjects they study, interpretations are bound to reflect the plurality of human experience and belief. Intellectual conflict among social scientists should not be regretted, in my view. People have their prejudices, as the saying goes—their distinctive sense of what motivates themselves and others, as well as their convictions about what makes institutions work. Philosophers and social scientists start from such everyday presuppositions; we crystallize them abstractly, elaborate them logically, and find methods to test them empirically. But we cannot eliminate these convictions, nor should we.[3]

Are political actors simply conniving, instrumental, egoistic, and ferociously competitive? Or are they also compelled by morality and communal feelings for others? These questions are topics for philosophy and the stuff of common sense, and they divide academic and public opinion over the topics of this book—power, culture, and mass communication. Readers of *The Performance of Politics* do not need to know how disputes about these topics divide academics, but they may be interested in them anyway. What follows is a Michelin guide for an armchair journey through these debates. I map the places of interest, offer evaluations, and provide recommendations. This guide is not, however, a substitute for actually traveling to the destination and sampling the fare oneself.

The Political and the Social

Power seems like a pretty simple idea, but for millennia it has remained an essentially contested concept. To simplify a complex and nuanced argument, one party to this dispute sees power primarily on a vertical axis. Power is not about developing links to others but about orders from above, about command and force. It is a matter of hierarchy, not solidarity, and of subordination, not respect. This view of the order of things rests on an instrumental idea of action. Twenty-five hundred years ago, Thrasymachus summed it up pretty well: "'Just' or 'right' means nothing but what is in the interest of the strongest party.... In all states alike, 'right' has the same meaning, namely what is for the interest of the party established in power, and that is the strongest."[4] This approach to power became associated in early modern philosophy with the so-called realism of Hobbes and Machiavelli and in modern social science with Marx.

Against such realism stands the normative view, which connects the exercise of power with morality. The key term here is legitimacy. To be legitimate, power must be deployed in a manner that can be justified according to an ethical ideal. Legitimate power solicits not only conflict but cooperation as well. When it succeeds, power becomes authority. Authoritative power is more stable and easier to deploy than naked compulsion or force. In early modern philosophy, John Locke's more consensual and democratic contract theory provides an answer to the *Leviathan* of Hobbes. The great German social scientist Max Weber introduces the idea of legitimacy to modern social scientific discussions of power, though he himself remains deeply ambivalent, developing an upgraded realist approach at the same time. Authoritative power is systematically conceptualized by the sociological theorist Talcott Parsons. The Marxist theorist Antonio Gramsci argues that, under the condition of ideological hegemony, those with less material power acquiesce voluntarily, thereby allowing dominant classes to rule more easily. Social philosopher Michel Foucault insists that power and knowledge are always intertwined but follows Nietzsche in conceptualizing legitimacy more as camouflage than ethical claim.[5]

These general and abstract disputations inform empirical argument about democratic politics. According to the tradition of Thrasymachus, the idea of speaking, acting, and moralizing citizens ruling themselves is naïve, a dangerous illusion. Marx economizes Thrasymachus when he argues that capitalist democracy can be only formal, never substantive, and that the ruling class dominates every political struggle. The German-born Italian political thinker Robert Michels bureaucratizes Thrasymachus when he asserts that oligarchy is inevitable because elites monopolize organizational resources. Weber sociologizes Thrasymachus when he argues that democracy can be sustained—against impersonal bureaucracy—only by the force of amoral demagogues and ruthless party organizations. Drawing on Marx, Michels, and Weber, C. Wright Mills describes America as ruled by a power elite. Combining military, economic, and political power, this callous clique wields its power against a pulverized mass, citizens pacified by a culture industry that has transformed the once-democratic public into mere publicity.[6]

Against this pessimism camouflaged as realism stands a line of social science thinkers who believe that democracy is not only desirable but also possible—because horizontal ties of solidarity can be built upon values, specified in law, and represented through elections. Alexis de Tocqueville elaborates the intertwining of religion, law, and democratic association in his studies of early nineteenth-century America. Emile Durkheim shows how solidarity can be woven into institutions via energetic symbolic actions that sustain collective symbolic representations. John Dewey writes, "Democracy is more than a form of government" and that "it is primarily a mode of associated living, of conjoint communicated experience," while George Herbert Mead explains how individuation emerges from common feeling and association. Hannah Arendt develops the most culturally sensitive democratic philosophy of recent times. Against visions of purely material and vertical power, she writes that "The reality of the world is guaranteed by the presence of others, by its appearing to all," that political action is "transacted in words," and that "to be political, to live in a polis" means that everything is "decided through words and persuasion and not through force and violence."[7]

The Performance of Politics is antirealist. Certainly, democratic theory should be hardheaded, not naïve or fanciful, but it should not conceive politics mechanistically, presuppose cynical and instrumental reason, or imagine democratic order as merely external or institutional. If we confine ourselves to the tradition of Thrasymachus, we have no access to the interior domain of politics, to the structures of feeling, the habits of the heart, and the worlds of moral sense and perception, which make living together in a democratic manner possible. We cannot illuminate the mysterious process by which citizens so often agree, willingly and without coercion, to uphold rules whose utility they scarcely understand and whose effect may be detrimental to their self-interest narrowly conceived. Democracies are not only about differences, interest, and antagonism; they are also sustained by shared morality and nurtured by community. This is exactly what Tocqueville meant by insisting that in democracies self-interest can be "rightly" understood, and not comprehended in only a narrow and calculating way.[8]

The continuing vitality of democratic discourse and the robustness of solidarity sustain a civil sphere that is relatively independent from money and brute force. In earlier work on civil culture and institutions, I develop a model of democratic societies that concentrates on shared emotions and symbolic commitments and on what and how people speak, think, and feel about politics.[9] I stress the critical role of social solidarity, the we-ness of a community, whether regional, national, or international, which defines feelings of connectedness in a manner that can transcend particularistic commitments, narrow loyalties, and segmented interests. The civil sphere is a form of social and cultural organization rooted simultaneously in a radical individualism and a thoroughgoing collectivism, a combination well captured in Jürgen Habermas's notion of the "sphere of private people come together as a public."[10] The phrase "We, the people," which opens the preamble to the U.S. Constitution, references the civil in struggles to broaden social participation and extend equality. Yet, if solidarity gestures only to collective obligation, it will support repression at the expense of liberty. In the wake of their successful revolution against kingship, Americans insisted that the Constitution proposing a new state be amended by a Bill of Rights enshrining individual liberties.

How does all this relate to the empirical study of elections? While not denying the existence of electoral campaigns and voting, those examining them through the lenses of Thrasymachus tend to brush their significance aside. They view campaigning and voting as merely political means to the end of social power, with "social" defined in a broadly economic-material way. Focusing on social power denies an independent significance to politics and to the meaning-in-the-moment that constitutes political action itself. In Harold Lasswell's classic formulation, politics becomes simply who gets what and why.[11] It is not about cultural justification, about aligning political struggle with moral right, about civil and anticivil meaning making, or about symbolizing candidates so they represent the collectivity in a discursive way. Modern political sociology elaborates this social reduction and focuses its empirical studies on social cleavages that determine electoral outcomes. As Seymour Martin Lipset formulated it, elections represent simply the "democratic translation of the class struggle." Daniel Bell once explained McCarthyism as "deep changes taking place in the social structure that are reworking the social map of the country." Contemporary political sociologists Clem Brooks and Jeff Manza explain today's voting patterns by the "post-industrial trends [that] have enhanced the electoral significance of the professional and managerial segments of the electorate." Emphasizing the external, material environment of political action makes political actors self-interested and calculating. Political campaigns become a market, the candidates sellers, the voters buyers. For Anthony Downs, "Each citizen casts his vote for the party he believes will provide him with more benefits than any other"; for Bernard Crick, politics is "the marketplace and the price mechanism of all social demands." Political scientists frequently employ the model of neoclassical economics, speaking of elections as "the marketplace of democracy" and conceptualizing "the median voter's policy preference" as driving "electoral competition between two viable candidates" in which "everyone is fully informed" and which produces "benefits to the general community."[12]

Accounts of the 2008 presidential election typically engage the same reductive language of social cause and political effect. In *How Barack Obama Won*, NBC News political director Chuck Todd and elections director Sheldon Gawiser write, "The actual results of the presidential race were as expected" and that they were "quite unremarkable if one understood how the fundamentals of the political landscape so favored the Democrats…in a year in which the economy was extremely weak and the Republican party brand was as poor as it had been since the Great Depression."[13] Looking "inside the American election of 2008," their account headlines, "Demographically Speaking: Times Are Tough for GOP."[14] Another postelection analysis, this one by a raft of academic political scientists, explains that "larger political and societal forces were at work and drove the election."[15] In a section titled "Social Groups and the 2008 Presidential Election," the volume's editor elaborates:

> As the campaign progressed, the group divisions among voters became clearer. There were few surprises. The electoral coalitions broke along traditional party lines—income, class, race, ideology, and gender—and in the expected directions. Obama attracted the working class, the better educated, liberals, Democrats, moderates, independents, and women, especially single and professional women [and] the exact opposite of Obama's pattern of support characterized McCain's.[16]

In the volume's conclusion, another political scientist explains that 2008 was a "transforming election" because it "represented a moment when a new demography caught up to a new politics."[17]

Against the social determinism of politics in 2008, *The Performance of Politics* proposes not that so-called social conditions do not matter but that the political has an independent force. Even Todd and Gawiser acknowledge that, among those Americans who saw the economy as tanking, 44 percent still voted for Republican John McCain, whose conservative, stand-pat policies did not promise economic change.[18] If elections really are socially determined, then how can this be? Similarly, while noting that the percentage of Democratic voters declined for three decades to rough parity with Republicans in 2004, these NBC journalists report an abrupt reversal between 2006 and 2008, with Republican identification dwindling and independent affiliation rising.[19] How could there have been such a history-shifting departure from a long-term pattern of secular social change? "The conditions of life can never 'explain' what we are or answer the question of who we are," Arendt contends, "for the simple reason they never condition us absolutely." If social conditions could actually determine the political, she continues, "Action would be an unnecessary luxury," merely "a capricious interference with general laws of behavior." Political action and speech are necessary precisely because they are not luxuries. They are the core of democracy, and they have significant and independent effect. "With word and deed we insert ourselves into the human world," Arendt explains, and "this insertion is not forced upon us by necessity." With political action, "something new is started which cannot be expected from whatever may have happened before," and "the new always happens against the overwhelming odds of statistical laws and their probability."[20]

Because politics matters, elections matter, and demographic groups are neither unitary nor determining. In February 2007, almost two years before the 2008 presidential election, *Rolling Stone* magazine described Obama's entry into the campaign as "one of the more startling and sudden acts in recent political history." Providing a rationale for his unexpected decision, Obama told the magazine he felt "a call from the crowds" as "a summons to a new role." Arendt is right to suggest that, in politics, "the new always appears in the guise of a miracle":[21]

> What is at stake is the revelatory character without which action and speech would lose all human relevance....The connotation of courage, which we now feel to be an indispensable quality of the hero, is in fact already present in a willingness to act and speak at all, to insert one's self into the world and begin a story of one's own....Courage and even boldness are already present in leaving one's private hiding place and showing who one is, in disclosing and exposing one's self.[22]

"For many years," write media scholars and election analysts Kathleen Hall Jamieson and Paul Waldman, "political scientists have endeavored to create models that would predict the outcome of presidential elections using only information available before the campaign begins in earnest."[23] If such predictive models really do hold sway, then the political disappears, and the significance of electoral democracy is whisked away. If elections simply transform social into political hierarchies, then focusing on democratic elections seems beside the point. In *The Performance of Politics,* I show how electoral campaigns stand in the way of such automatic translation. In order for the ruled to become the rulers—Aristotle's straightforward definition of democracy—voters must be protected by the relative autonomy of a civil sphere. Democracy allows the production of a new kind of power. In a democracy, it is civil power, not social power, that decides who will control the state. Civil power is solidarity translated into government. To the degree that the civil sphere is independent, "We, the people" can speak via communicative institutions that provide cultural authority and regulative institutions that carry legal force. The civil sphere regulates access to state power by constituting a new and different power of its own. To the degree that society is democratic, voting is the gatekeeper of state power. It is the civil power produced by electoral campaigns that opens and closes the gate.

The Cultural and the Performative

Philosophy may assert the independence of the political and justify it normatively, but the political actually achieves autonomy from the social only if nested inside the cultural, and this political theorists typically do not explain. Social meanings have their own internal logic. Patterned by binary codes and temporal narratives, culture structures are as forceful, organized, and independent as social structures of a more material kind. When political actors act and speak, they evoke meanings and symbolic weight. They see themselves in terms of exemplary models of speaking and acting that culture provides, and they wish to persuade audiences to view them in the same way. To enter into the state and to be in a position to pull the levers of organizational and material power, those who struggle for democratic power must first become authoritative. They gain authority by speaking on behalf of sacred values and against profane ones. By evoking such cultural valences, these claims for power gain legitimacy from citizen audiences before electoral decisions are made.

To understand modern politics, one must interpret and explain the structured meanings upon which political speech and action draw. The need to do so brings us right up to the edge of a truly cultural sociology. Before actually stepping into it, however, we must maneuver through another thicket of long-standing intellectual debate. Since the middle of the nineteenth century, sociologists of modernity have been announcing that tradition has vanished, that once-enchanted earlier societies have lost their magic, that iconic aura has been displaced by mechanical reproduction, and that alienation makes it impossible to experience meaning. As Marx and Engels put it in 1848, "All that is holy is profane." If the modern world is actually so deracinated, then contemporary efforts at symbolic action must be explained away. Symbols become superfluous superstructures. The motivation for ethical discourse is explained as an instrumental pursuit of material interest. Ideas are reduced to ideology. Traditional approaches to meaning in sociology treat culture as a dependent variable; only social power, social structures, and material interests are treated as independent variables that have a causal status. In this manner, sociology turns from culture to its unmoved mover, "society" as a noncultural force. Thus is the social reduction of politics camouflaged in cultural form.[24]

Instead of such a reductionist sociology *of* culture, I have argued for a *cultural* sociology. Just as we need to respect the independence of the political vis-à-vis the social, we must also give the independent structuring power of culture its due. Modernity has eliminated neither deep meaning nor encrusted tradition; it has, rather, changed the content of meaning and multiplied its forms. Modern culture still provides anchoring codes and narratives even if they often evoke rationality, individuality, skepticism, and social transformation more often than mystery, hierarchy, stasis, and metaphysical belief. As far as the role of meaning goes, according to Durkheim, no irrevocably great divide exists between the aboriginals who believed in totemic gods and "the religious man of today." Modern people still engage in emotional and ritual action, energizing symbols that can become powerful collective representations, dividing the sacred from profane.[25]

Not long after Durkheim's declaration and quite likely in response to it, there emerged a dramatic transformation in linguistic understanding that continues to ramify in the humanities and the social sciences. Ferdinand de Saussure and Roman Jakobson propose that words gain meaning not by referring to things "out there" in the real world but from their structured relation to other words inside of language. Meaning is relative and relational, organized by binaries. A color is called black not because it is a dark hue but because the English language pairs the idea of blackness with the color it designates as white. The physical hues we associate with the words *white* and *black* are defined relationally as opposites; only then do they become so in terms of empirical and social fact. In his later philosophical investigations, Ludwig Wittgenstein reaches the same conclusion by a different route. Before we can understand a word as denoting a specific worldly thing, we must see it in terms of the "language game" that identifies the relevant general category of things of which it is one part. So the meaning of a thing cannot exceed the conventions of cultural language at a given historical time.[26]

As these revolutions in philosophy and linguistics took hold, they turned intellectual attention away from the vexed problem of consciousness, accessible only via the mystery of empathy, to the actual words that sentient actors employ. Seen, heard, and written down, symbolic languages externalize subjective meaning. These cultural forms can be interpreted and analyzed in a more rational and disciplined manner, though the experiences and sensibilities of social analysts necessarily continue to come into play. This so-called linguistic turn facilitated a broader "cultural turn" in the human sciences. Not only speech but also culture itself comes to be modeled as language: Binary symbols prestructure social action, as language does with speech. Claude Lévi-Strauss was the first social scientist to move semiotics from language to the study of human societies, though he still held fast to the modernist faith that semiotic tools are confined to the "savage mind." Roland Barthes drew exactly the opposite conclusion, demonstrating the myriad manners in which binary symbolic relations structure modern meanings. As symbolic anthropology flourished, the concepts and methods of Mary Douglas, Victor Turner, and, above all, Clifford Geertz spread widely throughout the humanities and social sciences.[27]

Until well into the 1980s, cultural sociology remained an oxymoron, sociologists insisting on the great divide between meaning and modernity and the sociology *of* culture winning the day. Meaning was studied as the wagging tail of social power, as resistance to hegemony, disguised governmentality, organizational isomorphism, cultural capital, or symbolic politics.[28] As the cultural turn has broadened, more strongly cultural sociologies have finally emerged. Solidarity is modeled less as interest than discourse; stratification interpreted more in terms of symbolic rather than material boundaries; social movements are interpreted less as conflicts for power than as struggles over representations and framing; material life is seen more as material culture; and markets are perceived as economies of signs.[29] In my own studies of political and social conflict, I locate a binary discourse revolving around democratic purity and antidemocratic pollution. This discourse of civil society propels meaning making in the mass media and allows voters to make critical judgments about who's who in the struggle for electoral power. It is not issues per se that determine voters' political judgments and even less the social interests at stake. It is the manner in which these issues and interests are related to the underlying social language of civil purity and impurity.[30]

TABLE N.1. The Discourse of Civil Society

Civil	Anticivil
Motives	
Active	Passive
Autonomous	Dependent
Rational	Irrational
Reasonable	Hysterical
Calm	Excitable
Self-controlled	Wild/passionate
Realistic	Distorted
Sane	Mad
Relations	
Open	Secretive
Trusting	Suspicious
Critical	Deferential
Honorable	Self-interested
Altruistic	Greedy
Truthful	Deceitful
Straightforward	Calculating
Deliberative	Conspiratorial
Friendly	Antagonistic
Institutions	
Rule regulated	Arbitrary
Law	Power
Equality	Hierarchy
Inclusive	Exclusive
Impersonal	Personal
Contracts	Bonds of loyalty
Groups	Factions
Office	Personality

According to this cultural perspective, the factual status of "issues"—what is rationally ascertainable about social problems and the policies proposed to solve them—is relatively insignificant in the struggle for power. Problems and policies are ostensible referents. What students of social power miss is the symbolic language within which issues are framed and claims for legitimacy made. Journalists, bloggers, and voters themselves see campaigns as about personalities, issues, and ideologies, about being liberal or conservative, pro- or anti-abortion, military intervention, affirmative action, surveillance, gay marriage, immigration, free trade, financial regulation, health care, unions, the minimum wage. Nonetheless, it is symbolic identifications that are the ends of the struggle for power, whatever the means. Everything is done as if words and images matter, and they do. Campaigns refer to things that exist in the world, but they are not exclusively about these real things. In themselves, things are signifieds, social references redolent of symbolic signifiers. Every issue must be associated with the sacred or profane side of the civil binary, and this applies not only to conflicts inside the civil sphere but also to those concerning its boundaries. As former political press secretary and publisher of the *Columbia Journalism Review* Evan Cornog writes, "For all the campaign talk about résumés and experience, issues and qualifications, it is the battle of stories, not the debate on issues, that determines how Americans respond to a presidential contender."[31] Difference gathers temporal power in heroic narratives that promise the transformation of social life. Democratic stories are fueled by dramas in which protagonists cast themselves as civil heroes fighting against ruthless, scheming protagonists whose election would endanger the very fundaments of civil life.[32]

Yet, while a fundamental referent of political action, the codes and narratives that structure discourse in civil society are not determinate. There is agency. Political actors and campaigns *struggle* for power. They are compelled to create performances, and their success is uncertain and contingent. It depends on skill and fortune, on commanding an effective stage, on media interpretations, on shifting historical constellations, and on audiences being prepared and responding in felicitous ways. The discourse of civil society creates a vocabulary for political speech, but it is flesh and blood actors who make this script walk and talk, who speak the words, form intonations, create tropes, and time the rhetorical flow. These are not matters of culture's structure but of its pragmatics.[33]

To challenge more static understandings of language, John Austin introduced the idea of performativity.[34] When politicians emphatically state that the world is like this and declare in no uncertain terms that their opponent is doing that, they are making constative statements, statements that present themselves as descriptions, as denoting something out there in the real world. Performative statements, by contrast, rather than referring to a putatively existing fact, work to bring a condition into being through the very act of talking. When political candidates make emphatic declarations about the state of the world and ringing declarations about their opponents, they would like us to believe their words are constative. Mostly, however, they are performative. Politicians do things with words. Candidates are less describing the world than wanting to bring that world into being in the imaginations of their listeners. They want to convince us of how things are. If their performances are successful, we are persuaded. Whether we become convinced is less a matter of rightness in a moral or cognitive sense than aesthetic power—whether a political performance has "felicity." Is it structured in a manner that evokes our concerns, builds pictures in our minds, and allows us to share their worldly visions? About the time that Austin philosophizes performance, Erving Goffman draws on theatrical metaphors to develop a sociology of the performative in social interaction. Turner later describes the movement from ritual to theater as a pivotal transition marking modernity, and Geertz employs theatricality to understand cockfighting rituals in Bali. Crossing anthropology and theater studies, Richard Schechner creates the new discipline of performance studies.[35]

In my own, more recent theory of cultural pragmatics, I deconstruct social performance in terms of background representations, scripts, actors, means of symbolic production, mise en scène, social and interpretive power, and audiences. When felicitous performances fuse speaker and audience, these complex mediations became invisible, and audiences do not, in fact, see actions as if they are performed. We endow them with verisimilitude, so that scripted actions seem spontaneous and real. We believe that the words of politicians are true and their selves authentic. As societies become modern and more complex, however, the elements of performance become more separated one from another, and fusion becomes a much more difficult thing. Authenticity becomes problematic, and communication much more difficult to achieve. This diagram presents the historical separation of key performative elements schematically, and fusion and re-fusion as well.[36]

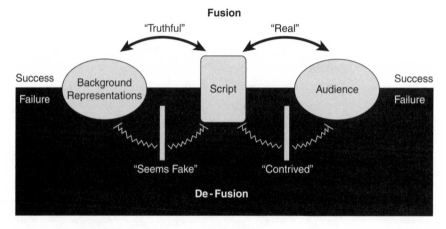

FIGURE N.1 Fusion

Cultural pragmatics undergirds *The Performance of Politics.*[37] It allows us to capture the self-interest and contingency of the struggle for power without jettisoning meaning and returning to Thrasymachus. In contemporary societies, audiences of political performances are often physically distant and emotionally disconnected, without affection or understanding for the mediated figures they see struggling for power. Citizen audiences do not feel compelled to believe the truth of what they hear or see, much less to attribute to political performances moral and emotional force. While political performances must achieve success, contemporary audiences are increasingly disconnected from the powers that be. The struggle to re-fuse speaker and audience, to connect with the members of civil society through felicitous performance of the codes and narratives that define it—this is what the democratic struggle for democratic power is all about, and it is what I have described in detail between June and November of 2008.

Media and Meaning

The democratic struggle for power is defined by the historical de-fusion of the elements of performance. The need to struggle for power responds to the separation, and protection, of those subject to power from those wielding it. Because politicians become less able to control citizen audiences, they are compelled to persuade them. When those subject to power win the right to vote, their interpretations and reactions decide whether or not state power can be gained. As the breadth of the democratic audience increases—with suffrage, territorial expansion, and demographic diversity—opportunities for direct communication between politicians and citizens correspondingly decrease. Few citizens see or hear political performances personally. In his refreshing critique of participatory and deliberative theories of democracy, Jeffrey Edward Green defends the role of the "citizen spectator" and the centrality of publicity. "The ideal that gives shape to democratic reform," he writes, "is the ideal that the People, not its leadership, controls the conditions under which leaders appear on the public stage." Green suggests that "the People's possession of the means of publicity" entails "a breaking down of leaders' control of their own public image making."[38] While the means of publicity is indeed crucial, however, the people do not contest directly with power but with media representations of it. It is the media that confront politicians, projecting interpretations that are framed by the profession of journalism and the discourse of civil society.

From the eighteenth century onward, political journalism emerges as part of the struggle to control publicity. These new media institutions disseminate political performances more broadly; at the same time, however, these media institutions remain tightly controlled by political speakers and the social interests and cultural interests that support them, a fusion that continues to mark political journalism throughout most of the next century. Even as political reporting forms an ever more significant filter between citizens and power, it remains tightly attached to ideology and party—a particularistic partisan press. So, even as political performers lose control of the means of symbolic production and direct interpretive power, there is not yet a fundamental conflict between politicians and media as we understand it today. Political media embrace bias, explicitly taking one side against another. Though independent organizationally, political journalism is not independent culturally inasmuch as it serves principally to amplify the messages of one side or another. Conservative, radical, religious, secular, and ethnic political movements each have their own media, and each blames the strident media of their opponents for distorting their views. Meanwhile, friendly media allow politicians to fuse easily with audiences on their own side. There is difference without real differentiation, mediation without true mediatization.[39] In the United States, media de-fusion deepens during the Progressive Era.

In the 1890s, mainstream political reformers begin challenging the excesses of industrial capitalism, take on the abuses of urbanism, and speak out on behalf of excluded classes, as well as ethnic and gender groups. These movements for civil repair stimulate and simultaneously depend upon newly crusading news media. By the 1920s, journalists begin seeing themselves as a professional group defined by the reformist ideals of the Progressive Era, which mirror the broader discourse of civil society. News pages are separated from editorial pages, and the expectation of politically independent news reporting, if not always the practice, firmly takes hold. Fifty years later, in the wake of Vietnam and Watergate, the independence of journalism deepens further still, with reporters becoming more skeptical and critical in their public interpretations of power. Journalists see themselves as professionally bound to subject the claims of power to civil values and as representing the citizen against those who would control the state.[40]

This historical account of growing media autonomy is disputed vociferously in academic circles. On one side, scholars in the Thrasymachus tradition maintain that media interpretations continue to serve social power, whether that of capitalist classes, media owners, or the state. Once there was a golden age when media were independent and critical, but the once-proud media now caters to state power and private profit, its public function transformed into publicity, its truth giving way to propaganda.[41] Other scholars deeply skeptical of media independence are less concerned with social power over the media than with the media's weakness of will, its failure to exercise control over itself. They charge contemporary journalists with transmitting spin rather than challenging it, with reporting the cynical manipulations of politicians rather than providing citizen audiences with the actual truth. When journalists "fail in their task of discovering and describing the knowable, relevant information at play in public discourse," Jamieson and Waldman argue, reporters contribute to the political cynicism of our already skeptical age, with citizen participation declining as a result.[42] As the media spoon-feed voters self-serving statements of political spinmeisters, they transform citizens into audiences. No longer able to separate fact from fiction, citizens become mere consumers, passively accepting power and absorbed in their private lives.[43]

The first group of media scholars is too critical by half, ignoring the media's increasing reflexivity vis-à-vis power.[44] The second wrongly identifies media skepticism with cynicism, suggesting as an alternative a rationalism that seems unrealistic if not naive. News reporting can never be hermetically sealed off from its social context, concerned solely with the reporting of empirical fact. Media interpretations of events reflect historical time and place, not free-floating objective evaluations. As Sonia Livingston suggests, "The media do not provide a (biased) window on the world, so much as a set of resources through which everyday meanings and practices are constituted."[45] The issue is not whether media produce value-free information—they can't—but whether media evaluations have independence from those of the other, nonjournalistic powers that be. Do political journalists align themselves with particular ideologies, enthusiastically supporting Left or Right, religion, class, ethnicity, or ideology in a propagandistic way? Or do they act more as a fourth estate by aligning their vocation with the discourse of civil society, serving their own interests in self-regulation and those of democracy at the same time?

News media do not produce value-free information, but they are brimming with attributions of fact, providing "raw data" for citizens about who is saying what to whom and when, what happened, and what the effects might be. News reports provide information, however, by telling stories, stringing independent observations into broader binary codes and narrative configurations. News reports present themselves as factual descriptions, yet they are culturally constructed symbolic representations at the same time. Reporters offer readers judgments about events in real time, about what is good and bad, and about what is harmful to democracy and helpful in repairing it. Reporters dramatize democratic protagonists as struggling with dangerously antidemocratic antagonists. Journalism offers representations of the public's varied and collective opinions; it does not merely provide facts upon which opinion is based. As Herbst writes, "Media portrayals of issues and narrative descriptions of policy debates in the news are themselves public opinion."[46] Not only fictional but also factual media have narrative interests at stake.[47]

Journalism constructs an opaque and unpredictable cultural screen between political claim and citizen audience. As *The Performance of Politics* suggests, far from taking media reflection as transparent, politicians and their teams expend extraordinary efforts to control it. As cable and Internet expand the breadth and reach of news broadcasting, the bristly net of media interpretation settles down ever more tightly over political campaigns. The blogosphere amplifies the digitally induced explosion of 24/7 media interpretation. As old and new layers of journalistic mediation grow omnipresent, politicians performing in the public sphere intensify efforts to buffer themselves against its intrusions. Influential journalists complain of their reduced "face time" with politicians, and campaigns assign "minders" to control reporters looking for information.[48] As journalism becomes more independent and probing, candidates and staff build protective walls, making themselves vulnerable to charges of becoming more artificial and controlled as a result.

A new level of media reflexivity has recently emerged. The earlier model of independence took a naturalistic stance. Journalists often came into conflict with politicians and power, but they generally refrained from publicly and directly questioning the realness of political presentations. Things are different today. Sophisticated print, television, and online journalism deconstruct the political image; refusing to accept the authenticity of front-stage performances, they publish backstage, behind-the-scenes narratives that reveal them to be constructed. The *New York Times* reports, "Strategists for Obama...have made it clear that they believe they need to take extra steps to control his image and protect against attack."[49] Sophisticated political news no longer presents candidates or political events as natural; it now covers the spinning of the thing as much as the thing in itself.

Why this new reflexivity? Not because politics has suddenly become deceptive and obsessed with spin, where once it was guided by sincerity and truth. Politics has always been performative. What's changed is that the elements of performance are more differentiated and de-fused. There are new roles, new paid specialties, and a new self-consciousness about performativity.

The earlier one travels back in the history of democratic mass politics, for example, the less likely one is to find speechwriters. When speechwriting does become more common, it is not a paid and specialized role. When it finally becomes a profession, it does not yet display itself on the public stage. Only over the last 30 years have speechwriters become a common trope of democratic politics, figures who step out of their role to take credit for the candidate's words.[50] Successful speechwriters give interviews and write books that brag about their own power at the expense of the candidate's. Contemporary journalists rarely fail to ask whether the words coming out of a candidate's mouth are actually the candidate's own, questioning that is facilitated by news organizations bringing former speechwriters such as William Safire (*New York Times*) and Pat Buchanan (CNN) onto their staffs.

Many other such observations could be made. Decades ago, there was no such thing as a press secretary; today, there are several in every campaign. Speeches were once delivered without armies of spinners descending upon journalists to mediate their interpretation; today, spinning and the media's discussion of spinning are public matters. Once, it was the candidate's friends who served as advisers. Today, the candidate hires professional teams of strategists, pollsters, advertisers, media buyers, and public relations experts, not to mention hairstylists and makeup artists, lighting specialists, and sometimes even wardrobe managers.

Such performative de-fusion makes it more difficult for those struggling for power to make their image seem natural and their messages real, and journalists have become centrally interested in explaining why. Everywhere there are media reporting about narrative, performance, and spinning, about stagings and settings, about scripted speeches and teleprompter reading, about focus groups and audience reception. Yet, even as the media expose political efforts at managing the image, the hope and reality of political authenticity remains. As in drama, so in politics: There remains the possibility that the citizen audience will engage in what Colerdige called the willing suspension of disbelief.

Method and Sources

This discussion has ranged widely over intellectual predispositions. Ultimately, however, the validity of *The Performance of Politics* rests on empirical claim. In philosophy, theories are asserted as matters of logic and analytical-rhetorical force and are illustrated with empirically oriented speculation. In social science, logic, analysis, and rhetoric remain significant, but argument must also be subjected to sustained factual inquiry, and researchers work assiduously to control investigator bias.

When cultural sociologists study politics, they must construct their arguments from the speech and actions of the social actors themselves. This restriction limits investigator speculation. To make their empirical case, cultural sociologists are compelled to immerse readers in the actual flows of social discourse so that they can themselves, at one remove, experience the fullness of social communication. The cultural sociologist is an ethnographer of public opinion. Failing to fully investigate public discourses that—to the investigator—seem untruthful or unappealing puts this ethnographic authority at risk. Yet, while aiming at flow, immersion, and fullness of range, the cultural sociologist exercises extraordinary selectivity. The reason is that public meanings cannot be discovered as such. Meaning can be represented only by indicators that stand in for it. When public opinion is operationalized via statistically random surveys, the resulting samples would seem to overcome the selectivity problem. But this is illusory. Pollsters supply respondents with a small number of preestablished questions, which reduce answers to brief

292 NOTE ON CONCEPT AND METHOD

abstractions that can be calibrated numerically. While the representational status of these "opinions" is useful for certain purposes, such spoon-fed, sliced-and-
diced responses do not supply symbolic material rich enough to reveal patterns
of meaning making. Thick, not thin, descriptions are needed, accounts that more
closely approximate actual thinking and speech.[51]

For thickness, one must have recourse to the social text reported by and
recorded in the mass media. In the media, we find not only factual information
about public actors and their speech but also cultural structures—public meanings themselves. While news media are not statistically representative, concerns
with sampling cannot be dismissed. Which news sources should be chosen? Which
best reveal the wide range of public discourses that animate political life? There
are thousands of media to choose among, from national to statewide to local, from
elite to popular, and from print to television to blogosphere. In *The Performance
of Politics*, the principal resource of choice is print media, and among these, "elite"
news outlets, most significantly the *New York Times* and the *Wall Street Journal*. In
this media ethnography, I reproduce long quotations from print media not primarily to supply facts but to give a feeling for the meaning and emotions circulating at a particular point in time.

For prophets of visuality and digital revolution, print sources will seem like
stodgy, old-fashioned, and very limiting choices. I suggest, to the contrary, that
reliance on these sources remains an empirical necessity. It reflects the longstanding sociological realities of media use and influence that continue to the present
day. A recent empirical study in the *Journal of Computer-mediated Communication*, for example, challenges the "widely heralded" claim that blogs represent a
new kind of "democratizing innovation" and questions "whether citizen media
outlets are really inverting the power structure between citizens and elite traditional media entities." Based on the quantitative technique of network analysis,
the study finds the same patterns of media influence that media research on print
and television has been documenting for decades: "Prior research has found
strong intermedia agenda setting effects between elite-to-less-elite traditional
mass media entities...[from] newspaper coverage to television news broadcasts
and...[from] newspaper coverage to wire services...[and] convergent agendas
between portal news outlets and traditional, elite media entities in television and
newspaper industries."[52] Looking at the 18 leading political blogs, the author concludes that, while "traditional media's agenda setting power is no longer universal,"
there remains "relative dominance" of the elite print media "as top sources within
each blog network's top 20 media choices." The elite print media "remains a driving 'A-list' force in the creation of blog agendas."

The principal reason for this continuing asymmetry is, to my mind, the
civil respect accorded independent and professional political journalism and, of

course, the significant resources that the print media continue to devote to news reporting. Citizen audiences are attracted to political blogs because, in sharp contrast with news journalism, they are openly engaged in ideological polemics; yet, paradoxically, leading blogs remain utterly dependent on news reporting for reliable political information and actually provide an echo chamber for it.[53] Furthermore, having "hijacked" the blog format, the elite print media's interactive websites now provide the same 24/7 access and mobility as other digital forms. No wonder "the only independent, citizen media bloggers that are able to gain traditional media's attention," according to one researcher, "were once journalists or maintain traditional media ties as in the case of the blogs *Talking Points Memo* and the *Huffington Post*."[54]

My interpretations of public meaning making often make reference to television news, websites, and blogs. I do so to indicate real-time flows of symbolic representation that print media do not provide (e.g., MSNBC coverage of the last day of the Democratic convention in chapter 2); to communicate the vividness of rapidly shifting meanings (e.g., discussions of "Victory and Defeat" in part III); to trace how terminal-to-terminal mediation allows virtual communication to intervene in the flow of representations in a distinctive milieu (e.g., as another channel for the performative interaction that marks the ground game in chapter 3); or to indicate the intensity of circulating meanings and images associated with a particular event (e.g., Tina Fey's all-too-real impersonation of Sarah Palin on SNL in chapter 8). Regarding the last point, I often report the frequency of YouTube hits for the virtual reproduction of the remarks or images of political actors or of the videos or ads issued by campaigns.

The agenda-setting power of the *New York Times* has long been noted. It deepened some two decades ago, when digitalization allowed the East Coast paper to print and distribute a truly national edition, and more recently to construct a website that has become the most visited of any news media in the world. Media scholars refer to the *Times*' "widely acknowledged ability to set news agendas for local and regional papers," to its providing "the lenses through which most citizens viewed their government," and to the *Times* as "the national paper of record," whose "news coverage [is] the most influential."[55] There is, moreover, a pronounced intertextuality between the print editions, blogs, and wire services of the *New York Times*, the *Washington Post*, and the *Los Angeles Times*, which together constitute three of the four elite print news organizations in the United States. The fourth is the *Wall Street Journal*. I reference articles in the *Post* and the *Los Angeles Times* vis-à-vis their New York counterpart only when they break or deepen a story in some distinctive way—for example, their reporting from Alaska exposing the Palin effect (chapter 8). By contrast, I cite *Wall Street Journal* reports nearly as frequently as those from the *New York Times*. There is longstanding and unresolved popular (and academic) argument about how far apart the *Times* and *Journal* actually are, ideologically speaking. Media watchdogs Irvine and Kincaid confirm that "The *Journal* has a long-standing separation between its conservative editorial pages and [its] liberal news pages." Outspoken investigative journalist Paul Sperry, a media fellow at Stanford University's conservative Hoover Institution, reports that writers in the *Journal*'s news division sometimes call those in the editorial division "Nazis," commenting that the two "departments are as politically polarized as North and South Korea." In a broad study of political leanings, Ho and Quinn find "a greater than 60% chance that the *New York Times* is the most liberal newspaper amongst all papers examined."[56]

My own sense is that, while *Journal* news reporters adhere to the same professional guidelines as other elite print journalists and move freely among jobs at all the leading papers, many editorial decisions at the *Journal*—about matters such as story placement, lead paragraphs, and headlining—reflect more conservative politics, which Rupert Murdoch's new ownership has hardly changed. Whatever the differences in actual content, there remains the fact, confirmed by other media research, that "the *readers* of the *New York Times* are more liberal and the readers of the *Wall Street Journal* are more conservative."[57] Thoroughly sampling the *Journal* ensures access to the political representations that sustain the conservative lifeworld during election campaigns, as well as access to the representations that are viewed as more conservative (even if they are not so) by the other, more liberal side. This is even more the case for the *Washington Times* and the *New York Post*, which are less institutions of professional journalism than conservative political voices of opinion dressed up in news media guise. The *Weekly Standard* is explicitly a journal of conservative opinion. I sample these media to ensure the widest possible discursive range, from the Left to the Right. Including a wide swath of meaning making does not, of course, preclude its being interpreted in a narrow-minded, shallow, or unimaginative way. Here another kind of interpretive control comes into play. Readers of cultural sociology often experience the same social events as those about which academic analysts write. Lay readers and university-employed intellectuals are members of overlapping social worlds and share wide swaths of meaningful understanding. The *Performance of Politics* draws primarily upon public discourse broadcast in American news media over five months from early summer to early autumn 2008. Today's readers will themselves have consumed much of the media during this period as interested citizens or more distant observers. They will deploy their own ethnographic sense in judging whether the interpretations in *Performance of Politics* have got it right.

The social scientist who intervenes in the streaming mass of media representation exercises extraordinary selectivity, and a severe reduction of empirical complexity is the result. Reconstructing meaning is the very point of cultural sociology.

Less concerned with material causality and demographics, its ambition is herme-neutical—to find deep underlying patterns, to trace the vectors of symbolic mean-ing and lines of interpretive force, and to make causal arguments about them. To demonstrate that there are coherent, if conflicting, subjectivities amid the buzzing and booming chaos of social reality is what cultural sociology is all about. Making wholes out of seemingly disconnected parts, what Dilthey describes as drawing the "hermeneutical circle," that is the method and the means.[58]

Scope

The *Performance of Politics* is about the contemporary struggle for presidential power in the United States. Do its findings extend to democratic struggles for power in other kinds of political and social systems? Certainly presidential and parliamentary systems organize the executive functions of government differently, and the struggle for state power is correspondingly affected. But to what degree? In parliamentary systems, elected party members choose one of their own members as prime minister; the masses of voters do not themselves elect the head of state. However, this may well be a distinction without a real difference in terms of the cultural dimensions of politics I consider here. Are parliamentary prime ministers merely party loyalists administering government? Do they eschew the symbolic role of collective representation, the cultural task of embodying the democratic discourse inside of civil society and on its boundaries, of narrating national social crisis in a heroic way? In the real political lives of modern parliamentary democra-cies, this hardly seems to be the case.

British history unrolls a sacred scroll of prime ministers who became tri-umphant heroes and casts down others as profane, those who faltered before the crisis of their times or who behaved in antidemocratic ways. This process of democratic collective representation unfolds alongside a powerful monarchy that would seem, in principle, to separate the expressive from the instrumental func-tions of government but in practice has not. Indeed, as leaders not only of party but also government, prime ministers often assume a symbolic superiority over rank-and-file party members more exaggerated than the distance between presi-dents and powerful, longer-serving senators in the United States. Voters in parlia-mentary systems know before national campaigns commence who each party's prime minister will be, and the symbolic investment of citizen audience and media in that single collective representation often outweighs party affiliation. It is also the case that parliamentary parties and their prime ministers rule in a more sov-ereign manner than American presidents, who face divided power, and they can serve longer terms and be voted into office time after time. Prime ministers have extraordinary performative opportunity to become legendary (or not) in their own times. Differences between the two political systems have less to do with the centrality of symbolic representation than with the temporal location of its generation. Unknown candidates for the American presidency must engage in months and even years of collective representation before election and undertake increasingly extended primary and general election campaigns. This is not the case in parliamentary systems. Still, the longer and more effective the symbolic preparation of a potential prime minister, the more likely the parliamentary struggle for collective representation is to succeed.

The argument for American exceptionalism extends beyond the peculiarity of this nation's presidency. The United States is often caricatured as the land of hype and Hollywood, a capitalist society that apotheosizes itself in grand symbolic fantasies, factional and fictional entertainment that allows battered masses momentary escape from mundane lives. As if other modern capitalist democracies do not have well-developed media spheres, public relations industries, television, Internet, films, and their own hucksterism and hype! The distance separating the culture and institutions of the United States from others is exaggerated—by Americans from self-love or self-hatred, by others from admiration, envy, or principled dislike. Of course, every democracy is historically distinctive. At the same time, one finds systemic features in mass democracies that are shared in common and of great significance.

It is my conviction that the theories and empirical findings reported here are broadly relevant to political performance as such, not exclusively to presidential government or contemporary American society.[59] In political sociology and electoral studies, power is typically conceived as control over instruments of domination, as maximizing resources, as asymmetrical exchange, as contingent struggle for strategic advantage, or as reproducing elite power, whether that of state, class, ethnicity, race, gender, or religion. This reduction of the political is echoed by weak programs that make culture subservient to social power. Neither form of social determination can conceptualize empirical processes central to the struggle for power in democratic societies. Inside the civil sphere, these conflicts revolve around persuasion, producing performances before idealized audiences of putatively rational, responsive, and solidary citizens. Gaining power depends on the success of symbolic representation. Meaning determines political fate. It only seems paradoxical that, in order to understand power, we must give relative autonomy to culture. Without a strong theory of meaning, we will not be able to understand how democratic politicians gain power in the state.

Appendix on the Poll of Polls

T HE "POLL OF POLLS" BRINGS TOGETHER THE BEST MEASUEMENTS of the national trends of public opinion for the Obama v. McCain presidential contest from June 1, 2008, until the election on November 4. It is a compilation of the periodic tracking polls from four sources: Real Clear Politics (RCP), Rasmussen Reports, Gallup Daily Tracking Poll, and ABC/ Washington Post.

Overview

These sources cover a range that eliminates extremes and provides representative sampling of results from four pollster types: aggregators, independent polling companies, old and establishment agencies, and news media. What is often called the "best in the business," Selzer & Company, to which the Daily Kos attributes a "stellar reputation,"[1] does not have the temporal consistency to chart the five-month period from June through November or the experience of a giant such as Rasmussen. Likewise, SurveyUSA and Pollster.com are reliable aggregate sources, but, in the end, RCP is preferable not only for sheer volume of data and usage but also, more importantly, because of the high professional esteem it is accorded even by competitors. At the other end of the spectrum, I have left out the notorious Zogby Poll, which polling experts across the board have rated as the worst despite its being quoted extensively by news media.

Size also matters, as does a proven track record. Nate Silver, of fiverthirtyeight. com (538), who first made a name for himself as the designer of a well-regarded method of predicting baseball statistics, says 538 received more than one million page views per day during the campaign,[2] but he is still the new kid stepping up to the plate. FiveThirtyEight's traffic is dwarfed by that of RCP, which was founded in 2000. Its site averaged just under seven million page views per day two weeks before the election, which, according to one of its founders, John McIntyre, was significantly higher than four years before.[3]

With regard to the choice of Rasmussen, it is qualified not only by virtue of its huge size but also, once again, because polling experts consistently hold it in high regard. Silver comments: "None of these tracking polls are perfect, although Rasmussen—with its large sample size and high pollster rating—would probably be the one I'd want with me on a desert island."[4] The Daily Kos cited Rasmussen's prediction accuracy in a postelection post, and a Fordham University study backs up that claim.

Gallup is trickier. Some polling analysts, as well as calculations from "report cards"—for example, SurveyUSA, 538, and the Daily Kos—are wary of its methodology. However, Gallup maintains a consistently large sample size, having interviewed no fewer than 1,000 out of a rolling sample of 2,700 registered U.S. voters nationwide each night during 2008. It is also one of the few companies to include a supplement of Spanish-language and cell phone numbers, creating a sample that represents 98 percent of the adult population, compared with 85 percent for landline-only samples.[5] A pioneer in public opinion polling, Gallup has maintained a strong industry reputation for absolute integrity since the 1930s. Despite critical comments, Silver considers its "strong professional ethics and sense of transparency" one of Gallup's strengths.[6]

The ABC/*Washington Post* polls stand out from all of the other media/newspaper outfits, an exception to the disdain that, along with Zogby, media/newspaper polls often provoke among polling experts. It showed up as fourth and second on SurveyUSA report cards issued after the primaries,[7] and it was rated the best of the newspaper polls and "average" in the field at large in 538's assessment in May 2008.[8]

Political bias toward the left or the right is a consideration, but it is not as significant as some say, and it is also often offset by other considerations. Silver of 538 underestimated Obama's margin of victory by four-tenths of one percent, and he is often considered a liberal pollster. Responding to a *New York Times* reporter who questioned his critical remarks about competitor RCP's conservative bias, Silver acknowledged that "the two sites had a friendly rivalry and grudging respect for each other,"[9] and he attests that RCP is "one of the first sites" he checked every day during the election.[10]

Virtually all pollsters fall prey to accusations of ideological or partisan bias. While I have not found evidence to support such accusations—against the four sources that compose the poll of polls—beyond a reasonable doubt, even if such biases do exist, the allegedly Republican/conservative-biased Rasmussen and RCP nicely balance out the ostensibly Democratic/liberal tendencies of the other two. More credible would be the worry over "house effects," or the tendency for a poll to lean consistently toward one candidate rather than the other. To consider these systematic effects as "bias" would be "misleading," according to Charles Franklin, professor of political science at the University of Wisconsin, Madison, and codeveloper of Pollster.com. Instead, as he explains, "[T]he differences are due to a variety of factors that represent reasonable differences in practice from one organization to another."[11] Thus, by using polling results from multiple sources with different statistical leanings—for example, Rasmussen has a slight Republican leaning effect, and ABC/*Washington Post* leans slightly toward Democrats[12]—I reduce the potential for interference from house effects.

Nuts and Bolts

My compilation evenly weights the four polling sources described earlier. Clearly, the parameters are not identical—some survey public opinion daily but release the results on different dates, while others sample more periodically. This explains some of the sharp ups and downs on the various graphs, for example, in the earlier months, when ABC/*Washington Post* polling was less frequent. To ameliorate these temporal irregularities, I include different graphing types (line, area), as well as multiple temporal periods (daily, three-day, and seven-day). This form of representation illuminates some of the nuances in the poll of polls.

Gallup Daily Polling

Gallup Daily describes its polling mission as "track[ing] Americans' views on politics, economics, and well-being, conducting 1,000 or more interviews each night and posting new numbers each day."[13] Its election-tracking results utilize combined data in three-day intervals, reporting the "percentage of registered voters who say they would support each candidate if the presidential election were held today." The sample sizes range from about 2,400 to 4,700 registered voters (generally, about 2,700), and the maximum margin of sampling error is ±2 percentage points. Gallup Daily contacts respondents on landline telephones (for respondents with a landline telephone) or cellular phones (for respondents who have only cell phone). There is considerable debate concerning Gallup's new models for targeting likely voters, but in the poll of polls I utilize only the surveys conducted among registered voters.

Rasmussen Reports

Rasmussen is the only one among the eight daily tracking polls that uses an automated polling methodology ("robocalls") to collect data for its surveys.[14] On the one hand, it asserts that this process is "identical to that of traditional, operator-assisted research firms such as Gallup, Harris, and Roper" and provides this rationale: "Automated polling systems use a single, digitally recorded, voice to conduct the interview while traditional firms rely on phone banks, boiler rooms, and operator-assisted technology." Their daily presidential tracking poll leads to consistency: "[T]he automated technology insures [sic] that every respondent hears exactly the same question, from the exact same voice, asked with the exact same inflection every single time." On the other hand, the New York Times won't publish the results from these types of polls, asserting they "employ an automated, recorded voice to call respondents who are asked to answer questions by punching telephone keys. Anyone who can answer the phone and hit the buttons can be counted in the survey—regardless of age."[15]

Rasmussen chooses its samples of "adults" using census data to reflect population demographics such as age, race, gender, and political parties, and for political surveys in particular, it utilizes a series of screening questions to determine "likely" voters (e.g., voting history, interest in the current campaign, and likely voting intentions). Finally, it considers partisanship "through a dynamic weighting system that takes into account the state's voting history, national trends, and recent polling in a particular state or geographic area." This is one reason that Nate Silver considers Rasmussen to have had the most stable results even if it does make Rasmussen's results a bit more (small c) conservative, reacting less strongly than others to changes in voters' moods. Silver also notes that the three-day rolling sample of 3,000 likely voters is the largest sample size of any of the tracking polls.[16]

ABC/Washington Post

The ABC/Washington Post national tracking poll ran from October 16 through November 3, 2008.[17] Aside from Gallup, it was the only other polling group to include cell phones. The "WaPo-ABC" daily polls utilized a multiple-night track (Thursday through Sunday nights) of interviews with approximately 450 randomly selected adults each day. For the last few days of the campaign, they increased the daily sample size to around 600, reporting that "These far-larger-than-usual sample sizes allow for analysis of some subgroups we can't normally assess in regular polling," citing Jewish voters, younger white evangelical Protestants, and younger white Catholics. Their stated sampling error is ±3 percentage points, with higher error margins for subgroups.[18] More impressive than their numbers, however, are the ABC News and (to a slightly lesser degree) *Washington Post* public statements concerning method, as well as methodology. Veteran polling expert Gary Langer elaborates the rigor of ABC's standards:

> The ABC News Polling Unit vets all survey research presented to ABC News to ensure it meets our standards for disclosure, validity, reliability and unbiased content. We recommend that our news division not report research that fails to meet these standards. On disclosure, in addition to the identities of the research sponsor and field work provider, we require a detailed statement of methodology, the full questionnaire and complete marginal data. If any of these are lacking, we recommend against reporting the results.... In terms of content, we examine methodological statements for misleading or false claims, questionnaires for leading or biasing wording or ordering, and analyses and news releases for inaccurate or selective conclusions. In addition to recommending against reporting surveys that do not meet these standards, we promote and strongly encourage the reporting of good-quality polls that break new ground in opinion research.[19]

Langer also elaborates the intricacies of sampling cell phones and the beast called "sampling error," referring the readers to an array of formal studies, several of which evaluate ABC polling results specifically. On November 4, Langer, who has won two Emmy awards for ABC's reporting of public opinion polls in Iraq, proudly announces in his blog:

> Our purpose hasn't been to dwell on the horse race, but rather to further our understanding of how the public has come to its choices in the 2008 election—to identify the issues and candidate attributes that mattered, to measure voters' responses to the thrust and parry of the race, to get a look inside the campaigns' own playbooks as they've formed and made their appeals and to have an alternative to the spin and speculation that rush in when empirical data are absent. *Public attitudes never are more important than in national elections.* Our aim at the ABC News Polling Unit this year, as in presidential elections since 1984, has been simple: Trying our best to understand them.[20]

Similarly, *The Washington Post* offers a "Detailed Methodology" as well as a "FAQs" webpage, with countless links for further study, including one to "find the hard core, wonky details of *Post* polling methodology."[21]

Real Clear Politics

RCP is not as forthcoming about its methodology as other aggregators, a matter of some debate among political bloggers, analysts, and, of course, other pollsters. Nate Silver of 538 has called out RCP on this issue, along with criticizing some of John McIntyre's poll choices:

> It is clear to me that there is substantial subjectivity in how RCP selects the polls to include in its averages. RCP does not publish an FAQ, or any other set of standards. Nor, in my conversation with John, was he willing to articulate one. In my view, the fact that RCP does not disclose a set of standards means *ipso facto* that they are making judgment calls—that there is some subjectivity involved—in how their polls are selected.[22]

At the same time, however, Silver makes clear, "[I]t does not necessarily follow that these judgment calls reflect any deliberate partisan leaning, i.e. any 'bias.'... I take John at his word that this is not the case."[23] Silver acquiesces to the inevitability of political subjectivity even as he defends his own poll-aggregating methods: "Look—I'm not going to tell you that my site is completely devoid of spin. I am a Democrat, and I see the world through a Democratic lens. But what I can promise you is that we'll keep the spin separate from our metrics.[24] McIntyre's primary response to these critiques is one with which Silver agrees. Ultimately, it is a matter of reflection of their "respective business models," he explains. "[RCP is] aiming for simplicity and ease of use, and trustworthiness. And they do these things well: RCP remains one of the first sites that I read every day."[25]

Meanwhile, RCP remains a top choice for countless political junkies from the Left *and* the Right. Among them are Arianna Huffington (who referred to it as the "gold standard" for polling in an October 2008 post), Howard Fineman, chief political correspondent for *Newsweek* during the 2008 campaign, and conservative *NYT* columnist David Brooks, who commented, "Some people wake up every morning with a raw egg and exercise. I wake up every morning with *RealClearPolitics.com*. It's the perfect one-stop shopping for the smartest commentary on politics and life."[26] Without discounting Silver's critique, which stands out among those by armchair pundits and highly ideological bloggers, I see little more than a quasi-friendly rivalry between the leader of the pack and a powerful up-and-coming force in the world of online political news and analysis.

While RCP does keep its precise methodology under wraps, several posts by Jay Cost, who maintains RCP's *HorseRaceBlog,* as well as public statements by cofounder John McIntyre, do make certain technical elements clear. Real Clear Politics uses an unweighted average, or mean, of a number of polls and calculates the standard deviation—how much the polls are disagreeing with each other. Just before the election, Cost posted an extensive statistical primer on how this works, which was a remarkably reflexive piece on polling methodology. Testing the deviation of individual polls from the RCP average, Cost found that 9 of the 15 polls fell significantly outside the average (4 for Obama, 5 for McCain), and another 3 were just on the boundary of significance (1 for Obama, 2 for McCain). As Cost went on to explain, this is all about sampling:

> The rules of statistics being what they are, we should expect a few polls here or there to fall outside the average by a statistically significant amount. But this is a lot…This variation cannot be chalked up to typical statistical "noise." Instead, it is more likely that pollsters are disagreeing with each other in their sampling methodologies. In other words, different pollsters have different "visions" of what the electorate will look like on November 4th, and these visions are affecting their results.[27]

The number of polls going into RCP's daily average varies, depending on individual polls' frequencies. For period covered by the poll of polls, there were results from a total of 28 different organizations, with intervals of three to four days containing anywhere from a handful in June through August to at least a dozen from mid-September onward. According to McIntyre, he requires at least three polls before producing an average. In response to concerns over keeping older polls in the averages, he emphasizes that they give more weight to recent polls and asserts that his site's numbers provide "a clearer picture of where things truly stand."[28]

What It's All For: Measuring the Three Boulders in the Campaign

From the aggregated trends revealed in the poll of polls, it is clear when the first boulder hits and the celebrity metaphor effect begins. Although McCain experiences a slight surge by the second week of July, it is is not until the end of the month that we see Obama's numbers dip and remain that way rather than bouncing around. McCain gains just 1–3 percentage points on average during the August period, but, coupled with Obama's drop, the race begins to take on a neck-and-neck stride, mirroring the start of June. At the end of August, Obama experiences a surge of support after his stellar convention performance but soon feels the effect of the curve ball hurled his way by McCain's announcement of Sarah Palin as his running mate.

Floating from Palin's initial popularity, the Republican campaign enjoys a new beginning in September with upward swings at the polls. But it is short lived. The

Palin image deflates, and from September 10 on, the Republican numbers begin to fall. Then McCain's failure to perform effectively in the early days of the financial crisis sends them tumbling. After September 15, McCain will not see 50 percent support levels again. He manages to stay in the mid-40s for a couple of weeks, but once the drama of the financial crisis has crystallized and the 30-day countdown to Election Day begins, the Republican numbers hover at a steady 41–43 percent, with only a minor surge in the last few days. It is not enough to counter the steady increases that Obama makes. For the second half of September, Obama's numbers climb to the highest level of support since his nomination, reaching from the high 40s to a solid 50 percent or more throughout October.

With one week to go, Obama leads McCain by 10 percentage points or more— the high- and low-ball figures range from 41 percent for McCain to 54 percent for Obama. Even by the most conservative estimates, the gap narrows only to 6 points by the morning of Election Day, and most other pollsters anticipate a 7–9 point final margin. The final results bear out the pollsters' predictions remarkably well. Aggregate pollsters Real Clear Politics and Pollster.com predicted the margin identically, within 1.1 points (which coincidentally was the average among all of the top polling outfits). The winner for accuracy however, was Nate Silver from FiveThirtyEight, calling the margin within just .4 of a point and McCain and Obama's share of the popular vote at 0.1 and 0.6, respectively.

Notes

PREFACE

1. Cf., Jill Abramson, "The Making of the President, Then and Now," *New York Times Book Review*, March 21, 2008, p. 14.

PROLOGUE

1. Colum McCann, "2008: Titles of the Times," in "The Decade We Had," *New York Times (NYT)*, December 27, 2009, "Week in Review," 12.

2. Frank Kermode, *The Sense of an Ending: Studies in the Theory of Fiction* (New York: Oxford University Press, 1970), 47. See, more generally, Phillip Sipiora, "Introduction: The Ancient Concept of *Kairos*," in P. Sipiora and James S. Baldwin, eds., *Rhetoric and* Kairos: *Essays in History, Theory, and Praxis*, 1–22 (New York: State University of Albany Press, 2002); John E. Smith, "Time and Qualitative Time," in Sipiora and Baldwin, eds., *Rhetoric and* Kairos, 46–57; and James L. Kenneav and Catherine R. Eskin, "*Kairos* in Aristotle's Rhetoric," *Written Communication* 17(3) 2000: 432–44.

3. Albert O. Hirschman, *Shifting Involvements: Private Interest and Public Action* (Princeton, N.J.: Princeton University Press, 1982).

4. Dan Balz and Haynes Johnson, *The Battle for America 2008: The Story of an Extraordinary Election* (New York: Viking, 2009), 12–13.

5. William J. Crotty, "Electing Obama: The 2008 Presidential Campaign," 20–47, in William J. Crotty, ed., *Winning the Presidency 2008* (Boulder, Colo.: Paradigm), 47.

6. On the broad political and cultural effects of Bobby Kennedy's murder, see Ron Eyerman, "Political Assassination, Trauma, and Narrative," in Jeffrey C. Alexander, Ronald Jacobs, and Philip Smith, eds., *Handbook of Cultural Sociology* (New York: Oxford University Press, 2011.

7. Michael Schudson, *The Good Citizen: A History of American Civil Life* (New York: Kessler, 1998).

CHAPTER 1

1. Later in this chapter I describe the civil sphere in more detail. For more about the concept, see "Note on Concept and Method."

2. Theodore H. White, *The Making of the President 1960* (New York: Atheneum), 3.

3. On this hidden power, see, for example, William G. Howell, *Power without Persuasion: The Politics of Presidential Action* (Princeton, N.J.: Princeton University Press, 2003) On the wide application of relatively invisible state power after Barack Obama's election, see John B. Judis, "The Quiet Revolution: Obama Has Reinvented the State in More Ways Than You Can Imagine" (*The New Republic*, February 1, 2010), which examines the first year of President Obama's activist efforts to strengthen federal regulatory agencies, the so-called fourth branch of government, after decades of being weakened by national conservative rule (available at http://www.tnr.com/print/article/politics/the-quiet-revolution).

4. Robert McKenzie and Allen Silver, *Angels in Marble: Working Class Conservatives in Urban England* (London: Heinemann, 1968).

5. John P. Avlon, "What Independent Voters Want," *Wall Street Journal* (*WSJ*), October 20, 2008, A19.

6. David S. Broder, "Why the Center Still Holds," *Washington Post* (*WP*), April 12, 2009, A17.

7. On the distance between the demographics of class and the political representations created to reach them during the final days of the 2008 campaign, see Jonathan Weisman and Ilan Brat, "Campaign '08: As Joe the Plumber Grows Famous, the Politics Get Murkier," *WSJ*, October 17, 2008, A8.

8. For a conservative intervention that made precisely these arguments—for the specificity of culture—during the heat of the campaign, see Lee Siegel, "Essay: The Triumph of Culture over Politics," *WSJ*, September 13, 2008, W1.

9. Jürgen Habermas, *Structural Transformation of the Public Sphere: An Inquiry into a Category of Bourgeois Society* (Cambridge, Mass.: MIT Press, 1989 [1962], parts I and II); *Theory of Communicative Action*, vol. 1, *Reason and the Rationalization of Society* (Boston: Beacon, 1984).

10. For example, Jim Rutenberg, "McCain Is Trying to Define Obama as Out of Touch," *NYT*, July 31, 2008, A1; or Ralph Z. Hallow, "Centrist Voters Tilt from Obama; Fears of Far Left Boost McCain," *Washington Times* (*WT*), August 11, 2008, A1.

11. E.E. Evans-Pritchard, *The Nuer: A Description of the Modes of Livelihood and Political Institutions of a Nilotic People* (Oxford: Clarendon Press 1940), 137.

12. Maureen Dowd, "Stalking, Sniffing, Swooning," *NYT*, July 27, 2008, http://www.nytimes.com/2008/07/27/opinion/27dowd.html.

13. "McCain Is Trying to Define Obama as Out of Touch."

14. What Barthes writes about the realism of photography applies to politics as well: It "innocents the semantic artifice of connotation" while presenting itself as denotative, as natural and sincere, as realistic and practical. In other words, the belief that the photographic image is a literal reference that mirrors an actual thing is an illusion that hides the aesthetic framing of the image, which is the very art of photography. Roland Barthes, "Rhetoric of the Image," in Roland Barthes, *Image, Music, Text*, 32–51 (New York: Hill and Wang, 1977), 45.

15. Adam Nagourney, "In Midsummer, Spring Training for the Fall Race," *NYT*, August 12, 2008, A18.

16. Jonathan Weisman and Laura Meckler, "Obama Sweeps to Historic Victory," *WSJ*, November 5, 2008, A1.

17. *Making of the President*, 255.

18. White, "Perspective 1960 #13, 'Ranging the Target,'" 307–13, in Edward T. Thompson, ed., *Theodore H. White at Large: The Best of His Magazine Writing, 1939–1986* (New York: Pantheon, 1992), 307 (original publication: *Saturday Review*, October 15, 1960).

19. *Making of the President*, 254.

20. "Ranging the Target," 307.

21. Ibid.

22. Stephanie Simon, "Democratic Convention: As Democrats Convene, McCain Strategists Take to 'War Room,'" *WSJ*, August 27, 2008, A4.

23. Barack Obama, *The Audacity of Hope: Thoughts on Reclaiming the American Dream* (New York: Crown, 2006), 121.

24. Jodi Kantor, interview by author, February 24, 2009.

25. Matthew Kaminski, "The Axelrod Method," *WSJ*, October 17, 2008, A13.

26. Jim Rutenberg, "An Infomercial, Big, Glossy, and Almost Unavoidable," *NYT*, October 30, 2008, A28.

CHAPTER 2

1. Adam Nagourney, "Carefully Shaped Message Now a Campaign Relic," *NYT*, September 16, A22.

2. "Swift boat tactics" refers to a controversial attack ad campaign organized by Republican strategist Steven Schmidt during the 2004 presidential race between George W. Bush and Democrat John Kerry. During his Vietnam service in the late 1960s, Kerry had commanded one of the so-called Swift boats deployed in river battles against the Viet Cong. Celebrated for bravery under fire, Kerry became a celebrated military hero. Returning home to protest the war for which he had fought and sacrificed, Kerry launched his liberal political career. The Schmidt attack ads claimed Kerry lied about his exploits and did not deserve his decorations. The attack ads were later discredited and became ignominious, a metaphor for dirty politics.

3. For the classic anthropological account of symbols as collective representations and symbolic actions as energizing ritual, see Emile Durkheim, *The Elementary Forms of Religious Life* (New York: Free Press, 1995 [1911]), which focuses on simple, Aboriginal societies in Australia but whose implications extend to the study of modern and postmodern societies today. By melding Durkheim's theory with Erving Goffman's microsociology of face-to-face encounters, Randall Collins has conceptualized how individual interactions become rituals by circulating emotional energy and creating solidarity. See Collins, *Interaction Ritual Chains* (Princeton, N.J.: Princeton University Press, 2004). Collins underplays the vital role that patterned discourses play in generating rituals and the way in which such ritually energized, symbolic texts have independent structuring power on their own,

quite independently of face-to-face interaction. As I explain in the "Note on Concept and Method," Durkheim's ideas must be brought into contact with semiotic and poststructural theories, not separated from them. Moreover, neither Durkheim nor contemporary neo-Durkheimians such as Collins conceptualizes the increasing difficulty of ritual connection as societies become more complex and segmented. The concept of performance provides a more supple and precise approach to symbolic action than ritual, as I explain in my "Note on Concept and Method." See note 5 below.

4. Serge Kovaleski, "Obama's Organizing years, Guiding Others and Finding Himself," *NYT,* July 7, 2008, A1; emphasis added.

5. They are, however, ritual-like, not rituals in the same sense as the repetitive, simplified, and habitual processes that classical anthropology discovered at the heart of aboriginal societies. Action is always performative but only occasionally ritualistic: Only when performances achieve intense fusion between actor and audience do they approach "ritual." This is immensely variable, as this book about political success and failure documents and explains.

6. Julie Bosman, "Obama Goes One on One, Battling 'Just a Speechmaker' Label," *NYT,* June 15, 2008, 18.

7. "CNN LIVE EVENT/SPECIAL; Hillary Clinton Suspending Campaign," CNN. com, June 7, 2008, http://transcripts.cnn.com/TRANSCRIPTS/0806/07/se.02.html.

8. Adam Nagourney and Mark Lebiovich, "Clinton Ends Campaign with Clear Call to Elect Obama," *NYT,* June 8, 2008, A1; emphasis added.

9. Adam Nagourney, "Heralding New Course, Democrats Nominate Obama," *NYT,* August 28, 2008, A1.

10. It might be argued that this media ethnography is not representative because (1) as a cable television channel, its audience is vastly smaller than that of network news and (2) MSNBC is more liberal than its competitors, CNN and Fox. As I indicate at the conclusion of this section, however, MSNBC's "fused" coverage was consistent with how the event was portrayed on the following day by a mainstream and influential national print medium, the *New York Times.* Further, in the conclusion to chapter 7—a chapter devoted to the celebrity metaphor and its dangers for the Obama campaign—I provide additional evidence that the fusion documented in this media ethnography reflected broad national currents and was not limited to the liberal side. For example, Charles Hurt, the editor emeritus of the conservative tabloid *New York Post,* owned by right-wing media mogul Rupert Murdoch, raved about Obama's speech and the audience reaction at Mile High Stadium, predicting that the event would have a powerful realigning effect on the campaign. Before the event, Hurt had expressed considerable skepticism. As I also show, former Reagan speechwriter Peggy Noonan offered a similarly positive account of the event in her *Wall Street Journal* column, as well as on the NBC *Today* show the next day. At the beginning of chapter 8, I describe how neoconservative strategist William Kristol offered a similarly positive account of the event in his Monday column in the *New York Times.* In data from the "Poll of Polls" presented at the end of chapter 7, the effect of Obama's fused performance is documented in a statistical way. Finally, I would note that MSNBC's viewers are not as one-sidedly liberal as it sometimes seems. During the 2006 midterm elections, 48 percent of MSNBC's regular viewers were Democratic, compared with 40 percent of viewers of nightly network news. By 2008, however, the party affiliations of MSNBC and

network news viewers were the same—45 percent (PEW Research Center for the People and the Press, "Audience Segments in a Changing News Environment," August 17, 2008, http://people-press.org/reports/pdf/444.pdf).

11. Although Mitchell has the right television drama, she may have had the wrong character. If Obama is seen as channeling fictional representations from *The West Wing*, their reference would have been Matt Santos, who appeared in the last two years of the series as the Democratic Hispanic candidate for president campaigning to succeed the Democratic incumbent Jed Bartlet.

Not long after the [2004] Convention [keynote] speech, Eli Attie, one of the writers and producers for NBC's hit television series "The West Wing," was starting to flesh out a character to succeed President Josiah (Jed) Bartlet, the wry and avuncular head of state played by Martin Sheen. Although the series, the creation of Aaron Sorkin, first went on the air during the Clinton years, many Democrats watched it during the Bush Presidency as a kind of alternative-reality show. Bartlet, a Nobel Prize–winning economist and a devout Catholic with liberal values, was, for that audience, everything Bush was not: mature, curious, assured, skeptical, and confident of his own intelligence.

Attie wanted the new character to be no less a liberal ideal, but this time he wanted someone of the "Post-Oprah" generation, as he put it, someone black or Hispanic, but not an older figure closely tied to the rhetoric of the civil-rights movement and identity politics. Attie had serious political experience. He had written speeches for the former New York mayor David Dinkins, and had been an aide to Richard Gephardt in Congress, and to Bill Clinton in the White House; he was Al Gore's chief speechwriter through the 2000 Presidential campaign. When he watched Obama, he thought he saw the model for his own character, Matt Santos: a young urban progressive with dignified bearing, a "bring-the-electorate-along-slowly candidate" who was neither white nor focused on race. "Faced with the task of fleshing out a fictional first-ever and actually viable Latino candidate for President, I had no precedent, no way to research a real-life version," he said.

Attie called David Axelrod, whom he had known from Democratic political campaigns, and asked him dozens of questions about Obama's history and psychology [and] Attie came to see Santos the way Axelrod saw Obama and the way Obama saw himself... "Those early conversations with David turned out to play a huge role in my shaping of the character," Attie said... In the final two seaons of the "The West Wing," which aired in 2005 and 2006, Matt Santos, played by Jimmy Smits, runs for President... A couple of years later, those seasons of "The West Wing" provide so eerily prescient that David Axelrod sent Attie an e-mail from the campaign trail reading, "We're living your scripts!" (David Remnick, *The Bridge: The Life and Rise of Barack Obama*, New York: Alfred A. Knopf, 2010, pp. 422–23).

12. Brian Stelter and Jim Rutenberg, "Obama's Speech Is a TV Hit, with Reviewers and Commentators Alike," *NYT*, August 29, 2008, A14.

13. Elizabeth Holmes, "McCain Shakes Up Campaign Organization," *WSJ*, July 3, 2008, A4.

14. Christina S. N. Lewis, "Picturing Obama," *WSJ*, July 17, 2008, D1; emphasis added.

15. Elizabeth Holmes and Amy Chozick, "Candidates Focus on States They Consider Key to Victory," *WSJ*, October 27, 2008, A6.

16. Andrew Breitbart, "Say It Ain't So, O!" *WT*, September 8, 2008, A4.

17. Adam Nagourney and Jeff Zeleny, "Obama Raises level of Attack as Party Frets," *NYT*, September 12, 2008, A1.

18. G. N. Miller, Carl Campanile, and Chuck Bennett, "This Is No Way to Treat a Lady—GOPers Stand Up for Sarah," *New York Post* (*NYP*), September 3, 2008, 5.

19. Fred Barnes, "Sarah Palin's Future," *Weekly Standard* (*WS*) 14(7), October 27, 2008.

20. John M. Broder and Julie Bosman, "In States Once Reliably Red, Palin and Biden Tighten Their Stump Speeches," *NYT*, November 2, 2008.

21. Elisabeth Bumiller, "With Palin at His Side, McCain Finds Energized Crowds," *NYT*, September 11, 2008, A23.

22. Monica Langley, "As Economic Crisis Peaked, Tide Turned against McCain," *WSJ*, November 5, 2008, Eastern edition, retrieved January 7, 2010, ProQuest Newsstand Complete.

23. Laura Meckler, Elizabeth Holmes, and Jim Carlton, "McCain's Surprise V.P. Choice," *WSJ*, August 30, 2008, A1.

24. Ibid., original emphasis.

25. Laura Meckler, "GOP Opens Convention with Unexpected Items Topping the Agenda," *WSJ*, September 2, 2008, A4.

26. Miller, Campanile, and Bennett, "This Is No Way to Treat a Lady."

27. Gerald F. Seib, "Palin Pitches Sam's Club Tent," *WSJ*, September 3, 2008, A2.

28. Adam Nagourney and Megan Thee, "Poll Finds Obama Gaining Support and McCain Weakened in Bailout Crisis," *NYT*, October 2, 2008, A27. For Palin's declining poll numbers during this period, see chapter 8.

29. Patrick Healy, "A Riveting Speaker, Waving the Flag," *NYT*, October 14, A19.

30. Samuel Taylor Coleridge, *Biographia Literaria*, Chapter XIV, 1817.

31. Jodi Kantor, "With Right Props and Stops, Clinton Transforms into Working-class Hero," *NYT*, May 6, 2008, A1; this source for quotations in next paragraph as well.

32. Jodi Kantor, interview by author, February 24, 2009.

33. John M. Broder, interview by author, February 19, 2009.

34. John M. Broder, "Amid Talk of the End and Boos from the Crowd, Clinton Carries On," *NYT*, May 6, 2008, A1 (for entire paragraph).

35. John M. Broder, interview by author, February 19, 2009 (quotes for entire paragraph).

CHAPTER 3

1. Christopher Cooper and Laura Meckler, "Obama Takes in a Record $150 Million, but McCain Narrows Gap in Some Polls," *WSJ*, October 20, 2008, A1.

2. Douglas B. Holt, *How Brands Become Icons: The Principles of Cultural Branding* (Boston: Harvard Business School Press, 2004).

3. Ibid.

4. Jeff Zeleny, "Obama Battles Block by Block to Get Voters to Polls," *NYT,* October 12, 2008, A34.

5. Laura Meckler and Nick Timiraos, "McCain Abandons Michigan as State Contests Shift," *WSJ,* October 3, 2008, A8.

6. For a compelling personal account by an academic sociologist who went door to door for Obama and established such personal connections, see Magali Sarfatti Larsons, "Si se puede! Working for Obama at K and A," *Sociological Forum* 24(2) (June 2009): 429–36.

7. Christopher Cooper and Susan Davis, "Obama Seeks to Add Black Voters," *WSJ,* June 30, 2008, A4.

8. Ibid.

9. Zeleny, "Obama Battles Block by Block to Get Voters to Polls."

10. Obama made these remarks at a roundtable discussion organized by the Woods Charitable Fund, in Chicago. Quoted in David Remnick, *The Bridge: The Life and Rise of Barack Obama*, p. 179.

11. This section draws from field notes recorded during a Camp Obama training day, which I attended as a participant-observer on September 6, 2008, in Denver, Colorado, at the invitation of Marshall Ganz. Ganz created the series of training camps for the national campaign. For decades one of Cesar Chavez's principal lieutenants in the campaign to organize farm workers in California, Ganz is now on the faculty of the Kennedy School of Government at Harvard University. His academic writing translates his practical experiences into a culturally oriented understanding of social movement organizing (e.g., Marshall Ganz, "Social Movement Leadership: Relationship, Story, Strategy, and Action," paper delivered at the American Sociological Association annual meeting, August 2008, Boston). It is a striking indication of the "realist" focus on money and technique that the workings of Camp Obama, Ganz's leadership in shaping the training, and the spirit and role of the Obama ground game received scant attention from the media, much less from academic students of the campaign. But see Zack Exley, "Stories and Numbers: A Closer Look at Camp Obama," *Huffington Post* (*HP*), August 29, 2007, http://www.huffingtonpost.com/zack-exley/stories-and-numbers-a-c_b_62278.html; and "The New Organizers, Part 1: What's Really behind Obama's Ground Game," *HP,* October 8, 2008, http://www.huffingtonpost.com/zack-exley/the-new-organizers-part-1_b_132782.html; John Hill, "Obama Basic Training: Volunteers Told to Share Personal Conversion Stories with Voters—Not Policy Views," *Sacramento Bee* [sacbee.com], January 21, 2008, http://www.sacbee.com/capitolandcalifornia/story/649427.html; Kelly Candaele and Peter Dreier, "The Year of the Organizer," *American Prospect,* February 1, 2008, http://www.prospect.org/cs/articles?article=the_year_of_the_organizer; Scott Martell, "Famed Organizer Sees History in the Making," *Los Angeles Times* (*LAT*), June 15, 2008, http://articles.latimes.com/2008/jun/15/nation/na-ganz15; Peter Dreir, "Will Obama Inspire a New Generation of Organizers?" *Dissent,* July 21, 2008, http://dissentmagazine.org/article/?article=1215; Alec MacGillis, "Obama Camp Relying Heavily on Ground Game," *WP,* October 12, 2008, http://www.washingtonpost.com/wp-dyn/content/article/2008/10/11/AR2008101102119.html.

12. Author interview with Katherine Venegas, April 16, 2009.

13. Ibid.

14. Ibid.

15. Rahaf Harfoush, *Yes We Did: An Inside Look at How Social Media Built the Obama Brand* (Berkeley: New Riders, 2009).

16. This refers to the number of times a video is seen in its entirety and does not include all of the hits where the user viewed only part of the video.

17. Posted by WeCan08, http://www.youtube.com/watch?v=jjXyqcx-mYY (19,992,543 views on or around January 20, 2010).

18. "Yes We Can" ranked number 2 for "Most Viewed (All Time)—News & Politics," number 11 for "Most Discussed (All Time)—News & Politics," with 87,684 user comments, and number 1 for "Top Favorited (All Time)—News & Politics," having been selected as a favorite 92,915 times. The number of views for *all* videos produced by the campaign is approximately 18 million. According to a scholarly study by Kevin Wallsten, "[T]he number of statements made by the campaign exerted a significant influence on the size of the online audience, the amount of discussion in the blogosphere and the number of media stories about the video. When the campaign sent emails and posted messages on their official blog about the video, Internet users, bloggers and journalists seem to have taken this as a cue that the video was something worth paying attention to" (Kevin Wallsten, "'Yes We Can': How Online Viewership, Blog Discussion, Campaign Statements and Mainstream Media Coverage Produced a Viral Video Phenomenon," paper presented at YouTube and the 2008 Election Cycle, the annual conference of the *Journal of Information Technology and Politics* (April 2009), 53, retrieved October 29, 2009. http://scholarworks.umass.edu/jitpc2009/1.

19. The three top videos posted by the McCain YouTube channel are "Celeb," "The One," and "Joe Biden on Barack Obama." The most popular video related to, but obviously not posted by, the McCain campaign is "McCain's YouTube Problem Just Became a Nightmare," from Brave New Films, posted on May 18, 2008. The website announces, "We are an organization that can produce a hard-hitting three-minute video in less than 24 hours that exposes John McCain's double talk, for instance, and receives *8 million views* [emphasis in original] around the world" (http://bravenewfilms.org/about/). The home page of their anti-McCain campaign proclaims, "The REAL McCain offered an accurate portrayal of Senator John McCain, which the corporate media repeatedly failed to provide throughout the 2008 election. This series featured 17 videos that received over 18 million views. The videos tackled every issue from McCain's out-of-touch stance on the economy to his refusal to support the GI Bill" (http://TheRealMcCain.com/).

CHAPTER 4

1. Janny Scott, "The Long Run: In 2000, a Streetwise Veteran Schooled a Bold Young Obama," *NYT*, September 9, 2007, http://www.nytimes.com/2007/09/09/us/politics/09obama.html.

2. Ibid.

3. As Obama ascended to a hero status in American myth, David Remnick, editor of *The New Yorker* magazine, was preparing his deeply researched and eloquent hagiography

subtitled "The Life and Rise of Barack Obama." It records numerous retrospective remembrances of the president-to-be as having been destined from the start of his adult life to become a hero.

About his early college years at Occidental, Obama's half-sister Maya Soetoro-Ng recalls that "I do remember Mom and I making jokes about, 'Oh yes, you're going to be the first black President.'" Cautioning that "I don't know why we would make those jokes," Soetoro-Ng speculates that perhaps "it was because he was always right," explaining "he was one of those people who even as a young man was like an old man, you know?" "When he went to college," she continues, "I would have been nine, ten, eleven, twelve, and we would joke about this." She admits that "on the one hand we were teasing him," on the other that "behind the joke there was the sense that he was going to do something important. I always felt that way about him, and my mother felt pretty early on that he belonged to something bigger" (Remnick, *The Bridge*, p. 90). Later, when Obama was working as a community organizer in Chicago, a young Protestant minister also professes to having sensed Obama's imminent destiny.

> Obama hoped to organize black neighborhoods whose residents were, for the most part, Baptists or Pentecostals. He moved from church to church, trying to enlist ministers in his effort. One day he rang the doorbell at Lilydale First Baptist Church on 113th Street. A young minister named Alvin Love answered and wondered, Who *is* this skinny kid? "I didn't know what an organizer was," Love said. [But] "I was trying to figure out how to get my church involved in the community [and] I saw him as a gift from Heaven" (ibid., p. 163).

During his years on the faculty at Chicago law school, "one senior faculty member, Richard Epstein, a libertarian," recalled that Obama "always had that aura: He said 'good morning' and you thought it was an event." (ibid., pp. 265–66). Between 1997 and 2000, during his time as an Illinois state legislator, Obama participated in the Saguaro Seminars at the invitation of Harvard government professor Robert Putnam. Asked what first brought Obama to his attention, Putnam remembered an incident from Obama's law school days: "My son was on the *Law Review* and played basketball with him. He came home to say he had met the most impressive person he has ever met in his life" (ibid., p. 305). In 2000, Obama felt great frustration after his loss to Congressman Bobby Rush in the Democratic primary. Despite this disappointment, Dan Shomon, his campaign manager, recounts that Obama "wasn't finished with" politics.

> Even when Barack was morose, when he was down and out after the race with Bobby, I never thought he would chuck politics. He had to pick up the pieces. But, ultimately, if it hadn't been for that race, there would be no Barack Obama. That was boot camp. That's what got him ready to do what he had to do" (ibid., p. 333).

When Obama ran for U.S. Senator in 2004, both his principal opponent in the Democratic primary and his Republican opponent in the general election were forced to withdraw because of sex scandals. "Obama enjoyed an easy path to office," Remnick duly notes, because he was "the beneficiary of one fantastic stroke or fortune after another" (ibid. p. 360).

When Bob Dylan spoke to the London *Times* in April 2009, just a few months after Obama's election, the legendary singer-poet gave voice to the mythical idea of Obama as not entirely of this earth: "He's like a fictional character, but he's real" (ibid., p. 41). This is the stuff of which heroes are made.

4. Scott, "Long Run."

5. Ibid.

6. Michael Powell, "Man in the News: Deliberative in a Manic Game—Barack Obama," *NYT,* June 4, 2008, A18, and for the remaining quotes in this paragraph.

7. George Gene Gustines, "Company for Batman and Robin," *NYT,* July 22, 2008, A14.

8. Jeffrey C. Alexander, "Modern, Anti, Post, and Neo: How Intellectuals Explain 'Our Time,'" in Jeffrey C. Alexander, *The Meanings of Social Life: A Cultural Sociology* (New York: Oxford University Press, 2004).

9. David Plouffe, *The Audacity to Win: The Inside Story and Lessons of Barack Obama's Historic Victory,* New York: Viking, 2009, pp. 113–14.

10. John M. Broder, "Obama, Adopting Economic Theme, Criticizes McCain," *NYT,* June 10, 2008, and for the following quotes in this paragraph.

11. "Defining Moments Ad," posted on October 24, 2008, by BarackObamadotcom, http://www.youtube.com/watch?v=vJvkRFKGgGw (334,895 views on YouTube since posting [on or around December 3, 2009]).

12. Ryan Lizza, "The Political Scene: Making It—How Chicago Shaped Obama," *New Yorker,* July 21, 2008, 49–65, and for all of the quotes in this paragraph and the next.

13. Stephen F. Hayes, "Democrats and Double Standards," *WS* 14(3), September 29, 2008.

14. Maureen Dowd, "Stalking, Sniffing, Swooning," *NYT,* July 27, 2008, http://www.nytimes.com/2008/07/27/opinion/27dowd.html.

15. Scott, "Long Run," and for the following quotes.

16. Ernst H. Kantorowicz, *The King's Two Bodies: A Study in Medieval Political Theology* (Princeton, N.J.: Princeton University Press, 1957).

17. John McCain and Mark Salter, *Faith of My Fathers: A Family Memoir* (New York: Harper, 1999), 342.

18. Ibid., 346.

19. Ibid., 18.

20. Ibid., 108, 129.

21. Ibid., 210–11, 257.

22. These quoted comments about *Faith of My Father* are among those reprinted on the back cover and front pages of the book's 2008 republication. That they were selected for their publicity value by the book's author and publisher makes them particularly revealing.

23. James M. Redfield, *Nature and Culture in the* Iliad (Durham: Duke University Press, 1994, expanded ed.), 27–28.

24. Elizabeth Holmes and Neil King Jr., "Will McCain's Hawkish View Play on National Stage?" *WSJ,* March 6, 2008, A6.

25. "McCain's Honor," editorial, *WSJ,* November 1, 2008, A10; this is the source of the quote in the next sentence as well.

26. McCain, *Faith of My Fathers*, 165.

27. Ibid., 214–15.

28. Ibid., 252.

29. Ibid., 222, 240–41.

30. Ibid., 76.

31. These quotations are from the book jacket blurbs; see n. 22, above.

32. "Barack Obama's Acceptance Speech," *NYT*, August 28, 2008, as recorded by *CQ Transcriptions*, http://www.nytimes.com/2008/08/28/us/politics/28text-obama.html.

33. For an account of the tensions between military and civil understandings of patriotism during the Clinton presidency, see Robin Wagner-Pacifici, "'Talking Lords Who Dare Not Face the Foe': Civilian Rule and the Military Notion of Patriotism in the Clinton Presidency," pp. 305–322 in John Bodnar, ed., *Bonds of Affection: Americans Define Their Patriotism* (Princeton, N.J.: Princeton University Press, 1996). Clinton was markedly less successful than Obama in avoiding polluting aspersions. Obama was not implicated by the polarizations of the Vietnam era. He never himself faced the draft. By 2008, domestic terrorism had receded as a voter concern. Disappointment with the course of the Iraq War diluted American enthusiasm for military heroism. There were also critical differences in the narrative characters and performative styles of the two Democratic leaders.

34. Stephen F. Hayes, "The Disappearing Issue of Election '08," *WS* 14(8), November 3, 2008.

35. My field notes from John McCain's appearance at a town meeting Republican campaign event in Bow, New Hampshire, September 4, 2007.

36. Hayes, "Disappearing Issue"; this is also the source of the remaining quotes in this paragraph and the following extract as well.

37. Fred Barnes, "The Warrior and the Priest," *WS* 14(4), October 6, 2008.

38. My field notes, Philadelphia, Pennsylvania, storefront office for the McCain-Palin '08 campaign, September 28, 2008.

39. As reported in Sara Murray and Stephanie Simon, "Democrats Begin Their Final Assault—Obama Targets Swing States like Colorado to Tilt Election," *WSJ*, August 25, 2008, A1.

40. As reported in Robin Toner and Adam Nagourney, "McCain Seen as Less Likely to Bring Change, Poll Finds," *NYT*, September 18, 2008, A1.

41. Elizabeth Holmes and Amy Chozick, "McCain Bristles over Russia's 'Aggression'— Rhetoric Reflects Campaign's Focus on Foreign Policy," *WSJ*, August 12, 2008, A2.

42. David E. Sanger, "Events in Iraq, Benefiting McCain, Are Likely to Be a Key Theme of His Run," *NYT*, September 3, 2008, A17.

43. From a Gallup Poll taken August 21–23, 2008. "Election 2008 Topics and Trends," *Gallup.com* (blog), retrieved October 9, 2008, http://www.gallup.com/poll/17785/election-2008.aspx#3.

44. Holmes and Chozick, "McCain Bristles over Russia's 'Aggression.'"

45. John M. Broder, "Biden Opens New Phase with Attack on McCain," *NYT*, August 28, 2008, http://www.nytimes.com/2008/08/28/us/politics/28biden.html.

46. Michael Falcone, "Biden and Palin Tussle over Taxes," *The Caucus* (NYT blog), September 18, 2008, http://thecaucus.blogs.nytimes.com/2008/09/18/biden-and-palin-tussle-over-taxes/.

47. Sheryl Gay Stolberg, "Bush Says McCain Is Choice to Lead in Time of Danger," *NYT,* September 3, 2008, A1; Elisabeth Bumiller and Michael Cooper, "Palin Assails Critics and Electrifies Party," *NYT,* September 4, 2008, A1; "Mike Huckabee's Convention Speech," *NYT,* September 3, 2008, *CQ Transcriptions,* http://www.nytimes.com/2008/09/03/us/politics/03text-huckabee.html.

48. Adam Nagourney and Michael Cooper, "McCain Sets Path; Vows to End 'Partisan Rancor,'" *NYT,* September 5, 2008, A1.

49. Ibid.

50. Laura Meckler, "Candidates Zero In on 'Change' as Key Message—Obama Emphasizes Reversing Bush; McCain Bucks Party," *WSJ,* September 8, 2008, A4, and below.

51. Herodotus, *The History,* VII, 10 (David Grene translation 1987), Chicago: University of Chicago Press.

52. Lee Siegel, "Essay: The Triumph of Culture over Politics," and below.

53. David D. Kirkpatrick, "Writing Memoir, McCain Found a Narrative for Life," *NYT,* October 13, A1, and below.

54. Janny Scott, "The Long Run: In Illinois, Obama Proved Pragmatic and Shrewd," *NYT,* July 30, 2007, http://www.nytimes.com/2007/07/30/us/politics/30obama.html, and below.

55. Janny Scott, "The Long Run: In 2000, a Streetwise Veteran Schooled a Bold Young Obama," *NYT,* September 9, 2007, http://www.nytimes.com/2007/09/09/us/politics/09obama.html.

56. Jodi Kantor, "Man in the News: For a New Political Age, a Self-made Man—Barack Hussein Obama," *NYT,* August 28, 2008, A1, and below.

57. See Part III, below, for chapters on celebrity metaphor, Palin effect, and financial crisis.

58. Sam Schulman, "Losing the Plot," *WS* 14(5), October 14, 2008, and below.

CHAPTER 5

1. Adam Nagourney, "In Political Realm, 'Family Problem' Emerges as Test and Distraction," *NYT,* September 2, 2008, A18.

2. Michael Cooper and Jim Rutenberg, "McCain Barbs Stirring Outcry as Distortions," *NYT,* September 13, A1.

3. For a historical discussion of how such polluting arguments have been employed since the classical age to disenfranchise various categories of voters, see Jeffrey C. Alexander, *The Civil Sphere* (New York : Oxford University Press, 2006), 114–23.

4. Alexis de Tocqueville introduces the idea of self-interest "rightly understood" in *Democracy in America* (vols. 1 and 2, New York: Library of America, 2004 [1835, 1840], book 2, chapter 8). For discussion of this distinction, see "Note on Concept and Method."

5. Jeff Zeleny, "Feeling a Challenge, Obama Sharpens His Silver Tongue," *NYT,* September 10, 2008, A20, and below.

6. "Gov. Palin's Worldview" (editorial), *NYT,* September 13, 2008, A18.

7. Adam Nagourney, "Concerns about Palin's Readiness as a Big Test for Her Nears," *NYT,* September 30, 2008, http://www.nytimes.com/2008/09/30/us/politics/30palin.html.

8. Adam Nagourney and Megan Thee, "Poll Finds Obama Gaining Support and McCain Weakened in Bailout Crisis."

9. Peter Baker and Jim Rutenberg, "The Long Road to a Clinton Exit," *NYT,* June 8, 2008, A1.

10. For voting as a closing ritual, see Inge Schmidt, When Good Ballots Go Bad: Voting Ritual (and Its Failure) in the United States, PhD diss., Department of Sociology, Yale University, 2010.

11. William Yardley, "Obama Supporters on the Far Left Cry Foul," *NYT,* July 13, 2008, A18.

12. Nat Hentoff, "Reality Sets In about Obama; Liberals Lament Flim-flam Candidate," *WT,* July 21, 2008, A27.

13. Gerald F. Seib, "Irked Extremes May Mean a Happy Political Middle," *WSJ,* July 29, 2008, A2.

14. "Obama's Summer of Discontent" (editorial), *WT,* August 26, 2008, A16.

15. Yardley, "Obama Supporters on the Far Left Cry Foul."

16. Seib, "Irked Extremes."

17. See "Note on Concept and Method" for more discussion of the elements of social performance. Scripts mediate between general background representations and concrete, situated actions. As foreground rather than background, they face both ways, not only symbolic and representational but also action specific at the same time. Scripts motivate specific actions, constituting their "efficient cause." Even so, evidence for their having done so is often post hoc. Frequently scripts are constructed for actions after the fact. They are attribution as much as description. Scripting after the fact is a way of documenting. It provides textual evidence that actions really are linked to the deep structures of democratic representation, structures that provide civil legitimacy.

18. Michael Luo and Jeff Zeleny, "Reversing Stand, Obama Declines Public Financing," *NYT,* June 20, 2008, A1, and below.

19. "Public Funding on the Ropes" (editorial), *NYT,* June 20, 2008, A20.

20. David Brooks, "The Two Obamas," *NYT,* June 20, 2008, http://www.nytimes.com/2008/06/20/opinion/20brooks.html, and below.

21. Luo and Zeleny, "Reversing Stand," and below.

22. Michael Powell, "For Obama, a Pragmatist's Shift toward the Center," *NYT,* June 27, 2008, A14, and below.

23. Linda Greenhouse, "Justices, Ruling 5–4, Endorse Personal Right to Own Gun," *NYT,* June 27, 2008, http://www.nytimes.com/2008/06/27/washington/27scotus.html; emphasis added, and below.

24. Powell, "For Obama, a Pragmatist's Shift," and below; emphasis added.

25. John Harwood, "Flip-flops Are Looking Like a Hot Summer Trend," *NYT,* June 23, 2006, and below. In writing that "the effect of a flip-flop is contingent on social context," sociologists Ruane and Cerulo do not sufficiently emphasize that this contextualization is a matter of attribution, of actors convincing audiences and journalists that this or that context is relevant rather than some other. Janet M. Ruane and Karen A. Cerulo, "The Forum: Second Thoughts on Presidential Politics," *Sociological Forum* 23(4), December 2008: 852–60, 853.

26. Michael Cooper and Jeff Zeleny, "Obama Fuels Pullout Debate with Remarks," *NYT,* July 4, 2006, and below.

27. Richard A. Oppel Jr. and Jeff Zeleny, "For Obama, a First Step Is Not a Misstep," *NYT,* July 22, 2008, A1.

28. David D. Kirkpatrick, "Response to 9/11 Offers Outline of McCain Doctrine," *NYT,* August 16, 2008, http://www.nytimes.com/2008/08/17/us/politics/17mccain.html.

29. David D. Kirkpatrick, "From a Heckler to a Deal Maker: After 2000 Run, McCain Learned to Work Levers of Power," *NYT,* July 21, 2008, A1.

30. Speech of Rudy Giuliani at the Republican convention, *NYT,* September 3, 2008, as recorded by *CQ Transcriptions,* http://elections.nytimes.com/2008/president/conventions/videos/20080903_GIULIANI_SPEECH.html.

31. Brian Knowlton and David D. Kirkpatrick, "McCain Moves to Shore Up Republicans' House Divided," *NYT,* February 7, 2008; David D. Kirkpatrick, "McCain's Critics on Right Look Again," *NYT,* February 11, 2008, http://www.nytimes.com/2008/02/01/us/01conservatives.html; Kirkpatrick, "McCain's Effort to Woo Conservatives Is Paying Off," *NYT,* September 3, 2008, http://www.nytimes.com/2008/09/03/us/politics/03conservatives.html.

32. Patrick Healy, "Target: Barack Obama. Strategy: What Day Is It?" *NYT,* July 4, 2008, A14, and below.

33. Kirkpatrick, "From Heckler to Deal Maker," and below.

34. Jackie Calmes and Alex Frangos, "Candidates Mobilize as Race Grinds On; McCain's Breaks with GOP Leave Scars but Could Increase His Electability," *WSJ,* February 7, 2008, Eastern ed., retrieved January 7, 2010, ProQuest Newsstand Complete.

35. Jackie Calmes, "The *Wall Street Journal/NBC News* Poll: McCain, GOP May Have Cause for Hope; Latest Poll Helps Detail Reasons the Democrats Remain Deadlocked," *WSJ,* March 13, 2008, Eastern ed., retrieved January 7, 2010, ProQuest Newsstand Complete, and below.

36. Alison Mitchell, "The Mantle of the Maverick Suits McCain," *NYT,* July 7, 1999, http://www.nytimes.com/2008/09/03/us/politics/03conservatives.html; David D. Kirkpatrick, "John McCain, Flexible Aggression," *NYT* election special issue, October 25, 2008, http://www.nytimes.com/2008/10/26/weekinreview/26kirkpatrick.html.

37. Karen Tumulty, "John McCain, Maverick No More," *TIME.com* (blog), July 12, 2007, http://www.time.com/time/magazine/article/0,9171,1642900,00.html; see also Byron York, "Maverick No More: But Will Conservatives Embrace John McCain?" *National Review* 60, February 11, 2008, 17.

38. Peggy Noonan, "Declarations: Let McCain Be McCain," *WSJ,* June 28, 2008, Eastern ed., retrieved January 7, 2010, ProQuest Newsstand Complete.

39. Gerald F. Seib, "Candidates May Draw New Map," *WSJ,* April 8, 2008, Eastern ed., retrieved January 7, 2010, ProQuest Newsstand Complete.

40. Kimberley Strassel, "The Weekend Interview with Steny Hoyer: Ready for Real Change," *WSJ,* April 26, 2008, Eastern ed., retrieved January 7, 2010, ProQuest Newsstand Complete.

41. Laura Meckler and Elizabeth Holmes, "Campaign '08: McCain Sets Stage for Fall Run; Senator Stakes Out Positions and Fills Campaign Coffers," *WSJ,* May 9, 2008, Eastern ed., retrieved January 7, 2010, ProQuest Newsstand Complete.

42. Ibid.

43. Laura Meckler, "Campaign '08: McCain vs. Obama: In the General Election, Sharp Battle Lines over Policy," *WSJ*, June 6, 2008, Eastern ed., retrieved January 7, 2010, ProQuest Newsstand Complete.

44. Bob Davis, "McCain's Economy Platform: Big Tax Cuts, with Caveats," *WSJ*, March 3, 2008, Eastern ed., retrieved January 7, 2010, ProQuest Newsstand Complete, and below.

45. Jim Rutenberg, "McCain Is Trying to Define Obama as Out of Touch," *NYT*, July 31, 2008, and below. For an extended discussion, see chapter 7.

46. Karl Rove, "Conventions Need a Believable Script," *WSJ*, August 21, 2008, emphasis added.

47. "Original Mavericks," http://www.youtube.com/watch?v=bVIaqCjvLpU, posted by JohnMcCaindotcom on September 7, 2008 (305,274 views on or around December 3, 2009). See also "Alaska Maverick," posted by JohnMcCaindotcom on September 3, 2008 (293,874 views on or around December 3, 2009), http://www.youtube.com/watch?v=AIn_fFWPaUU&feature=channel. The Obama campaign responded a day later with an ad titled "No Maverick," posted by BarackObamadotcom on September 8, 2009 (531,936 views on or around December 3, 2009), http://www.youtube.com/watch?v=NBtbG5xjFBY).

48. Brad Haynes, "GOP Fight in Nevada Could Cause McCain Trouble," *WSJ*, August 23, 2008, A4.

49. Peter Baker, "Party in Power, Running as If It Weren't," *NYT*, September 4, 2009, http://www.nytimes.com/2008/09/05/us/politics/05assess.html.

CHAPTER 6

1. Glenn R. Simpson and Amy Chozick, "Obama's Muslim-Outreach Adviser Resigns," *WSJ*, August 6, 2008, A4.

2. For two contemporary conservative arguments that justify inequality by defending the virtues of noncivil qualities, see Samuel P. Huntington, *Who Are We? The Challenge to America's National Identity* (New York: Simon and Schuster, 2004), and Harvey Mansfield, *Manliness* (New Haven: Yale University Press, 2006).

3. Gerald F. Seib and Laura Meckler, "Voter Unease with Obama Lingers Despite His Lead," *WSJ*, July 24, 2008, A1.

4. Ibid.

5. Gerald F. Seib, "Palin Pitches Sam's Club Tent," *WSJ*, September 3, 2008, A2, and below.

6. Julie Bosman and John M. Broder, "Obama's Campaign Opens a New Web Site to Strike Back at 'Dishonest Smears,'" *NYT*, July 13, 2008, A24.

7. Jeff Zeleny, "Campaign Flashpoint: Patriotism and Service," *NYT*, July 1, 2008, A18.

8. John M. Broder, "At Obama Event, a Comedian's Jokes Fall Flat," *NYT*, July 13, 2008, A20.

9. Jeff Zeleny, "Obama Talks about Rumors," *Caucus*, April 21, 2008, http://thecaucus.blogs.nytimes.com/2008/04/21/obama-talks-about-rumors/.

10. Nicholas D. Kristof, "The Push to 'Otherize' Obama," *NYT*, September 21, News of the Week in Review, 9.

11. Jeffrey C. Alexander, ed., *Real Civil Societies: Dilemmas of Institutionalization* (London: Sage, 1998), and Jeffrey C. Alexander, *The Civil Sphere* (New York: Oxford University Press, 2006), chapter 8.

12. Elizabeth Holmes and Amy Chozick, "Candidates' Business Advisers Get Heat," *WSJ*, June 14, 2008, A5.

13. Ibid.

14. Michael Cooper and Michael Luo, "At Debate on the Economy, Republicans Become Kindest of Candidates," *NYT*, January 25, 2008, http://www.nytimes.com/2008/01/25/us/politics/25repubs.html.

15. Laura Meckler, "McCain Disputes Adviser," *WSJ*, July 11, 2008, A5.

16. Ralph Z. Hallow, "Gramm 'Jumped,' Not Pushed from McCain Campaign," *WT*, July 20, 2008, A4.

17. Meckler, "McCain Disputes Adviser," and below.

18. "John McCain's Housing Crisis," *The Board: A Blog by the Editorial Writers of the New York Times*, August 21, 2008, http://theboard.blogs.nytimes.com/2008/08/21/john-mccains-housing-crisis/.

19. See "Seven," posted by BarackObamadotcom on August 21, 2008 (1,044,292 views on or around December 3, 2009), http://www.youtube.com/watch?v=vpmFd25tRqo.

20. "Out of Touch," posted by BarackObamadotcom on August 22, 2008 (359,690 views on or around December 3, 2009), http://www.youtube.com/watch?v=NZdi1JnMxFU.

21. Seib, "Palin Pitches Sam's Club Tent," and below.

22. Hallow, "Gramm 'Jumped.'"

23. Gerald F. Seib, "Seeking Economic Pole Position," *WSJ*, September 9, 2008, A2.

24. Bill Carter, "Rivals CNN and Fox News Spar over Obama Report," *NYT*, January 24, 2007, http://www.nytimes.com/2007/01/24/us/politics/24obama.html.

25. Kristof, "Push to 'Otherize' Obama."

26. "Republicans Decry Use of 'Hussein' in Obama's Name," *CNN Politics.com*, February 28, 2008, http://www.cnn.com/2008/POLITICS/02/28/tennessee.gop/index.html.

27. Austin Bogues, "Words; Rhymes with…Obama," *NYT*, July 19, 2008, http://query.nytimes.com/gst/fullpage.html?res=9D0CE5DA113CF93AA25754C0A96E9C8B63.

28. John K. Wilson, "Jerome Corsi's Lies: Inside the Deceptions of the Best-selling Anti-Obama Book," *HP*, August 14, 2008, http://www.huffingtonpost.com/john-k-wilson/jerome-corsis-lies-inside_b_119036.html.

29. Glenn R. Simpson and Amy Chozick, "Obama's Muslim-Outreach Adviser Resigns," *WSJ*, August 6, 2008, A4, and below.

30. Alexander Mooney, "New Yorker Editor Defends Controversial Obama Cover," *Election Center 2008*, CNN.com, July 14, 2008, http://www.cnn.com/2008/POLITICS/07/15/obama.cover/index.html.

31. Douglas Belkin, Stephanie Simon, and Suzanne Sataline, "Critics of McCain Web Ad Say It Links Obama to Antichrist," *WSJ*, August 8, 2008, A5.

32. "The One," posted by JohnMcCaindotcom on August 1, 2008, http://www.youtube.com/watch?v=mopkn01PzM8. This video was the "most discussed" and the second "most viewed" (26,352 comments and 1,644,611 views on or around November 13, 2008) during the campaign, according to McCain's YouTube website (JohnMcCaindotcom).

33. Belkin, Simon, and Sataline, "Critics of McCain Web Ad."

34. "Barack Obama Addresses A.M.E. Church General Conference," posted by Barackobama.com on July 6, 2008, http://www.youtube.com/watch?v=WVKxwECwRLE&feature=player_profilepage.

35. Kristof, "Push to 'Otherize'"; "Presidential Race Remains Even," Pew Research Center for the People and the Press, September 18, 2008, complete report retrieved October 9, 2008, http://people-press.org/reports/pdf/450.pdf, and below.

36. Kristof, "Push to 'Otherize.'"

37. Hannah Strange and Philippe Naughton, "Hillary Clinton: My Teary Moment Won Me New Hampshire," January 9, 2008, http://www.timesonline.co.uk/tol/news/world/us_and_americas/us_elections/article3160177.ece

38. Ibid.

39. Jodi Kantor, "A Show of Emotion That Reverberated beyond the Campign," NYT, January 9, 2008, http://www.nytimes.com/2008/01/09/us/politics/09moment.html.

40. Ibid.

41. Mike Barnicle (guest), "Hilary Clinton Complains about Media's Treatment of Women; Interview With Laura Dern," CNN Reliable Sources, May 25, 2008, CNN Transcript, retrieved May 5, 2010, from Lexis Nexis Academic; Chris Matthews, "The Clintons Never Quit," Anderson Cooper 360 Degrees, July 11, 2008, CNN transcript, retrieved May 5, 2010.

42. Michelle Malkin, "BIG STORY," The Big Story with John Gibson, December 17, 2007, FNN transcript, retrieved May 5, 2010, from Lexis Nexis Academic.

43. Katharine Q. Seelye and Julie Bosman, "Media Charged With Sexism in Clinton Coverage," NYT, June 13, 2008, http://www.nytimes.com/2008/06/13/us/politics/13women.html.

44. Jodi Kantor and Jeff Zeleny, "Michelle Obama Adds New Role to Balancing Act," NYT, May 18, 2008, http://www.nytimes.com/2007/05/18/us/politics/18michelle.html, and below.

45. From a speech given by Michelle Obama at a get-out-the-vote rally in Los Angeles on February 3, 2009 ("LA Rally—Full Video," posted by Barackobama.com on February 3, 2008, http://www.youtube.com/watch?v=JZiNtTq10i0).

46. See excerpt from CSPAN coverage titled "Michelle Obama: 'For the First Time in My Adult Lifetime, I Am Really Proud of My Country,'" February 18, 2008, http://www.breitbart.tv/html/49244.html, and excerpt from MSNBC with clarifying remarks made in Providence, R.I., two days later, "Michelle Obama—I Am Proud of This Country," February 20, 2008, http://www.youtube.com/watch?v=40S4JAfb00w.

47. Matt Stearns, "Michelle Obama's 'Proud of my Country' Comment Provokes Thunder on the Right," McClatchey.com, February 20, 2008, http://www.mcclatchydc.com/104/story/28263.html.

48. Michael Powell and Jodi Kantor, "After Attacks, Michelle Obama Looks for a New Introduction," NYT, June 18, 2008.

49. Stearns, "Thunder on the Right."

50. Nancy Gibbs, "The War over Michelle Obama," Time.com, May 22, 2008, http://www.time.com/time/magazine/article/0,9171,1808642,00.html.

51. Christopher Hitchens, "Are We Getting Two for One? Is Michelle Obama Responsible for the Jeremiah Wright Fiasco?" Slate Magazine, posted May 5, 2008, http://www.slate.com/id/2190589/.

52. Mark Steyn, "Mrs. Obama's America," cover story, *National Review Online*, April 21, 2008, http://nrd.nationalreview.com/article/?q=MWU0YzQwZTZjODZhZTNkODc50 DlhMGU1MDkzZjRjODc.

53. Michelle Malkin, cited in Robin Abcarian, "Campaign '08: The Democrats," *LAT*, June 11, 2008, http://articles.latimes.com/2008/jun/11/nation/na-michelle11; Gibbs, "War over Michelle Obama"; Steyn, "Mrs. Obama's America."

54. Steyn, "Mrs. Obama's America."

55. Powell and Kantor, "After Attacks," and below.

56. See "Michelle Obama on The View," posted by BarackObamadotcom on June 18, 2008, one of the campaign's most viewed videos (number 13 at 1,472,917 views on or around December 3, 2009), http://www.youtube.com/watch?v=59tw01fJwtQ.

57. Powell and Kantor, "After Attacks," and following. The following day, Fox News anchor Joe Scarborough grilled David Axelrod about Mrs. Obama's "makeover" and her new talking points outlined in the *Times*, prompting the campaign manager to finally retort, "I absolutely reject the notion of any kind of makeover. Absolutely not. I don't know where they got that from. None necessary" ("Decision '08," *Morning Joe*, Fox News Network, June 18, 2008).

58. *US Weekly* 698, June 30, 2008, and below.

59. Jodi Kantor, "Reluctant No More, and Taking Center Stage," *NYT*, August, 26, 2008, A14, and below.

60. Ibid.

61. See "Michelle Obama at the 2008 DNC," posted by Barackobama.com on August 26, 2008 (903,981 views on or around December 3, 2009), http://www.youtube.com/watch?v=sTFsB09KhqI; "Michelle Obama Keynote Address at DNC," posted by CSPAN on August 25, 2008 (428,665 views on or around December 3, 2009), http://www.youtube.com/watch?v=790hG6qBPx0. In addition, the campaign produced a short biography of Michelle Obama that played on Monday night at the convention, featuring her mother as narrator ("Michelle Obama: South Side Girl," posted by BarackObamadotcom on August 25, 2008 [383,441 views on or around December 3, 2009], http://www.youtube.com/watch?v=2Utt-6HumUU).

62. "Michelle Obama's Speech at the Democratic National Convention," *NYT*, as recorded by *CQ Transcriptions*, August 25, 2008, http://elections.nytimes.com/2008/president/conventions/videos/20080825_OBAMA_SPEECH.html, and below.

63. Kate Zernike, "Both Sides Seeking to Be What Women Want," *NYT*, September 15, 2008, A22, and below.

64. Ibid.

65. "Editorial: Candidate McCain's Big Decision," *NYT*, September 2, 2008, http://www.nytimes.com/2008/09/03/opinion/03wed1.html.

66. Jodi Kantor and Rachel Swarns, "A New Twist in the Debate on Mothers," *NYT*, September 1, 2008, A1.

67. Andrea Mitchell, *Hardball with Chris Matthews* (HB), August 29, 2008, MSNBC transcript, retrieved January 24, 2010, from Lexis Nexis Academic.

68. Christina Bellantoni, "Obama, Biden Speak to Press on Palin," *Bellantoni on Politics* (WT) (blog), August 29, 2008, http://washingtontimes.com/weblogs/bellantoni/2008/Aug/29/obama-biden-speak-to-press-on-palin/.

69. Jodi Kantor, Kate Zernike, and Catrin Einhorn, "Fusing Politics and Motherhood in a New Way," *NYT,* September 7, 2008, http://www.nytimes.com/2008/09/08/us/politics/08baby.html.

70. Elisabeth Bumiller and Michael Cooper, "Palin Assails Critics and Electrifies Party," *NYT,* September 4, 2008, A1; "Palin's Speech at the Republican National Convention," *NYT,* September 3, 2008, as recorded by *CQ Transcriptions,* http://elections.nytimes.com/2008/president/conventions/videos/20080903_PALIN_SPEECH.html.

71. Chris Matthews, "For September 3, 2008," MSNBC coverage of Republican National Convention, MSNBC transcript, retrieved January 25, 2010, Lexis Nexis Academic.

72. Ibid.

73. Kim Severson, "They Raise Children, Pray and Rally around a Running Mate," *NYT,* September 5, 2008, A22, and below.

74. Kantor and Swarns, "New Twist," and below.

75. Ibid.

76. Ibid.

77. *US Weekly,* September 15, 2008, issue 709.

78. David Brooks, "What the Palin Pick Says," *NYT,* September 2, 2008, A23.

79. William Kristol, "A Star Is Born?" *NYT,* September 1, 2008, A17.

80. Janny Scott, "Code-breaking: What Politicians Say When They Talk about Race," *NYT,* March 23, 2008, A1.

81. Describing Barack Obama as "successful, well educated, and cosmopolitan," African American legal scholar and Stanford professor Richard Thompson Ford insists "he is not atypical: there are millions of successful Blacks who share these characteristics with Obama."

> They represent a large and growing share of the Black students I teach at Stanford Law School; they are an ever larger share of the Black undergraduate students I encounter at Stanford, and I suspect an even larger share of the Black grade school students nationwide who are likely to attend college in the future... Since the civil rights legislation of the 1960s, life has gotten much, much better for Blacks with the resources, skills, and socialization necessary to enter the American mainstream. Racism has consistently and steadily declined, and opportunities for well-eduated Blacks have expanded even more quickly than a rapidly expanding economy. The bad news: things got much, much worse for those without such advantages" ("Barack Is the New Black: Obama and the Promise/Threat of the Post-Civil Rights Era," *Du Bois Review* 6:1 [2009]: 37–38, 42–43).

82. For the distinction between assimilative and multicultural modes of civil incorporation, see Alexander, *Civil Sphere,* part IV.

83. Adam Nagourney and Megan Thee, "Poll Finds Obama Candidacy Isn't Closing Divide on Race," *NYT,* July 16, 2008, A1, and below. After the election, at least, some leading academic experts in the social science of race agreed that white racism has sharply declined and the willingness to elect a Black president dramatically increased. This is the gist of a special post-election "Obama Issue" of Harvard's *Du Bois Review: Social Science Research on Race* (volume 6:1) which appeared in Spring 2009. In their editorial introduction, the *Review*'s editors Lawrence D. Bobo and Michael C. Dawson write that "Obama's entire candidacy,

and his ultimate success, was premised on the fact of an enormous transformation in racial attitudes and outlooks in the United States." Despite the fact that "negative stereotypes of African Americans remain alive and well," Bobo and Dawson point to two decades of poll data demonstrating the "unabated decline in the number of White Americans who say they wold not support a Black candidate nominated by their own party" ("A Change Has Come: Race, Politics, and the Path to the Obama Presidency," *Du Bois Review* 6 [1] 2009: 1-14, pp. 3–4). Ford relates such indicators to deeper economic, cultural, and behavioral changes within the Black community.

> Whites are beginning to make distinctions between those Blacks whom they associate with negative racial stereotypes and those whom they see, increasingly, as an ethnic group—people with slightly different accents, culinary styles, and traditions, but otherwise assimilated to mainstream norms of behavior. It's the difference between associating a Black face with gangbangers, crack addicts, and panhandlers and associating that face with jazz, soul food, and Kwanzaa ("Barack Is the New Black," p. 46; cf. n. 81, above).

84. Ibid.

85. Adam Nagourney, "In Voting Booth, Race May Play a Bigger Role," *NYT*, October 14, 2008, A20.

86. Patrick Healy, "Target: Barack Obama. Strategy: What Day Is It?" *NYT*, July 4, 2008, http://www.nytimes.com/2008/07/04/us/politics/04strategy.html

87. Christopher Cooper and Susan David, "Obama Seeks to Add Black Voters," *WSJ*, June 30, 2008, A4, and below.

88. Gerald F. Seib and Laura Meckler, "Voter Unease with Obama Lingers despite His Lead," *WSJ*, July 24, 2008, A1, and below.

89. Andrew Ferguson, "We Can't Handle the Truth," *WS* 13(43), July 28, 2008.

90. Andy Soltis, "Barack Brother in Shack Shock," *NYP*, August 21, 2008, 7, and below.

91. Andrew Breitbart, "The Inconvenient Obama," *WT*, August 25, 2008, A4, and below.

92. Richard Burr, "Unsuper Delegate: Detroit's Kwame Kilpatrick, Unwelcome in Denver," *WS* 13(47), September 1, 2008, retrieved January 20, 2009, http://dailystandardblog.com/Content/Public/Articles/000/000/015/456nywuk.asp?pg=2, and below.

93. Ibid.

94. Henry Payne, "Cross Country: Start Your Engines: Michigan Will Have a Real Race This Year," *WSJ*, September 20, 2008, A13, and below.

95. Adam Nossiter, "For Some, Uncertainty Starts at Racial Identity," *NYT*, October 15, 2008, A21, and below.

96. Jennifer Steinhauer, "Volunteers for Obama Face a Complex Issue," *NYT*, October 14, 2008.

97. Healy, "Target: Barack Obama. Strategy: What Day Is It?"

98. John Harwood, "McCain Takes a Page from Clinton's Playbook," *NYT*, August 4, 2008, A12.

99. Jacob Weisberg, "If Obama Loses: Racism Is the Only Reason McCain Might Beat Him," Slate Magazine, August 23, 2008, http://www.slate.com/id/2198397/.

100. Kristof, "Push to 'Otherize' Obama."

101. Brent Staples, "Barack Obama, John McCain and the Language of Race," *NYT*, September 22, 2008, A22, and below.

102. Remnick, *The Bridge*, p. 467.

103. Quoted in ibid.

104. Ben Wallace-Wells, "Destiny's Child," http://www.Rollingstone.com, February 22, 2007.

105. Janny Scott, "In Illinois, Obama Proved Pragmatic and Shrewd," *NYT*.

106. Janny Scott, "A Biracial Candidate Walks His Own Fine Line," *NYT*, December 29, 2008, http://www.nytimes.com/2007/12/29/us/politics/290bama.html.

107. Foxnews.com, "Jesse Jackson Apologizes for Crude Obama Remarks," July 9, 2008, http://www.foxnews.com/politics/elections/2008/07/09/jesse-jackson-apologizes-for-obama-remarks/; video posted July 10, 2008, http://video.foxnews.com/v/3908576/.

108. Arch Puddington, "Review: Trials of a Civil-Rights Pioneer…and Questions of Who Is 'Black Enough,'" *WSJ*, October 18, 2008, W8. In an interview after Obama's election, Harvard scholar Henry Louis Gates asked his colleague William Julius Wilson, for four decades America's leading social scientific student of race, "Were you surprised at the continuing Black nationalist critiques that he's not Black enough?" Wilson responded, "those critiques are ridiculous…It just saddens me to hear those ill-informed Black nationalist critiques" (Henry Louis Gates, Jr., "A Conversation with William Julius Wilson on the Election of Barack Obama," *Du Bois Review* 6 [1] 2009: 15–23, pp. 16–17.) Ford expands on the fierce generational tensions inside the African-American political community.

> The older generation of Black activists—and this included many who in fact held public office—tried to pressure *other people* to take action on their behalf. The basic model was oppositional and the tools used—mau-mauing, dramatic confrontation, public embarrassment, the guilt trip—were the tools of the weak. By contrast Obama didn't raise the roof about social injustice, hoping that those in control would take some notice—he had every expectation that *he* would be in control. Obama and the Black politicians of his new generation didn't speak truth to power—they were power. And they used the language and tools of the powerful: moderation and compromise, backed up by the proverbial big stick…Obama was judicious and measured, rather than righteous and opinionated; he avoided controversy, while [Jesse] Jackson [Sr.] and [Al] Sharpton chased it…Obama was not alone in his new, less confrontatonal style of politics. He was part of a cohort of new Black politicians who have won office not by appealing to narrow racial solidarities but instead by drawing broad support from voters of all races….The old style of Black politics, which relied heavily on racial bloc voting and influence peddling within the Black community, may be obsolete ("Barack Is the New Black," 38–40, original italics).

Obama's personal and public struggle against the more confrontational and Black-centered politics of the civil rights movement forms one of the central themes in Remnick's biography, *The Bridge: The Life and Rise of Barack Obama*.

109. Barack Obama, *Dreams from My Father: A Story of Race and Inheritance* (New York: Three Rivers Press, 2004 [1995]), 51.

110. Ibid., 106.

111. Ibid., 111.

112. Ibid., 134–35.

113. "Obama Speech: 'A More Perfect Union'" (5,423,603 views on or around November 13, 2008; 6,279,694 views on or around January 21, 2009), posted March 18, 2008, by BarackObamadotcom, captioned as follows: "Barack Obama speaks in Philadelphia, PA, at Constitution Center on matters not just of race and recent remarks but of the fundamental path by which America can work together to pursue a better future," http://www.youtube.com/watch?v=pWe7wTVbLUU.

114. Obama, *Audacity of Hope,* 231.

115. Janny Scott, "Obama Chooses Reconciliation over Rancor," *NYT,* March 19, 2008, A1, and below.

116. BarackObamadotcom, "Obama Speech: 'A More Perfect Union.'"

117. Scott, "Obama Chooses Reconciliation over Rancor."

118. Full text available at *The Huffington Post,* http://www.huffingtonpost.com/2008/03/18/obama-race-speech-read-t_n_92077.html. It is Obama's evocation of such broader, civil solidarity that so appeals to Wilson in the post-election interview with Gates:

> GATES: What was the lowest moment during the primary season for you?
>
> WILSON: The public's reaction to that video clip of Reverend Wright's incendiary comments. I thought that Obama might not be able to recover from the political fallout. I was very, very worried until he gave that brilliant race speech... That speech is a model for what I consider to be effective political framing. Because in appealing to the goodwill of the American people, he emphasized points that I'm sure resonated with them, including points that highlighted the importance of helping people to help themselves. You see, Americans tend to support programs that attempt to develop a level playing field ("Conversation with William Julius Wilson," pp. 15–16).

119. Ibid.

120. Obama first used this term in reference to Geraldine Ferraro, on NBC's *Today* show: "Part of what I think Geraldine Ferraro is doing, and I respect the fact that she was a trailblazer, is to participate in the kind of slice-and-dice politics that's about race and about gender and about this and that, and that's what Americans are tired of because they recognize that when we divide ourselves in that way we can't solve problems" ("Ferraro Leaves Clinton Campaign in Flap over Race," *Reuter's.com* [blog], March 12, 2008, http://www.reuters.com/article/idUSN1159673020080312).

121. CNN reports that when McCain's campaign manager, Rick Davis, stated on July 31, 2008, that Obama had "falsely accused" the campaign of "injecting race into the presidential contest," spokesperson Bill Burton immediately responded with a statement asserting Obama's position: "[He] in no way believes that the McCain campaign is using race as an issue, but he does believe they're using the same old low-road politics to distract voters from the real issues in this campaign, and those are the issues he'll continue to talk about" (Dana Bush, "McCain Campaign Charges Obama Playing Race Card," *CNN Political Ticker* [CNN.com, blog], July 31, 2008, http://politicalticker.blogs.cnn.com/2008/07/31/mccain-campaign-charges-obama-playing-race-card/).

122. John M. Broder, "Obama Cites Attack Ads as a Failing of the System," *NYT*, June 21, 2008, http://www.nytimes.com/2008/06/21/us/politics/21donate.html, and below.

123. "Obama's Bad Turn," editorial, *WSJ*, August 1, 2008, A12, and below.

124. Charles Hurt, "Barack Lowers His Worth with Cheap 'Dollar' Shot," *NYP*, August 1, 2008, 9, and below.

125. Tara Wall, "The Color of Politics: Subtle Shades of Gray on the Campaign Trail," *WT*, August 5, 2008, A23.

126. Stephen F. Hayes, "The Disappearing Issue of Election '08," *WS* 14(8), November 3, 2008, and below.

127. Elisabeth Bumiller and John M. Broder, "In V.F.W. Speech, McCain Attacks Obama on War," *NYT*, August 18, 2008, http://www.nytimes.com/2008/08/19/us/politics/19campaign.html.

128. Michael Luo, "McCain Now Hammers Obama on Cuba," *Caucus*, May 20, 2008, http://thecaucus.blogs.nytimes.com/2008/05/20/mccain-now-hammers-obama-on-cuba/.

129. Elisabeth Bumiller, "McCain Slams Obama on National Security," *The Caucus*, August 18, 2008, http://thecaucus.blogs.nytimes.com/2008/08/18/mccain-slams-obama-on-national-security/.

130. John M. Broder and Isabel Kershner, "Obama Will Meet Palestinian Leaders in the West Bank," *NYT*, July 15, 2008, http://query.nytimes.com/gst/fullpage.html?res=9C01E1D6123AF936A25754C0A96E9C8B63.

131. "Bush's Address to the Republican National Convention," *NYT*, as recorded by *CQ Transcriptions*, September 2, 2008, http://elections.nytimes.com/2008/president/conventions/videos/transcripts/20080902_BUSH_SPEECH.html.

132. "Palin's Speech at the Republican National Convention," *NYT*, as recorded by *CQ Trasncriptions*, September 3, 2008, http://elections.nytimes.com/2008/president/conventions/videos/transcripts/20080903_PALIN_SPEECH.html.

133. Jeff Zeleny and John M. Broder, "On Eve of Primary, Clinton Ad Invokes bin Laden," *NYT*, April 22, 2008, http://www.nytimes.com/2008/04/22/us/politics/22campaign.html.

134. "Obama and the Flag," *Hannity and Colmes* (H&C), October 5, 2007, Fox News Network (FNN) transcript, retrieved January 17, 2009, Lexis Nexis Academic.

135. Mark Finkelstein, "Obama: No Hand on Heart for National Anthem," *NewsBusters.org* (blog), October 20, 2007, http://newsbusters.org/blogs/mark-finkelstein/2007/10/20/obama-no-hand-heart-pledge-either-will-msm-notice.

136. Zeleny and Broder, "On Eve of Primary."

137. Ferguson, "We Can't Handle the Truth."

138. "Remarks of Illinois State Sen. Barack Obama against Going to War with Iraq," October 2, 2002, transcript available at *Organizing for America*, http://www.barackobama.com/2002/10/02/remarks_of_illinois_state_sen.php.

139. Bumiller and Broder, "In V.F.W. Speech, McCain Attacks Obama on War."

140. Julie Bosman, "The Ad Campaign: Obama Defines Himself," *NYT*, July 20, 2008, http://www.nytimes.com/2008/06/20/us/politics/200adbox.html.

141. Carlotta Gall and Jeff Zeleny, "Obama's Visit Renews Focus on Afghanistan," *NYT*, July 20, 2008, A1.

142. Maureen Dowd, "Ich Bin Ein Jet-Setter," *NYT,* July 20, 2008.

143. Richard A. Oppel, Jr. and Jeff Zeleny, "For Obama, A First Step is Not a Misstep," *NYT,* July 22, 2008, A1.

144. Carlotta Gall and Jeff Zeleny, "Obama Opens a Foreign Tour in Afghanistan," *NYT,* July 20, 2008.

145. Oppel Jr. and Zeleny, "For Obama, a First Step Is Not a Misstep," and below.

146. Jeff Zeleny, "A Candidate's Brief Taste of a Region's Complexities," *NYT,* July 23, 2008, A16, and below.

147. Jeff Zeleny, "Obama Meets with Israeli and Palestinian Leaders," *NYT,* July 24, 2008, A20, and below.

148. Alessandra Stanley, "Obama Overseas! In Presidential Mode! Back Home, It's McCain in a Golf Cart," *NYT,* July 23, 2008, A16.

149. Jeff Zeleny and Nicholas Kulish, "Obama, in Berlin, Calls for Renewal of Ties with Allies," *NYT,* July 25, 2008, A19, and below.

150. Marc D. Charney, "In Berlin, Oratory with Echoes," *NYT, Week in Review,* July 27, 2008, http://query.nytimes.com/gst/fullpage.html?res=9C07EED9123DF934A15754C0A96 E9C8B63.

151. Jeff Zeleny and Steven Erlanger, "3 Hours in Paris, and Smiles All Around," *NYT,* July 26, 2008, A15, and below.

152. "Al-Malik's Big Boost for Obama's Campaign," *The Week,* August 1, 2008, 4.

153. Frank Rich, "How Obama Became Acting President," *NYT,* July 27, 2008.

154. Ginger Adams Otis, "Middle East Minefield for Barack," *NYP,* July 20, 2008, p. 5, and below.

155. Zeleny, "Obama Meets with Israeli and Palestinian Leaders."

156. Christina Bellantoni, "McCain Assails Snub of Troops; Disputes Rival's Explanation," *WT,* July 27, 2008, A1, and below.

157. Frank J. Gaffney Jr., "Citizen Obama?" *WT,* July 20, 2008, and below.

158. Elisabeth Bumiller, "Hey, Obama: There's Bratwurst in Ohio, Too (but No Cheering Masses)," *NYT,* July 25, 2008, A18, and below.

159. Elisabeth Bumiller, "McCain, at Bush Home, Faults Obama on War Plan," *NYT,* July 22, 2008, A14.

160. Bumiller, "Hey, Obama," and below.

161. Jeff Zeleny, "Going for That Presidential Look, but Trying Not to Overdo It," *NYT,* July 27, 2008, A19, and below.

162. Ibid.

CHAPTER 7

1. Peggy Noonan, "Let McCain Be McCain," *WSJ Opinion Journal,* June 27, 2008, http://online.wsj.com/article/SB121450930616708139.html.

2. For a brief analysis of the turning points indicated in the poll of polls and a more extended rationale for its construction, see the appendix.

3. Fred Barnes, "The Takeaway from the First Debate," *WSJ,* September 29, A25.

4. Amy Chozick, "Obama Heads to Election with Some Weaknesses—Limping to Victory after Strong Start," *WSJ,* June 5, 2008, A6.

5. Elizabeth Holmes, "Week 1 of Push to Focus McCain: Tighter Message, Some Gaffes," *WSJ*, July 12, 2008, A4.

6. Elizabeth Holmes, "McCain Shakes Up Campaign Organization," *WSJ*, July 3, 2008, A4.

7. Holmes, "Week 1 of Push."

8. Mark Leibovich, "McCain Battles a Nemesis, the Teleprompter," *NYT*, July 6, 2008, A1.

9. Holmes, "Week 1 of Push."

10. Holmes, "McCain Shakes Up Campaign Organization."

11. William Kristol, "So Where's Murphy?" *NYT*, July 7, 2008, A17, and below.

12. Holmes, "McCain Shakes Up Campaign Organization," and below.

13. Holmes, "Week 1 of Push."

14. Robert Draper, "The Making (and Remaking) of the Candidate: When a Campaign Can't Settle on a Central Narrative, Does It Imperil Its Protagonist?" *NYT Magazine*, October 26, 2008, 52ff, and below.

15. David Asman, "Interview with Arizona Senator Jon Kyl," *Your World with Neil Cavuto*, July 24, 2008, FNN transcript, retrieved January 24, 2009, Lexis Nexis Academic. In addition, *Media Matters'* research column reports that the words appeared in on-screen text as Asman introduced Sen. Jon Kyl (R-AZ) to discuss Obama's performance that day in Germany and American voters' reaction to it, along with a 20-second video clip from the show (Media Matters for America, "Fox News Wonders: "Obama a Rock Star over There: Red Flag for All Americans Here?" *mediamatters.org Latest Research* [blog], July 25, 2008, http://mediamatters.org/research/200807250003).

16. Bill Sammon (guest), "Candidates Trade Barbs over Canceled Hospital Visit," H&C, July 25, 2008, retrieved January 17, 2009, Lexis Nexis Academic.

17. "Interview with John Bolton," H&C, July 21, 2008, FNN transcript, retrieved January 17, 2009, Lexis Nexis Academic.

18. Charles Hurt, "On a Futile Mission to Find 'Facts' He Likes," *NYP*, July 22, 2008, 6.

19. Sean Hannity, "Obama Cancels Plans to Visit Troops," H&C, July 24, 2008, FNN transcript, retrieved January 17, 2009, Lexis Nexis Academic.

20. Mort Kondracke and Fred Barnes, "Beltway Boys for July 26, 2008," *Beltway Boys*, FNN transcript, retrieved January 17, 2009, Lexis Nexis Academic.

21. S. A. Miller and Jennifer Harper, no headline, *WT*, July 22, 2008, A1.

22. "Obama Love 3.0," posted July 26, 2008, by JohnMcCaindotcom, http://www.youtube.com/watch?v=u6CSix3Dy04; Elisabeth Bumiller, "McCain Intensifies His Attack," *NYT*, July 23, 2008, A16.

23. Jon Scott, Jane Hall, Cal Thomas, Jim Pinkerton, and Kristin Powers, "Fox News Watch for July 26, 2008," FNN transcript, retrieved January 17, 2009, Lexis Nexis Academic.

24. Wesley Pruden, "The Messiah Who Can't Break Away," *WT*, July 29, 2008, A4.

25. "Fox News Watch for July 26, 2008."

26. Kondracke and Barnes, "Beltway Boys."

27. Karl Rove, "Transcript: '*Fox News on Sunday*,'" July 27, 2008, http://www.foxnews.com/story/0,2933,391789,00.html.

28. See "Celeb," posted by JohnMcCaindotcom on July 30, 2008, http://www.youtube. com/watch?v=oHXYsw_ZDXg. In less than 24 hours, the video had received more than a quarter million views and, after three days online, a million more (1,339,267). It took just ten days to reach nearly two million views (1,939,667), hitting 2,187,161 by Election Day, making it the most viewed McCain campaign video, beating out "The One" (1,765,702 views); Joseph Curl, "Obama Persona Inspires Comedians," *WT,* August 8, 2008, A1.

29. Michael Falcone, "Obama Gets 'Celebrity Treatment' in New McCain Ad," *The Caucus, NYT,* July 30, 2008, http://thecaucus.blogs.nytimes.com/2008/07/30/obama-gets-celebrity-treatment-in-new-mccain-ad/.

30. Dan Schnur, "The Race for '08: Going Negative," *Good Morning America,* July 31, 2008, ABC News transcript, Retrieved January 25, 2010, Lexis Nexis Academic.

31. John G. Geer (guest), "Campaign Attack Ads: An American Tradition?" *Talk of the Nation,* NPR transcript, July 31, 2008, http://www.npr.org/templates/transcript/transcript. php?storyId=93137804, and below.

32. Tom Brokaw, *Meet the Press* (NBC News TV program), August 3, 2008. Federal News Service transcript, Retrieved January 25, 2010, Lexis Nexis Academic.

33. "Outrage over Paris, Britney and Obama Connection," *Showbiz Tonight,* CNN. com transcripts, July 31, 2008, http://transcripts.cnn.com/TRANSCRIPTS/0807/31/sbt.01. html, and below.

34. Globe Staff, "McCain Mocks Obama in a New Video on Web," *Boston Globe,* August 2, 2008, A4.

35. Jill Hazelbaker, "Examining the Week's Political News Stories," *This Week in Politics,* August 3, 2008, CNN transcript, Retrieved January 25, 2010, Lexis Nexis Academic.

36. "Obama's Bad Turn," *WSJ.*

37. June Kronholz, "Ready, Aim, Backfire: Nasty Political Ads Fall Flat," *WSJ,* October 16, 2008, A16, and below.

38. Stephen Dinan, "McCain Ad Rips Celebrity Obama; Compares Him to Britney, Paris," *WT,* July 31, 2008, A1, and below.

39. Charles Hurt, "Barack Lowers His Worth."

40. Hannity and Powers, "Analysis with Karl Rove," H&C, July 30, 2008, FNN transcript, retrieved January 17, 2009, Lexis Nexis Academic.

41. "New Campaign Ads from Obama and McCain Campaigns; Nicolle Wallace, Republican Strategist, and Robert Gibbs, Democratic Strategist, Discuss," *Today Show,* July 31, 2008, NBC news transcript, Retrieved January 25, 2010, Lexis Nexis Academic, and below.

42. Stephen Dinan, "Ad Rips Celebrity Obama," *WT,* July 31, 2009, http://www. washingtontimes.com/news/2008/jul/31/mccain-ad-rips-celebrity-obama/.

43. Susan Estrich, "Country First," H&C, July 29, 2008, FNN transcript, retrieved January 17, 2009, Lexis Nexis Academic; video at http://video.foxnews.com/v/3909811.

44. Katie Couric, "Campaign '08; Obama, McCain Continue Attacks, Counterattacks over Pop Celebrity Ad," *CBS Evening News,* July 31, 2008, CBS News transcript, retrieved January 25, 2010, Lexis Nexis Academic.

45. Jake Tapper, "Race for '08: Going Negative."

46. Charles Gibson, "Plan of Attack," *World News with Charles Gibson,* July 31, 2008, NBC News transcript, retrieved January 25, 2010, Lexis Nexis Academic,.

47. Mara Liasson, "Obama, McCain Trading Jabs," *Morning Edition,* NPR transcript, August 1, 2008, http://www.npr.org/templates/story/story.php?storyId=93162553.

48. Jane Valez-Mitchell, "Outrage over Paris, Britney and Obama Connection," *Showbiz Tonight,* July 31, 2008, CNN transcript, retrieved January 25, 2010, Lexis Nexis Academic.

49. "Hastert on Impact of McCain Celebrity Ad," H&C, Fox News interview archive, August 7, 2008, http://www.foxnews.com/story/0,2933,400045,00.html.

50. Mort Kondracke, Brit Hume, Fred Barnes, and Mara Liasson, "Fox News All Stars," *FOX News Special Report with Brit Hume,* July 30, 2008, FNN transcript, retrieved January 17, 2010, Lexis Nexis Academic.

51. Christina Bellantoni, "McCain's Mockery Hits Rival as 'the One,'" *WT,* August 2, 2008, A1.

52. George Stephanopoulos, "Race for '08: Going Negative."

53. Interview with John M. Broder, February 19, 2009, and below.

54. USNews.com, "Political Humor: The Latest from Late-night Comedians," *Political Bulletin,* July 30, 2008, http://www.usnews.com/usnews/politics/bulletin/bulletin_080730.htm.

55. "Fox News All Stars," July 30, 2008.

56. Diane Sawyer, "Race for '08: Going Negative."

57. Jack Tapper in ibid.

58. Michelle Cottle in ibid.

59. Jeffrey T. Kuhner, "Celebrity Contender," *WT,* August 17, 2008, B3.

60. "An American Tradition?" *Talk of the Nation.*

61. Mike Barnicle, "Hardball for August 4, 2008," HB, MSNBC transcript, retrieved January 17, 2009, Lexis Nexis Academic.

62. Andrea Mitchell in ibid.

63. "Hastert on Impact of McCain Celebrity Ad," H&C, August 7, 2008.

64. Greg Pierce, "Inside Politics," *WT,* August 4, 2008, A6.

65. Ginger Adams Otis, "McC Spots are 'Cheap' Shots," *NYP,* August 3, 2008, 6; Tom Topousis, "Mama Rips McC: Leave Paris Alone!" *NYP,* August 4, 2008, 4.

66. PewResearchCenter Publications, August 5, 2008, http://pewresearch.org/pubs/919/spears-hilton-obama.

67. See "Gallup Daily: Election 2008," *Gallup.com,* http://www.gallup.com/poll/107674/Interactive-Graph-Follow-General-Election.aspx, results for July 29–31, 2008; Stephen Dinan, "McCain Takes Lead on YouTube Hits," *WT,* August 7, 2008, A1; Michael Finnegan, "TIMES/BLOOMBERG POLL: Obama and McCain in a Statistical Tie," *LAT,* August 20, 2008, http://articles.latimes.com/2008/aug/20/nation/na-p01120; Maggie Haberman, "McSurge—Poll Roll Blows Away O Lead; McCain Juggernaut Wipes Out O's Lead in Prez Polls," *NYP,* August 21, 2008, 1; Michael Cooper and Dalia Sussman, "Poll Shows Tight Race with Focus on Economy," *NYT,* August 21, 2008, A14.

68. Otis, "McC Spots are 'Cheap' Shots."

69. Topousis, "Mama Rips McC"; Ginger Adams Otis, "McC Spots are 'Cheap' Shots."

70. Pierce, "Inside Politics."

71. Dinan, "McCain Takes Lead."

72. Pruden, "Now a Campaign like All Others"; Dinan, "McCain Takes Lead."

73. Dinan, "McCain Takes Lead"; Christina Bellantoni, "Obama Responds to McCain with Own Negative Ad," *WT,* August 12, 2008, A1.

74. Maggie Haberman, "McSurge: Poll Roll Blows Away O Lead."

75. "Obama's Summer of Discontent," editorial, *WT,* August 26, 2008, A16.

76. "Chuck Todd, Andrea Mitchell, and Joshua Green of *The Atlantic* discuss the Presidential Campaign," *Meet the Press,* August 17, 2008, Federal News Service transcript, retrieved January 25, 2010, Lexis Nexis Academic, and below.

77. "Republican Strategist Ed Rollins on the Presidential Race," *The Early Show,* August 7, 2008, CBS News transcript, retrieved January 25, 2010, Lexis Nexis Academic.

78. "Race for '08: Going Negative."

79. *CBS Evening News,* July 31, 2008.

80. Monica Langley, "Democratic Convention: Meet Obama's Media 'Enforcer,'" *WSJ,* August 28, 2008, A4.

81. "New Campaign Ads," *Today,* July 31, 2008, and below.

82. Ibid.

83. Amanda Scott, "Message from David Plouffe: 'A Nasty Turn,'" Organizing for America, July 31, 2008, http://my.barackobama.com/page/community/post/amandascott/gGxYzH.

84. Michael Cooper, "McCain Says He Is Proud of 'Celebrity' Ad," *The Caucus,* July 31, 2008, http://thecaucus.blogs.nytimes.com/2008/07/31/mccain-says-he-is-proud-of-celebrity-ad/; also, see http://my.barackobama.com/page/content/mccainslowroadexpress/. A few days after the website launched, on August 4, 2008, the Obama campaign produced a TV ad by the same name (http://www.youtube.com/watch?v=RceGdwa9GRg).

85. "Senator John Kerry and Senator Joseph Lieberman Discuss 2008 Presidential Race," *Meet the Press,* August 3, 2008, NBC News transcript, retrieved January 25, 2010, Lexis Nexis Academic, and below.

86. Topousis, "Mama Rips McC."

87. Kate Sheehy, "New Paris Hilton Video Mocks 'Old' McCain," *NYP,* August 6, 2008, 25.

88. Michael Saul, "Who You Callin' a Celeb, Mac?" *Daily News,* August 12, 2008, 14, and below.

89. Kyle Smith, "Magilla Guerilla—At Film Fest, There's Only One Man They Love More Than O," *NYP,* September 14, 2008, 28.

90. "Republican Strategist Ed Rollins on the Presidential Race," *The Early Show.*

91. Charles Hurt, "Voters OD on Media 'O'-verkill," *NYP,* August 7, 2008, 18.

92. Carl Campanile, "O, What a Taxman: Mac," *NYP,* August 16, 2008, 2.

93. Maggie Haberman, "McSurge—Poll Roll Blows Away O Lead."

94. Carl Campanile, "Angry Ad Blitz a Real Snoot-out," *NYP,* August 23, 2008.

95. Jeffrey T. Kuhner, "Celebrity Contender."

96. Adam Nagourney, "Anxious Party Hopes to Show Strong Obama," *NYT,* August 25, 2008, A1, and below.

97. Bob Herbert, "Voters Want More from Obama," *NYT,* August 23, 2008, A19.

98. Frank Rich, "Last Call for Change We Can Believe In," *NYT,* August 24, 2008, and below.

99. Maureen Dowd, "High Anxiety in the Mile-high City," *NYT,* August 27, 2008, A23, and below.

100. Jim Rutenberg and Jeff Zeleny, "Democrats Work to Minimize Stadium Setting's Political Risks," *NYT,* August 28, 2008, A22.

101. Stephanie Simon, "Stadium Setting a Spectacular Gamble, Especially If Weather Turns Ugly," *WSJ,* August 26, 2008, http://online.wsj.com/article/SB121971501325271597. html.

102. Bill O'Reilly, "Talking Points Memo: Hilary and Barack," *The O'Reilly Factor,* August 28, 2008, http://www.foxnews.com/story/0,2933,412484,00.html.

103. Donald Lambro, "A Changeless Party?" *WT,* August 25, 2008, A12, and below.

104. Jeremy Olshan and Geoff Earle, "Temple of Dem on Mt. O-lympus—GOP Mocks Grand Stage for Bam as Greek Hubris," *NYP,* August 28, 6.

105. Charles Hurt, "Now Beware the Wily Mac," *NYP,* August 29, 2008, 6.

106. Charles Hurt, "Something New and Powerful," *NYP,* August 29, 2008, 29.

107. Jim Rutenberg and Jeff, Zeleny, "Democrats Try to Minimize Stadium's Political Risks," *NYT,* August 27, 2008, and below.

108. Jodi Kantor, "For a New Political Age, a Self-made Man," *NYT,* August 28, 2008, A1, and below.

109. For a television ethnography that describes the fusion Obama and the Democrats achieved with their audiences near and far on this last day of the Denver convention, see chapter 2. The quotations from Matthews, Todd, and Brokaw in the paragraph following are cited from this earlier discussion of the MSNBC television coverage that day.

110. James Poniewozik, "What's Wrong with Celebrity?" *Time* magazine, August 25, 2008, 21.

111. Hurt, "Something New and Powerful," and below.

112. "Barack Obama Speaks at Democratic Convention; Peggy Noonan of the *Wall Street Journal* Discusses Subject," *Today Show,* August 29, 2008, NBC News transcript, retrieved January 25, 2010, Lexis Nexis Academic, and below.

CHAPTER 8

1. William Kristol, "A Star Is Born?" *NYT,* September 1, 2008, A17.

2. Elisabeth Bumiller and Michael Cooper, "Selecting Palin, McCain Falls Back on History of Instinctive, Often Risky Moves," *NYT,* August 31, 2008, A26.

3. Kristol, "A Star Is Born?"

4. Ibid. Indeed, Palin's debut on the stage contributed to the highest week of media coverage during the 2008 election (August 25–31). According to the News Coverage Index of the Pew Center for Excellence in Journalism, campaign news accounted for 69 percent of the newshole for that week, and the narratives about the candidates' VP picks and events related to the Democratic convention made up more than 80 percent of that coverage.

5. Ken Khachigian, "Who'll Be McCain's Veep? Who Cares?" *WSJ,* July 25, 2008, A13, and below.

6. Laura Meckler, Elizabeth Holmes, and Jim Carlton, "McCain's Surprise V.P. Choice—Alaska's Gov. Palin Targets Those Stung by Clinton's Loss," *WSJ,* August 30, 2008, A1.

7. Richard Wolffe, *Renegade: The Making of a President* (New York: Crown, 2009), 226; Robert Draper, "The Making (and Remaking) of the Candidate," *New York Times Magazine,* October 22, 2008.

8. Donald Lambro, "Where There's Fervor," *WT,* September 4, 2008, A16.

9. Meckler, Holmes, and Carlton, "McCain's Surprise V.P. Choice," and below.

10. Draper, "Making (and Remaking) of the Candidate," and below.

11. Pete Baker, "The Party in Power, Running as if It Weren't," *NYT,* September 5, 2008, A1.

12. Stephen F. Hayes, "How Palin Got Picked," *WS* 13(48), September 8, 2008, and below.

13. Andrew Breitbart, "Say It Ain't So, O!" RealClearPolitics.com, September 8, 2008, http://www.realclearpolitics.com/articles/2008/09/say_it_aint_so_o.html.

14. Baker, "Party in Power, Running as if It Weren't," and below.

15. David Brooks, "What the Palin Pick Says," *NYT,* September 2, 2008, A23.

16. Laura Meckler, "GOP Opens Convention with Unexpected Items Topping the Agenda," *WSJ,* September 2, 2008, A4.

17. Patrick Healy, "A Riveting Speaker, Waving the Flag," *NYT,* October 14, 2008, A19.

18. Gerald F. Seib, "Palin Pitches Sam's Club Tent," and below.

19. "Transcript: Weekend of September 7, 2008," *The Chris Matthews Show,* http://www.thechrismatthewsshow.com/html/transcript/index.php?selected=1&id=127.

20. Meckler, "GOP Opens Convention with Unexpected Items."

21. Seib, "Palin Pitches Sam's Club Tent."

22. Meckler, Holmes, and Carlton, "McCain's Surprise V.P. Choice," and following.

23. Chris Matthews and Andrea Mitchell, *Hardball,* August 30, 2008, MSNBC.

24. Monica Davey, "Daughter's Pregnancy Interrupts G.O.P. Convention Script," *NYT,* September 2, 2008, A19.

25. David Brooks, "A Glimpse of the New," *NYT,* September 4, 2008.

26. The following quotations from Kim Severson, "They Raise Children, Pray and Support Palin," *NYT,* September 4, 2008.

27. G. N. Miller, Carl Campanile, and Chuck Bennett, "This Is No Way to Treat a Lady—GOPers Stand Up for Sarah," *NYP,* September 3, 2008, 5.

28. Kantor, Zernike, and Einhorn, "Fusing Politics and Motherhood in a New Way."

29. Michael Scherer, "The Sarah Show: A Front-Row View of Sarah Palin's Campaign and Why Her Grip on Women's Voters Is Likely to Last," *Time* magazine 172(12) September 22, 2008.

30. Bumiller, "Palin Disclosures Spotlight McCain's Screening Process."

31. Meckler, "McCain's Surprise V.P. Choice."

32. Kristol, "A Star Is Born?"

33. Katherine Roberts, "A Western State of Mind," *NYT,* September 14, 2008, and below.

34. Draper, "Making (and Remaking) of the Candidate," and below.

35. Ibid.

36. Ellen Byron, Jennifer Saranow, and Rachel Dodes, "Palin's Style Sparks Buying Frenzy, and Fashion Firms Rush to Cash In," *WSJ,* September 12, 2008, A1, and below.

37. "Eye-catching Trend; Palin's Specs Draw Attention," *Good Morning America,* September 7, 2008, ABC News transcript, retrieved January 25, 2010, Lexis Nexis Academic, and below.

38. Mary Ann Giordano, "Action Figures: Back Off, GI Joe," *NYT,* September 14, 2008, A20.

39. Jan Hoffman, "The Upshot on Palin and Her Updo, *NYT,* September 12, 2008.

40. Ellen Byron, Jennifer Saranow, and Rachel Dodes, "Palin's Style Sparks Buying Frenzy, and Fashion Firms Rush to Cash In; Wig Sellers Capitalize on Upswept Hairdo; Naughty Monkey's Red Heels Get a Lift," *WSJ,* September 12, 2008, A1.

41. Chris Matthews, Michelle Bernard, and Pat Buchanan, "Hardball for September 4, 2008," HB, MSNBC transcript, retrieved January 17, 2009, Lexis Nexis Academic.

42. Jeff Zeleny, "Feeling a Challenge, Obama Sharpens His Silver Tongue," *NYT,* September 10, 2008, A20, and below.

43. Adam Nagourney and Jeff Zeleny, "Obama Plans Sharper Tone as Party Frets," *NYT,* September 11, 2008.

44. Wolffe, *Renegade,* 226, and below.

45. Monica Langley, "As Economic Crisis Peaked, Tide Turned against McCain," *WSJ,* November 5, 2008.

46. Lambro, "Where There's Fervor."

47. Wolffe, *Renegade,* 226.

48. Patrick Healy and Michael Cooper, "Rival Tickets Are Redrawing Battlegrounds: Palin Helps G.O.P. Put More States in Play," *NYT,* September 7, 2008, A1.

49. David Brooks, "Surprise Me Most," *NYT,* September 9, 2008, A27.

50. John P. Avlon, "What Independent Voters Want: They Tend to Be Fiscally Conservative and Strong on Security," *WSJ,* October 20, 2008, A1.

51. Wolffe, *Renegade,* 226.

52. Langley, "As Economic Crisis Peaked."

53. Nagourney and Zeleny, "Obama Plans Sharper Tone as Party Frets."

54. Zeleny, "Feeling a Challenge."

55. Nagourney and Zeleny, "Obama Plans Sharper Tone as Party Frets," and below.

56. Zeleny, "Feeling a Challenge."

57. E. J. Dionne Jr., "Tiptoeing through the Mud," *WP,* September 12, 2008, A15, and below.

58. Thomas L. Friedman, "From the Gut," *NYT,* September 10, 2008, A25, and below.

59. Jim Rutenberg and Monica Davey, "Squad of G.O.P. Aides Prepares Palin for Interviews," *NYT,* September 10, 2008, A23, and below.

60. Rutenberg and Davey, "Squad of G.O.P. Aides Prepares Palin."

61. Howard Kurtz, "Palin and Press: A Testy Start," *WP,* September 8, 2008, C2.

62. "Coping with Sarah Palin; Palin's Silence Questioned," *World News Sunday,* September 7, 2008, ABC News transcript, retrieved January 25, 2010, Lexis Nexis Academic, and below.

63. Hannity and Colmes. "Fred Thompson Weighs In on Election," H&C, September 8, 2008, FNN transcript, retrieved January 24, 2009, Lexis Nexis Academic.

64. Shailagh Murray, "Obama Rails against Attacks from Palin, GOP; Democrat Denounces 'Slash-and-Burn Politics,'" *WP,* September 5, 2008, A31.

65. Chuck Todd and Andrea Mitchell, "For August 29, 2008," HB, MSNBC transcript, retrieved January 24, 2010, Lexis Nexis Academic, and below.

66. Meckler, "McCain's Surprise V.P. Choice," and below.

67. Peter Wallsten, "McCain's Choice of Palin Is a Risk," *Latimes.com*, August 30, 2008.

68. Elisabeth Bumiller and Michael Cooper, "Conservative Ire Pushed McCain From Lieberman," *NYT* August 30, 2008, A26, and below.

69. Jodi Kantor and Rachel Swarns, "A New Twist in the Debate on Mothers," *NYT*, September 1, 2008, A1, and below. For a fuller discussion of the gender-family controversy and the Palin campaign, see chapter 6.

70. Adam Nagourney, "In Political Realm, 'Family Problem' Emerges as Test and Distraction," *NYT*, September 2, 2008, A18.

71. Monica Davey, "Palin Daughter's Pregnancy Interrupts G.O.P. Convention Script," *NYT*, September 1, 2008, and below.

72. Meckler, "GOP Opens Convention with Unexpected Items," and below.

73. Kristol, "A Star Is Born?"

74. Peter Wallsten, "Stakes of McCain Bet Are Clearer; Details Emerge One after Another, and the Campaign Can't Be Sure What Will Capture or Hold Public Interest," *LAT*, September 2, 2008, A11, and below.

75. Elisabeth Bumiller, "Palin Disclosures Spotlight McCain's Screening Process; Daughter's Pregnancy One of Several Revelations," *NYT*, September 2, 2008, A1, and below.

76. Nagourney, "In Political Realm," and below.

77. Brooks, "What the Palin Pick Says," and below.

78. Nagourney, "In Political Realm," and below.

79. Davey, "Palin's Daughter's Pregnancy Interrupts," and below.

80. Jim Rutenberg, "The Caucus: Fallout for Larry King," *NYT*, September 3, 2008, A16, and below.

81. Howard Fineman, "Hardball for September 2, 2008," HB, MSNBC transcript, retrieved January 24, 2010, Lexis Nexis Academic.

82. Kurtz, "Palin and Press," and below.

83. Seib, "Palin Pitches Sam's Club Tent"; emphasis added.

84. June Kronholz, "Palin's Pitch to Parents of Disabled Raises Some Doubts—Support Is Pledged, but the GOP Ticket Seeks Spending Cuts," *WSJ*, September 8, 2008, A5, and below.

85. Laura Meckler, "Palin, on TV, Says U.S. Should Defend Its Allies," *WSJ*, September 12, 2008, A6, and below.

86. Jim Rutenberg and Monica Davey, "Squad of G.O.P. Aides Prepares Palin for Interviews," http://www.nytimes.com/2008/09/11/us/politics/11palin.html.

87. "In Search of Gov. Palin," editorial, *NYT*, September 10, 2008, A24, and below.

88. E. J. Dionne Jr., "Pulling the Curtain on Palin," *WP*, September 9, 2008, A23, and below.

89. Tim Rutten, "Palin's Privacy versus Her Public Stance. She, her husband and daughter got to make private decisions privately. But her public views would deny that same right to other Americans." Latimes.com, September 3, 2008.

90. Lisa Fletcher, "Northern Exposure; Life in Wasilla," *Nightline*, September 5, 2008, ABC News transcript, retrieved January 25, 2010, Lexis Nexis Academic.

91. Kurtz, "Palin and Press."

92. Maureen Dowd, "My Fair Veep," *NYT*, September 10, 2008, A25.

93. Karl Vick and James V. Grimaldi, "Palin's Family Has Always Held a Place in Her Politics," *WP*, September 7, 2008, A1, and below.

94. James V. Grimaldi, "Palin's Ex-Brother-in-Law Says He Regrets Bad Blood," *WP*, September 6, 2008, A7, and below.

95. Savannah Guthrie, "Investigation into Sarah Palin's Firing of Top Law Enforcement Official," *Saturday Today*, September 6, 2008, NBC News transcript, retrieved January 25, 2010, Lexis Nexis Academic, and below.

96. "An In-depth Look at Sarah Palin," *CNN Newsroom*, September 6, 2008, CNN transcript, retrieved January 25, 2010, Lexis Nexis Academic, and below.

97. Vick and Grimaldi, "Palin's Family Has Always held a Place," and below.

98. Karl Vick, "Governor Is Asked to Release E-mails," *WP*, September 10, 2008, A4, and below.

99. James V. Grimaldi and Karl Vick, "Palin Billed State for Nights Spent at Home; Taxpayers. Also Funded Family's Travel," *WP*, September 9, 2008, A1, and below.

100. Michael M. Phillips, "Alaska Officials Weigh Subpoenas for Palin Staff over Firing," *WSJ*, September 8, A5, and below.

101. Michael M. Phillips, "In Palin's Past, the Personal Got Political; An Aide's Affair May Have Become Grounds for Firing," *WSJ*, September 9, 2008, A6, and below.

102. Jim Carlton, "Ethics Adviser Warned Palin about Trooper Issue; Letter Described Situation as 'Grave,' Called for Apology," *WSJ*, September 11, 2008, A8, and below.

103. Nathan Thornburgh, "Mayor Palin: A Rough Record," *Time.com*, September 2, 2008.

104. "An In-depth Look at Sarah Palin," *CNN Newsroom*.

105. "Whole Truth about Some Claims Made by Sarah Palin," *NBC Nightly News*, September 9, 2008, NBC News transcript, retrieved January 25, 2010, Lexis Nexis Academic.

106. "Facts behind Palin's Involvement in Bridge to Nowhere," *CBS Evening News*, September 9, 2008, CBS News transcript, retrieved January 25, 2010, Lexis Nexis Academic.

107. "Palin and the Librarian; Did Palin Try to Ban Books?" *Good Morning America*, September 10, 2008, ABC News transcript, retrieved January 25, 2010, Lexis Nexis Academic.

108. Jo Becker, Peter S. Goodman, and Michael Powell, "Once Elected, Palin Hired Friends and Lashed Foes; Governor's Style of Politics Is Highly Personal," *NYT*, September 14, 2008, A1, and below.

109. Michael Powell, interview by author, September 26, 2008, and below.

110. Rutenberg and Davey, "Squad of G.O.P. Aides Prepares Palin," and below.

111. Dowd, "My Fair Veep."

112. "Excerpts: Charlie Gibson Interviews Sarah Palin," Abcnews.go.com, September 11, 2008.

113. Jim Rutenberg, "In First Big Interview, Palin Says 'I'm ready' for the Job," *NYT*, September 12, 2008, A1.

114. Alessandra Stanley, "TV Watch: Showing a Confidence, in Prepared Answers," *NYT,* September 12, 2008, A19, and below.

115. "Matt Damon Rips Sarah Palin," posted by CBS News on September 10, 2008, http://www.youtube.com/watch?v=C6urw_PWHYk.

116. Alessandra Stanley, "TV Watch: A Question Reprised, but the Words Came None Too Easily for Palin," *NYT,* September 25, 2008, http://www.nytimes.com/2008/09/26/us/politics/26watch.html, and below.

117. As with the Gibson piece, Palin's postinterview popularity on YouTube depended on the numerous short clips of particular sound bites, such as "Couric Stumps Palin with Supreme Court Question," at 1,158,379 views, on or around December 9, 2009 (http://www.youtube.com/watch?v=0rXmuhWrlj4); "Sarah Palin Can't Name a Newspaper She Reads," at 1,367,808 views for the month of October alone and more than 1.9 million on or around December 9, 2009 (http://www.youtube.com/watch?v=xRkWebP2Q0Y); and CBS's own brief (1:29) clip titled "Palin on Foreign Policy," at an astounding 3,248,111 views on or around December 9, 2009 (http://www.youtube.com/watch?v=nokTjEdaUGg).

118. Rich Lowry, "Palin on CBS," *The Corner (National Review* blog), September 27, 2008, http://corner.nationalreview.com/post/?q=MDY2MDBjNGQ1MWY40TY3N2JhZD k20TcwOTkxMTYzZWY.

119. Rod Dreher, "Palin Debacle on CBS Evening News," *CRUNCHY CON (beliefnet. com* blog), September 25, 2008, http://blog.beliefnet.com/crunchycon/2008/09/palin-deba-cle-on-cbs-evening-n.html.

120. Jack Cafferty, "President & Dems vs. House GOP; Dems: McCain Hurt Negotiations; Obama Ready to Debate," *The Situation Room,* September 26, 2008, CNN transcript, retrieved January 20, 2010, Lexis Nexis Academic. In fact, Cafferty's remarks were watched and rewatched millions of times online, with one YouTube video alone receiving more than 3 million hits during the election ("Jack Cafferty Tells Us How He Really Feels about Palin," posted September 26, 2008, by *TPMTV* [Talking Points Memo TV], http://www.youtube.com/watch?v=L8__aXxXPVc).

121. Kathleen Parker, "Palin Problem: She's Out of Her League," *National Review Online,* September 26, 2008, and below.

122. David Brooks, "Why Experience Matters," *NYT,* September 16, 2008, A29, and below.

123. Rachel Sklar, "SNL Opener: Tina Fey Does Palin," *HP,* September 14, 2008, http://www.huffingtonpost.com/2008/09/14/snl-opener-tina-fey-does_n_126256.html.

124. "Do you think Tina Fey did a good job playing Sarah Palin on the season premiere of SNL?" *The Insider* (CBS blog), September 15, 2008, http://www.theinsider.com/polls/1192922_Do_you_think_Tina_Fey_did_a_good_job_playing_Sarah_Palin_on_the_season_premiere_of_SNL. The final polls results were these: "Yes, the acting was dead on, and I hope to see more of Tina as Palin this season" (86 percent) and "No, I thought it was nothing like Sarah Palin" (14 percent).

125. Andrew Wallenstein, "NBC's Web Sites See Surge in Traffic," *HollywoodReporter. com,* September 18, 2008, http://www.hollywoodreporter.com/hr/content_display/news/e3i8fcb5100629836e60f2b946f58f168aa. Tens of millions watched the Tina Fey spots in one form or another online, including one video that featured the SNL version immediately

followed by the actual CBS interview ("SNL Sarah Palin Interview vs. Real Sarah Palin"), which alone garnered more than 1.3 million views (http://www.youtube.com/watch?v=tjZW4z9zqqY, posted September 28, 2008).

126. A segment from CNN's *Late Edition,* posted on September 28, 2008 ("CNN Laughs It Up over Sarah Palin Interview"), returns as number five in the "most viewed" results for a YouTube search using simply "Sarah Palin," at 4,675,256 views, on or around December 9, 2009 (http://www.youtube.com/watch?v=zeMypXCUWMw). A CELEBTV.com copy of the September 16 SNL skit, with "Hillary," is number one and has been viewed nearly 10 million times on or around December 9, 2009 ("Sarah Palin, Tina Fey, on SNL," posted September 28, 2008, http://www.youtube.com/watch?v=FdDqSvJ6aHc).

127. Rebecca Dana, "So Four Candidates Enter the Election...TV Comedians Feast on Political Fodder," *WSJ,* October 9, 2008, A10.

128. "Gov. Palin's Worldview," editorial, *New York Times,* September 12, 2008, and below.

129. Michael Cooper and Jim Rutenberg, "McCain Barbs Stirring Outcry as Distortions," *NYT,* September 13, 2008, A1, and below.

130. Jonathan Weisman, "Obama Campaign Begins Counterattack," *WP,* September 13, 2008, A3.

131. See the *Huffington Post* blog entry at http://www.huffingtonpost.com/2008/09/12/mccain-grilled-on-the-vie_n_125972.html (September 12, 2008).

132. "John McCain Buried in Pile of Angry 'View' Hosts," *Wonkette: The DC Gossip,* wonkette.com (blog), September 12, 2008, http://wonkette.com/402744/john-mccain-buried-in-pile-of-angry-view-hosts/.

133. Cooper and Rutenberg, "McCain Barbs Stirring Outcry as Distortions," and below.

134. "The Reality behind the Claims," *NYT,* September 13, 2008, A14, and below.

135. Zeleny, "Feeling a Challenge."

136. Wolffe, *Renegade,* 227.

137. Cooper and Rutenberg, "McCain Barbs Stirring Outcry," and below.

138. "'Honor' Ad," posted September 14, 2008, by BarackObamadotcom, http://www.youtube.com/watch?v=CK3Y1KPzW9k.

139. Sara Murray, "Palin Bump Falls Flat in Some Swing States," *WSJ,* September 12, 2008, A6, and below.

140. Robin Toner and Adam Nagourney, "McCain Seen as Less Likely to Bring Change, Poll Finds," *NYT,* September 18, 2008, A1, and below.

141. Laura Meckler, "Financial Crisis Has Little Sway in Presidential Poll," *WSJ,* September 24, 2008, A16.

142. Gary Langer, "Sarah Palin Boom Busts: Poll Casts Doubt on Experience prior to Vice Presidential Debate," *ABC News Polling Unit,* October 2, 2008, http://abcnews.go.com/PollingUnit/Politics/story?id=5930646&page=1; see charts and full questionnaire at "Views of Palin Sour Sharply; Six in 10 Doubt Her Readiness," *ABC NEWS/WASHINGTON POST POLL: PALIN/BIDEN,* October 2, 2008, http://abcnews.go.com/images/PollingUnit/1074a3PalinBiden.pdf.

143. Adam Nagourney, "Concerns about Palin's Readiness as a Big Test for Her Nears," *NYT,* September 30, 2008, A16.

CHAPTER 9

1. Vikas Bajaj, "A Wall Street Goliath Teeters amid Fears of a Widening Crisis," *NYT,* September 14, 2008, A1.

2. Alex Berenson, "A Financial Drama with No Final Act in Sight," *NYT,* September 14, 2008.

3. Elisabeth Bumiller, "With Palin at His Side, McCain Finds Energized Crowds," *NYT,* September 11, 2008, A23.

4. Paul Krugman, "Blizzard of Lies," *NYT,* September 12, 2008, A23; also Frank Rich, "The Palin-Whatshisname Ticket," and Thomas Friedman, "Making America Stupid," *NYT,* September 14, 2008.

5. Adam Nagourney, "Carefully Shaped Message Now a Campaign Relic," *NYT,* September 16, 2008, A22. For an analysis of Nagourney's story as a revealing, if exaggerated, argument about the difficulty of communication in the context of performative defusion, see pp. 17–18 above.

6. "Andrea Mitchell of NBC News, Joe Scarborough of MSNBC, David Brooks of the *New York Times,* and Jon Meacham of *Newsweek* Discuss the 2008 Presidential Campaign," *Meet the Press,* October 19, 2008, NBC News transcript, retrieved January 19, 2009, Lexis Nexis Academic.

7. Jenny Anderson, Andrew Ross Sorkin, and Ben White, "Financial Crisis Reshapes Wall Street's Landscape; Merrill Is Sold; Failing to Find Buyer, Lehman Bros. Is Set to Wind Down," *NYT,* September 15, 2008, A1.

8. *NYT,* September 16, 2008, A1.

9. *NYT,* September 18, 2008, A1.

10. Floyd Norris and Vikas Bajaj, "News Analysis: A Jittery Road Ahead," *NYT,* September 15, 2008, A1.

11. Anderson, Sorkin, and White, "Financial Crisis Reshapes," and below.

12. Michiko Kakutani, "Exuberant Riffs on a Land Run Amok," *NYT,* September 15, 2008, E6.

13. "Washington Takes on the Feel of Wartime" is the jump head on p. 15 for Jackie Calms, "Political Memo: Dazed Capital Feels Its Way, Eyes on the Election," *NYT,* September 20, 2008, A1, and below.

14. Monica Langley, "As Economic Crisis Peaked, Tide Turned against McCain," *WSJ,* November 5, 2008, A1.

15. John Harwood, "Policies Sound the Same, but Goals Are Different," *NYT,* September 22, 2008, A16.

16. Elizabeth Holmes, Laura Meckler, and Nick Timiraos, "The Financial Crisis: McCain, Obama Jockey for Position on Economy," *WSJ,* September 19, 2008, A7.

17. Kate Phillips, "Last Words: Economic Game-Changer," *The Caucus,* September 15, 2008, http://thecaucus.blogs.nytimes.com/2008/09/15/last-words-perhaps/.

18. A YouTube search returns about 100 videos on the topic, with the most views going to a compilation of this and the several other times McCain has declared strong "fundamentals," posted by Brave New Films on September 30, 2008 ("John McCain: Economic Disaster," http://www.youtube.com/watch?v=C4egXbhSOhk [436,476 views on or around January 20, 2010]). The Obama campaign's response, titled simply

"Fundamentals," received just over 207,000 views (on or around December 9, 2009) on YouTube (posted by BarackObamadotcom on September 15, 2008, http://www.youtube.com/watch?v=6reQLzgywzk).

19. "Mr. McCain and the Economy," editorial, *NYT,* September 17, 2008, A26, and below.

20. Holmes, Meckler, and Timiraos, "Financial Crisis."

21. John M. Broder, "With Economy Slowing, All Speeches Are Turning to It," *NYT,* January 12, 2008, A1.

22. John M. Broder, "Obama, Adopting Economic Theme, Criticizes McCain," *NYT,* June 10, 2008, A1.

23. Amy Chozick and Laura Meckler, "Obama, Bernanke Talk Economy—Democrat Seeks Tougher Oversight," *WSJ,* July 30, 2008, A5.

24. Bob Davis, Damian Paletta, and Rebecca Smith, "Unraveling Reagan: Amid Turmoil, U.S. Turns Away from Decades of Deregulation," *WSJ,* July 25, 2009, A1.

25. Chozick and Meckler, "Obama, Bernanke Talk Economy."

26. Jeff Zeleny, "Obama Looks to Shift Focus of Campaign to Economy," *NYT,* September 17, 2008, A21, and below.

27. Marjorie Connelly, "Growing Interest in Campaign," *NYT,* September 20, 2008, A13.

28. Ibid.

29. Jeff Zeleny, "Obama Cautions Florida Voters on McCain," *NYT,* September 21, 2008, A24, and below. See also "The McCain Gamble," posted by BarackObamadotcom on September 12, 2008, http://www.youtube.com/watch?v=oHazb4FAREE.

30. Zeleny, "Obama Looks to Shift Focus," and below.

31. See "Plan for Change Ad," posted by BarackObamadotcom on September 16, 2008, http://www.youtube.com/watch?v=ONM7148cTyc (approx. 275,000 views in the first 48 hours: total = 739,770 views on or around December 9, 2009); Julie Bosman, "No Attacks, Just an Economic Plan," *NYT,* September 18, 2008, A22.

32. Michael Cooper, "McCain Laboring to Hit Right Note on the Economy," *NYT,* September 17, 2008, A1, and below.

33. Calms, "Political Memo: Dazed Capital Feels Its Way."

34. Holmes, Meckler, and Timiraos, "Financial Crisis."

35. Laura Meckler, Elizabeth Holmes, and Nick Timiraos, "Candidates Keep Their Bailout Stances to Themselves—As Senators, Both Will Vote on Plan; Concept Embraced," *WSJ,* September 23, 2008, A18.

36. Lanny J. Davis, "The GOP Leads a 'Socialist' Bailout," *WSJ,* September 22, 2008, A21.

37. Gail Collins, "The McCain of the Week," *NYT,* September 18, 2008, A35.

38. Robert Draper, "The Making (and Remaking) of a Candidate," *New York Times Magazine,* October 22, 2008, and below.

39. Laura Meckler, Elizabeth Holmes, and Christopher Cooper, "Financial Crisis Upends Campaign—Obama Rebuffs McCain's Request to Postpone Debate; Voters Divided over Bailout," *WSJ,* September 25, 2008, A1, and below.

40. Langley, "As Economic Crisis Peaked, Tide Turned against McCain."

41. Draper, "Making (and Remaking) of a Candidate," and below.

42. Elisabeth Bumiller and Jeff Zeleny, "First Debate Up in Air as McCain Steps off the Trail," *NYT,* September 25, 2008, A1.

43. Elisabeth Bumiller and Jeff Zeleny, "With Debate Uncertain, Candidates Meet Bush," *NYT,* September 26, 2008, A1.

44. Meckler, Holmes, and Cooper, "Financial Crisis Upends Campaign," and below.

45. Draper, "Making (and Remaking) of a Candidate," and below.

46. John D. McKinnon, Laura Meckler, and Christopher Cooper, "The Financial Crisis: An Inside View of a Stormy White House Summit," *WSJ,* September 27, 2008, A2, and below.

47. Greg Hitt, Sarah Lueck, and Deborah Solomon, "Bailout Compromise Gets New Life," *WSJ,* September 27, 2008, A1.

48. McKinnon, Meckler, and Cooper, "Inside View of a Stormy White House Summit," and below.

49. Sheryl Gay Stolberg and Elisabeth Bumiller, "A Balancing Act as McCain Faces a Divided Party and a Skeptical Public," *NYT,* September 27, 2008, A15.

50. Draper, "Making (and Remaking) of a Candidate," and below.

51. Ibid.

52. Langley, "As Economic Crisis Peaked, Tide Turned against McCain."

53. Daniel Henninger, "The Financial Crisis Is McCain's Katrina," *WSJ,* October 16, 2008, A13.

54. "The First Debate," editorial, *NYT,* September 27, 2008, A20; emphasis added.

55. McKinnon, Meckler, and Cooper, "Inside View of a Stormy White House Summit"; emphasis added.

56. Meckler, Holmes, and Cooper, "Financial Crisis Upends Campaign."

57. Gerald F. Seib, "Capital Journal: Foreign-policy Exchanges Highlight Sharp Differences," *WSJ,* September 27, 2008, A6.

58. Michael Cooper and Elisabeth Bumiller, "Qualified Support for Bailout; Sharp Exchanges on Foreign Issues," *NYT,* September 27, 2008, A1.

59. Patrick Healy, "On Bailout, Candidates Were Surely Themselves," *NYT,* September 29, 2008, A16, and below.

60. William Kristol, "How McCain Wins," *NYT,* September 29, 2008, A21, and below.

61. Langley, "As Economic Crisis Peaked, Tide Turned against McCain."

62. Michael Cooper and Jeff Zeleny, "With Deal's Collapse, the McCain Camp Attacks," *NYT,* September 30, 2008, A25.

63. Adam Nagourney and Megan Thee, "Poll Finds Obama Gaining Support and McCain Weakened in Bailout Crisis," *NYT,* October 2, 2008, A27, and below.

64. Laura Meckler and Nick Timiraos, "McCain Abandons Michigan as State Contests Shift," and below.

65. Seib, "Capital Journal: McCain's Best Shot."

66. Laura Meckler, "Independent Voters Move toward Obama—New Poll Indicates That Democrat Is Benefiting from Financial Crisis," *WSJ,* October 7, 2008, A12, and below.

67. Michael Cooper, "McCain Abandons His Efforts to Win Michigan," *NYT,* October 3, 2008, A20.

68. Adam Nagourney and Elisabeth Bumiller, "Republicans Voicing Concern after Rough Week for McCain," *NYT,* October 12, 2008, A1.

69. Gerald Seib, "A McCain Comeback May Rely on Feeling the Nation's Anger," *WSJ*, October 7, 2008.

70. Kate Phillips, "Palin: Obama Is 'Palling around with Terrorists,'" *The Caucus*, October 4, 2008, http://thecaucus.blogs.nytimes.com/2008/10/04/palin-obama-is-palling-around-with-terrorists/, and below.

71. Julie Bosman, "Palin Plays to Conservative Base in Florida Rallies," *NYT*, October 8, 2008, A20, and below.

72. Indeed, one of the most watched (number four with 747,438 views on or around December 9, 2009) of the McCain campaign's videos was "Ayers," nearly two minutes on how Obama is hiding his friendship with "domestic terrorist" Ayers even though he "launched his political career in Ayers's living room." However, the friendship with "terrorist William Ayers" is not the issue—it's "Barack Obama's judgment and candor" ("Ayers," posted by JohnMcCaindotcom on October 8, 2009, http://www.youtube.com/watch?v=ONfJ7YSXE5w).

73. Julie Bosman, "Palin Plays to Conservative Base in Florida Rallies," *NYT*, October 7, 2008.

74. "Politics of Attack," editorial, *NYT*, October 8, 2008, A30, quoted from the *Washington Post*.

75. See "Dangerous," posted by JohnMcCaindotcom on October 5, 2008, http://www.youtube.com/watch?v=PjEKRIBDv6Q&feature=channel. It is one a series of TV ads launched between October 5 and October 10, which all ask, "Who is Barack Obama?" and provide an answer. "Ambition" says he is a man of "blind ambition" and "bad judgment" who associates with terrorists "when convenient" (posted October 9, 2008, http://www.youtube.com/watch?v=M9JNna5EmJg&feature=channel). "ACORN" reaffirms these traits and describes his ties to a group that engaged in "intimidation tactics" and "nationwide voter fraud" (posted October 10, 2008, http://www.youtube.com/watch?v=0dlnt9maBJA&feature=channel).

76. "Full Remarks of McCain in Albuquerque, New Mexico," *The Page: Politics up to the Minute* (*TIME.com* blog), October 7, 2008, http://thepage.time.com/full-remarks-of-mccain-in-albuquerque-new-mexico/.

77. Elisabeth Bumiller, "McCain Excites Crowd with Criticism of Obama," *NYT*, October 9, 2008, A23, and below.

78. Elisabeth Bumiller and Patrick Healy, "McCain Joins Attacks on Obama over Radical," *NYT*, October 10, 2008, A23, and below.

79. Elisabeth Bumiller, "McCain Excites Crowd."

80. Ibid.

81. Jim Rutenberg, "A Day after McCain and Obama Face Off, a Debate over Who Won," *NYT*, September 28, 2008, A26.

82. Sarah Wheaton, "The Republican Nominee: A Primer on Testiness," *NYT*, October 2, 2008, A28.

83. Katharine Q. Seelye, "Two Words Touch Off a Lot More of Them," *NYT*, October 9, 2008, A22.

84. Elisabeth Bumiller, "Tempering Attacks, McCain Says He's a Leader for Troubled Times," *NYT*, October 14, 2008, A17, and below.

85. "Politics of Attack," editorial.

86. Maureen Dowd, "Tao of Lee Atwater," *NYT,* October 8, 2008, A31, and below.

87. Mark Leibovich, "For Karl Rove, a Busy New Career and a 'Rovian' Legacy," *NYT,* October 11, 2008, A11, and below.

88. See Jeffrey C. Alexander, "Watergate as Democratic Ritual," in Jeffrey C. Alexander, *The Meanings of Social Life: A Cultural Sociology,* 155–178 (New York: Oxford University Press, 2004 [1987]), and Michael Schudson, *Watergate in American Memory: How We Remember, Forget, and Reconstruct the Past* (New York: Perseus, 1992).

89. Michael Cooper and Megan Thee, "Poll Says McCain Is Hurting His Bid by Using Attacks; Recent Shift Backfires; Numbers Up for Obama Ahead of the Final 3 Weeks of the Race," *NYT,* October 15, 2008, A1, and below.

90. David Brooks, "Thinking about Obama," October 17, 2008, A33, and below.

91. Brian Stelter, "The Caucus: Popular, and Over at Last," *NYT,* October 17, 2008, A20.

EPILOGUE

1. Peter Baker, "A Year Later, a Daily Grind: The Glow of Obama's Election Has Long Faded," *NYT,* November 4, 2009, A19, and below.

2. See Inge Schmidt, "When Good Ballots Go Bad: Voting Ritual (and Its Failure) in the United States," PhD diss., Department of Sociology, Yale University, 2010.

3. A special "Obama Issue" of the *Journal of Visual Culture* published in August 2009 gives breathless scholarly voice to the iconic spirit that marks the transition period. Avowing that "Obama is unquestionly the most visible of U.S. presidents to date," W.J.T. Mitchell, a leading philosopher of the visual, suggests "this is partly an effect of ... the personal beauty of himself and his family, his sculpted facial features, his body image especially in motions that reveal athleticism" ("Obama as Icon," *Journal of Visual Culture* 8 [2] 2009: 125–129, p. 125). Celebrating Shephard Fairey's Obama posters, so ubiquitous that they provided an official emblem for the inauguration, John Armitage and Joy Garnet exclaim that the images "bring people together in struggle and they show that this struggle can be given expression ... through transformations of single news photograph into artworks that describe [a] man whose very likeness has come to embody hope" ("Obama and Shephard Fairey: The Copy and Political Iconography in the Age of the Demake [*sic*]," in ibid., 172–183, p. 183).

4. For a related analysis of the fate of heroes, one that more closely hues to the Weberian framework of charisma and its institutionalization, see Bernhard Giesen, "Inbetweenness and Ambivalence," in J. Alexander, Ronald Jacobs, and Philip Smith, eds., *The Oxford Handbook of Cultural Sociology* (New York: Oxford, 2011).

NOTE ON CONCEPT AND METHOD

1. Jeffrey C. Alexander, *Positivism, Presuppositions, and Current Controversies,* vol. 1 of Jeffrey C. Alexander, *Theoretical Logic in Sociology* (4 vols.) (Berkeley: University of California Press, 1982).

2. Jeffrey C. Alexander, *The Civil Sphere* (New York: Oxford University Press, 2006), 39–42, 110–14.

3. Steven Sherwood, Jeffrey C. Alexander, and Philip Smith, "Risking Enchantment: Theory and Methodology in Cultural Analysis," *Culture* 8(1) 1993: 10–14.

4. Plato, *The Republic*, trans. Francis MacDonald Cornford (New York: Oxford University Press, 1965), part I, chapter 3, 18.

5. Thomas Hobbes, *Leviathan: The Matter, Form, and Power of a Common Wealth Ecclesiastical and Civil,* 1651; John Locke, *The Second Treatise on Government: An Essay concerning the True Original, Extent, and End of Civil Government,* 1694; Max Weber, "Politics as a Vocation" and "Structures of Power," pp. 79–128, 159–179, in Hans Gerth and C. Wright Mills, *From Max Weber* (New York: Oxford University Press, 1956); Talcott Parsons, "On the Concept of Political Power" in Parsons, *Politics and Social Structure* (New York: Free Press, 1969), pp. 352–404; Antonio Gramsci, *Selections from the Prison Notebooks* (New York: International Publishers, 1971), pp. 12–13, 234, 263, 268; Michel Foucault, *Discipline and Punish: The Birth of the Prison* (New York: Vintage), 1970.

6. Karl Marx and Friedrich Engels, *Manifesto of the Communist Party,* in *Karl Marx and Friedrich Engels, Selected Works,* vol. 1, 18–48 (Moscow: International Publishers, 1962 [1848]) ; Robert Michels, *Political Parties: A Sociological Study of the Oligarchical tendencies of Modern Democracy* (New York: Free Press, 1962 [1911]); Max Weber, "Appendix II: Parliament and Government in a Reconstructed Germany," in Max Weber, *Economy and Society,* vol. 2, 1381–1469; C. Wright, Mills, *The Power Elite* (New York: Oxford University Press, 1956).

7. Alexis de Tocqueville, *Democracy in America,* vols. 1 and 2 (New York: Library of America, 2004 [1835, 1840]); Emile Durkheim, *The Elementary Forms of Religious Life* (New York: Free Press, 1995 [1911]), and *Professional Ethics and Civic Morals* (London: Routledge and Kegan Paul, 1957); John Dewey, *Democracy and Education* (New York: Free Press, 1966 [1916]), 87; George Herbert Mead, *Mind, Self, and Society* (Chicago: University of Chicago Press, 1964); Hannah Arendt, *The Human Condition* (Chicago: University of Chicago Press, 1958), 199, 26.

8. Alexis de Tocqueville introduces this idea of self-interest "rightly understood" in *Democracy in America,* vols. 1 and 2 (New York: Library of America, 2004 [1835, 1840]), book 2, chapter 8. He does so to distinguish narrow and egoistic interest (*l'intérêt*) from a more solidaristic kind (*l'intérêt bien entendu*). With this latter conception, Tocqueville indicates "the disinterested, spontaneous impulses that are part of man's nature" (611), as compared with the more consciously calculated and selfish estimates of material well-being that propel the capitalist marketplace and also frame the approach to action in many political and economic theories today. Self-interest rightly understood, Tocqueville writes, suggests motives and relations that "are disciplined, temperate, moderate, prudent, and self-controlled" (612), which rather precisely describes the civil rationality of contemporary voters as they are discursively constructed today. Tocqueville credits "mores"—the accepted English translation of *les moeurs*—as the social force that allows democratic citizens to understand their own interests more broadly, and he defines mores in a cultural manner, as "habits, opinions, usages, beliefs" (356). The most recent English translation of *Democracy in America,* excellent in other respects, translates *l'intérêt bien entendu* as "self-interest prop-

erly understood," unfortunately shifting the English rendition of a concept that has become a classic theoretical term in democratic theory.

9. Alexander, *Civil Sphere*.

10. Jürgen Habermas, *The Structural Transformation of the Public Sphere: An Inquiry into a Category of Bourgeois Society* (Cambridge, Mass.: MIT Press, 1989 [1963].

11. Harold D. Lasswell, *Politics: Who Gets What, When, How* (New York: McGraw-Hill, 1936).

12. Robert Dahl, *Who Governs? Democracy and Power in an American City* (New Haven: Yale University Press, 1961); Seymour Martin Lipset, "Elections: The Expression of the Democratic Class Struggle," in Lipset, *Political Man: The Social Bases of Politics*, 230–78 (Baltimore: Johns Hopkins University Press, 1981 [1960]); Daniel Bell, "Interpretations of American Politics," in Daniel Bell, ed., *The Radical Right*, 47–74 (New York: Doubleday, 1963); Clem Brooks and Jeff Manza, "The Social and Ideological Bases of Middle-class Political Realignment in the United States, 1972–1992," *American Sociological Review* 61 (April 1997): 191–208; Anthony Downs, *An Economic Theory of Democracy* (New York: Harper and Row, 1957), 36; Bernard Crick, *In Defence of Politics* (Harmondsworth, UK: Penguin, 1962), 23. For less instrumental, more meaning- and emotion-centered studies of elections in contemporary political science, see, for example, Donald Green, Bradley Palmquist, and Eric Schickler, *Partisan Hearts and Minds: Political Parties and the Social Identities of Voters* (New Haven: Yale University Press, 2002); Ted Brader, *Campaigning for Hearts and Minds: How Emotional Appeals in Political Ads Work* (Chicago: University of Chicago Press, 2006); Andrew Gelman, David Park, Boris Shor, Joseph Bafumi, and Jeronimo Cortina, *Red State, Blue State, Rich State, Poor State: Why Americans Vote the Way They Do* (Princeton: Princeton University Press, 2008). For a critique of reductionism in contemporary political sociology, see Jeffrey C. Alexander, "Power, Politics, and the Civil Sphere," in Kevin Leight and Craig Jenkins, eds., *Handbook of Politics: State and Society in Global Perspective* (New York: Springer, 2010).

13. Chuck Todd and Sheldon Gawiser, *How Barack Obama Won: A State-by-State Guide to the Historic 2008 Presidential Election* (New York: Vintage, 2009), 16.

14. Ibid., 29.

15. William J. Crotty, "Preface and Acknowledgments," ix–x, in William J. Crotty, ed., *Winning the Presidency 2008* (Boulder: Paradigm, 2009), ix.

16. William J. Crotty, "Electing Obama: The 2008 Presidential Campaign," 20–47, in ibid., 40.

17. John Kenneth White, "A Transforming Election: How Barack Obama Changed American Politics," 185–208, in Crotty, *Winning the Presidency 2008*, 204.

18. Todd and Gawiser, *How Barack Obama Won*, 43.

19. Ibid., 44–45.

20. Arendt, *Human Condition*, 13, 8, 176–78.

21. Ibid., 178.

22. Ibid., 178, 182, 186.

23. Kathleen Hall Jamieson and Paul Waldman, *Electing the President, 2000: The Insiders' View* (Philadelphia: University of Pennsylvania Press, 2001), 2.

24. For demagicalization, see Max Weber, "Introduction" and part II, section IV in Max Weber, *The Protestant Ethic and the Spirit of Capitalism* (New York: Scribner, 1927

[1904–1905]); for aura and mechanical reproduction, see Walter Benjamin, "The Work of Art in the Age of Mechanical Reproduction," in Walter Benjamin, *Illuminations*, 211–44 (New York: Harcourt, Brace, 1968); for alienation, Karl Marx, "Economic and Philosophical Manuscripts," in *Karl Marx: Early Writings*, ed. T. B. Bottomore, 61–219 (New York: McGraw-Hill, 1963 [1844]); for "all that is holy," Karl Marx and Friedrich Engels, *Manifesto of the Communist Party*; for superstructures, see Karl Marx, *The German Ideology* (Moscow: International Publishers, 1970 [1846]); for meaning as a dependent variable in the sociology of culture, see Jeffrey C. Alexander and Philip Smith, "The Strong Program in Cultural Sociology: Elements of a Structural Hermeneutics," in Jeffrey C. Alexander, *The Meanings of Social Life: A Cultural Sociology*, 11–26 (New York: Oxford University Press, 2003).

25. Alexander and Smith, "Strong Program in Cultural Sociology," and Jeffrey C. Alexander and Philip Smith, "The Strong Program: Mission, Origins, Achievements, and Prospects," in John R. Hall, Laura Grindstaff, and Ming-Cheng Lo, eds., *Handbook of Cultural Sociology* (New York: Routledge, 2010); more generally, Alexander, *Meanings of Social Life*; Durkheim, *Elementary Forms*, 1.

26. Ferdinand de Saussure, *Course in General Linguistics* (New York: McGraw Hill, 1966 [1916]); Roman Jakobson, *On Language* (Cambridge, Mass.: Harvard University Press, 1990); Ludwig Wittgenstein, *Philosophical Investigations* (London: Macmillan, 1953).

27. Richard Rorty, ed., *The Linguistic Turn: Essays in Philosophical Method* (Chicago: University of Chicago Press, 1967); Roger Friedland and John Mohr, eds., *Matters of Culture: Cultural Sociology in Practice* (New York: Cambridge University Press, 2003); Claude Lévi-Strauss, *The Savage Mind* (Chicago: University of Chicago Press, 1967), and *Tristes Tropiques* (New York: Athenaeum 1973 [1955]); Roland Barthes, *Mythologies* (New York: Hill and Wang, 1972 [1957]); Mary Douglas, *Purity and Danger: An Analysis of Concepts of Pollution and Taboo* (New York: Praeger, 1967); Victor Turner, *The Ritual Process: Structure and Anti-structure* (New York: de Gruyter, 1969); Clifford Geertz, *The Interpretation of Cultures* (New York: Basic Books, 1973).

28. For Birmingham, Stuart Hall, Chas Critcher, Tony Jefferson, John N. Clarke, and Brian Roberts, *Policing the Crisis: Mugging, the State, and Law and Order* (London: Macmillan, 1978); for governmentality, Graham Burchell, Colin Gordon, and Peter Miller, eds., *The Foucault Effect: Studies in Governmentality* (Chicago: University of Chicago Press, 1991); for isomorphism, John Meyer and Brian Rowan, "Institutionalized Organizations: Formal Structure as Myth and Ceremony," *American Journal of Sociology* 83 (1977): 340–63; for cultural capital, Pierre Bourdieu, *Distinction: A Social Critique of the Judgment of Taste* (Cambridge, Mass.: Harvard University Press, 1984); see also Murray Edelman, *The Symbolic Uses of Politics* (Champaign: University of Illinois Press, 1964).

29. William H. Sewell Jr., *Work and Revolution in France: The Language of Labor from the Old Regime to 1848* (New York: Cambridge University Press, 1980); Michelle Lamont, *Money, Manners, and Morals: The Culture of the French and American Upper-middle Class* (Chicago: University of Chicago Press, 1992); Ron Eyerman and Andrew Jameson, *Social Movements: A Cognitive Approach* (Cambridge, UK: Polity, 1991); Viviana Zelizer, *Pricing the Priceless Child: The Changing Social Value of Children* (New York: Basic Books, 1985); Daniel Miller, *Material Culture and Mass Consumption* (Oxford: Blackwell, 1987); Scott Lash and John Urry, *Economies of Signs and Space* (London: Sage, 1994).

30. Jeffrey C. Alexander, "Citizen and Enemy as Symbolic Classification: On the Polarizing Discourse of Civil Society," in M. Lamont and Marcel Fournier, eds., *Cultivating Differences: Symbolic Boundaries and the Making of Inequality*, 289–308 (Chicago: University of Chicago Press, 1992); Jeffrey C. Alexander and Phillip Smith, "The Discourse of American Civil Society: A New Approach for Cultural Studies," *Theory and Society* 22(2) 1993: 151–207; and Alexander, *Civil Sphere*.

31. Evan Cornog, *The Power and the Story: How the Crafted Presidential Narrative Has Determined Political Success from George Washington to George W. Bush* (New York: Penguin, 2004), 5.

32. For narratives, see Hayden White, *The Content of the Form: Narrative Discourse and Historical Representation* (Baltimore: Johns Hopkins University Press, 1987), and Roland Barthes, "Introduction to the Structural Analysis of Narratives," in Roland Barthes, *Image-Music-Text* (New York: Hill and Wang, 1977); for the entwinement of narratives and the discourse of civil society, see Ronald Jacobs, *Race, Media, and the Crisis of Civil Society: From Watts to Rodney King* (New York: Cambridge University Press, 2000), and Philip Smith, *Why War? The Cultural Logic of Suez, the Gulf War, and Iraq* (Chicago: University of Chicago Press, 2005); for heroes, see Thomas Carlyle, *On Heroes, Hero Worship, and the Heroic in History* (Berkeley: University of California Press, 1993 [1841]); Joseph Campbell, *The Hero with a Thousand Faces* (Princeton: Princeton University Press, 1949); John Carroll, *The Western Dreaming: How the Western World Is Dying for Want of a Story* (New York: Harper Collins, 2001); and Bernhard Giesen, *Triumph and Trauma* (Boulder: Paradigm, 2004).

33. Jeffrey C. Alexander, "Cultural Pragmatics: Social Performance between Ritual and Strategy," in Jeffrey C. Alexander, Bernhard Giesen, and J. Mast, *Social Performances: Symbolic Action, Cultural Pragmatics, and Ritual*, 29–90 (New York: Cambridge University Press, 2006).

34. John L. Austin, *How to Do Things with Words* (Cambridge, Mass.: Harvard University Press, 1962).

35. Erving Goffman, *The Presentation of Self in Everyday Life* (New York: Doubleday, 1956); Victor W. Turner, *From Ritual to Theatre: The Human Seriousness of Play* (New York: PAJ, 1982); Clifford Geertz, "Deep Play: Notes on the Balinese Cockfight," in Geertz, *Interpretation of Cultures*, pp. 412–453; Richard Schechner, *Performance Theory* (New York: Routledge, 1988).

36. Alexander, "Cultural Pragmatics," 67.

37. In his PhD dissertation, Politics and Performance: The Cultural Pragmatics of the Clinton Presidency (UCLA 2006), Jason L. Mast has employed cultural pragmatics to develop a performative perspective on presidential politics during the Clinton years; see also Mast, "The New Cultural Sociology of Politics: The Cultural Pragmatics of the Clinton Years," in Alexander, Jacobs, and Smith, eds., *Oxford Handbook of Cultural Sociology*.

38. Jeffrey Edward Green, *The Eyes of the People: Democracy in an Age of Spectatorship* (New York: Oxford University Press, 2010), pp. 33 and 129-30.

39. Knut Lundby, ed., *Mediatization: Concept, Changes, Consequences* (New York: Lang, 2009); Roger Silverstone, *Media and Morality: On the Rise of the Mediapolis* (Cambridge, UK: Polity, 2007); Sonia Livingstone, "On the Mediation of Everything," *Journal of Communication* 59(1): 1–18. While mediatization is an evocative new concept in contemporary media theory,

it remains ambiguous and vaguely conceptualized. Pointing to the fact that institutions and even private individual actions are increasingly framed publicly by mass media, the concept risks a dangerous overgeneralization by failing to specify what exactly such mediatization does—and does not do. Are the various mass media sui generis, such that they provide meaning in themselves, or do they, rather, project meanings from cultural structures outside themselves? Are there values that are distinctively embedded in, for example, contemporary new media? Is mediatization omniscient, as well as omnipresent, or are mass media still continuously pulled and shaped by social actors and groups? *The Performance of Politics* bears on these questions.

40. Michael Schudson, *Why Democracies Need an Unlovable Press* (Cambridge, UK: Polity, 2008), and "The Objectivity Norm in American Journalism," *Journalism* 2(2) 2001: 149–70; Jeffrey C. Alexander, "The Mass News Media in Systemic, Historical, and Comparative Perspective," in E. Katz and T. Szecsko, eds., *Mass Media and Social Change*, 17–52 (London: Sage, 1981), and Alexander, *Civil Sphere*, 75–85.

41. Habermas, *Structural Transformation*, 181–221; Mills, *Power Elite*, 305–324; Nicholas Garnham, *Capitalism and Communication* (London: Sage, 1990); Pierre Bourdieu, *On Television* (New York: New Press, 1999).

42. Kathleen Hall Jamieson and Paul Waldman, *The Press Effect: Politicians, Journalists, and the Stories That Shape the Political World* (New York: Oxford University Press, 2003), 165 and passim.

43. Joseph N. Cappella and Kathleen Hall Jamieson, *The Spiral of Cynicism: The Press and the Public Good* (New York: Oxford University Press, 1997). For an influential screed about television making passive consumers out of formerly active citizens, see Robert Putnam, *Bowling Alone: The Collapse and Revival of American Community* (New York: Simon and Schuster, 2000). For the case against dividing active citizens from television viewing audiences, see Sonia Livingstone and Peter Lunt, *Talk on Television: Audience Participation and Public Debate* (London: Routledge, 1994), and, more broadly, Pippa Norris, *A Virtuous Circle: Political Communications in Postindustrial Societies* (New York: Cambridge University Press, 2000).

44. For media scholarship conceptualizing such reflexivity, see John B. Thompson, "The New Visibility," *Theory, Culture, and Society* 22(6) (2005): 31–51; Schudson, *Why Democracies Need an Unlovable Press*.

45. Sonia Livingstone, "On the Relation between Audiences and Publics," in Sonia Livingstone, ed., *Audiences and Publics: When Cultural Engagement Matters for the Public Sphere*, 17–41 (Bristol, UK: Intellect Books, 2005), 21.

46. Susan Herbst, *Reading Public Opinion: How Political Actors View the Democratic Process* (Chicago: University of Chicago Press, 1998), 67.

47. Ronald N. Jacobs, "Producing the News, Producing the Crisis: Narrrativity, Television, and New Work," *Media, Culture, and Society* 18(3) (1996): 373–97; Jeffrey C. Alexander and Ronald N. Jacobs, "Mass Communication, Ritual, and Civil Society," in T. Liebes and J. Curran, eds., *Media, Ritual and Identity*, 23–41 (London: Routledge, 1998).

48. In my interviews with *New York Times* reporters who profiled Obama, as well as other candidates, during the 2008 campaign, I heard repeated complaints about minders and lack of both access and face time.

49. Jim Rutenberg and Jeff Zeleny, "Obama's Campaign Tightens Control of Image and Access," *NYT*, June 19, 2008, A1.

50. Elvin T. Lim, *The Anti-intellectual Presidency: The Decline of Presidential Rhetoric from George Washington to George W. Bush* (New York: Oxford University Press, 2008).

51. Geertz, "Thick Description: Toward an Interpretive Theory of Culture," in Geertz, *Interpretation of Cultures*, pp. 3–30.

52. Sharon Meraz, "Is There an Elite Hold? Traditional Media to Social Media Agenda Setting Influence in Blog Networks," *Journal of Computer-mediated Communication* 14 (2009): 682–707, quoting pp. 683–84.

53. Schudson, *Why Democracies Need an Unlovable Press*, 9, 25, 137–38, 150.

54. Meraz, "Is There an Elite Hold?" 701.

55. Fiona Clark and Deborah L. Illman, "Content Analysis of *New York Times* Coverage of Space Issues for the Year 2000," *Science Communication* 25(3) (2003): 24; Stephen J. Farnsworth and S. Robert Lichter, "The Mediated Congress: Coverage of Capitol Hill in the *New York Times* and the *Washington Post*," *Harvard International Journal of Press/Politics* 10 (2005): 94; William L. Benoit, Kevin A. Stein, and Glenn J. Hansen, "*New York Times* Coverage of Presidential Campaigns," *Journalism and Mass Communication Quarterly* 82(2) (2005): 360.

56. Reed Irvine and Cliff Kincaid, "Post Columnist Concerned about Media Bias," *Media Monitor* (*Accuracy in Media* blog), September 17, 2007, http://www.aim.org/media-monitor/post-columnist-concerned-about-media-bias/; Paul Sperry, "Myth of the Conservative Wall Street Journal," *WorldNetDaily*, June 25, 2002, http://www.wnd.com/index.php?pageId=14357; Daniel E. Ho and Kevin M. Quinn, "Measuring Explicit Political Positions of Media," *Quarterly Journal of Political Science* 3 (2008): 363.

57. Chun-Fang Chiang, "Political Differentiation in Newspaper Markets," working paper, National Taiwan University (February 2009), http://homepage.ntu.edu.tw/~chunfang/newspaper_markets.pdf; emphasis added.

58. Wilhelm Dilthey, "The Construction of the Historical World in the Human Studies," in Wilhelm Dilthey, ed., *Dilthey: Selected Writings*, 168–245 (New York: Cambridge University Press, 1976).

59. Given limitations of space, I here am able only to suggest this is the case. To make a stronger case would require extensive comparison, including examining democratic struggles for power in non-Western societies. Despite significant substantive differences, however, it is my impression that similar cultural processes are implicated in the struggles for democratic power in, for example, Korea, Taiwan, and Japan.

APPENDIX ON THE POLL OF POLLS

1. See poblano (aka Nate Silver), "Pollster Report Card," *Daily Kos*, March 3, 2009, http://www.dailykos.com/storyonly/2008/3/4/1172/31168/539/468308.

2. Bernie Becker, "Political Polling Sites Are in a Race of Their Own," *NYT*, October 22, 2008, http://www.nytimes.com/2008/10/28/us/politics/28pollsite.html?fta=y.

3. Ibid.

4. Nate Silver, "Tracking Poll Primer," *FiveThirtyEight*, October 21, 2008, http://www.fivethirtyeight.com/2008/10/tracking-poll-primer.html. Further, Rasmussen accounts for

about 37 percent of the input into 538's tracking poll; see Silver, "House Effects in Da House," *FiveThirtyEight,* August 25, 2008, http://www.fivethirtyeight.com/2008/08/house-effects-in-da-house.html.

5. See http://www.gallup.com/poll/110380/How-does-Gallup-Daily-tracking-work.aspx.

6. Silver, "Tracking Poll Primer."

7. SurveyUSA, "2008 Pollster Report Card, Updated to Include Potomac Primaries," *SurveyUSA Breaking News,* February 13, 2008, http://www.surveyusa.com/index.php/2008/02/13/2008-pollster-report-card-updated-to-include-potomac-primaries/.

8. "Pollster Ratings, v3.1.1," *FiveThirtyEight,* May 2, 2008, http://www.fivethirtyeight.com/2008/05/pollster-ratings-v311.html.

9. Becker, "Political Polling Site Are in a Race of Their Own."

10. Silver, "RCP and the R2K Tracking Poll," *FiveThirtyEight,* September 22, 2008, http://www.fivethirtyeight.com/2008/09/rcp-and-r2k-tracking-poll_6506.html.

11. Charles Franklin, "How Pollsters Affect Poll Results," *Pollster.com* (blog), August 24, 2008, http://www.pollster.com/blogs/how_pollsters_affect_poll_resu.php.

12. Ibid.

13. See "GALLUP DAILY Measures Explained," *Gallup.com,* no date, http://www.gallup.com/poll/113842/GALLUP-DAILY-Measures-Explained.aspx).

14. See "Methodology," *Rasmussen Reports* (blog), no date, http://www.rasmussenreports.com/public_content/about_us/methodology.

15. "The *New York Times* Polling Standards," *NYT,* September 10, 2008, http://www.nytimes.com/ref/us/politics/10_polling_standards.html.

16. Silver, "Tracking Poll Primer," October 21, 2008.

17. Prior to this period, I utilize data from their June, July, and August monthly polls, as well as the four polls taken in September and early October, which were also four-day rolling samples.

18. Jon Cohen, "WaPo-ABC Daily Tracking—Release #1," *WP* (blog), October 20, 2008; http://voices.washingtonpost.com/behind-the-numbers/2008/10/wapo-abc_daily_tracking_1.html; Jennifer Agiesta, "WaPo-ABC Tracking: Nine Divided by 56 is..." *WP,* November 1, 2008, http://voices.washingtonpost.com/behind-the-numbers/2008/11/wapo-abc_tracking_nine_divided.html.

19. Langer, "ABC News' Polling Methodology and Standards: The Nuts and Bolts of Our Public Opinion Surveys," *WP,* November 25, 2009, http://abcnews.go.com/US/PollVault/story?id=145373&page=1.

20. Langer, "Final Tracking," *The Numbers* (ABC News blog), November 4, 2008, http://blogs.abcnews.com/thenumbers/2008/11/final-tracking.html; emphasis added.

21. "*Washington Post* Polls: Detailed Methodology," *WP,* March 31, 2009, http://www.washingtonpost.com/wp-dyn/content/article/2009/03/31/AR2009033101229.html; "About *Washington Post* Polls," *WP,* March 31, 2009, http://www.washingtonpost.com/wp-dyn/content/article/2009/03/31/AR2009033101241.html.

22. Silver, "RCP Follow-up," *FiveThirtyEight,* October 2, 2008, http://www.fivethirtyeight.com/2008/10/rcp-follow-up.html.

23. Ibid.

24. Silver, "Real Credibility Problems," *FiveThirtyEight,* October 2, 2008, http://www. fivethirtyeight.com/2008/09/real-credibility-problems.html.

25. Silver, "RCP and the R2K Tracking Polls."

26. "RealClearPolitics.com Launches New Web Site, Announces Financing," *PR Newswire,* March 14, 2006. Additionally, Jim VandeHei, executive editor and a founder of the *Politico* site, a Web-based political journal, stated via e-mail: "The site is an essential stop for anyone interested in politics…They do a better job than anyone in the business at flagging the must-read political stories and analysis on the Web each day." Steve Johnson, "Real Clear Politics real Clear on Its Growth, Mission," *Hypertext* (*chicagotribune. com* blog), February 7, 2008, http://featuresblogs.chicagotribune.com/technology_ internetcritic/2008/02/real-clear-poli.html.

27. Jay Cost, "A Note on the Polls," *RCP HorseRaceBlog,* October 24, 2008, http://www. realclearpolitics.com/horseraceblog/2008/10/a_note_on_the_polls_1.html.

28. Carl Bialik, "Election Handicappers Are Using Risky Tool: Mixed Poll Averages," *The Numbers Guy* (*WSJ* blog), February 15, 2008, http://online.wsj.com/public/article/ SB120303346890469991.html.

Index